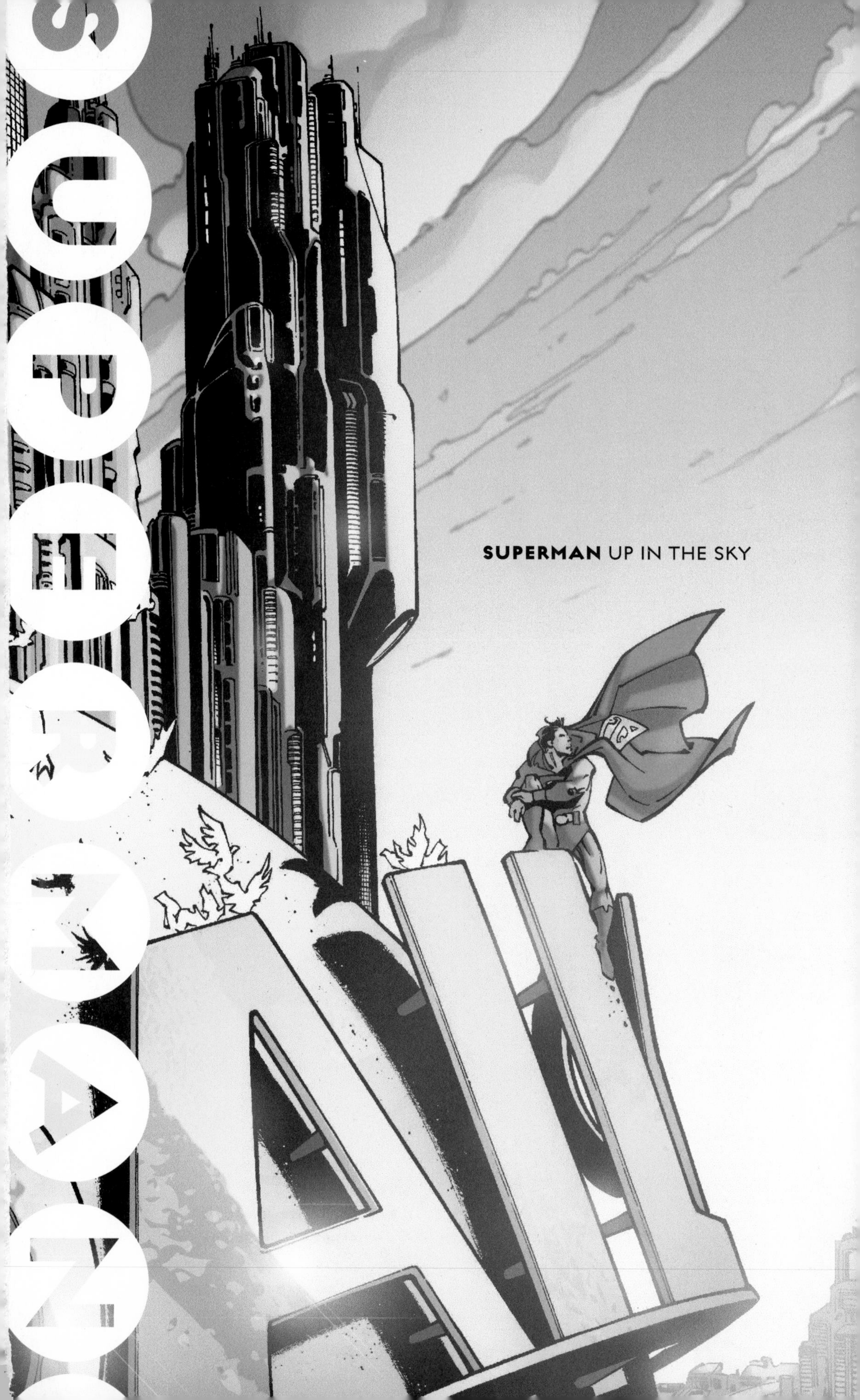

SUPERMAN UP IN THE SKY

SUPERMAN UP IN THE SKY

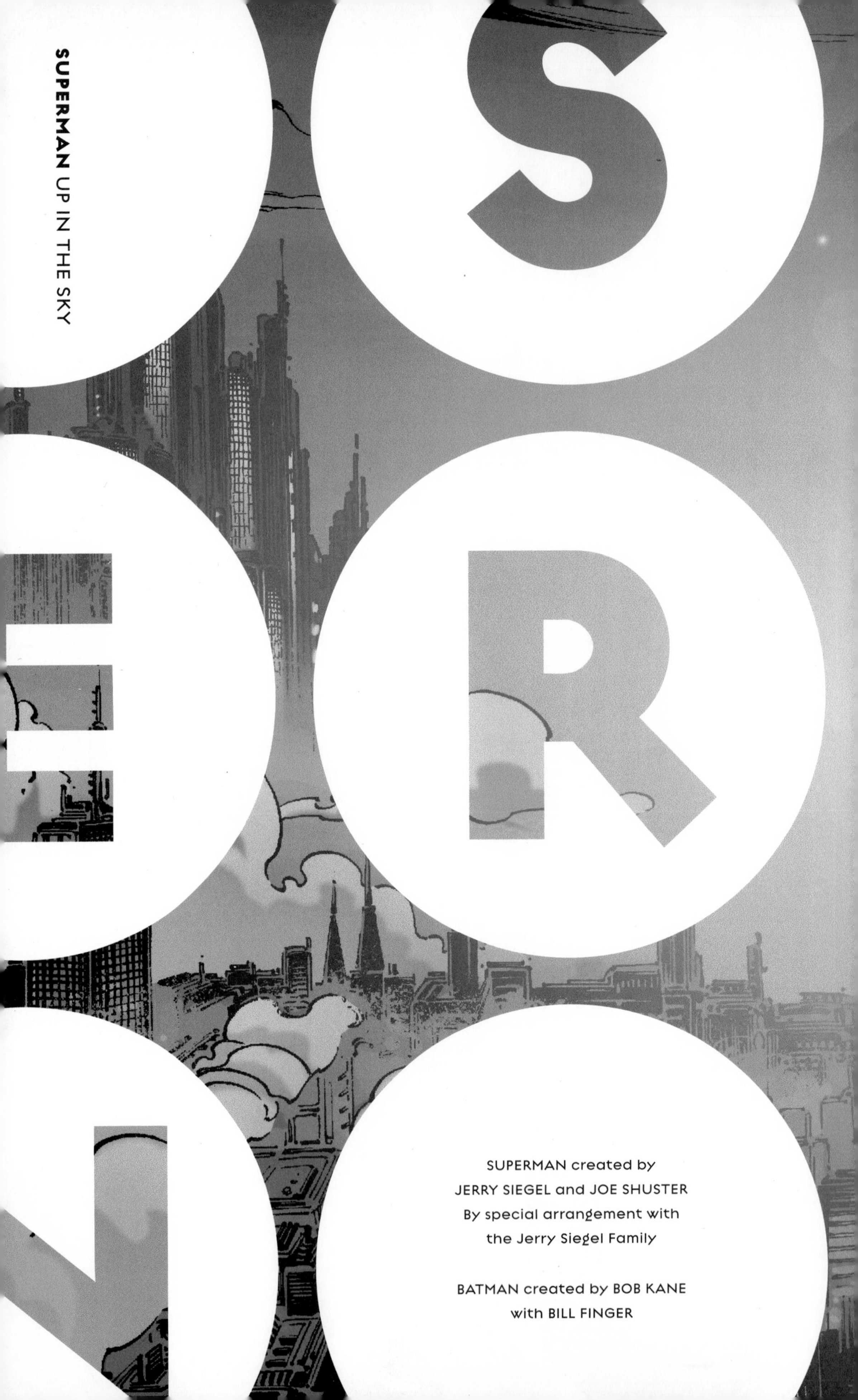

SUPERMAN created by
JERRY SIEGEL and JOE SHUSTER
By special arrangement with
the Jerry Siegel Family

BATMAN created by BOB KANE
with BILL FINGER

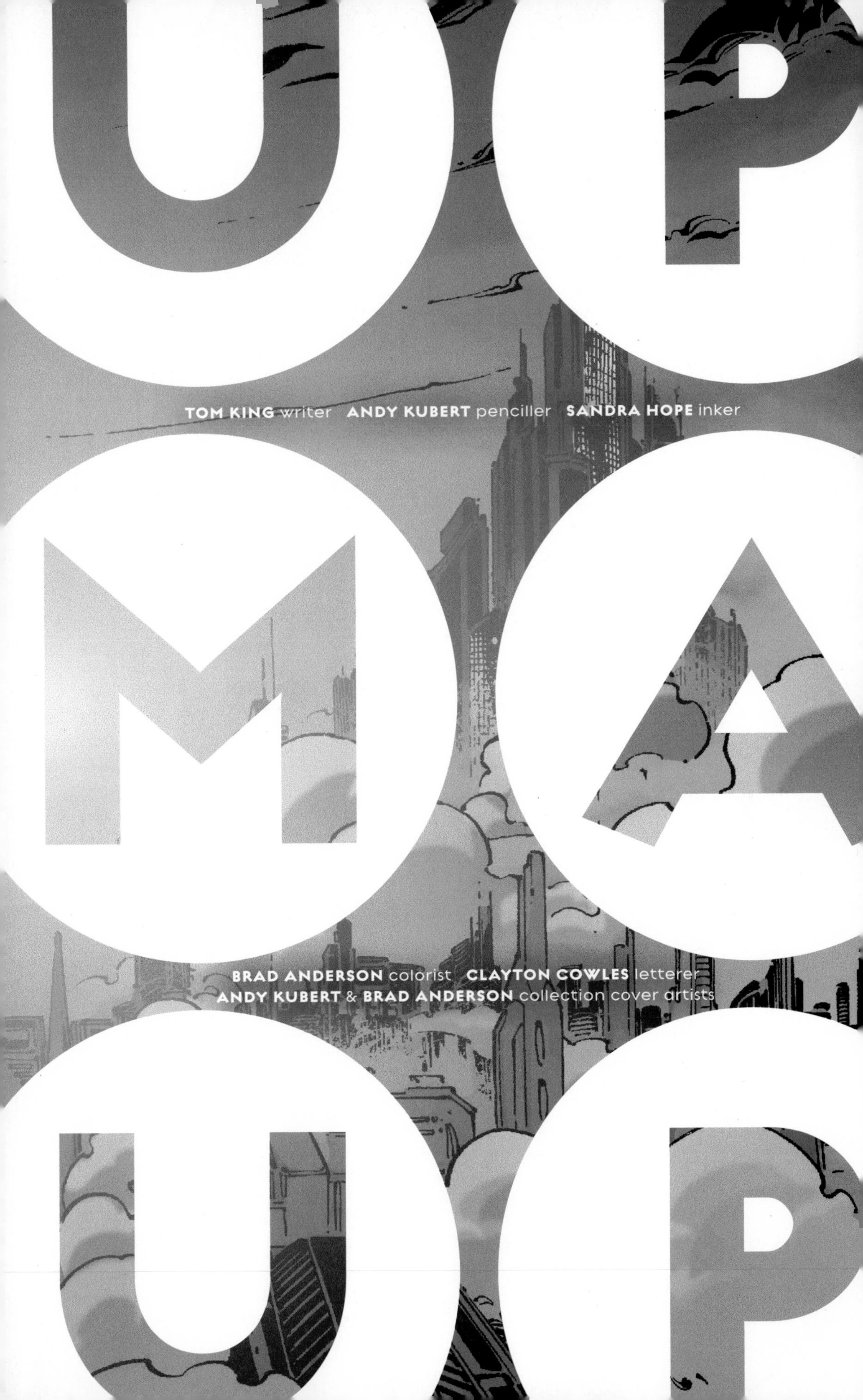
UP
MA
UP

TOM KING writer **ANDY KUBERT** penciller **SANDRA HOPE** inker

BRAD ANDERSON colorist **CLAYTON COWLES** letterer
ANDY KUBERT & **BRAD ANDERSON** collection cover artists

JAMIE S. RICH Editor – Original Series
BRITTANY HOLZHERR Associate Editor – Original Series
JEB WOODARD Group Editor – Collected Editions
ERIKA ROTHBERG Editor – Collected Edition
STEVE COOK Design Director – Books
MONIQUE NARBONETA Publication Design
TOM VALENTE Publication Production

BOB HARRAS Senior VP – Editor-in-Chief, DC Comics
PAT McCALLUM Executive Editor, DC Comics

DAN DiDIO Publisher
JIM LEE Publisher & Chief Creative Officer
BOBBIE CHASE VP – New Publishing Initiatives & Talent Development
DON FALLETTI VP – Manufacturing Operations & Workflow Management
LAWRENCE GANEM VP – Talent Services
ALISON GILL Senior VP – Manufacturing & Operations
HANK KANALZ Senior VP – Publishing Strategy & Support Services
DAN MIRON VP – Publishing Operations
NICK J. NAPOLITANO VP – Manufacturing Administration & Design
NANCY SPEARS VP – Sales
MICHELE R. WELLS VP & Executive Editor, Young Reader

SUPERMAN: UP IN THE SKY

DC Comics, 2900 West Alameda Ave., Burbank, CA 91505
Printed by LSC Communications, Kendallville, IN, USA. 3/13/20. First Printing.
ISBN: 978-1-4012-9456-4

Library of Congress Cataloging-in-Publication Data is available.

PEFC Certified

This product is from
sustainably managed
forests and controlled
sources

PEFC/29-31-337   www.pefc.org

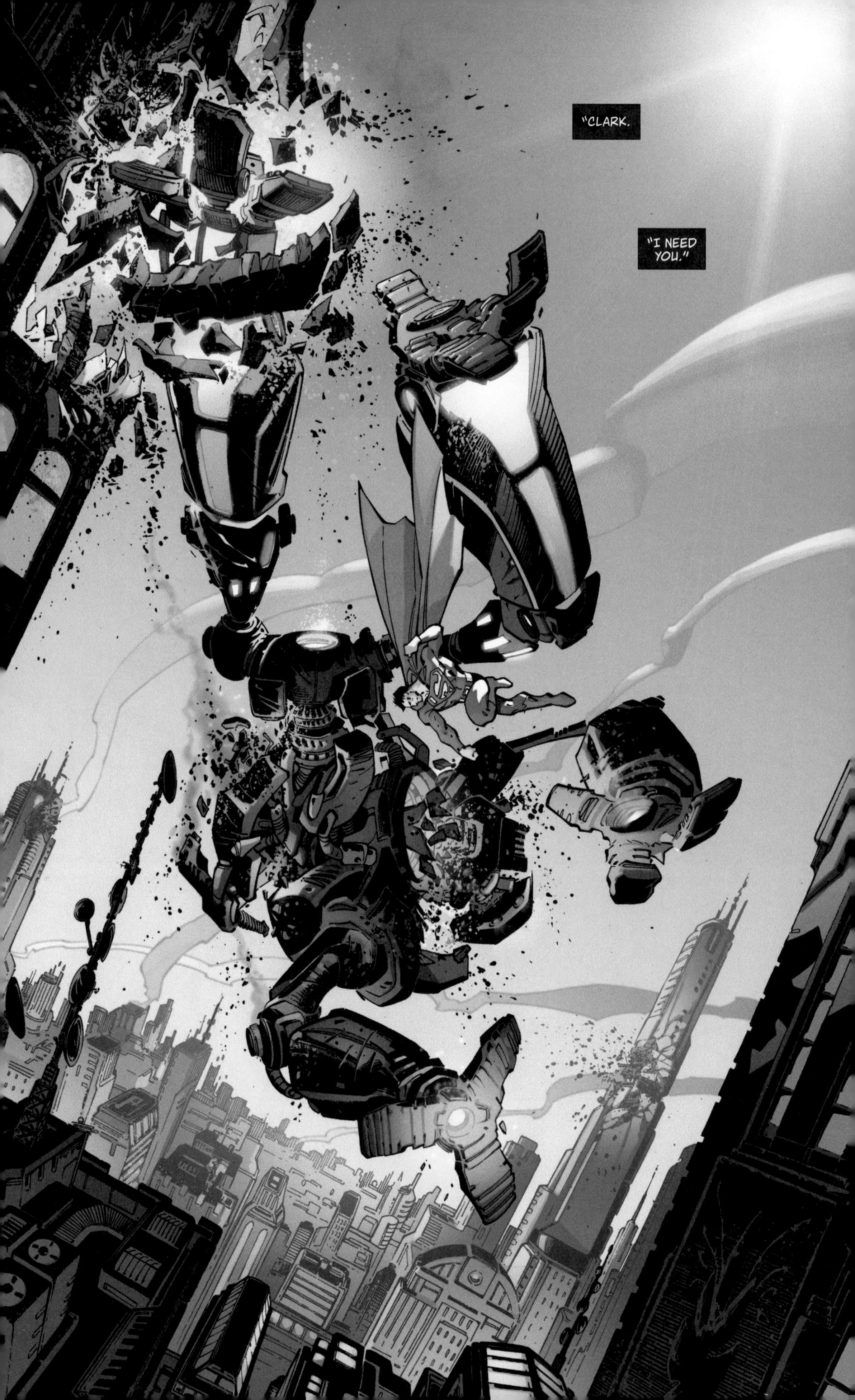
"CLARK.
"I NEED YOU."

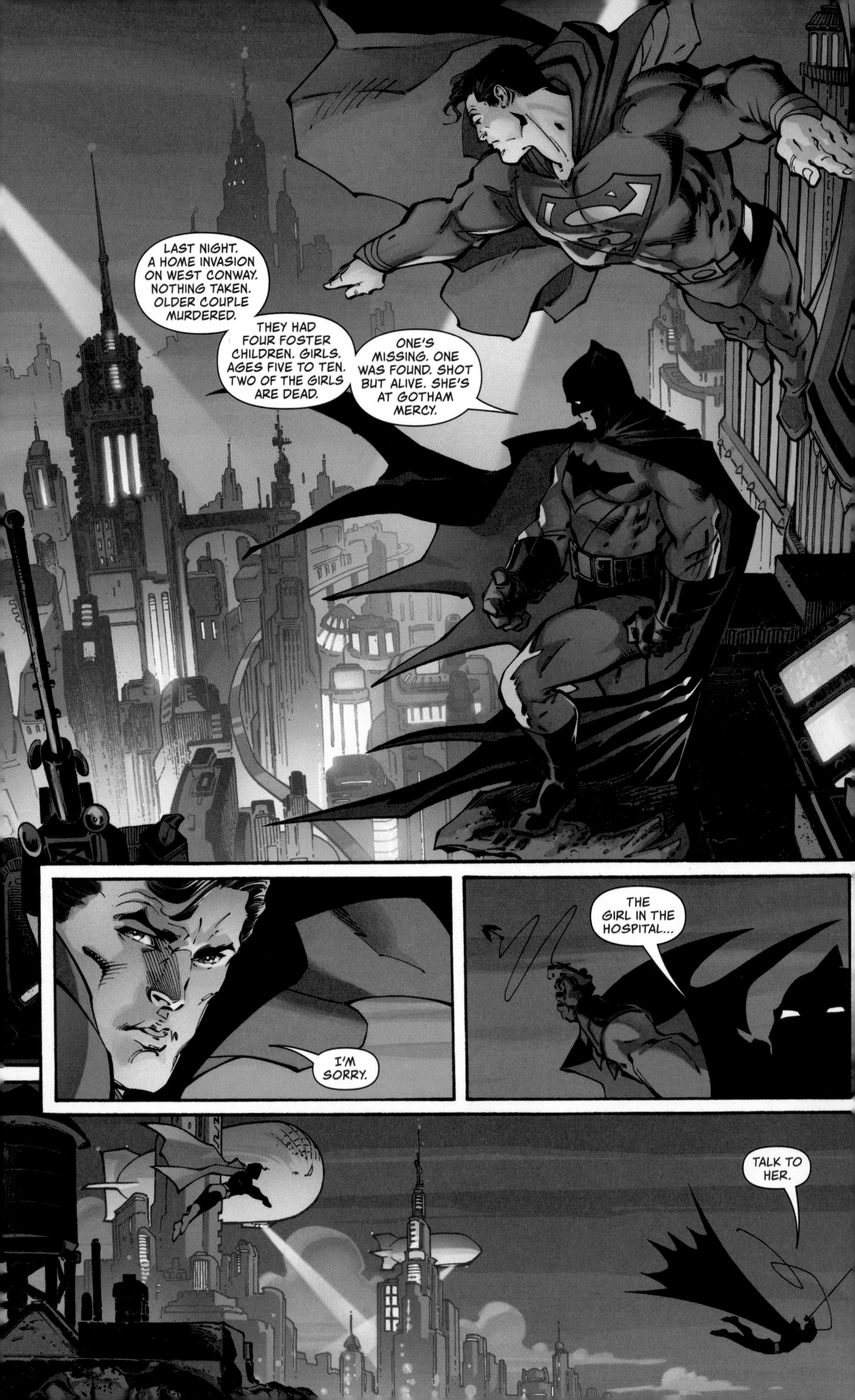
LAST NIGHT. A HOME INVASION ON WEST CONWAY. NOTHING TAKEN. OLDER COUPLE MURDERED.
THEY HAD FOUR FOSTER CHILDREN. GIRLS. AGES FIVE TO TEN. TWO OF THE GIRLS ARE DEAD.
ONE'S MISSING. ONE WAS FOUND. SHOT BUT ALIVE. SHE'S AT GOTHAM MERCY.
I'M SORRY.
THE GIRL IN THE HOSPITAL...
TALK TO HER.

WE...WE WERE IN THE *BASEMENT* AND THEN WE HEARD *REALLY* LOUD NOISES. THE NOISES WERE, LIKE, *BIG* NOISES. AND THEY *SHOOK* THINGS.

WE WERE PLAYING *SUPERHEROES.* MS. JAN GIVES US *SUPERHERO* TOYS.

I HAVE *YOUR* TOY. BUT *ALICE* ALWAYS TAKES IT FROM ME. SUPERMAN'S *HER* FAVORITE.

WE WERE *GOING* TO GO UPSTAIRS AND LOOK. ALICE AND ME.

BUT *THEN* WE HEARD MS. JAN *SCREAMING,* AND WE *DIDN'T* GO UPSTAIRS.

THERE'S A *BACK* DOOR IN THE BASEMENT AND WE WENT *OUTSIDE.*

ALICE *STILL* HAD YOUR TOY, EVEN THOUGH IT'S MINE.

THERE'S A *BUSH* IN THE BACKYARD AND WE *TRIED* TO HIDE IN IT. IT PINCHED.

WELL, THERE WAS *ANOTHER* BIG NOISE, AND I GOT *SO* HURT, AND I WAS CRYING.

ALICE WAS *YELLING,* AND THEN SHE *WASN'T* YELLING. A MAN *WAS* THERE. IN A *SPACEMAN* SUIT!

I COULDN'T SEE BECAUSE I WAS IN THE *HIDING* PLACE, *BUT* I SAW A *LITTLE* BIT.

HE *REACHED* IN, I CLOSED *MY* EYES, AND ALICE SCREAMED *SO* LOUD.

I WAS HURT AND, LIKE, WET AND RED AND HE TOOK HER.

SHE *STILL* HAD MY TOY. OR, LIKE, I MEAN, *YOUR* TOY.

AND... COULD YOU...

FROM WHAT YOU COULD SEE.

WHERE DID HE TAKE HER?

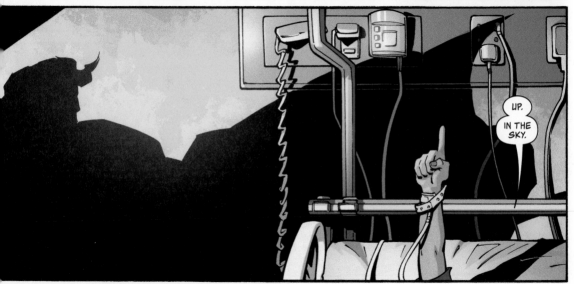

UP. IN THE SKY.

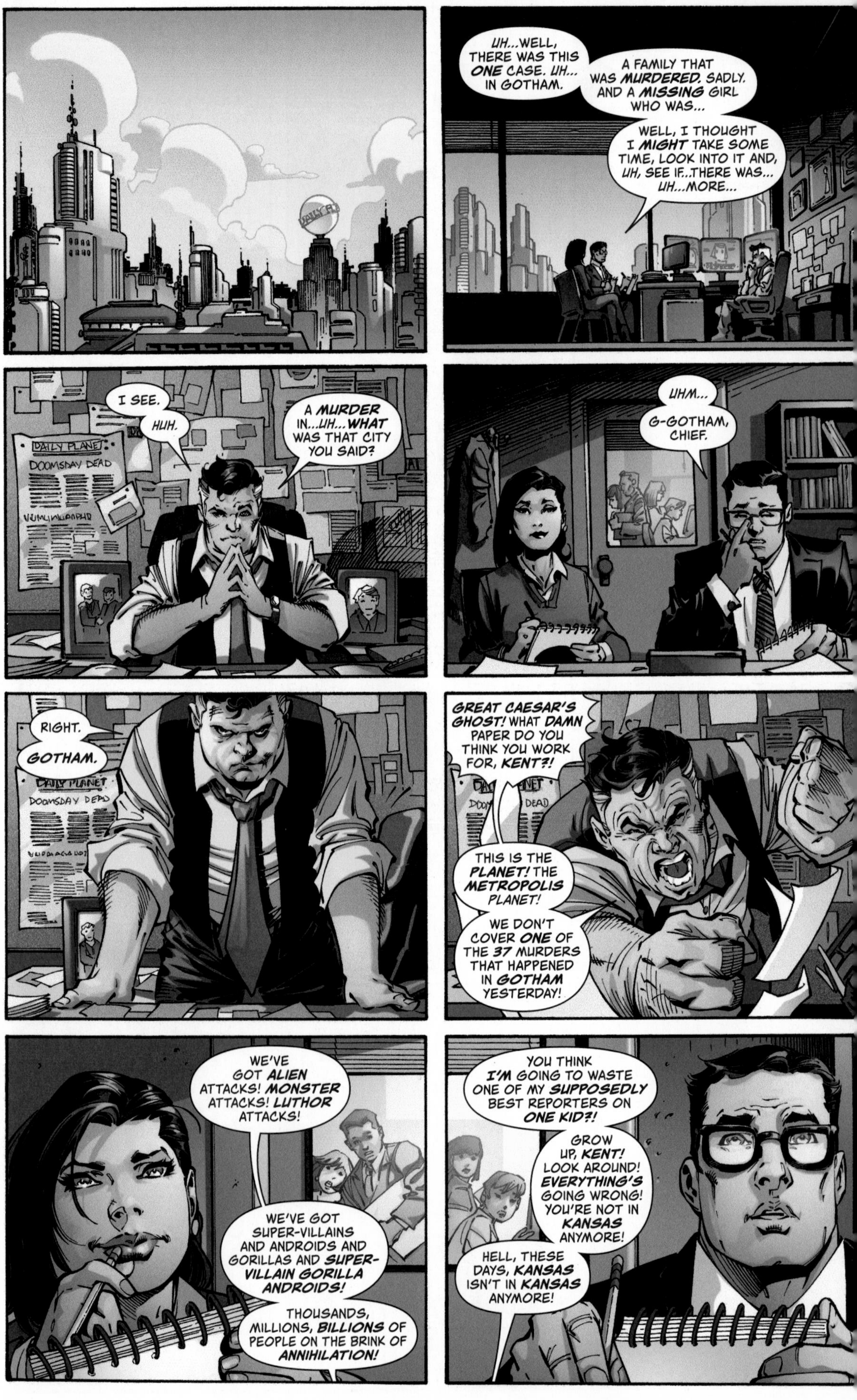
DAILY PLANET
UH...WELL, THERE WAS THIS ONE CASE. UH... IN GOTHAM.
A FAMILY THAT WAS MURDERED. SADLY. AND A MISSING GIRL WHO WAS...
WELL, I THOUGHT I MIGHT TAKE SOME TIME, LOOK INTO IT AND, UH, SEE IF...THERE WAS... UH...MORE...
I SEE.
HUH.
A MURDER IN...UH...WHAT WAS THAT CITY YOU SAID?
DAILY PLANET
DOOMSDAY DEAD
UHM...
G-GOTHAM, CHIEF.
RIGHT.
GOTHAM.
DAILY PLANET
DOOMSDAY DEAD
GREAT CAESAR'S GHOST! WHAT DAMN PAPER DO YOU THINK YOU WORK FOR, KENT?!
THIS IS THE PLANET! THE METROPOLIS PLANET!
WE DON'T COVER ONE OF THE 37 MURDERS THAT HAPPENED IN GOTHAM YESTERDAY!
WE'VE GOT ALIEN ATTACKS! MONSTER ATTACKS! LUTHOR ATTACKS!
WE'VE GOT SUPER-VILLAINS AND ANDROIDS AND GORILLAS AND SUPER-VILLAIN GORILLA ANDROIDS!
THOUSANDS, MILLIONS, BILLIONS OF PEOPLE ON THE BRINK OF ANNIHILATION!
YOU THINK I'M GOING TO WASTE ONE OF MY SUPPOSEDLY BEST REPORTERS ON ONE KID?!
GROW UP, KENT! LOOK AROUND! EVERYTHING'S GOING WRONG! YOU'RE NOT IN KANSAS ANYMORE!
HELL, THESE DAYS, KANSAS ISN'T IN KANSAS ANYMORE!

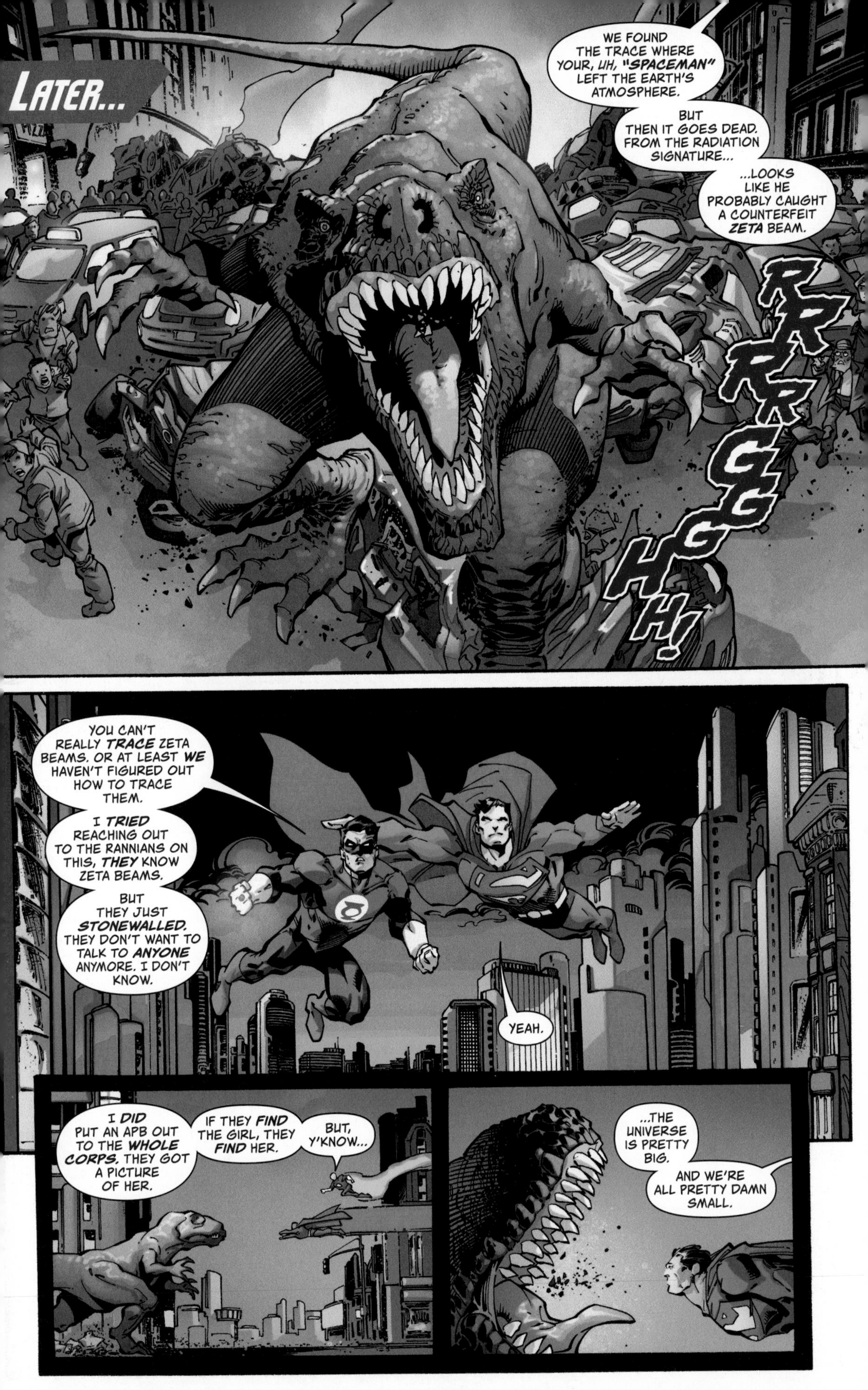
LATER...
WE FOUND THE TRACE WHERE YOUR, UH, "SPACEMAN" LEFT THE EARTH'S ATMOSPHERE.
BUT THEN IT GOES DEAD. FROM THE RADIATION SIGNATURE...
...LOOKS LIKE HE PROBABLY CAUGHT A COUNTERFEIT ZETA BEAM.
RRRRGGGHHH!
YOU CAN'T REALLY TRACE ZETA BEAMS. OR AT LEAST WE HAVEN'T FIGURED OUT HOW TO TRACE THEM.
I TRIED REACHING OUT TO THE RANNIANS ON THIS, THEY KNOW ZETA BEAMS.
BUT THEY JUST STONEWALLED. THEY DON'T WANT TO TALK TO ANYONE ANYMORE. I DON'T KNOW.
YEAH.
I DID PUT AN APB OUT TO THE WHOLE CORPS. THEY GOT A PICTURE OF HER.
IF THEY FIND THE GIRL, THEY FIND HER.
BUT, Y'KNOW...
...THE UNIVERSE IS PRETTY BIG.
AND WE'RE ALL PRETTY DAMN SMALL.

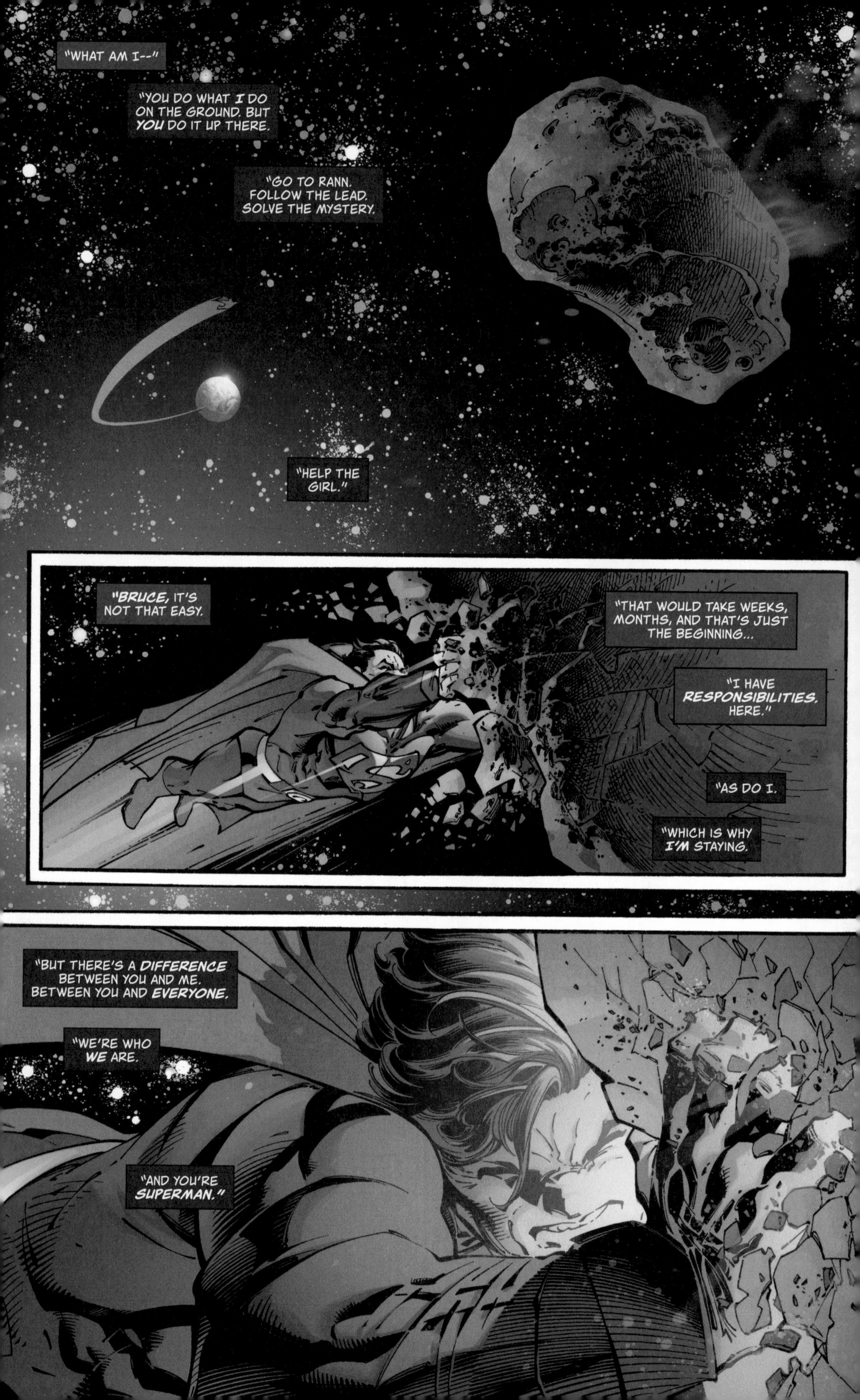
"WHAT AM I--"
"YOU DO WHAT I DO ON THE GROUND. BUT YOU DO IT UP THERE.
"GO TO RANN. FOLLOW THE LEAD. SOLVE THE MYSTERY.
"HELP THE GIRL."
"BRUCE, IT'S NOT THAT EASY.
"THAT WOULD TAKE WEEKS, MONTHS, AND THAT'S JUST THE BEGINNING...
"I HAVE RESPONSIBILITIES. HERE."
"AS DO I.
"WHICH IS WHY I'M STAYING.
"BUT THERE'S A DIFFERENCE BETWEEN YOU AND ME. BETWEEN YOU AND EVERYONE.
"WE'RE WHO WE ARE.
"AND YOU'RE SUPERMAN."

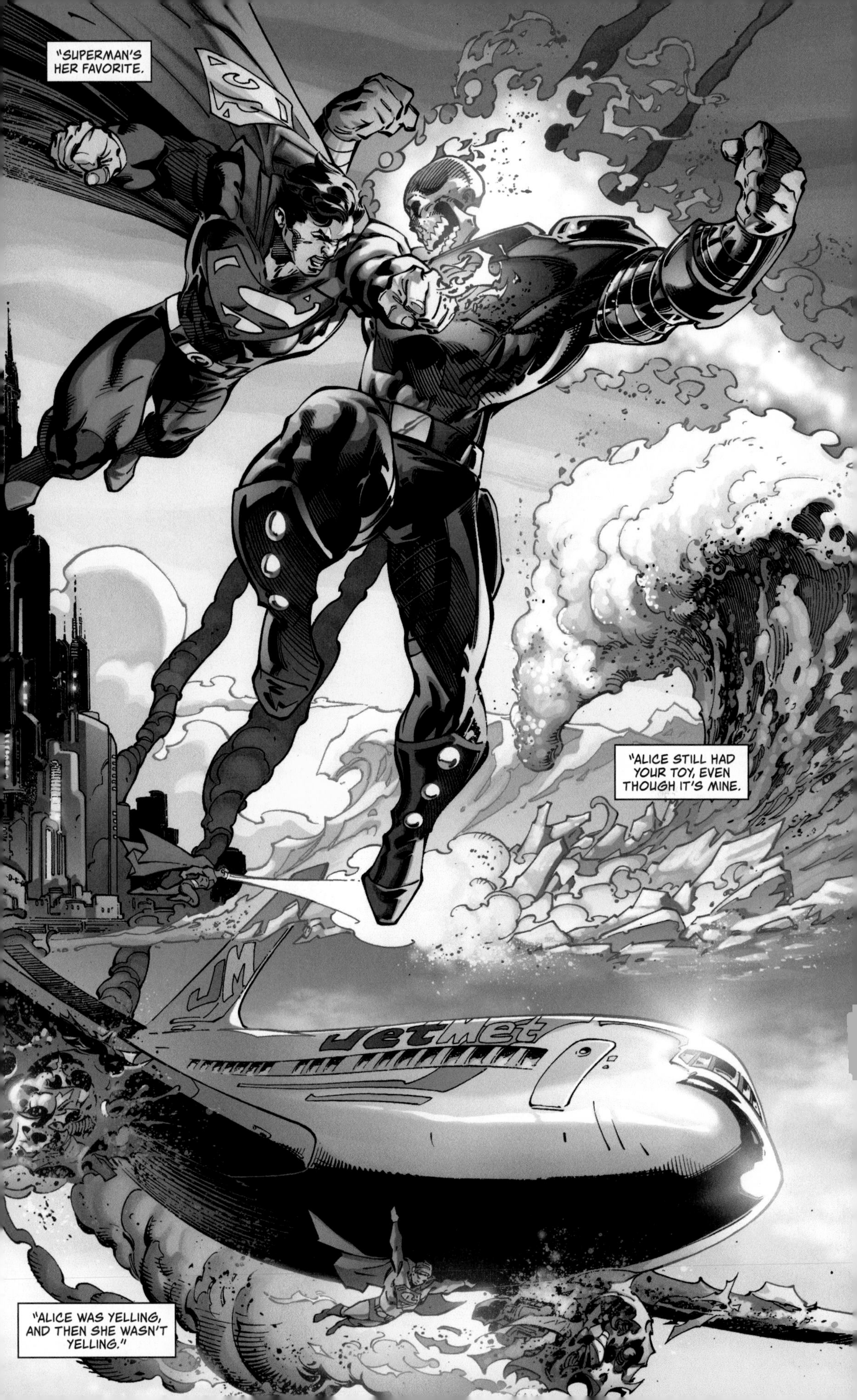
"SUPERMAN'S HER FAVORITE.
"ALICE STILL HAD YOUR TOY, EVEN THOUGH IT'S MINE.
JetMet
"ALICE WAS YELLING, AND THEN SHE WASN'T YELLING."

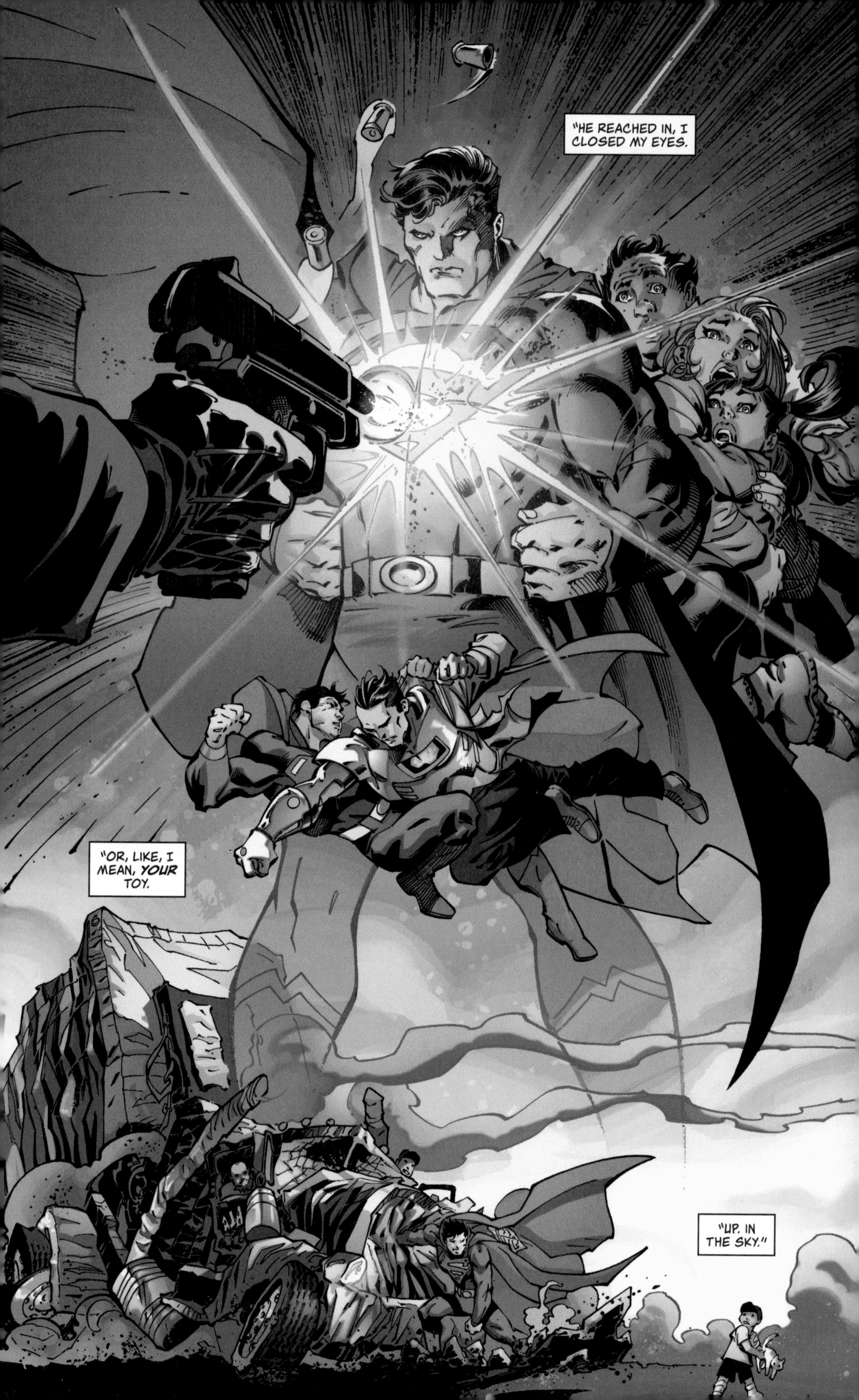
"HE REACHED IN, I CLOSED MY EYES.
"OR, LIKE, I MEAN, YOUR TOY.
"UP. IN THE SKY."

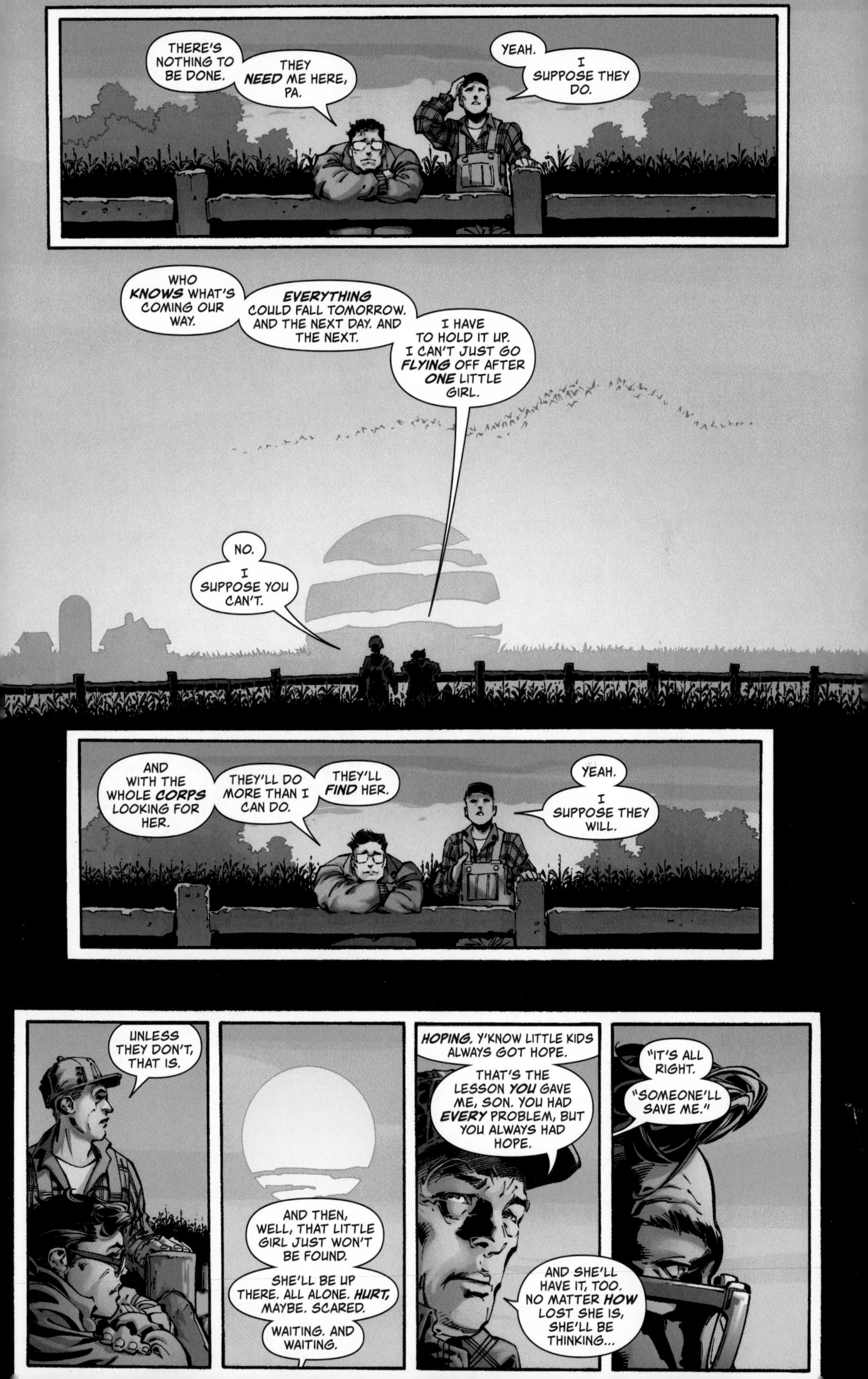
THERE'S NOTHING TO BE DONE.
THEY NEED ME HERE, PA.
YEAH.
I SUPPOSE THEY DO.
WHO KNOWS WHAT'S COMING OUR WAY.
EVERYTHING COULD FALL TOMORROW. AND THE NEXT DAY. AND THE NEXT.
I HAVE TO HOLD IT UP. I CAN'T JUST GO FLYING OFF AFTER ONE LITTLE GIRL.
NO.
I SUPPOSE YOU CAN'T.
AND WITH THE WHOLE CORPS LOOKING FOR HER.
THEY'LL DO MORE THAN I CAN DO.
THEY'LL FIND HER.
YEAH.
I SUPPOSE THEY WILL.
UNLESS THEY DON'T, THAT IS.
AND THEN, WELL, THAT LITTLE GIRL JUST WON'T BE FOUND.
SHE'LL BE UP THERE. ALL ALONE. HURT, MAYBE. SCARED.
WAITING. AND WAITING.
HOPING. Y'KNOW LITTLE KIDS ALWAYS GOT HOPE.
THAT'S THE LESSON YOU GAVE ME, SON. YOU HAD EVERY PROBLEM, BUT YOU ALWAYS HAD HOPE.
AND SHE'LL HAVE IT, TOO. NO MATTER HOW LOST SHE IS, SHE'LL BE THINKING...
"IT'S ALL RIGHT.
"SOMEONE'LL SAVE ME."

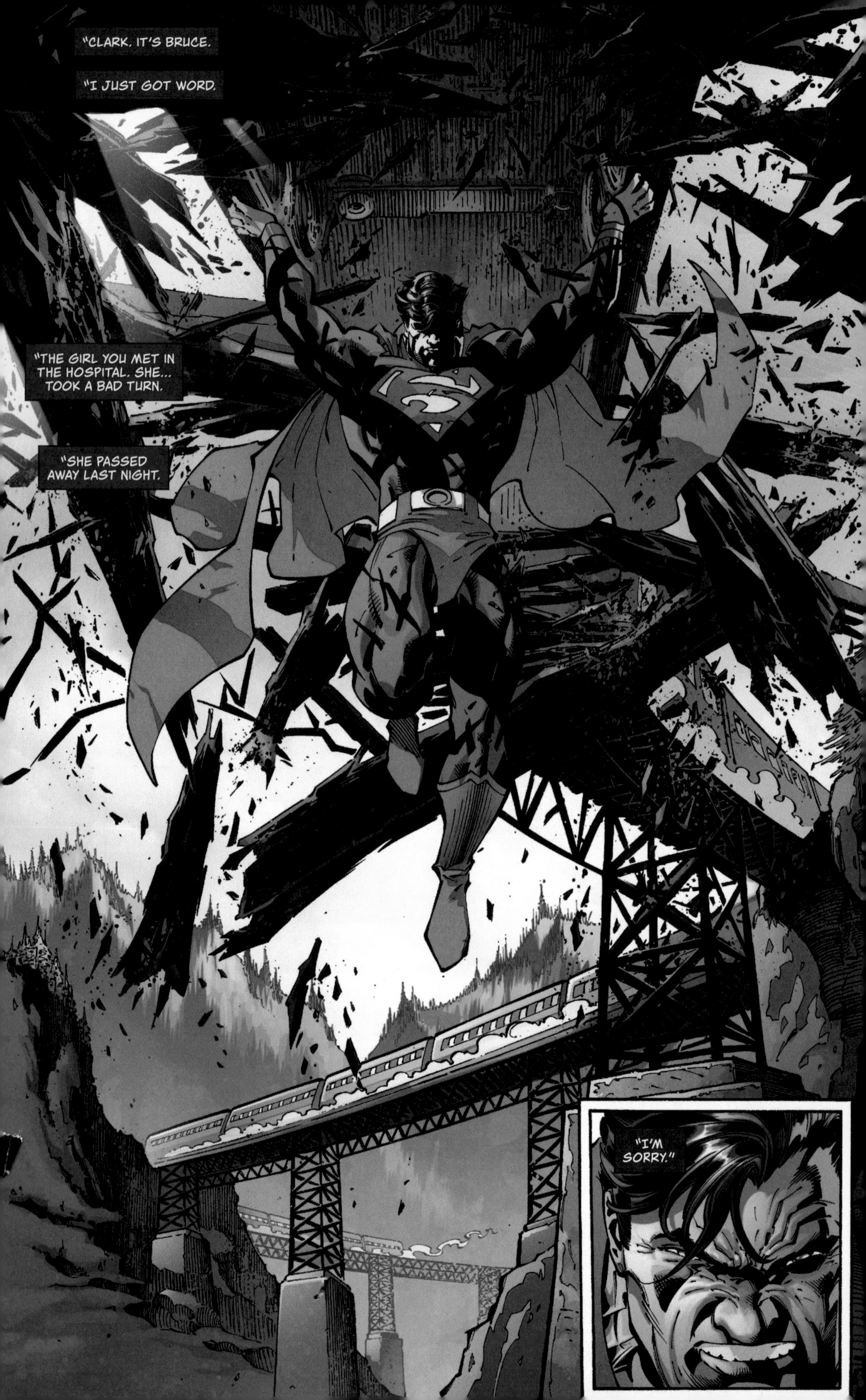
"CLARK. IT'S BRUCE.
"I JUST GOT WORD.
"THE GIRL YOU MET IN THE HOSPITAL. SHE... TOOK A BAD TURN.
"SHE PASSED AWAY LAST NIGHT.
"I'M SORRY."

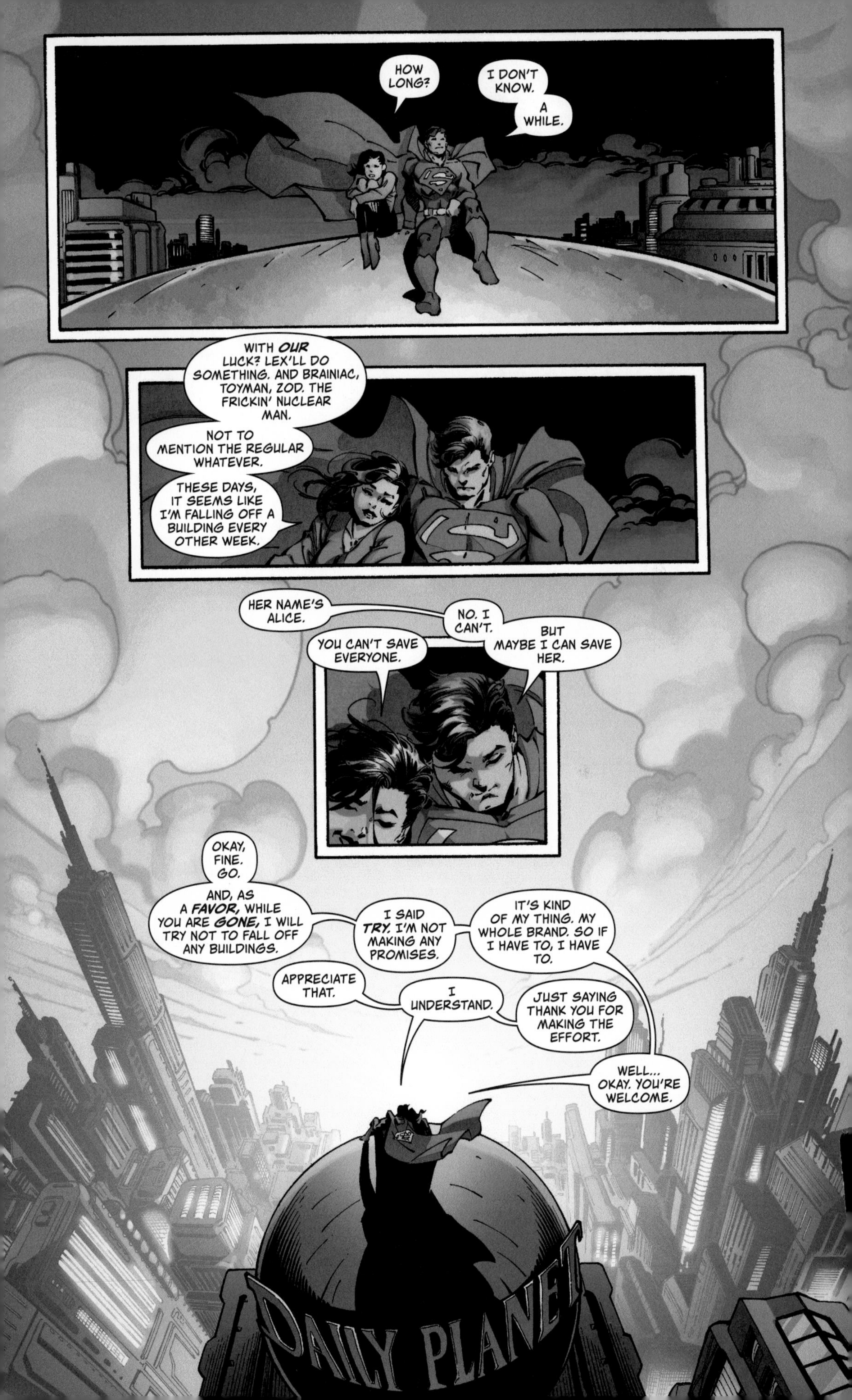
HOW LONG?
I DON'T KNOW. A WHILE.
WITH OUR LUCK? LEX'LL DO SOMETHING. AND BRAINIAC, TOYMAN, ZOD. THE FRICKIN' NUCLEAR MAN.
NOT TO MENTION THE REGULAR WHATEVER.
THESE DAYS, IT SEEMS LIKE I'M FALLING OFF A BUILDING EVERY OTHER WEEK.
HER NAME'S ALICE.
YOU CAN'T SAVE EVERYONE.
NO. I CAN'T.
BUT MAYBE I CAN SAVE HER.
OKAY, FINE. GO.
AND, AS A FAVOR, WHILE YOU ARE GONE, I WILL TRY NOT TO FALL OFF ANY BUILDINGS.
APPRECIATE THAT.
I SAID TRY. I'M NOT MAKING ANY PROMISES.
I UNDERSTAND.
IT'S KIND OF MY THING. MY WHOLE BRAND. SO IF I HAVE TO, I HAVE TO.
JUST SAYING THANK YOU FOR MAKING THE EFFORT.
WELL... OKAY. YOU'RE WELCOME.
DAILY PLANET

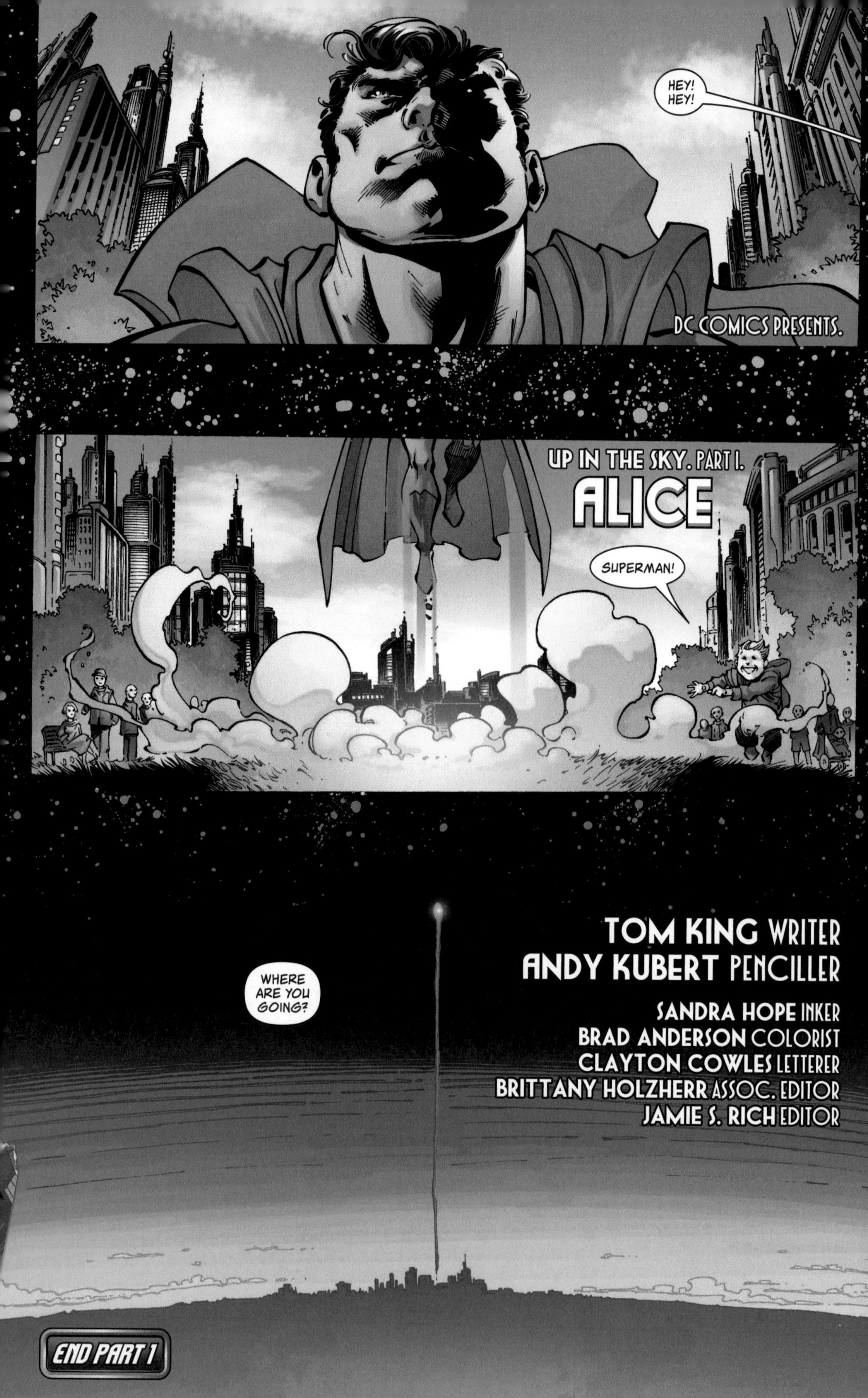
HEY! HEY!
DC COMICS PRESENTS.
UP IN THE SKY. PART I.
ALICE
SUPERMAN!
WHERE ARE YOU GOING?
TOM KING WRITER
ANDY KUBERT PENCILLER
SANDRA HOPE INKER
BRAD ANDERSON COLORIST
CLAYTON COWLES LETTERER
BRITTANY HOLZHERR ASSOC. EDITOR
JAMIE S. RICH EDITOR
END PART 1

I'M *SORRY*, AS I'VE TOLD THE CORPS-- REPEATEDLY--

TRACKING THESE *SO-CALLED* COUNTERFEIT ZETA BEAMS CRIMINALS ARE USING NOW...

WELL, IT'S *ABSOLUTELY* IMPOSSIBLE.

BUT THEY JUST *COMPLAIN.* "YOU HAVE THE DATA! HOW HARD COULD IT BE?"

OF COURSE WE HAVE THE DATA! THE ZETA BUILT *RANN* AS MUCH AS WE BUILT *THE ZETA!*

ANY USE OF *THAT* TECHNOLOGY WILL BE *MONITORED* AND RECORDED HERE!

THE *PROBLEM* IS WE HAVE *TOO MUCH* DATA.

AN *ACTIVE* ZETA EXISTS *EVERYWHERE* AT ONCE.

TRACKING IT IS LIKE TRYING TO CONTAIN THE UNIVERSE IN A THOUGHT.

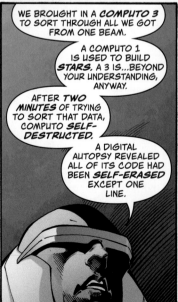

WE BROUGHT IN A *COMPUTO 3* TO SORT THROUGH ALL WE GOT FROM ONE BEAM.

A COMPUTO 1 IS USED TO BUILD *STARS.* A 3 IS...BEYOND YOUR UNDERSTANDING, ANYWAY.

AFTER *TWO MINUTES* OF TRYING TO SORT THAT DATA, COMPUTO *SELF-DESTRUCTED.*

A DIGITAL AUTOPSY REVEALED ALL OF ITS CODE HAD BEEN *SELF-ERASED* EXCEPT ONE LINE.

"*I CAN'T.*"

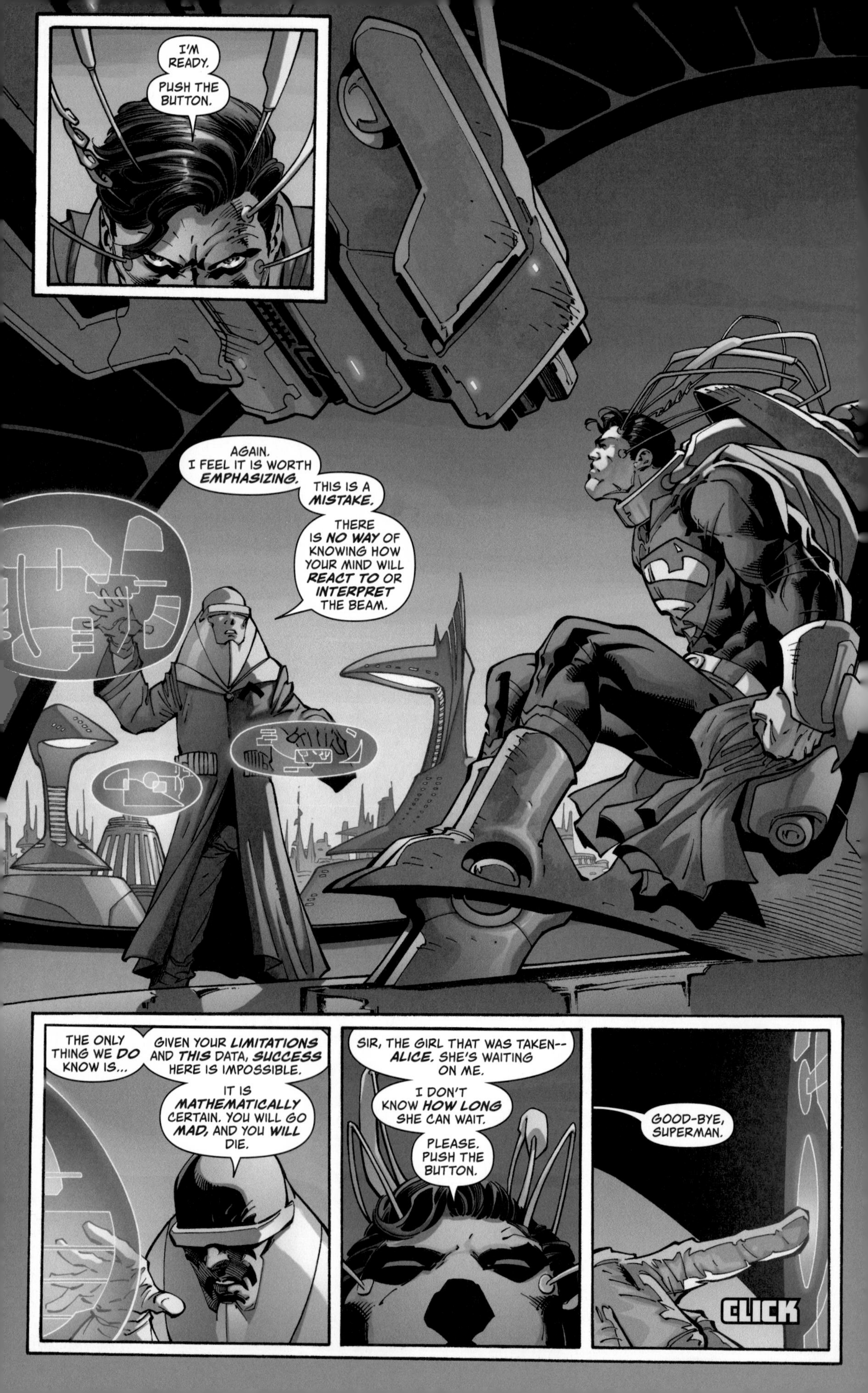
I'M READY.
PUSH THE BUTTON.
AGAIN. I FEEL IT IS WORTH EMPHASIZING.
THIS IS A MISTAKE.
THERE IS NO WAY OF KNOWING HOW YOUR MIND WILL REACT TO OR INTERPRET THE BEAM.
THE ONLY THING WE DO KNOW IS...
GIVEN YOUR LIMITATIONS AND THIS DATA, SUCCESS HERE IS IMPOSSIBLE.
IT IS MATHEMATICALLY CERTAIN. YOU WILL GO MAD, AND YOU WILL DIE.
SIR, THE GIRL THAT WAS TAKEN-- ALICE. SHE'S WAITING ON ME.
I DON'T KNOW HOW LONG SHE CAN WAIT.
PLEASE. PUSH THE BUTTON.
GOOD-BYE, SUPERMAN.
CLICK

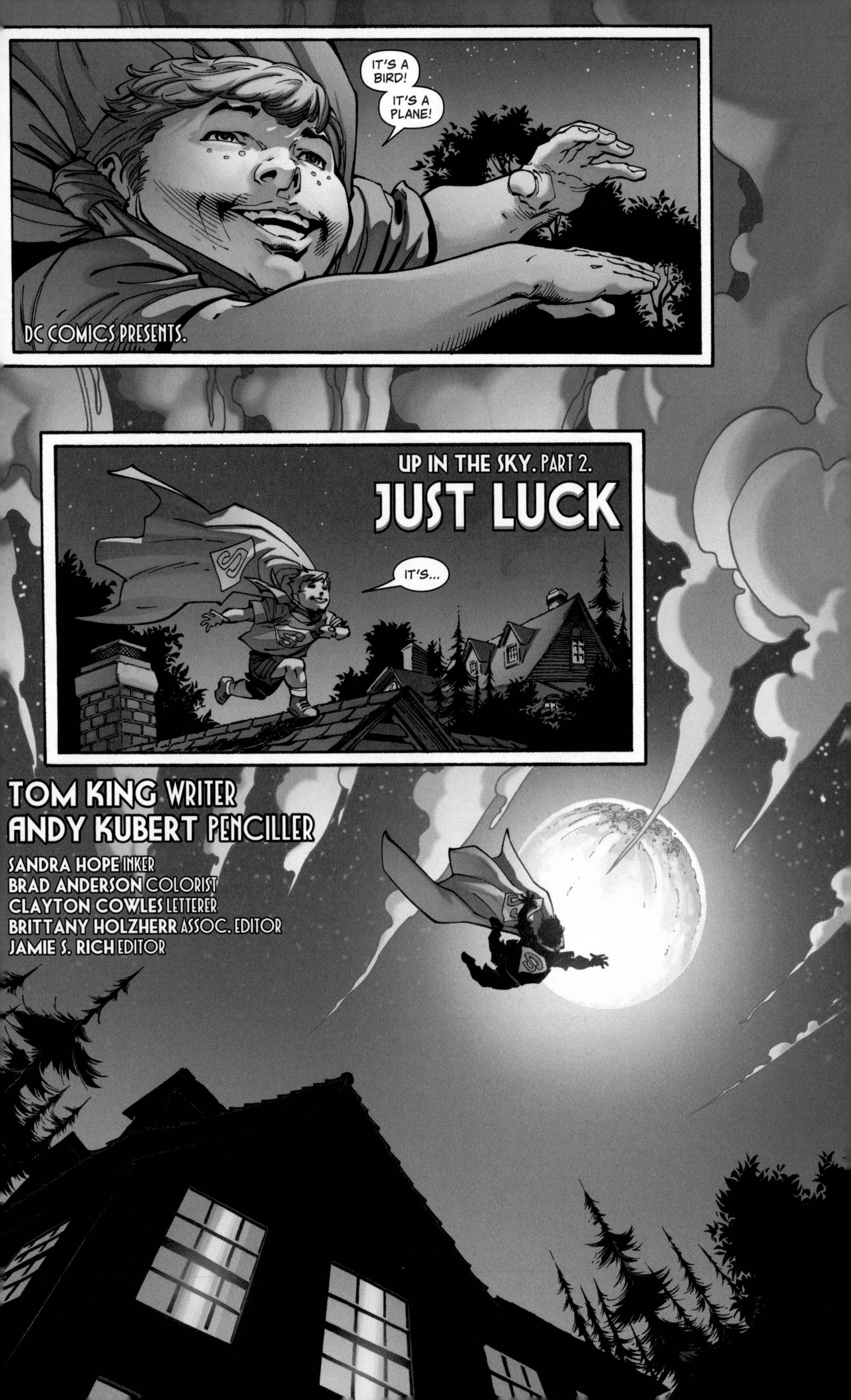

IT'S A BIRD!
IT'S A PLANE!
DC COMICS PRESENTS.
UP IN THE SKY. PART 2.
JUST LUCK
IT'S...
TOM KING WRITER
ANDY KUBERT PENCILLER
SANDRA HOPE INKER
BRAD ANDERSON COLORIST
CLAYTON COWLES LETTERER
BRITTANY HOLZHERR ASSOC. EDITOR
JAMIE S. RICH EDITOR

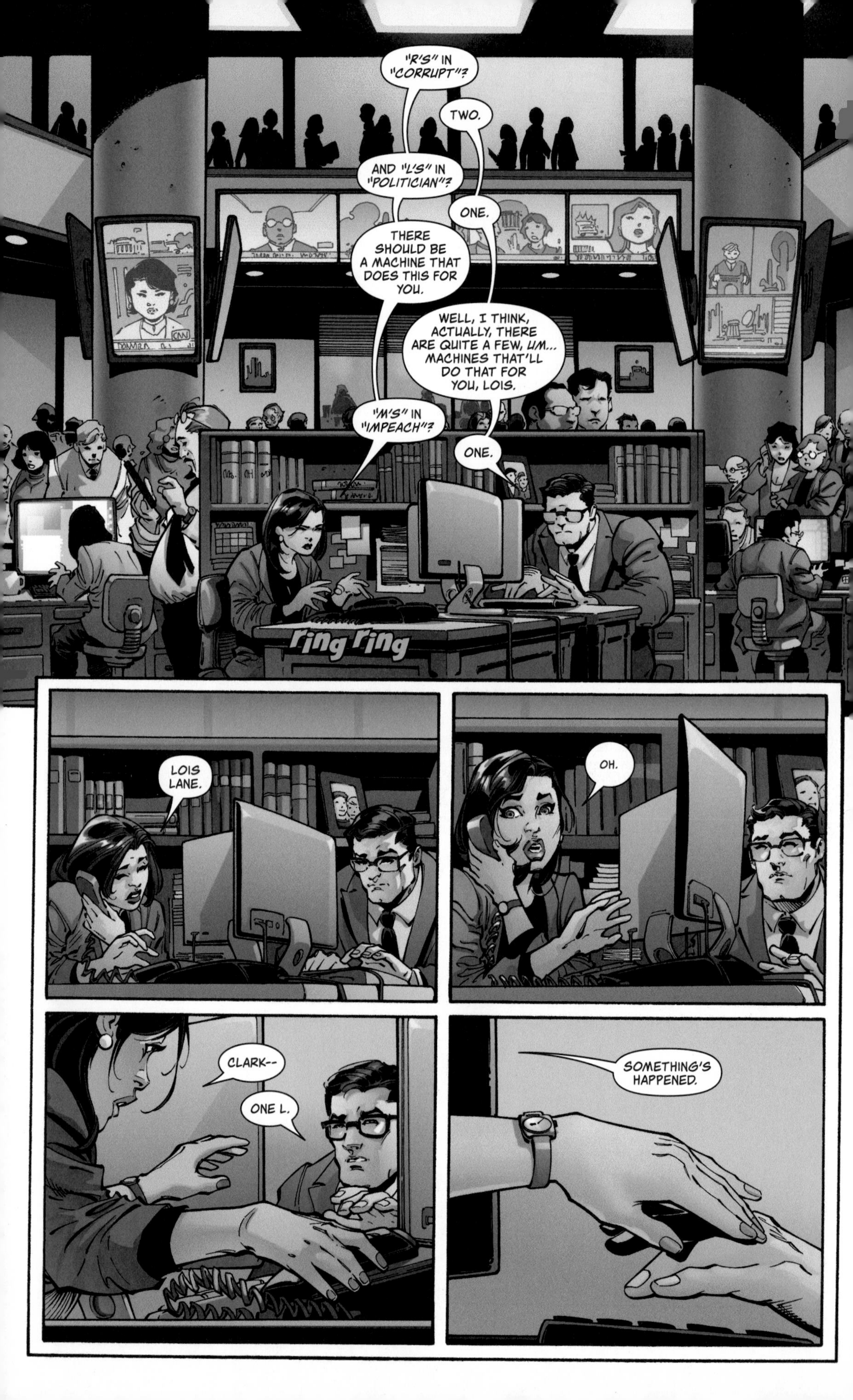
"R'S" IN "CORRUPT"?
TWO.
AND "L'S" IN "POLITICIAN"?
ONE.
THERE SHOULD BE A MACHINE THAT DOES THIS FOR YOU.
WELL, I THINK, ACTUALLY, THERE ARE QUITE A FEW, UM... MACHINES THAT'LL DO THAT FOR YOU, LOIS.
"M'S" IN "IMPEACH"?
ONE.
ring ring
LOIS LANE.
OH.
CLARK--
ONE L.
SOMETHING'S HAPPENED.

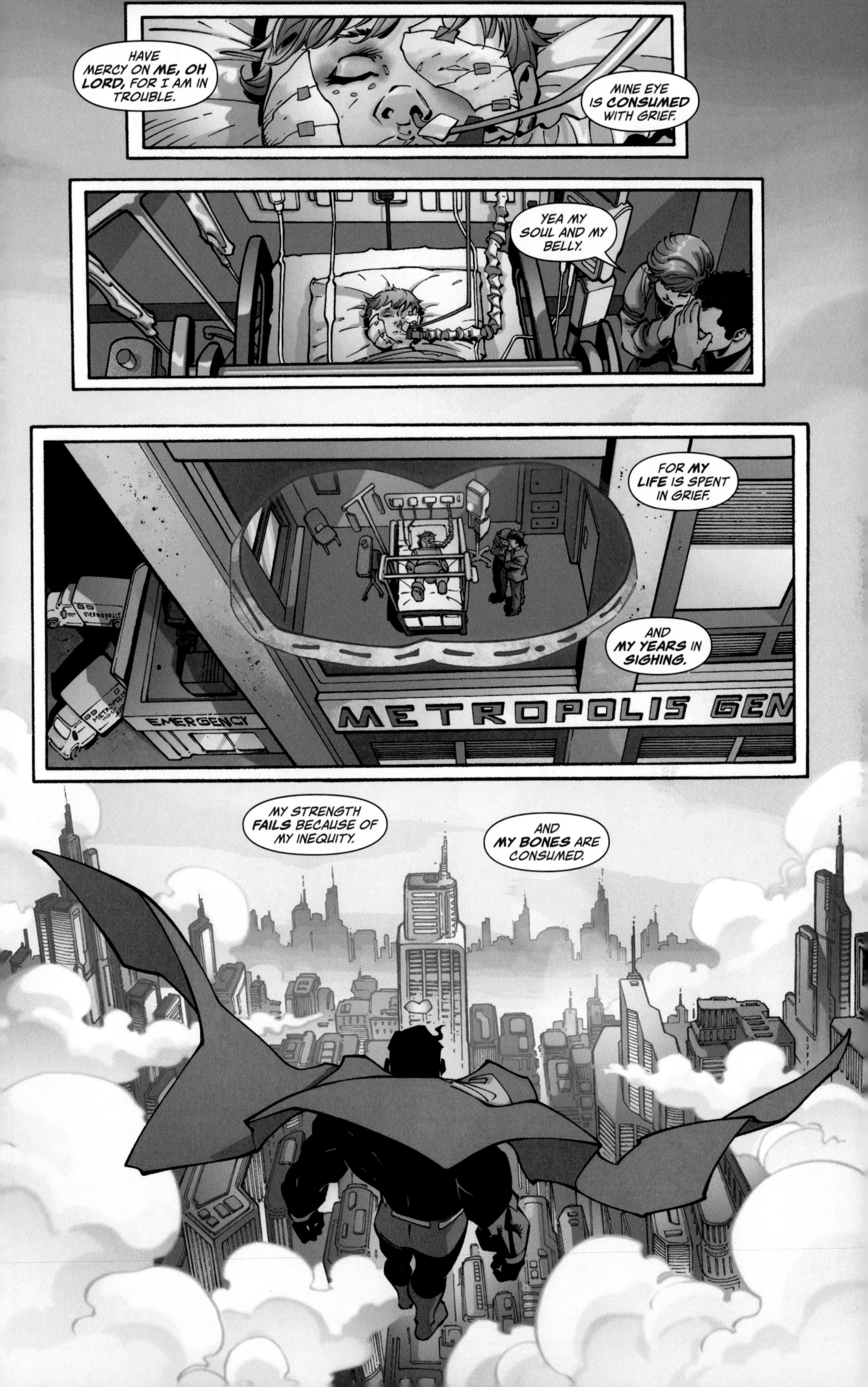
HAVE MERCY ON ME, OH LORD, FOR I AM IN TROUBLE.
MINE EYE IS CONSUMED WITH GRIEF.
YEA MY SOUL AND MY BELLY.
FOR MY LIFE IS SPENT IN GRIEF.
AND MY YEARS IN SIGHING.
METROPOLIS GEN
EMERGENCY
MY STRENGTH FAILS BECAUSE OF MY INEQUITY.
AND MY BONES ARE CONSUMED.

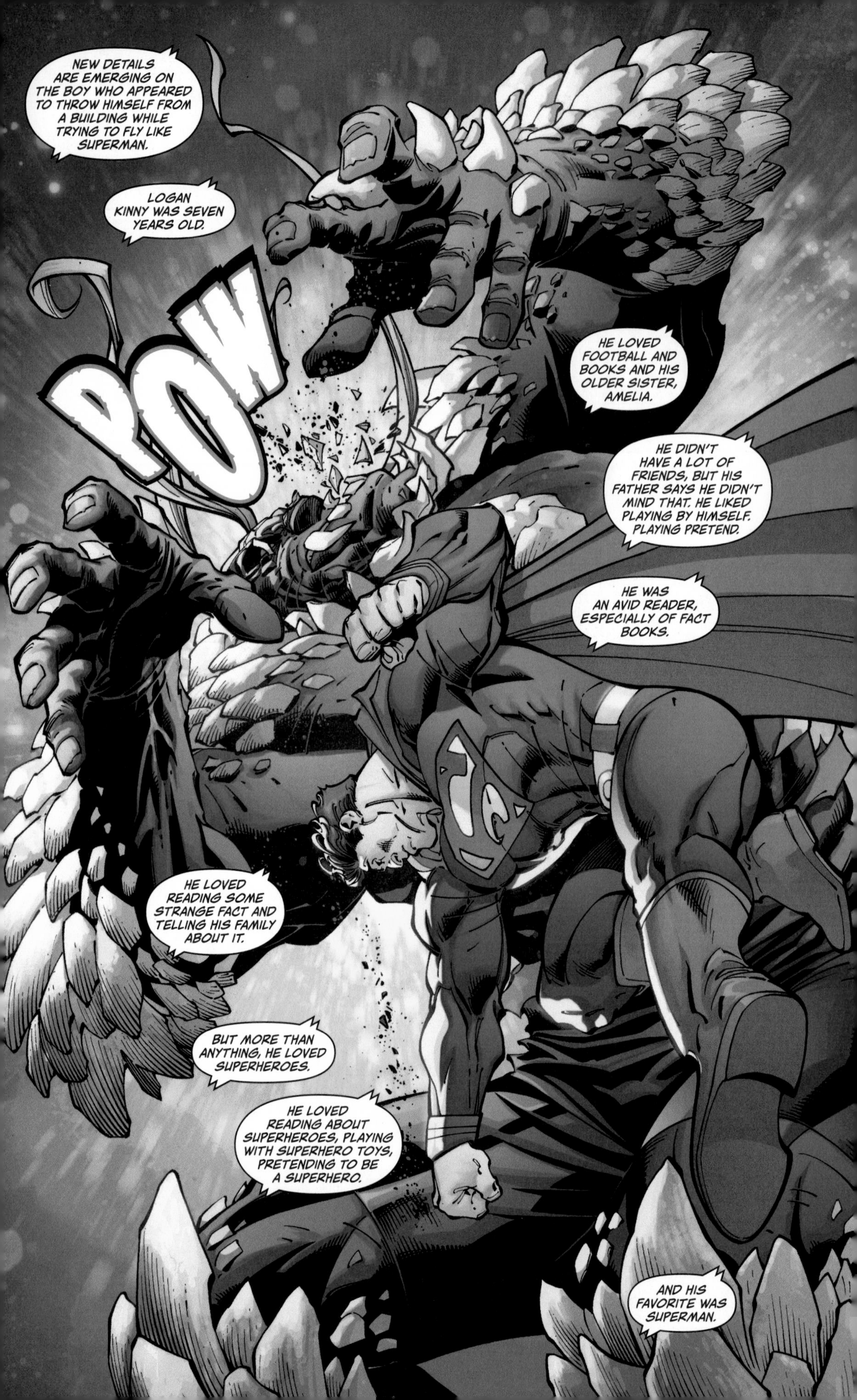
NEW DETAILS ARE EMERGING ON THE BOY WHO APPEARED TO THROW HIMSELF FROM A BUILDING WHILE TRYING TO FLY LIKE SUPERMAN.
LOGAN KINNY WAS SEVEN YEARS OLD.
POW
HE LOVED FOOTBALL AND BOOKS AND HIS OLDER SISTER, AMELIA.
HE DIDN'T HAVE A LOT OF FRIENDS, BUT HIS FATHER SAYS HE DIDN'T MIND THAT. HE LIKED PLAYING BY HIMSELF. PLAYING PRETEND.
HE WAS AN AVID READER, ESPECIALLY OF FACT BOOKS.
HE LOVED READING SOME STRANGE FACT AND TELLING HIS FAMILY ABOUT IT.
BUT MORE THAN ANYTHING, HE LOVED SUPERHEROES.
HE LOVED READING ABOUT SUPERHEROES, PLAYING WITH SUPERHERO TOYS, PRETENDING TO BE A SUPERHERO.
AND HIS FAVORITE WAS SUPERMAN.

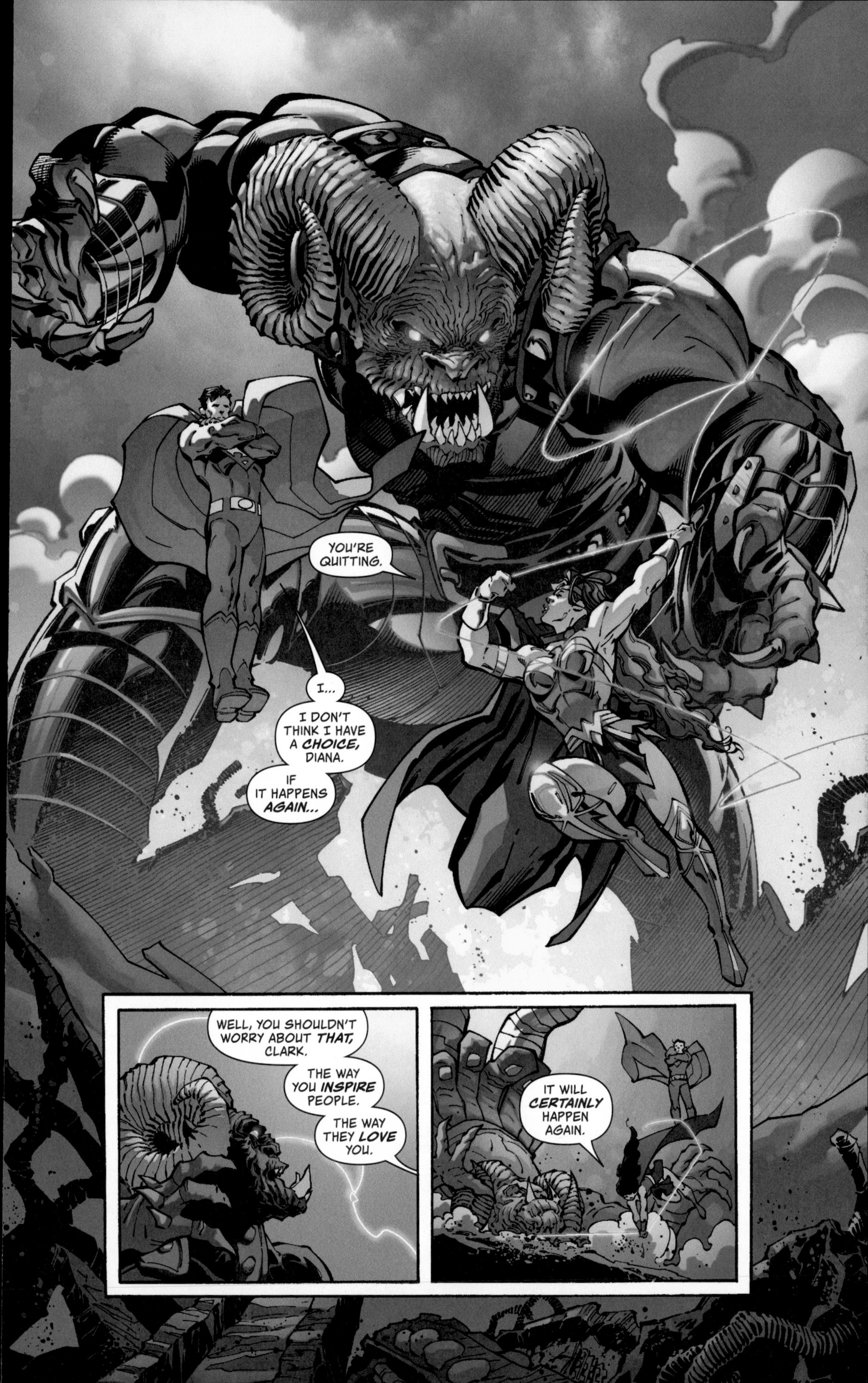
YOU'RE QUITTING.
I...
I DON'T THINK I HAVE A CHOICE, DIANA.
IF IT HAPPENS AGAIN...
WELL, YOU SHOULDN'T WORRY ABOUT THAT, CLARK.
THE WAY YOU INSPIRE PEOPLE.
THE WAY THEY LOVE YOU.
IT WILL CERTAINLY HAPPEN AGAIN.

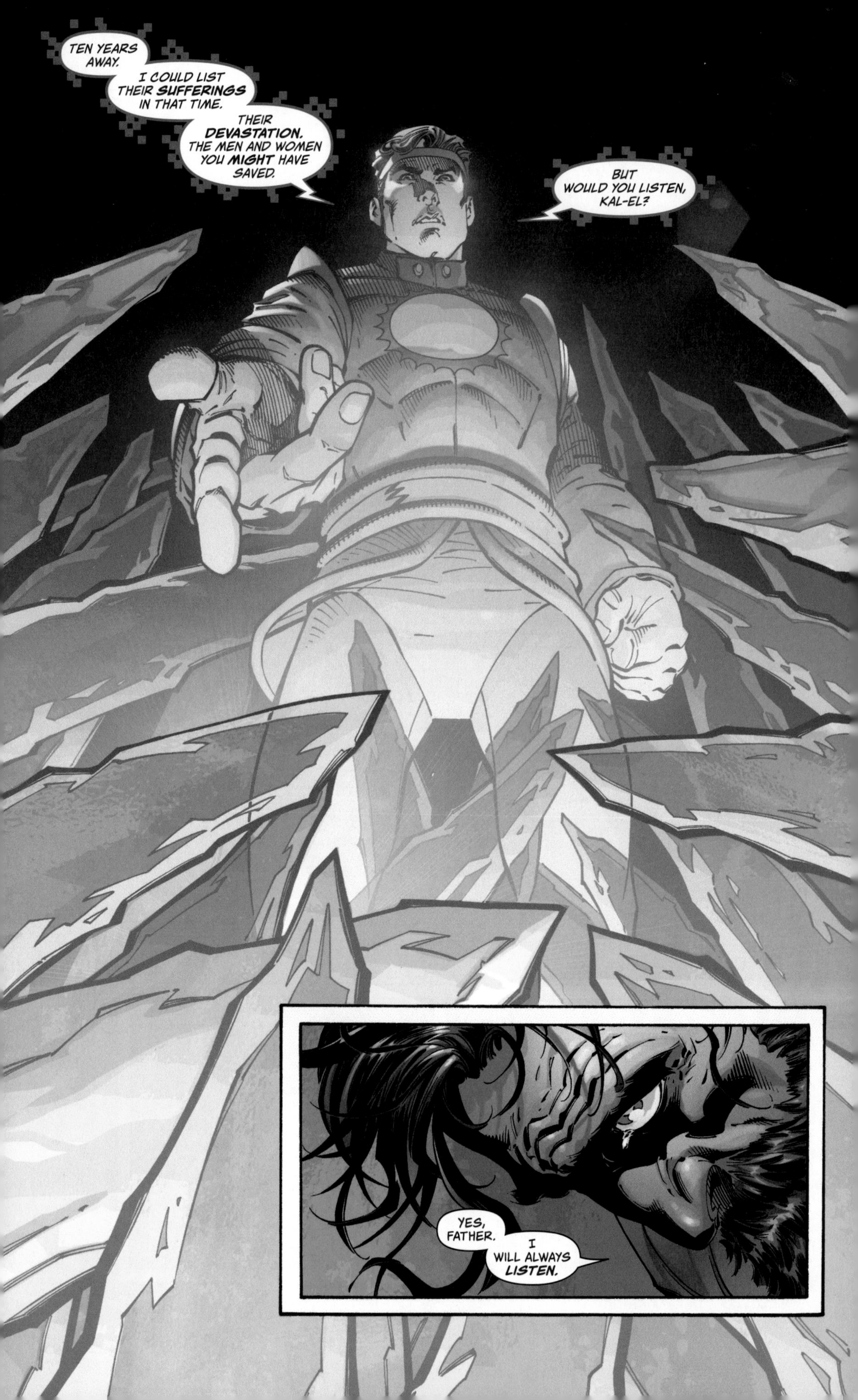
TEN YEARS AWAY.
I COULD LIST THEIR SUFFERINGS IN THAT TIME.
THEIR DEVASTATION. THE MEN AND WOMEN YOU MIGHT HAVE SAVED.
BUT WOULD YOU LISTEN, KAL-EL?
YES, FATHER.
I WILL ALWAYS LISTEN.

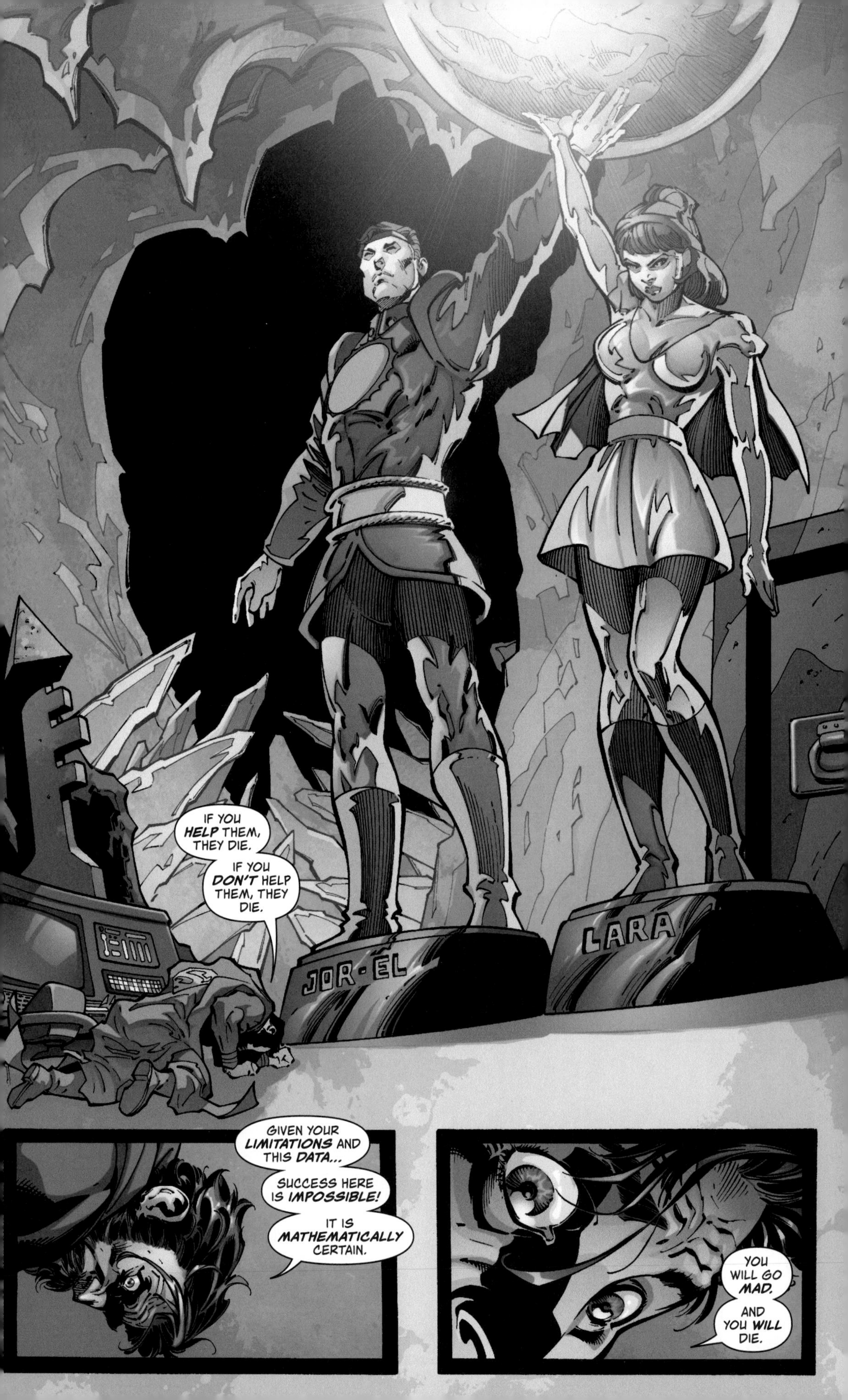
IF YOU HELP THEM, THEY DIE.
IF YOU DON'T HELP THEM, THEY DIE.
JOR-EL
LARA
GIVEN YOUR LIMITATIONS AND THIS DATA...
SUCCESS HERE IS IMPOSSIBLE!
IT IS MATHEMATICALLY CERTAIN.
YOU WILL GO MAD.
AND YOU WILL DIE.

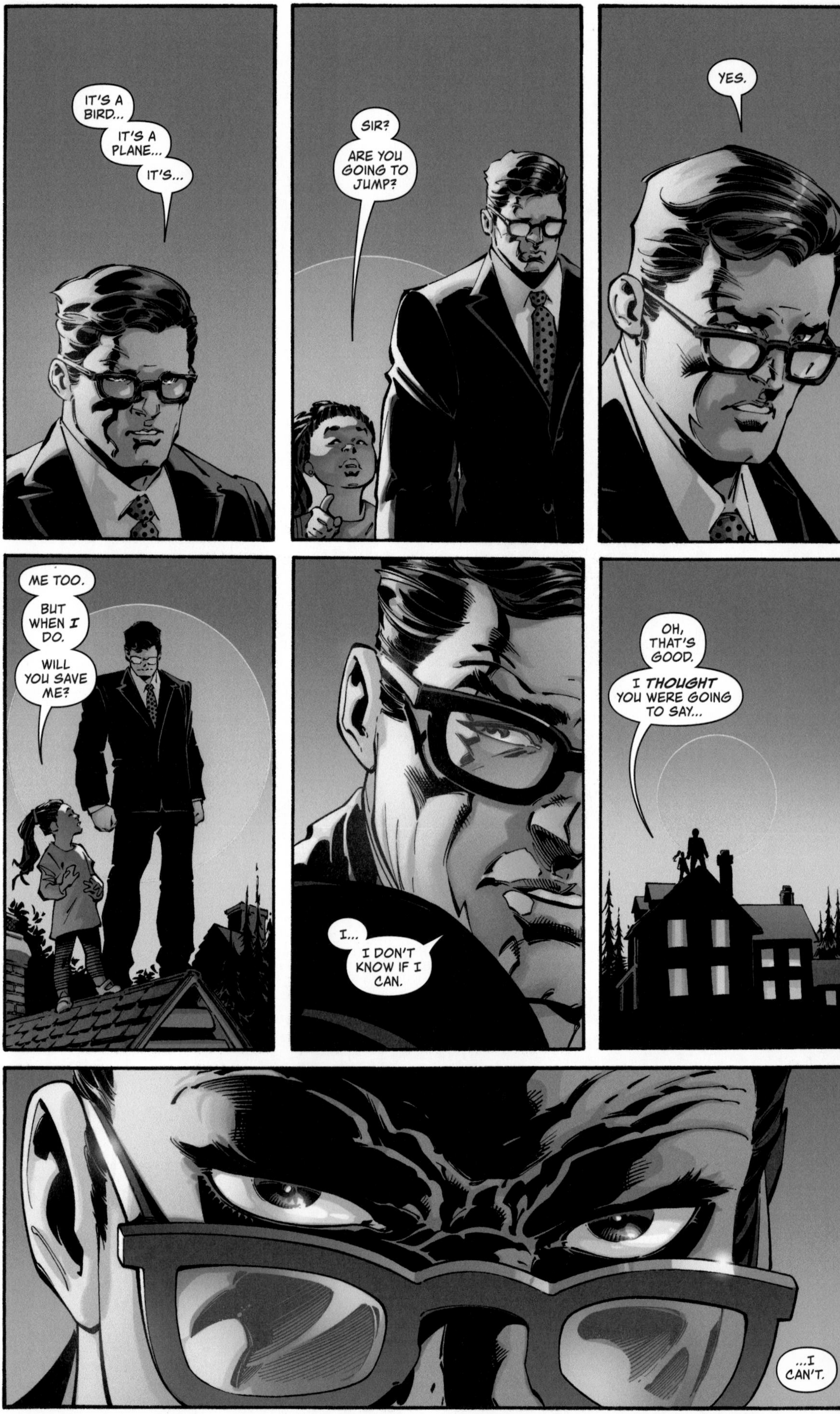
IT'S A BIRD...
IT'S A PLANE...
IT'S...
SIR?
ARE YOU GOING TO JUMP?
YES.
ME TOO.
BUT WHEN *I* DO.
WILL YOU SAVE ME?
I...
I DON'T KNOW IF I CAN.
OH, THAT'S GOOD.
I *THOUGHT* YOU WERE GOING TO SAY...
...I CAN'T.

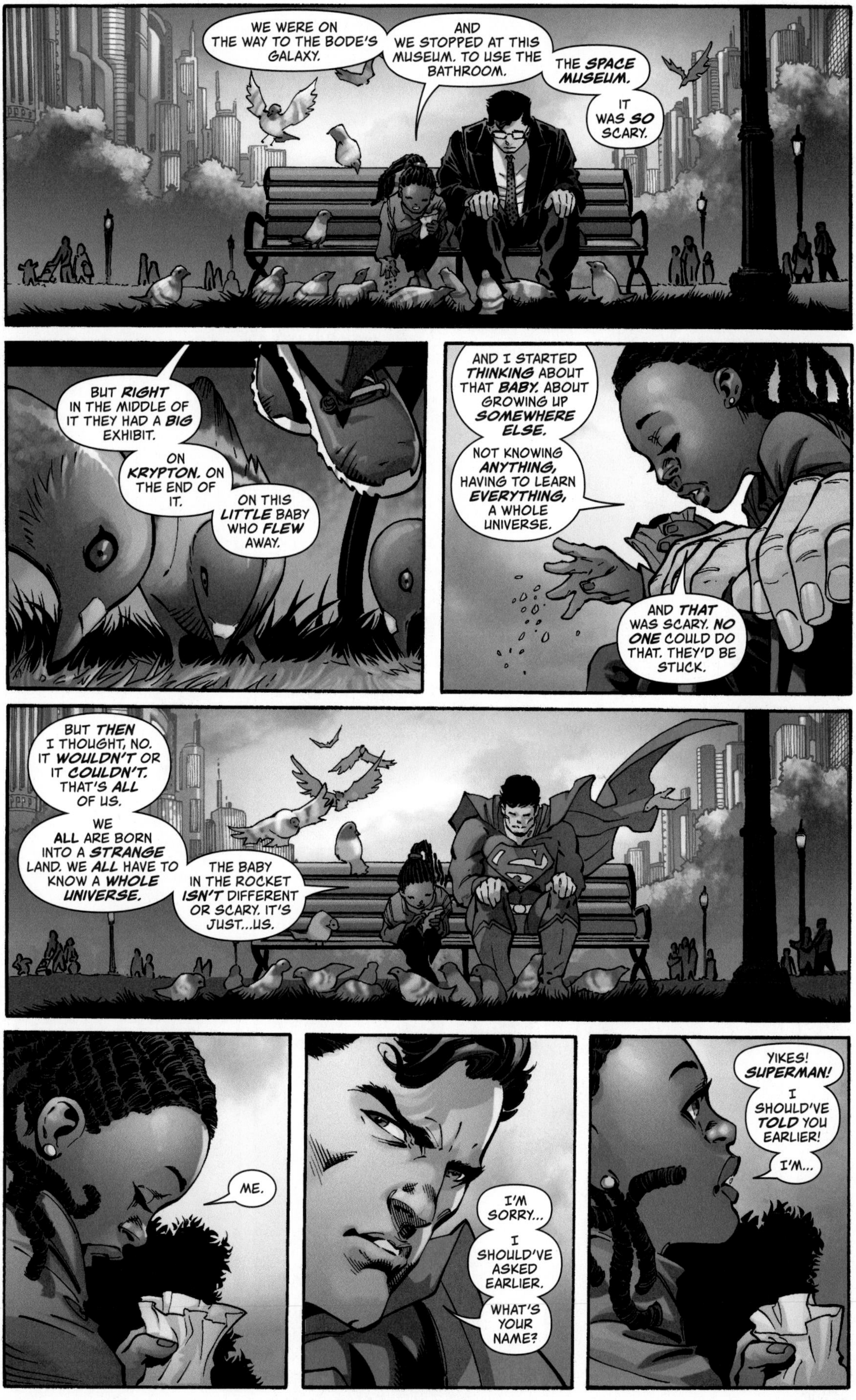
WE WERE ON THE WAY TO THE BODE'S GALAXY.
AND WE STOPPED AT THIS MUSEUM. TO USE THE BATHROOM.
THE SPACE MUSEUM.
IT WAS SO SCARY.
BUT RIGHT IN THE MIDDLE OF IT THEY HAD A BIG EXHIBIT.
ON KRYPTON. ON THE END OF IT.
ON THIS LITTLE BABY WHO FLEW AWAY.
AND I STARTED THINKING ABOUT THAT BABY. ABOUT GROWING UP SOMEWHERE ELSE.
NOT KNOWING ANYTHING, HAVING TO LEARN EVERYTHING, A WHOLE UNIVERSE.
AND THAT WAS SCARY. NO ONE COULD DO THAT. THEY'D BE STUCK.
BUT THEN I THOUGHT, NO. IT WOULDN'T OR IT COULDN'T. THAT'S ALL OF US.
WE ALL ARE BORN INTO A STRANGE LAND. WE ALL HAVE TO KNOW A WHOLE UNIVERSE.
THE BABY IN THE ROCKET ISN'T DIFFERENT OR SCARY. IT'S JUST...US.
ME.
I'M SORRY...
I SHOULD'VE ASKED EARLIER.
WHAT'S YOUR NAME?
YIKES! SUPERMAN!
I SHOULD'VE TOLD YOU EARLIER!
I'M...

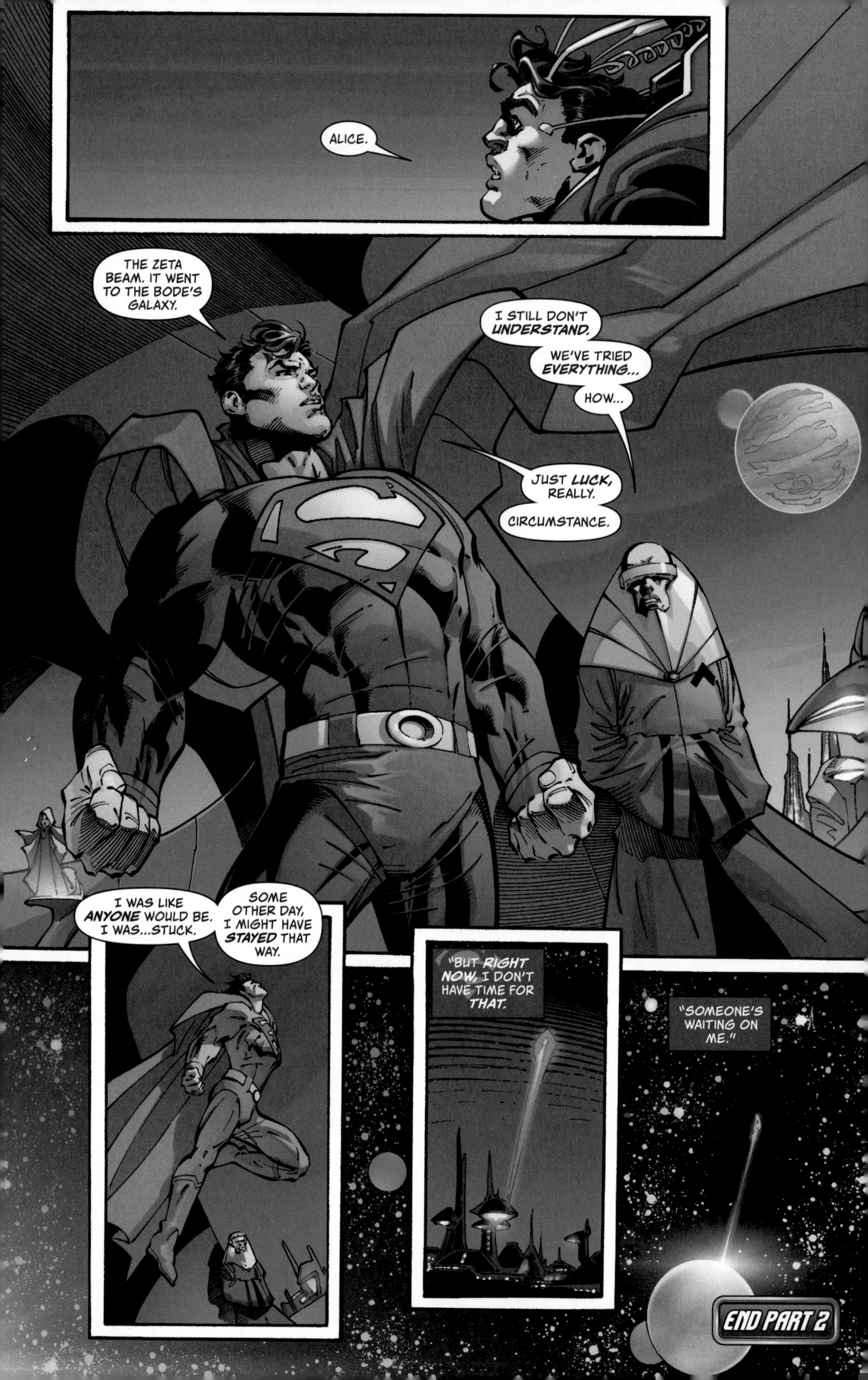
ALICE.
THE ZETA BEAM. IT WENT TO THE BODE'S GALAXY.
I STILL DON'T UNDERSTAND.
WE'VE TRIED EVERYTHING...
HOW...
JUST LUCK, REALLY.
CIRCUMSTANCE.
I WAS LIKE ANYONE WOULD BE. I WAS...STUCK.
SOME OTHER DAY, I MIGHT HAVE STAYED THAT WAY.
"BUT RIGHT NOW, I DON'T HAVE TIME FOR THAT.
"SOMEONE'S WAITING ON ME."
END PART 2

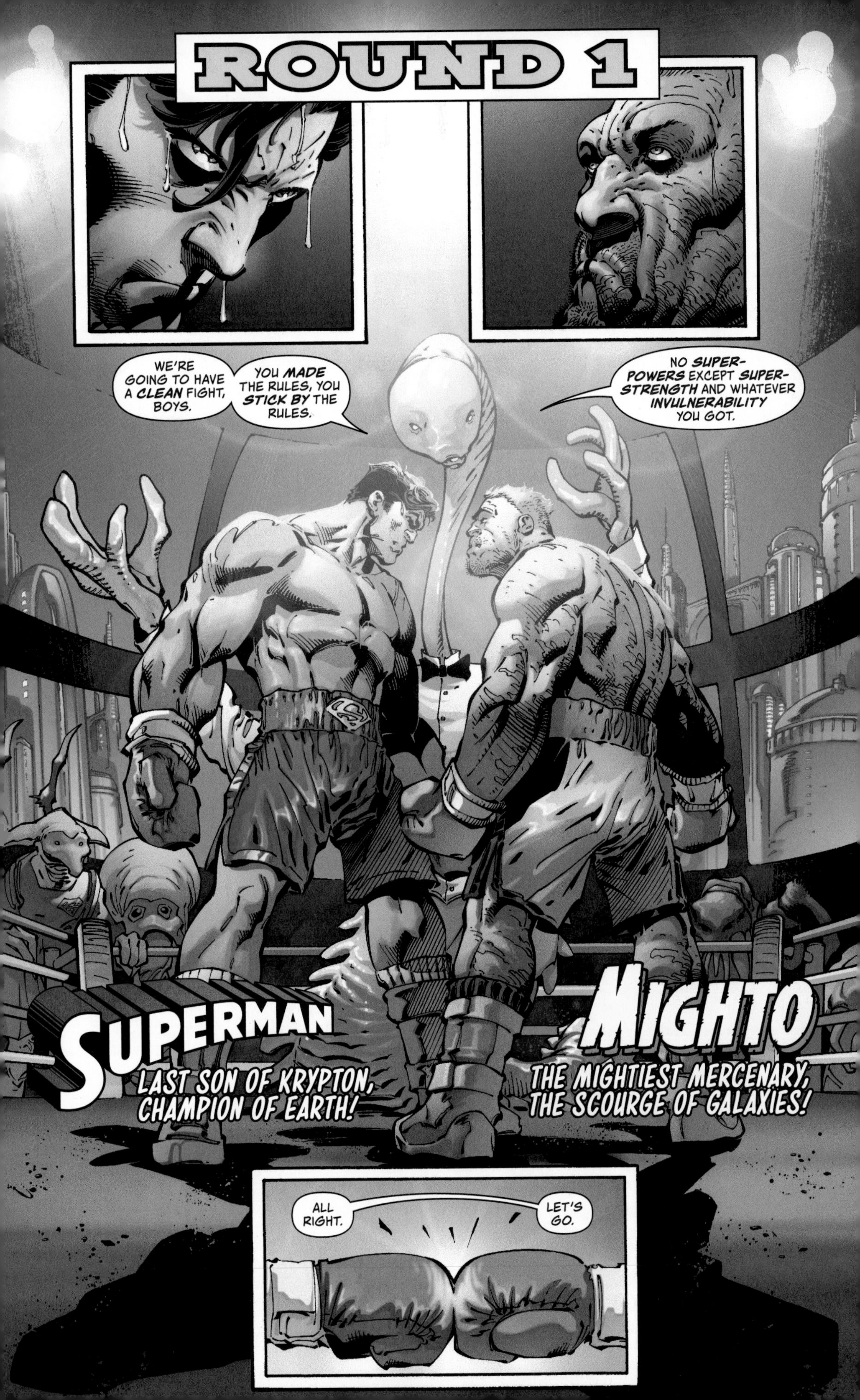
ROUND 1
WE'RE GOING TO HAVE A CLEAN FIGHT, BOYS.
YOU MADE THE RULES, YOU STICK BY THE RULES.
NO SUPER-POWERS EXCEPT SUPER-STRENGTH AND WHATEVER INVULNERABILITY YOU GOT.
SUPERMAN
LAST SON OF KRYPTON, CHAMPION OF EARTH!
MIGHTO
THE MIGHTIEST MERCENARY, THE SCOURGE OF GALAXIES!
ALL RIGHT.
LET'S GO.

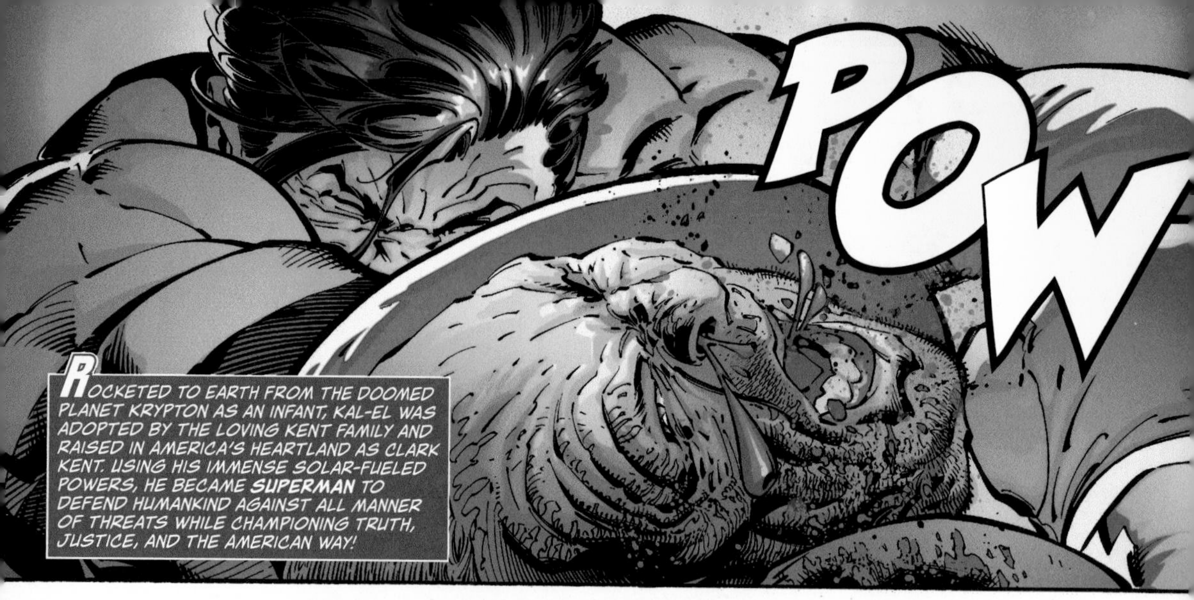
POW
ROCKETED TO EARTH FROM THE DOOMED PLANET KRYPTON AS AN INFANT, KAL-EL WAS ADOPTED BY THE LOVING KENT FAMILY AND RAISED IN AMERICA'S HEARTLAND AS CLARK KENT. USING HIS IMMENSE SOLAR-FUELED POWERS, HE BECAME SUPERMAN TO DEFEND HUMANKIND AGAINST ALL MANNER OF THREATS WHILE CHAMPIONING TRUTH, JUSTICE, AND THE AMERICAN WAY!

ROUND 2

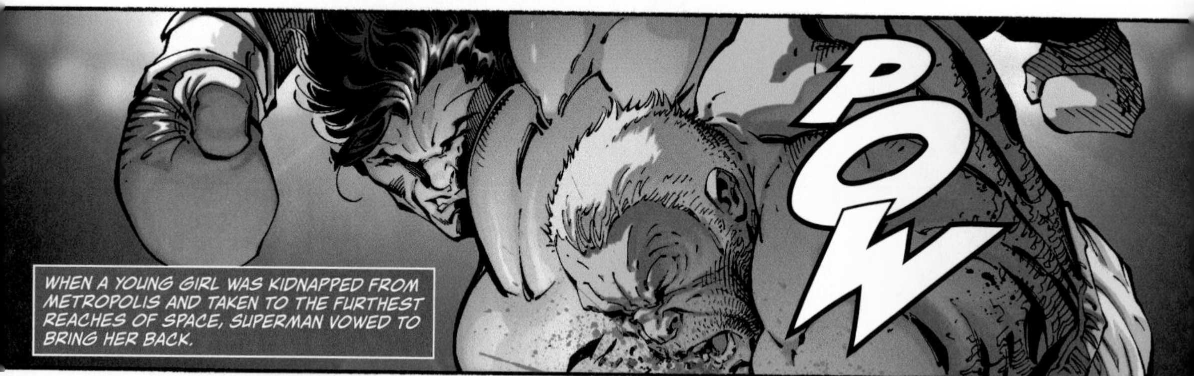
POW
WHEN A YOUNG GIRL WAS KIDNAPPED FROM METROPOLIS AND TAKEN TO THE FURTHEST REACHES OF SPACE, SUPERMAN VOWED TO BRING HER BACK.

DC COMICS PRESENTS

SUPERMAN: UP IN THE SKY. PART 3.

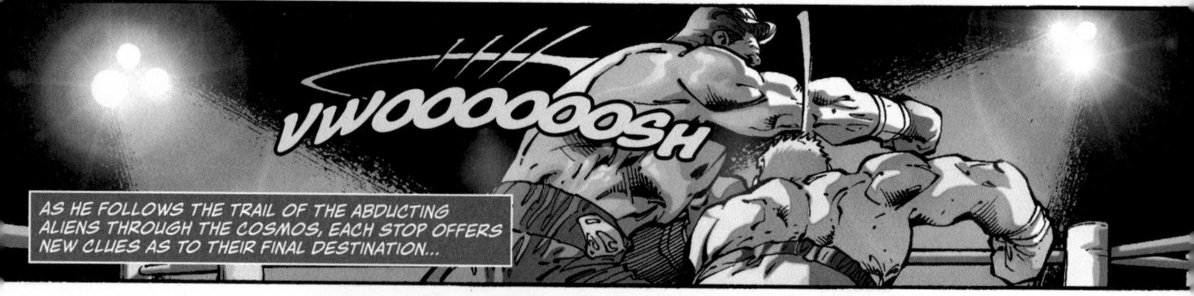
VWOOOOOOOSH
AS HE FOLLOWS THE TRAIL OF THE ABDUCTING ALIENS THROUGH THE COSMOS, EACH STOP OFFERS NEW CLUES AS TO THEIR FINAL DESTINATION...

FIGHT!!!

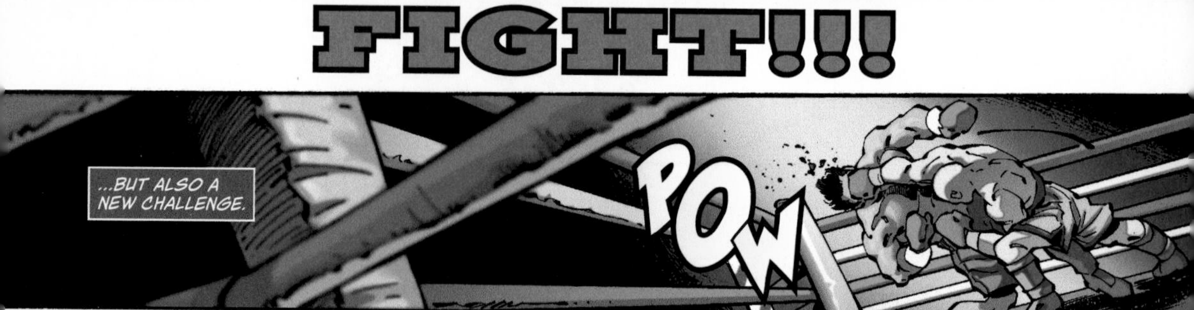
...BUT ALSO A NEW CHALLENGE.
POW

TOM KING WRITER **ANDY KUBERT** PENCILLER
SANDRA HOPE INKER **BRAD ANDERSON** COLORIST **CLAYTON COWLES** LETTERER
BRITTANY HOLZHERR ASSOC. EDITOR **JAMIE S. RICH** EDITOR

ROUND 3

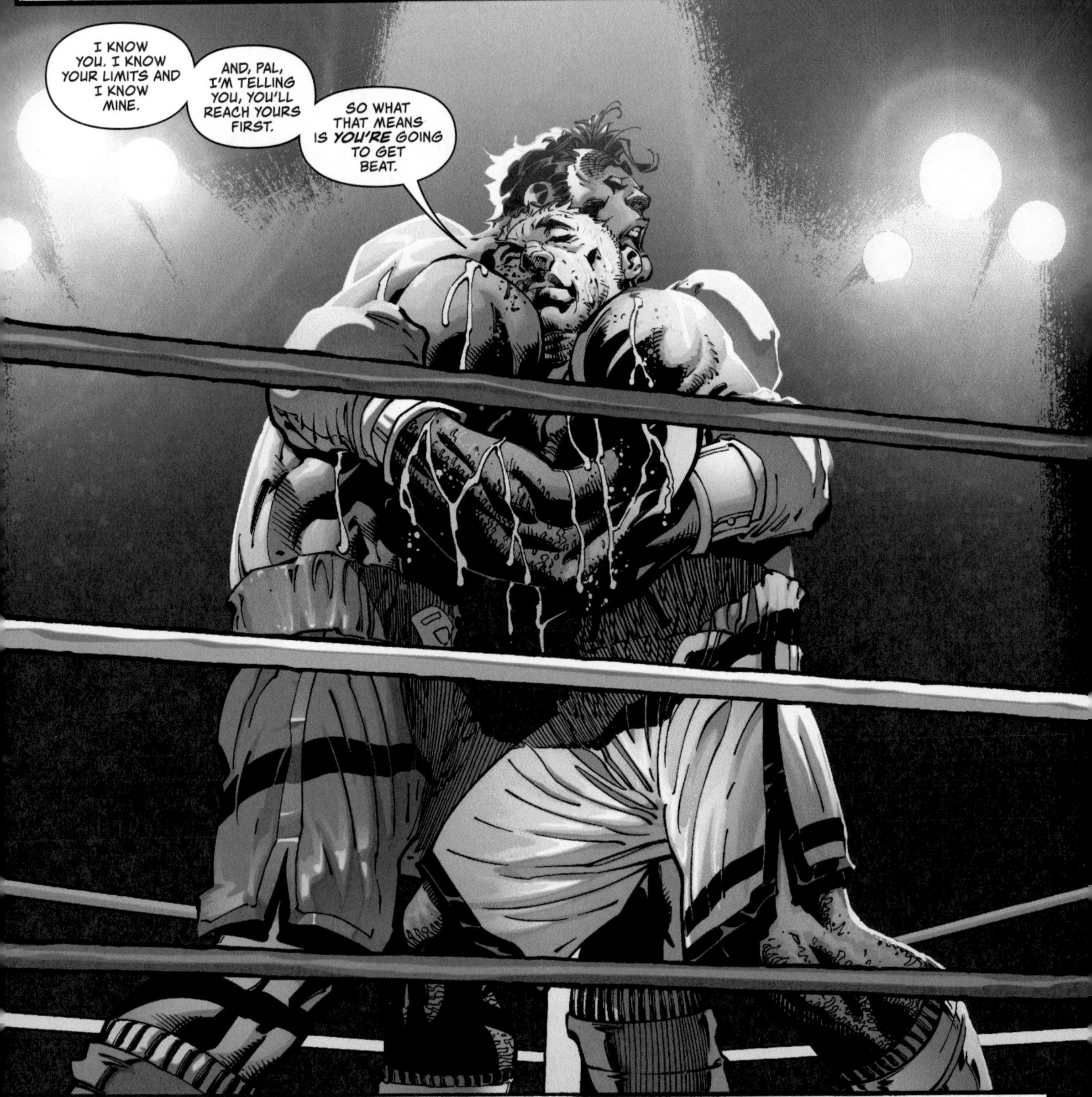
I KNOW YOU. I KNOW YOUR LIMITS AND I KNOW MINE.
AND, PAL, I'M TELLING YOU, YOU'LL REACH YOURS FIRST.
SO WHAT THAT MEANS IS *YOU'RE* GOING TO GET BEAT.

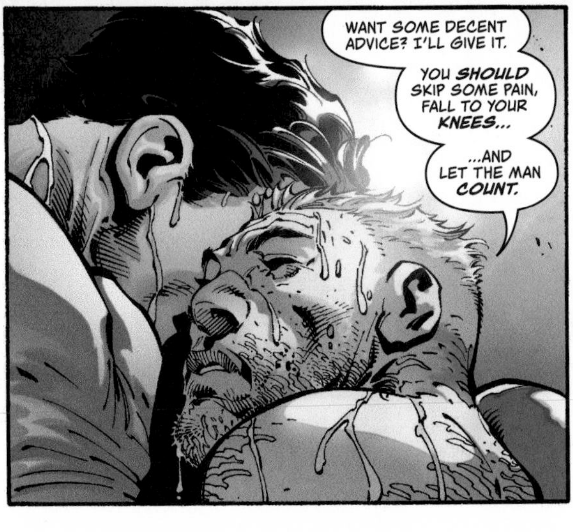
WANT SOME DECENT ADVICE? I'LL GIVE IT.
YOU *SHOULD* SKIP SOME PAIN, FALL TO YOUR *KNEES...*
...AND LET THE MAN *COUNT.*

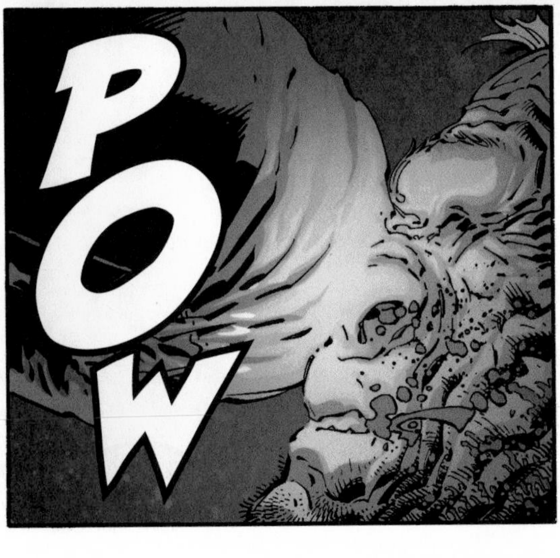
POW

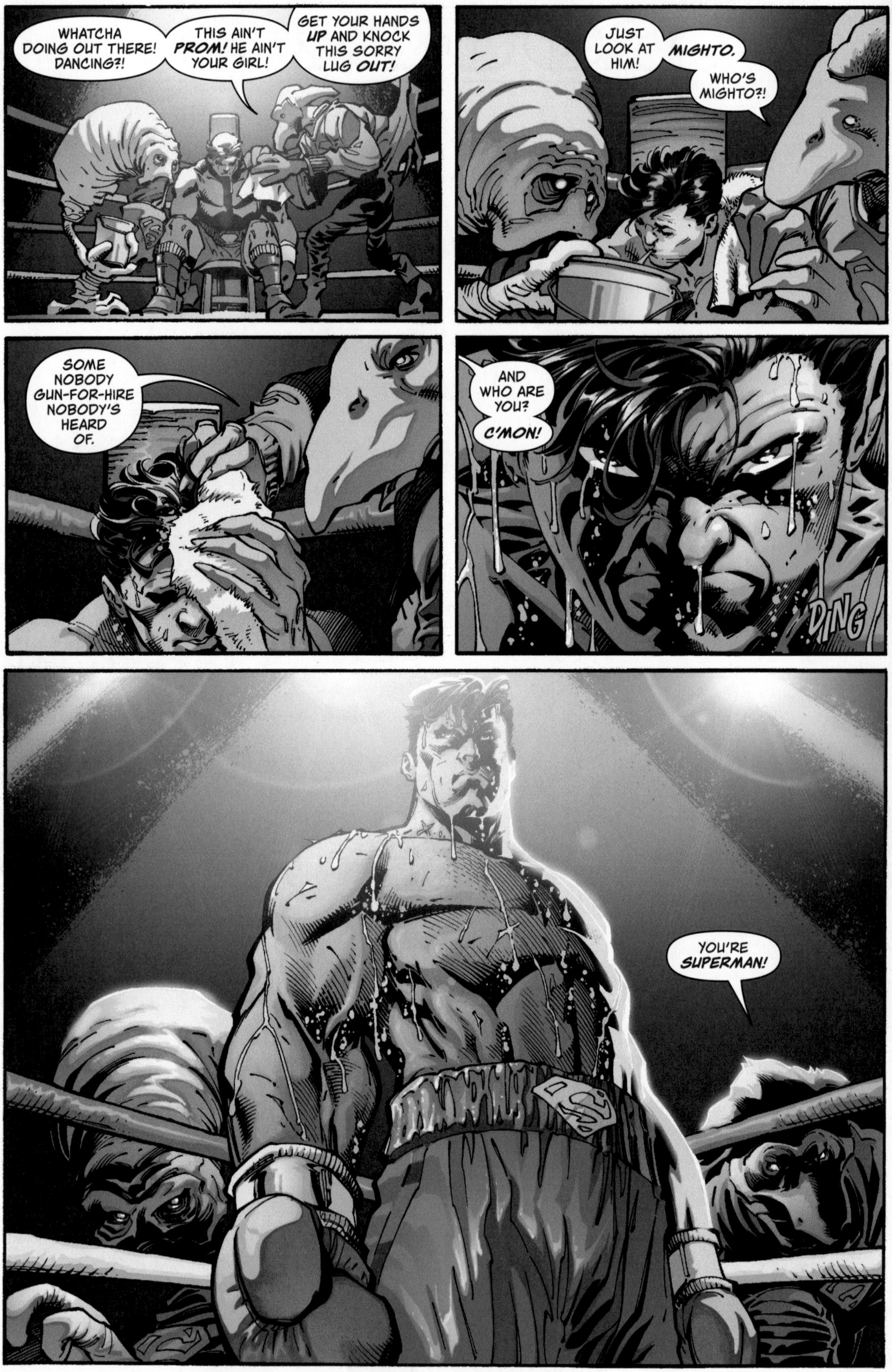
WHATCHA DOING OUT THERE! DANCING?!
THIS AIN'T PROM! HE AIN'T YOUR GIRL!
GET YOUR HANDS UP AND KNOCK THIS SORRY LUG OUT!
JUST LOOK AT HIM!
MIGHTO.
WHO'S MIGHTO?!
SOME NOBODY GUN-FOR-HIRE NOBODY'S HEARD OF.
AND WHO ARE YOU?
C'MON!
DING
YOU'RE SUPERMAN!

ROUND 4

ROUND 5

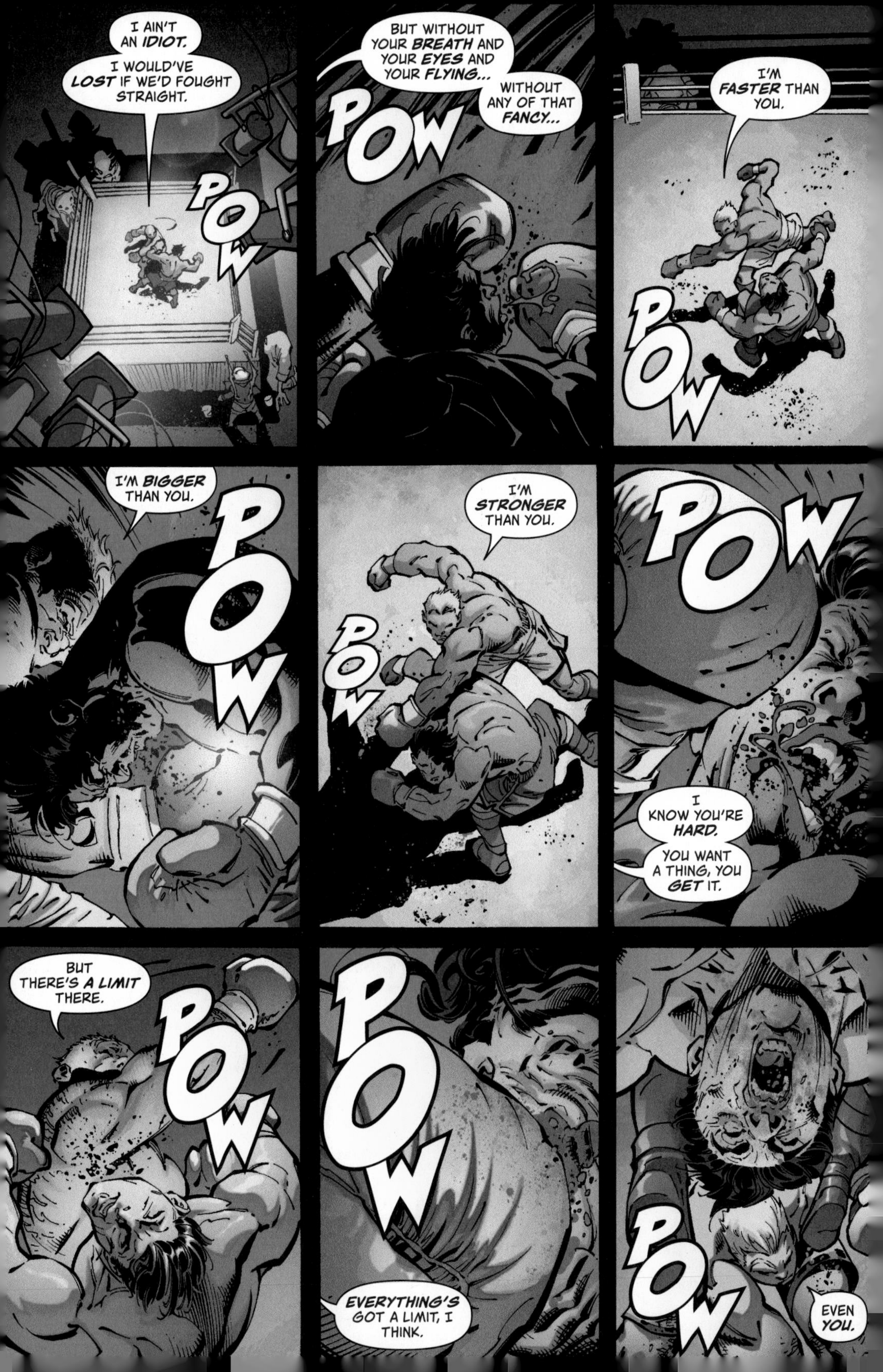

I AIN'T AN IDIOT.
I WOULD'VE LOST IF WE'D FOUGHT STRAIGHT.
POW
BUT WITHOUT YOUR BREATH AND YOUR EYES AND YOUR FLYING...
WITHOUT ANY OF THAT FANCY...
POW
I'M FASTER THAN YOU.
POW
I'M BIGGER THAN YOU.
POW
I'M STRONGER THAN YOU.
POW
POW
I KNOW YOU'RE HARD.
YOU WANT A THING, YOU GET IT.
BUT THERE'S A LIMIT THERE.
POW
POW
EVERYTHING'S GOT A LIMIT, I THINK.
POW
EVEN YOU.

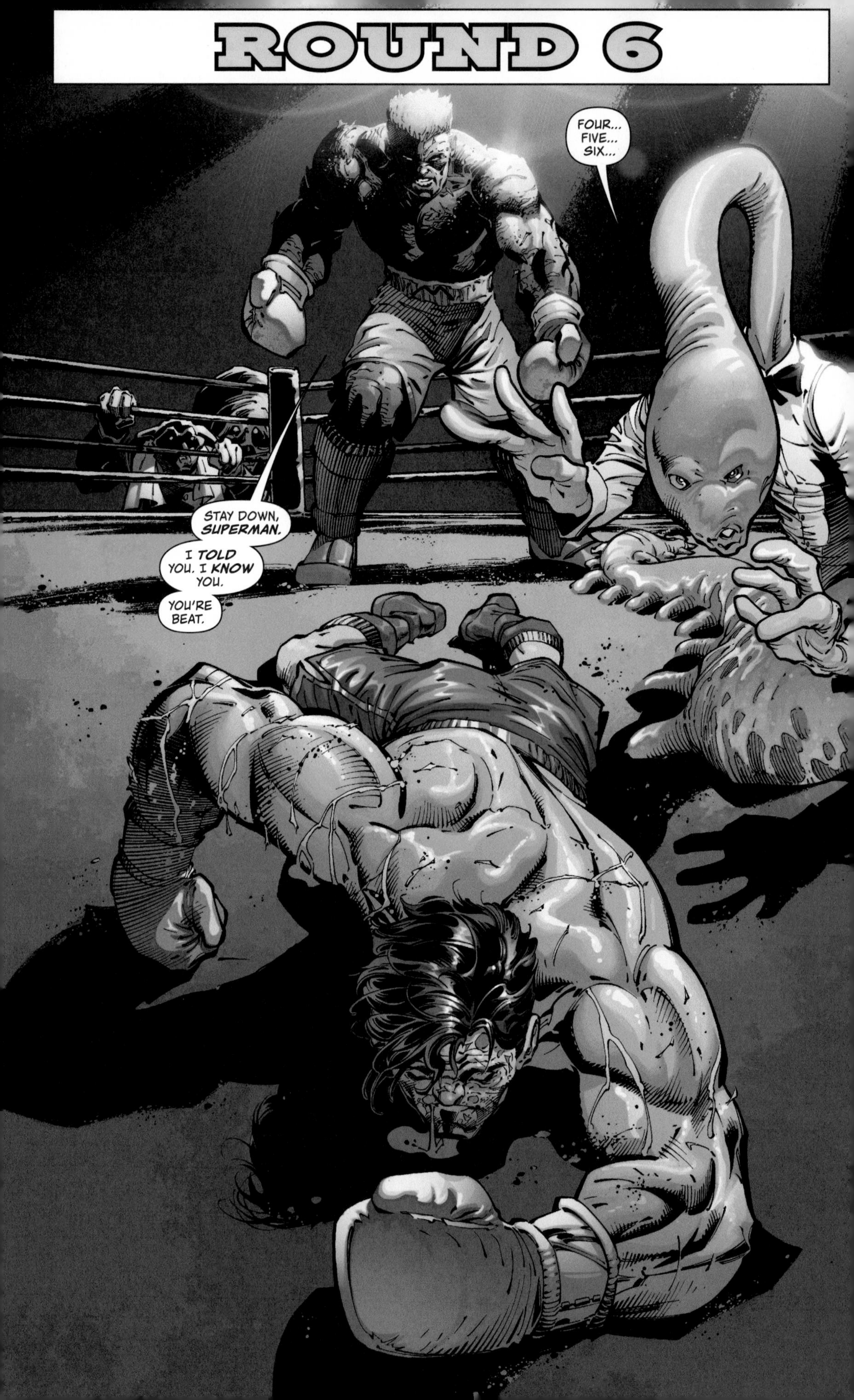
ROUND 6
FOUR... FIVE... SIX...
STAY DOWN, SUPERMAN.
I TOLD YOU. I KNOW YOU.
YOU'RE BEAT.

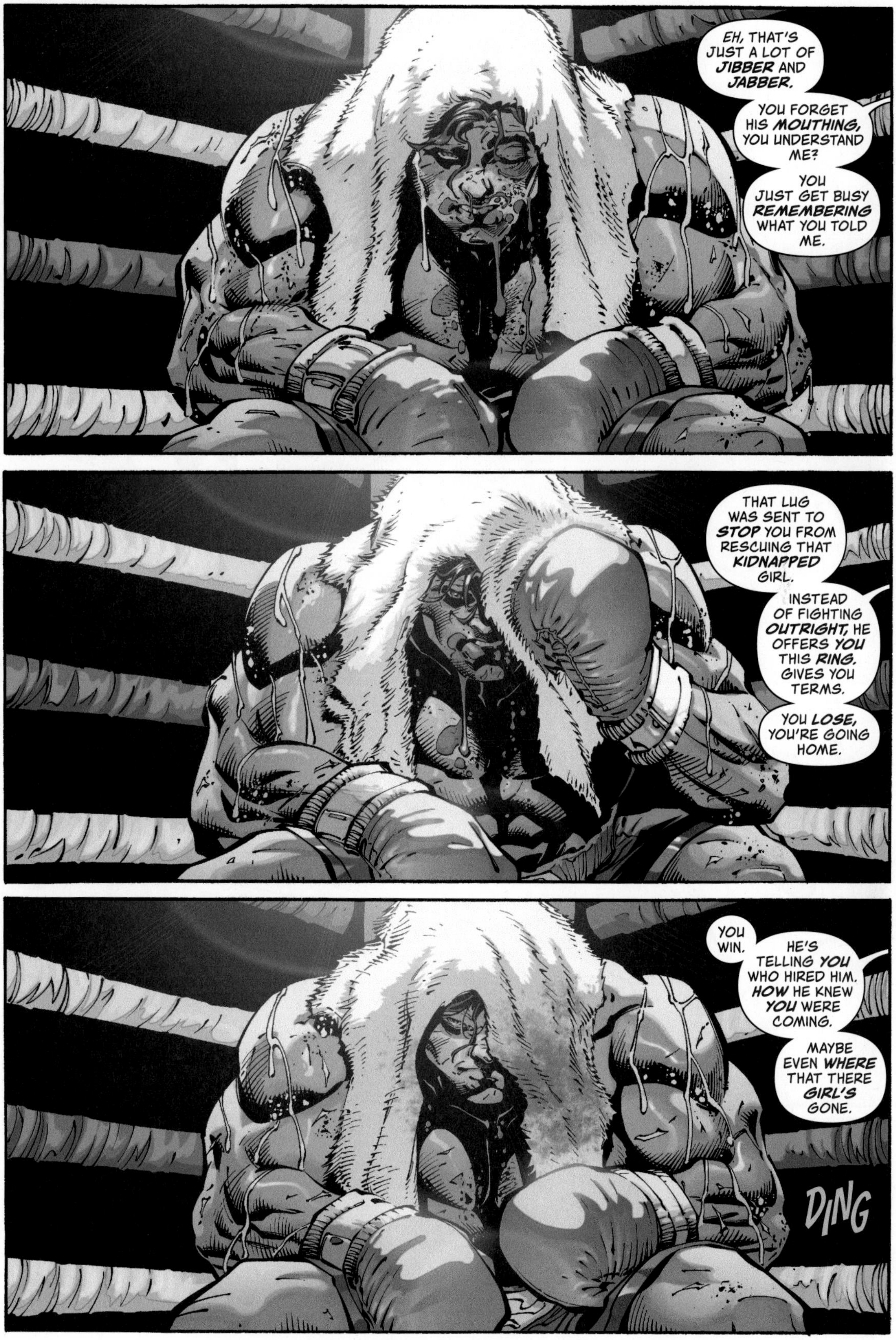
EH, THAT'S JUST A LOT OF JIBBER AND JABBER.
YOU FORGET HIS MOUTHING, YOU UNDERSTAND ME?
YOU JUST GET BUSY REMEMBERING WHAT YOU TOLD ME.
THAT LUG WAS SENT TO STOP YOU FROM RESCUING THAT KIDNAPPED GIRL.
INSTEAD OF FIGHTING OUTRIGHT, HE OFFERS YOU THIS RING. GIVES YOU TERMS.
YOU LOSE, YOU'RE GOING HOME.
YOU WIN.
HE'S TELLING YOU WHO HIRED HIM. HOW HE KNEW YOU WERE COMING.
MAYBE EVEN WHERE THAT THERE GIRL'S GONE.
DING

ROUND 7

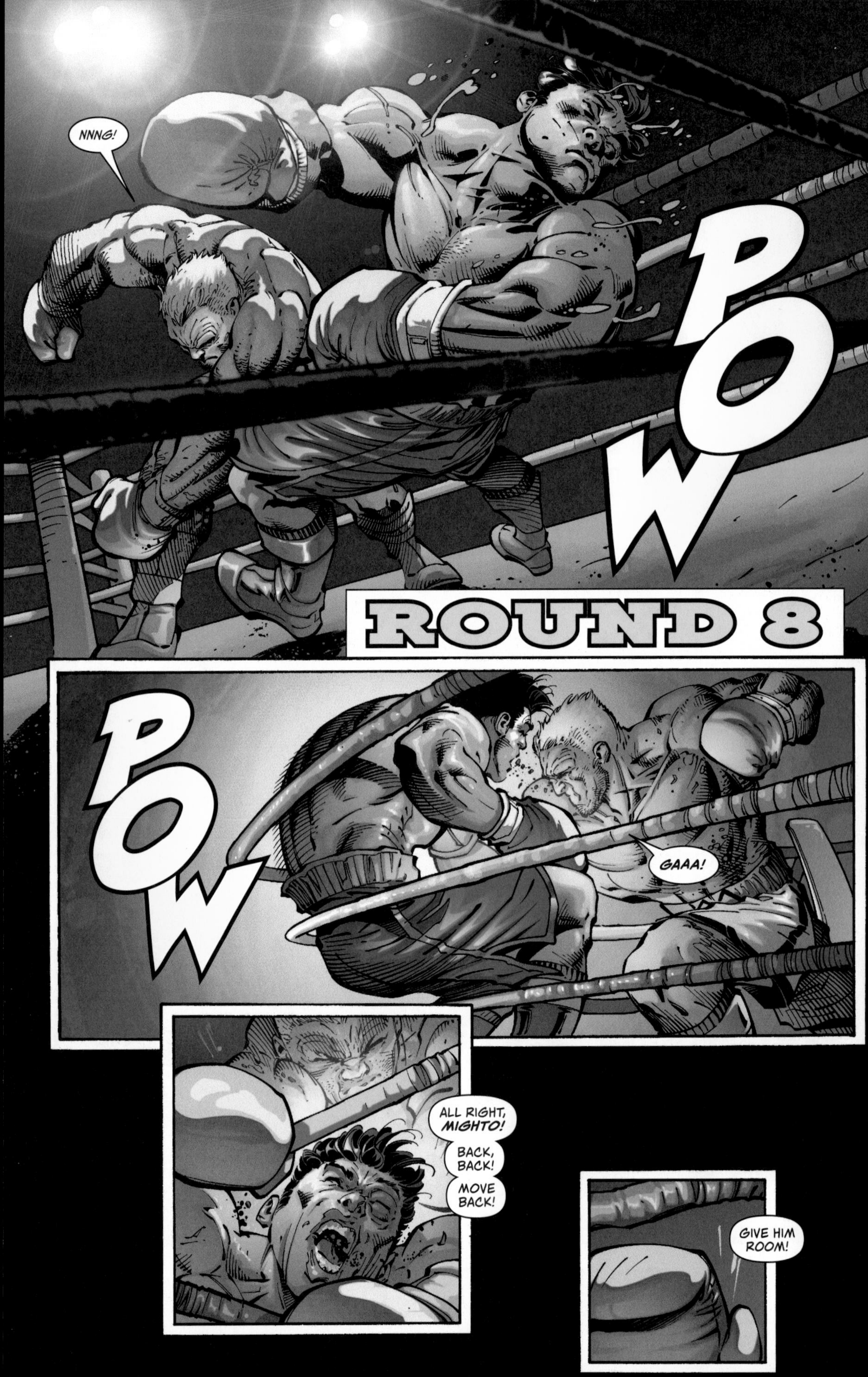
NNNG!
POW
ROUND 8
POW
GAAA!
ALL RIGHT, MIGHTO!
BACK, BACK!
MOVE BACK!
GIVE HIM ROOM!

ROUND 9

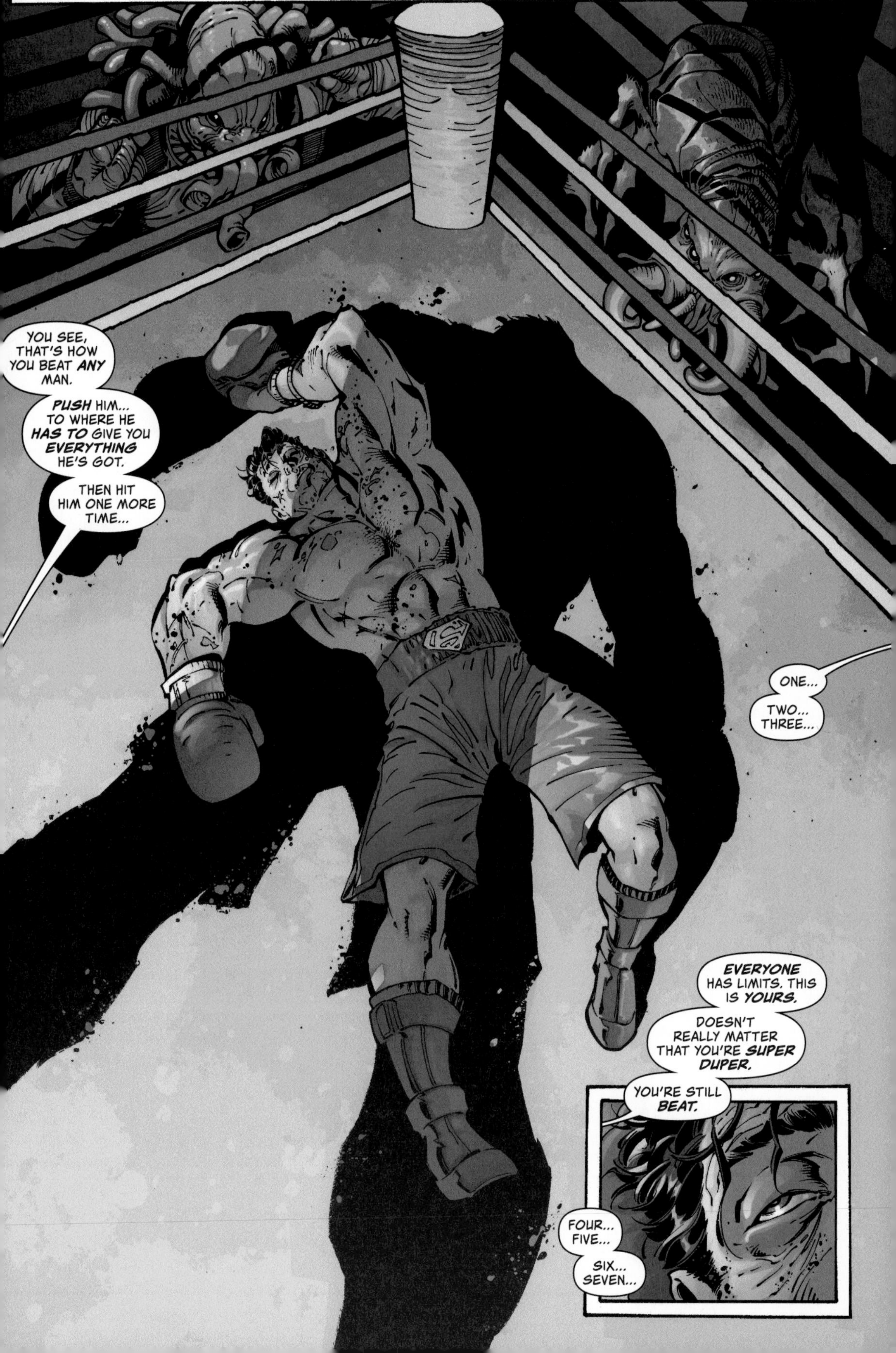
YOU SEE, THAT'S HOW YOU BEAT ANY MAN.
PUSH HIM... TO WHERE HE HAS TO GIVE YOU EVERYTHING HE'S GOT.
THEN HIT HIM ONE MORE TIME...
ONE...
TWO... THREE...
EVERYONE HAS LIMITS. THIS IS YOURS.
DOESN'T REALLY MATTER THAT YOU'RE SUPER DUPER.
YOU'RE STILL BEAT.
FOUR... FIVE...
SIX... SEVEN...

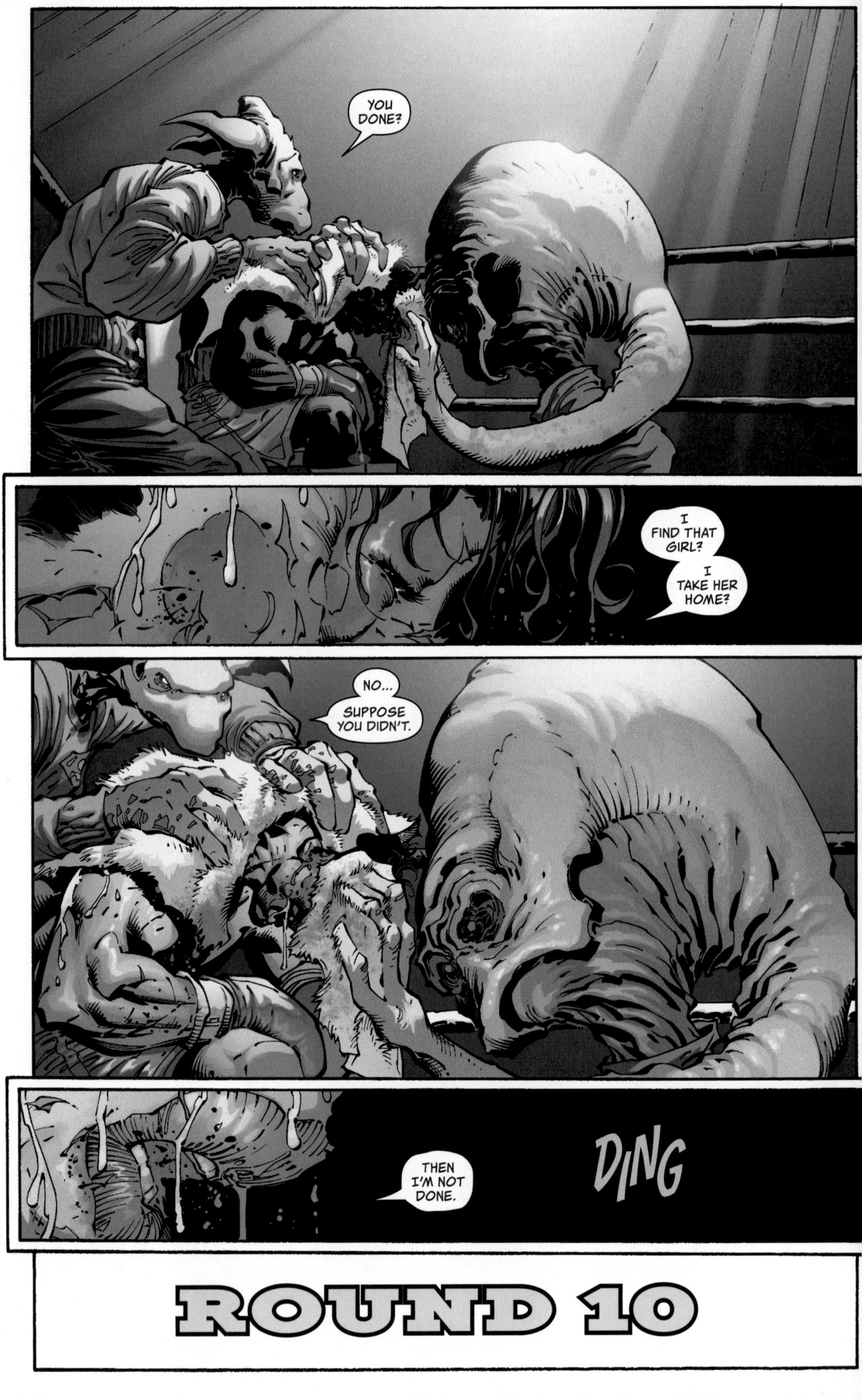
YOU DONE?
I FIND THAT GIRL?
I TAKE HER HOME?
NO... SUPPOSE YOU DIDN'T.
THEN I'M NOT DONE.
DING
ROUND 10

ROUND 11

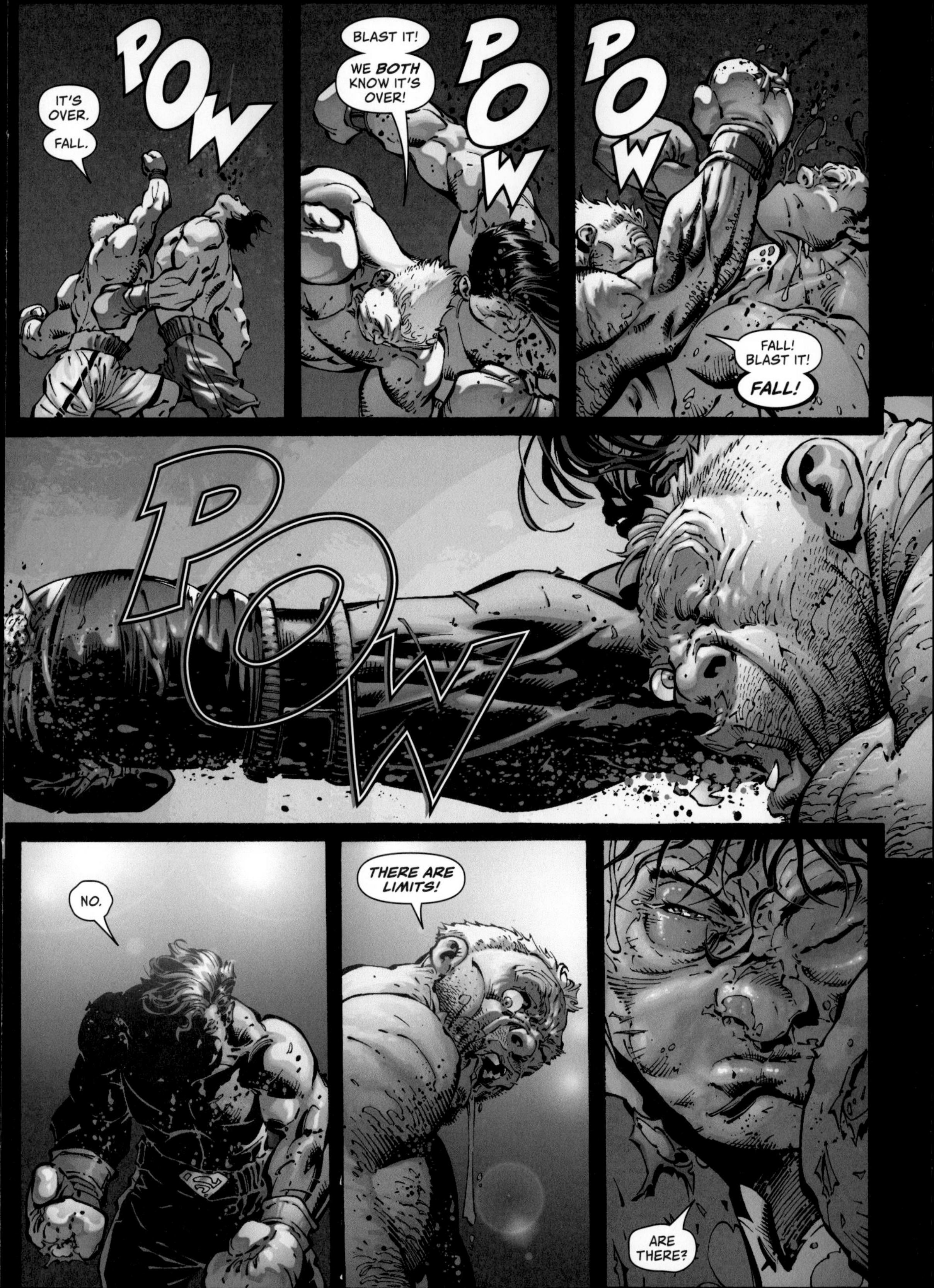

IT'S OVER.
FALL.
POW
BLAST IT!
WE *BOTH* KNOW IT'S OVER!
POW
POW
FALL! BLAST IT!
FALL!
POW
NO.
THERE ARE LIMITS!
ARE THERE?

ROUND 12

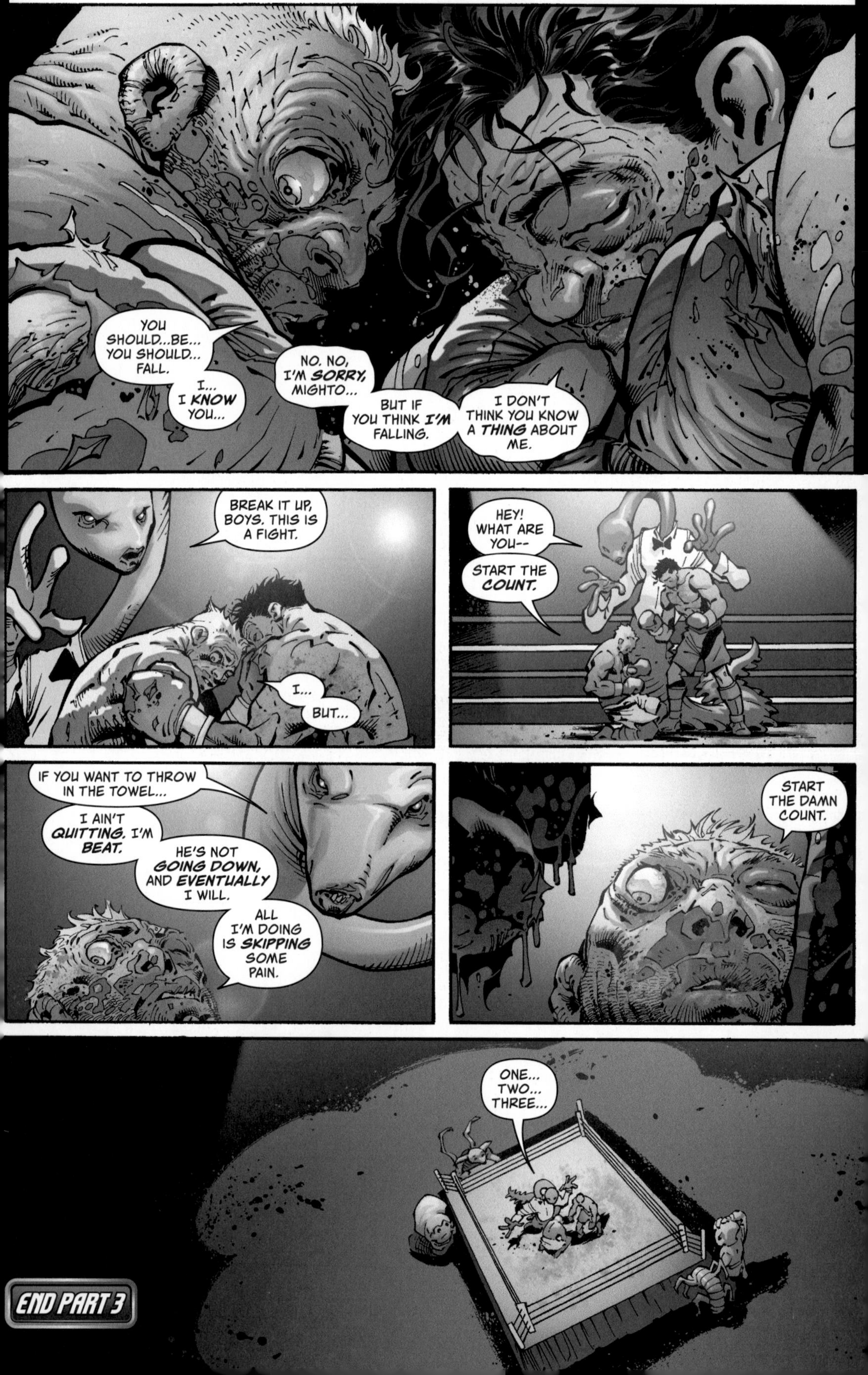
YOU SHOULD...BE... YOU SHOULD... FALL.
I... I KNOW YOU...
NO. NO, I'M SORRY, MIGHTO...
BUT IF YOU THINK I'M FALLING.
I DON'T THINK YOU KNOW A THING ABOUT ME.
BREAK IT UP, BOYS. THIS IS A FIGHT.
I...
BUT...
HEY! WHAT ARE YOU--
START THE COUNT.
IF YOU WANT TO THROW IN THE TOWEL...
I AIN'T QUITTING. I'M BEAT.
HE'S NOT GOING DOWN, AND EVENTUALLY I WILL.
ALL I'M DOING IS SKIPPING SOME PAIN.
START THE DAMN COUNT.
ONE... TWO... THREE...
END PART 3

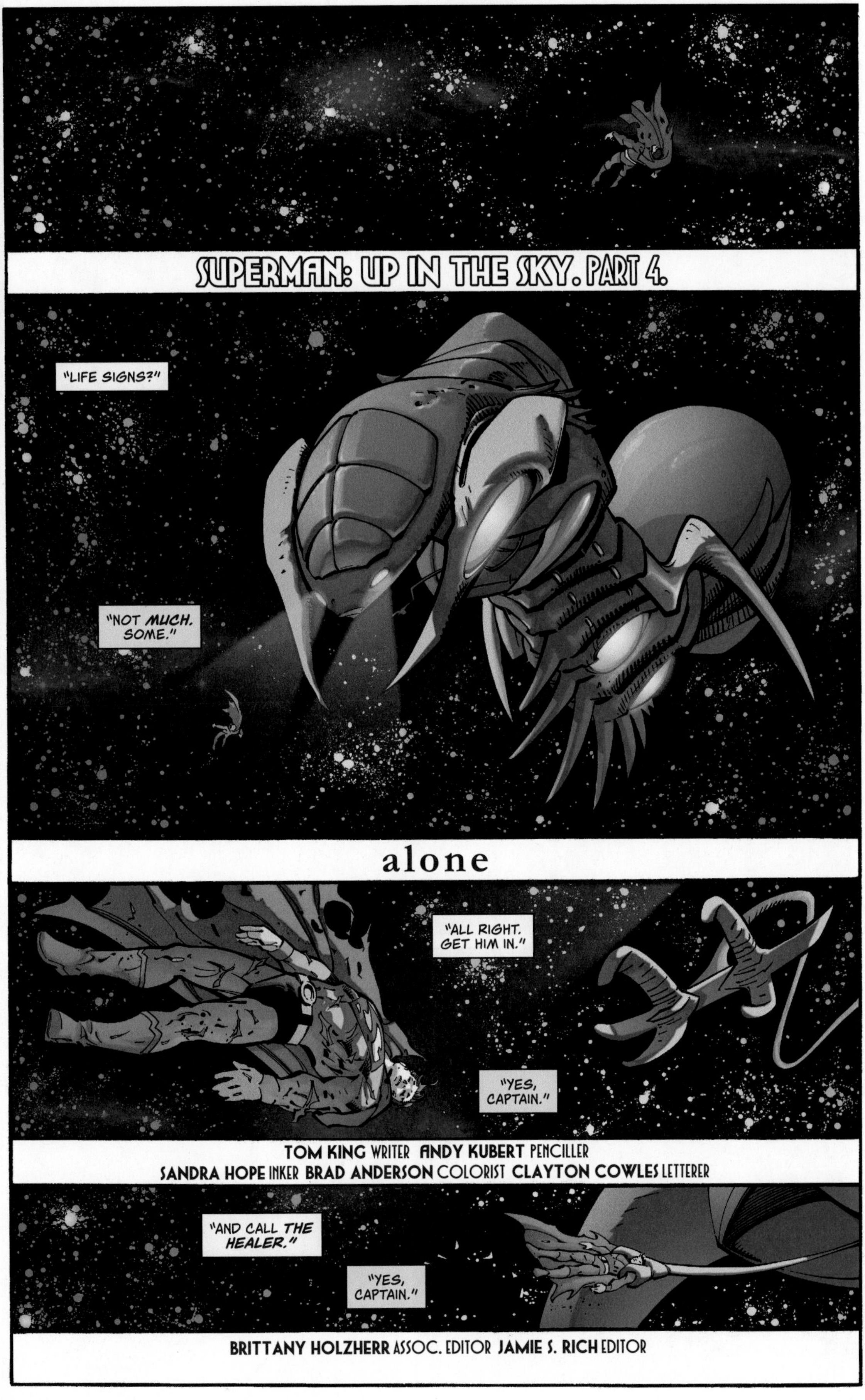
SUPERMAN: UP IN THE SKY. PART 4.
"LIFE SIGNS?"
"NOT *MUCH.* SOME."
alone
"ALL RIGHT. GET HIM IN."
"YES, CAPTAIN."
TOM KING WRITER ANDY KUBERT PENCILLER
SANDRA HOPE INKER BRAD ANDERSON COLORIST CLAYTON COWLES LETTERER
"AND CALL *THE HEALER.*"
"YES, CAPTAIN."
BRITTANY HOLZHERR ASSOC. EDITOR JAMIE S. RICH EDITOR

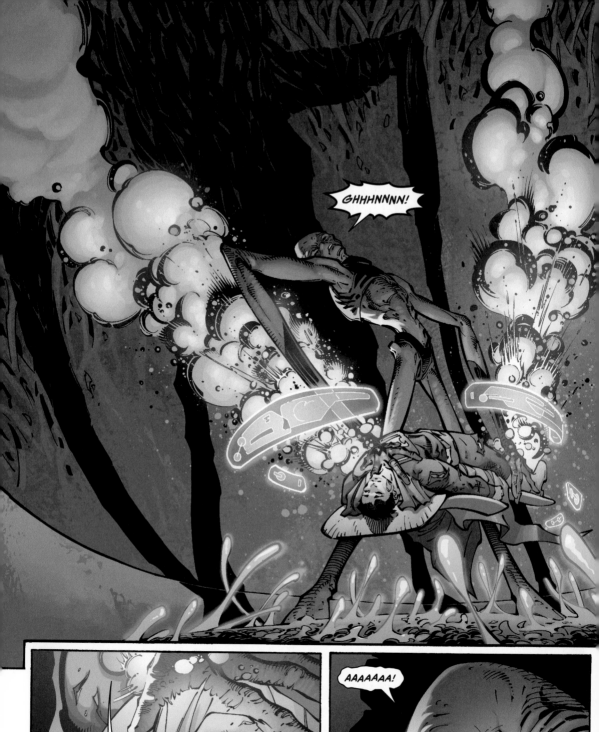

GHHHNNNN!

NNNNNN!

AAAAAAA!

LOIS!

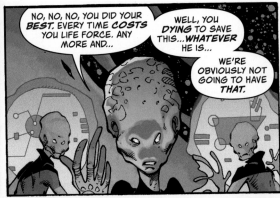

NO, NO, NO, YOU DID YOUR *BEST*. EVERY TIME *COSTS* YOU LIFE FORCE. ANY MORE AND...

WELL, YOU *DYING* TO SAVE THIS...*WHATEVER* HE IS...

WE'RE OBVIOUSLY NOT GOING TO HAVE *THAT*.

YES, CAPTAIN.

I DON'T SEE ANY *HAPPY ALTERNATIVE* HERE. UNFORTUNATELY.

LET THE *WOUND* RUN ITS COURSE.

WE'LL DROP THE BODY OFF AT THE NEXT *WAY STATION*.

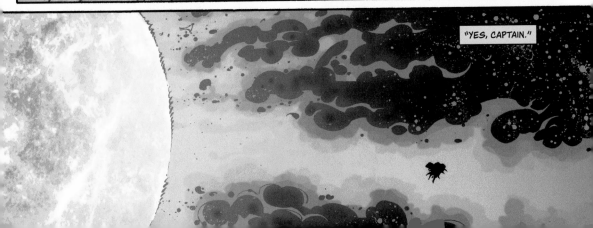

"YES, CAPTAIN."

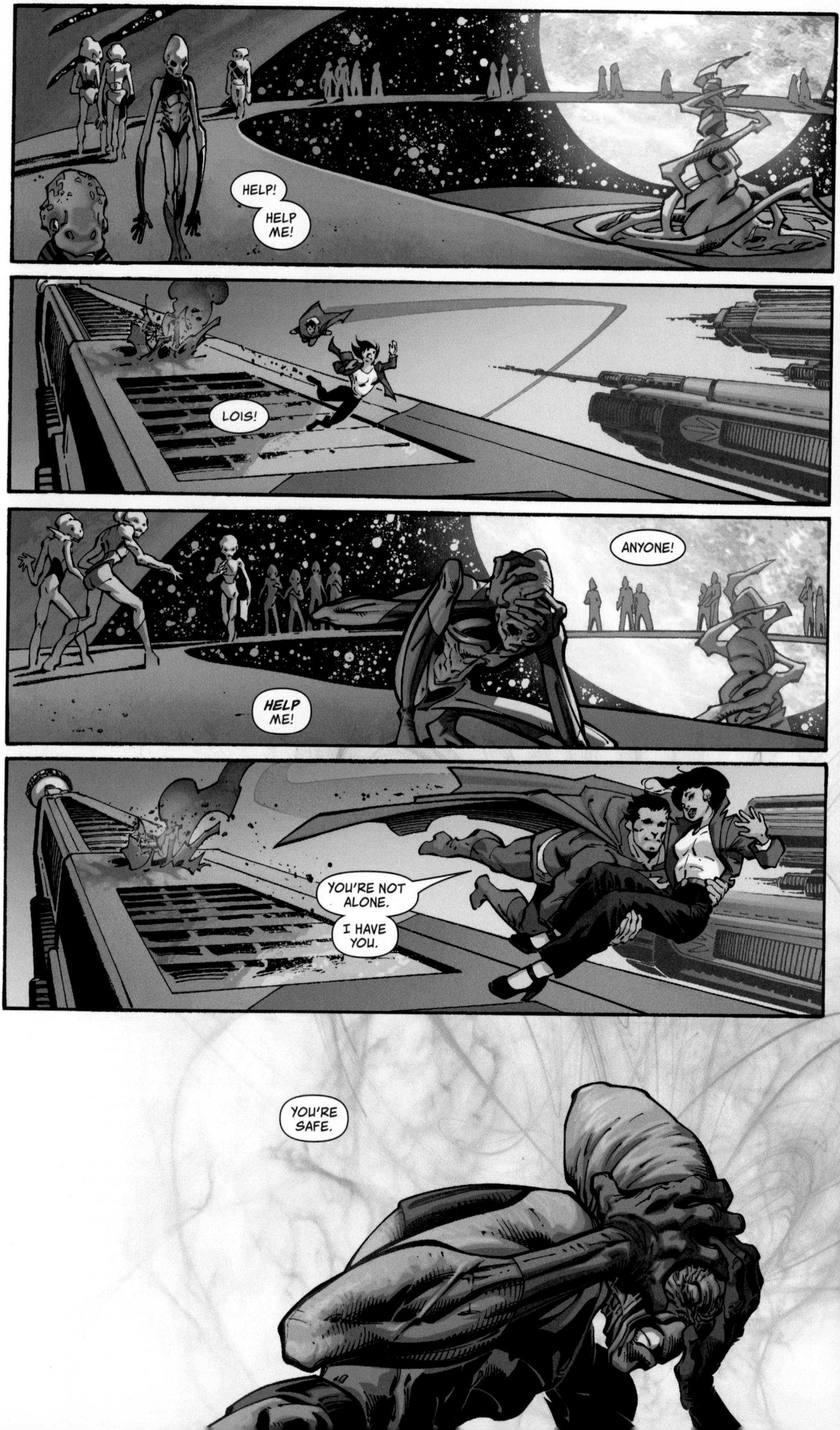
HELP!
HELP ME!
LOIS!
ANYONE!
HELP ME!
YOU'RE NOT ALONE.
I HAVE YOU.
YOU'RE SAFE.

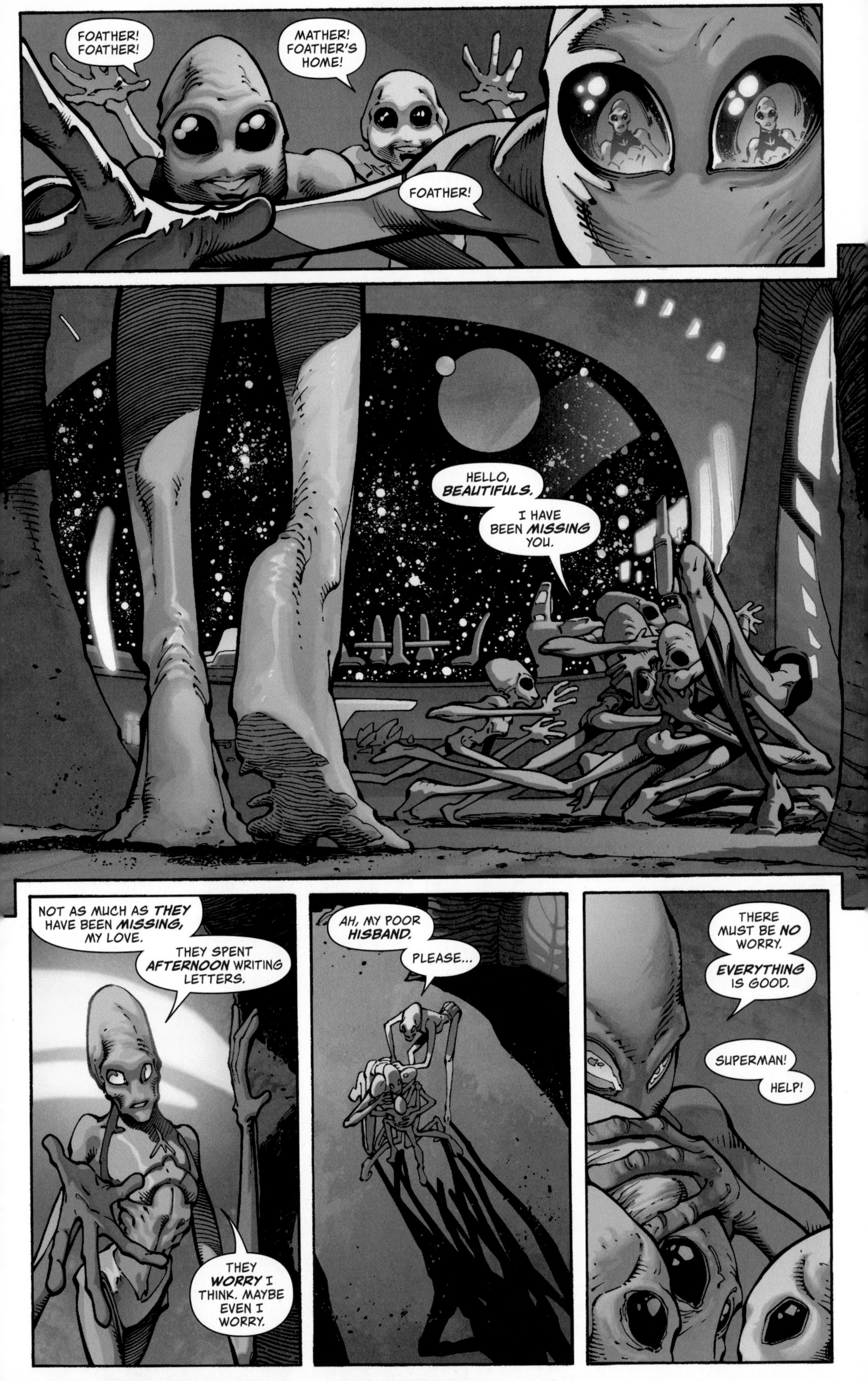

FOATHER! FOATHER!
MATHER! FOATHER'S HOME!
FOATHER!
HELLO, BEAUTIFULS.
I HAVE BEEN MISSING YOU.
NOT AS MUCH AS THEY HAVE BEEN MISSING, MY LOVE.
THEY SPENT AFTERNOON WRITING LETTERS.
THEY WORRY I THINK. MAYBE EVEN I WORRY.
AH, MY POOR HISBAND.
PLEASE...
THERE MUST BE NO WORRY.
EVERYTHING IS GOOD.
SUPERMAN!
HELP!

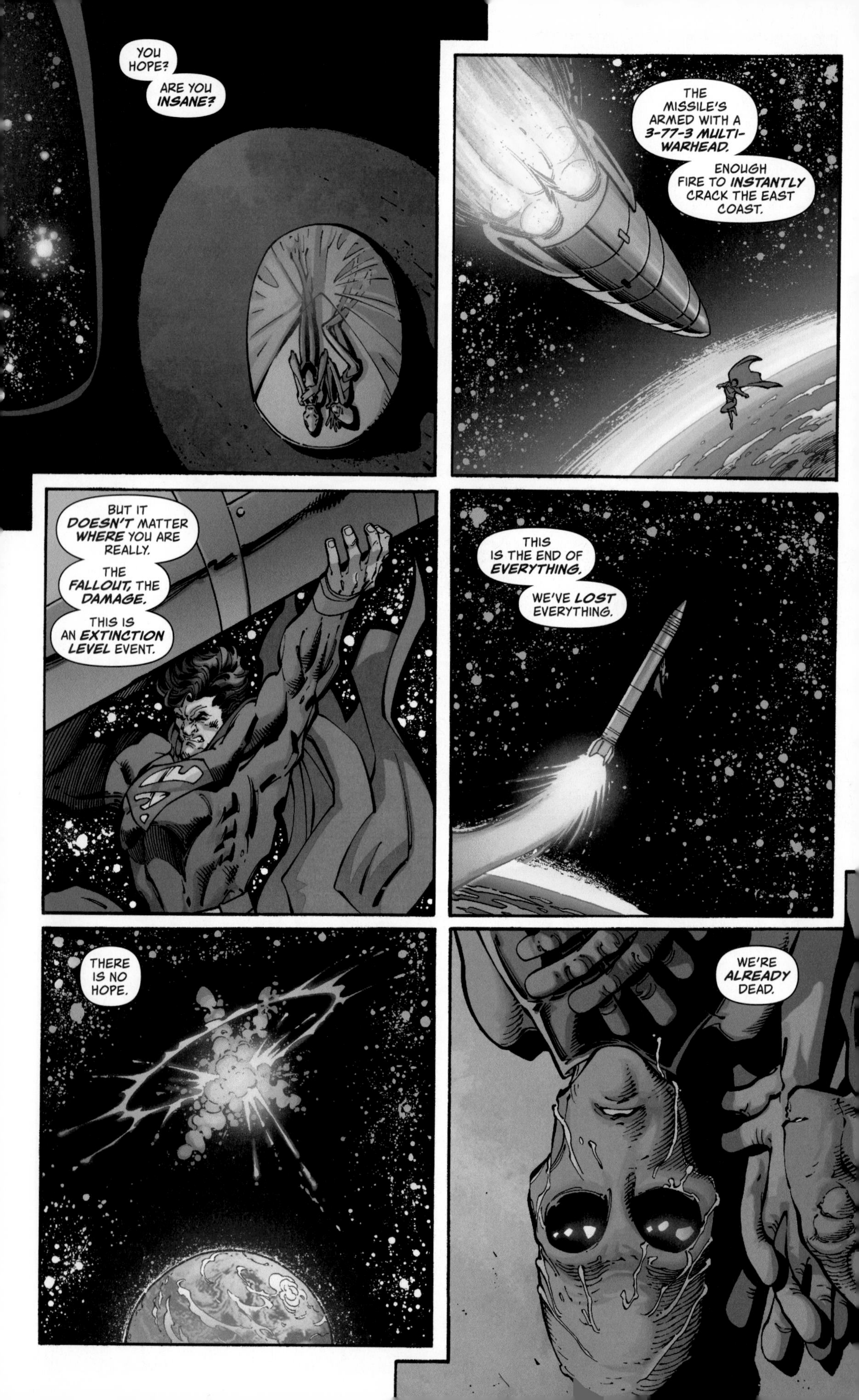
YOU HOPE?
ARE YOU INSANE?
THE MISSILE'S ARMED WITH A 3-77-3 MULTI-WARHEAD.
ENOUGH FIRE TO INSTANTLY CRACK THE EAST COAST.
BUT IT DOESN'T MATTER WHERE YOU ARE REALLY.
THE FALLOUT, THE DAMAGE.
THIS IS AN EXTINCTION LEVEL EVENT.
THIS IS THE END OF EVERYTHING.
WE'VE LOST EVERYTHING.
THERE IS NO HOPE.
WE'RE ALREADY DEAD.

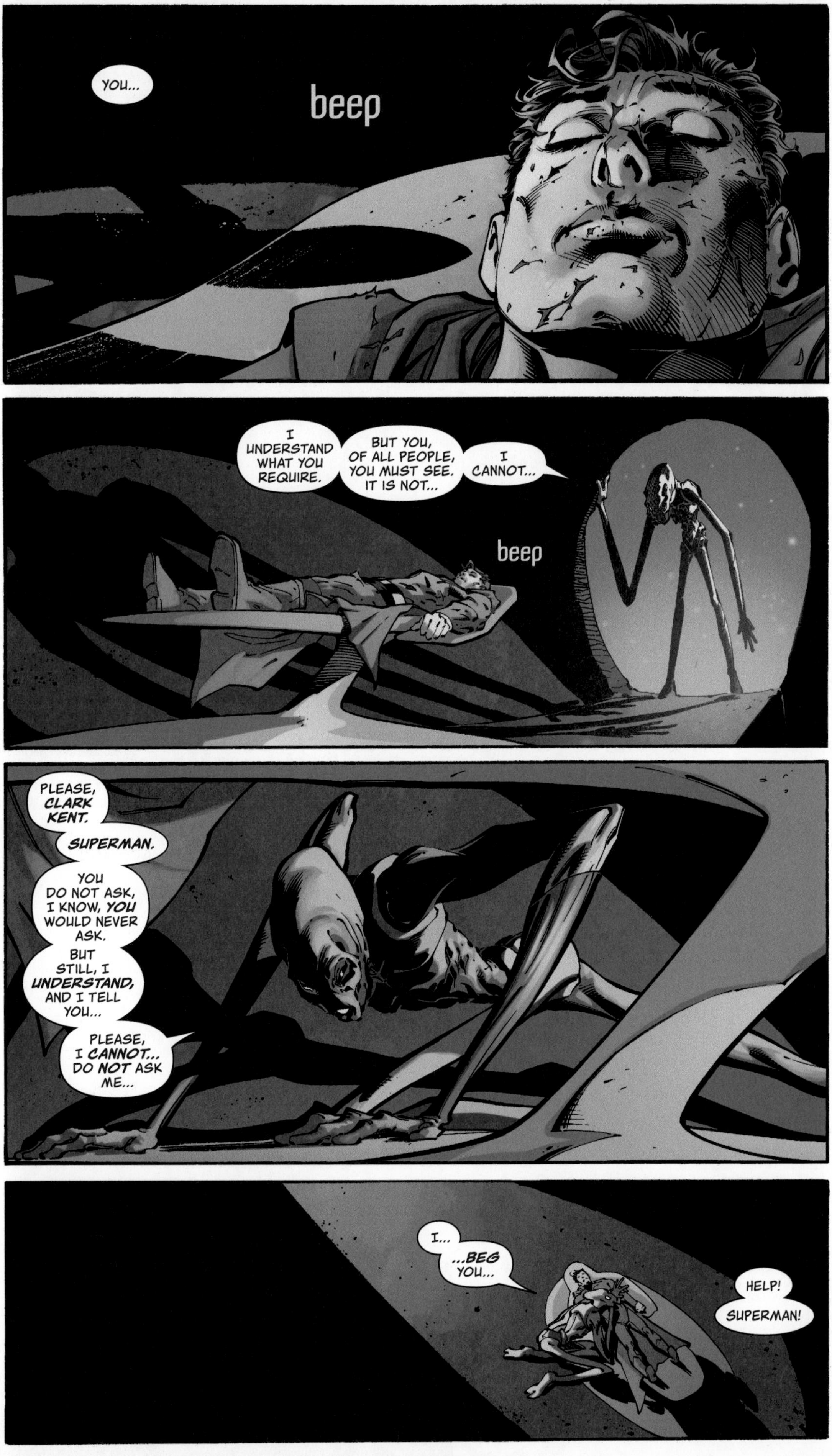
YOU...
beep
I UNDERSTAND WHAT YOU REQUIRE.
BUT YOU, OF ALL PEOPLE, YOU MUST SEE. IT IS NOT...
I CANNOT...
beep
PLEASE, CLARK KENT.
SUPERMAN.
YOU DO NOT ASK, I KNOW, YOU WOULD NEVER ASK.
BUT STILL, I UNDERSTAND, AND I TELL YOU...
PLEASE, I CANNOT... DO NOT ASK ME...
I...
...BEG YOU...
HELP!
SUPERMAN!

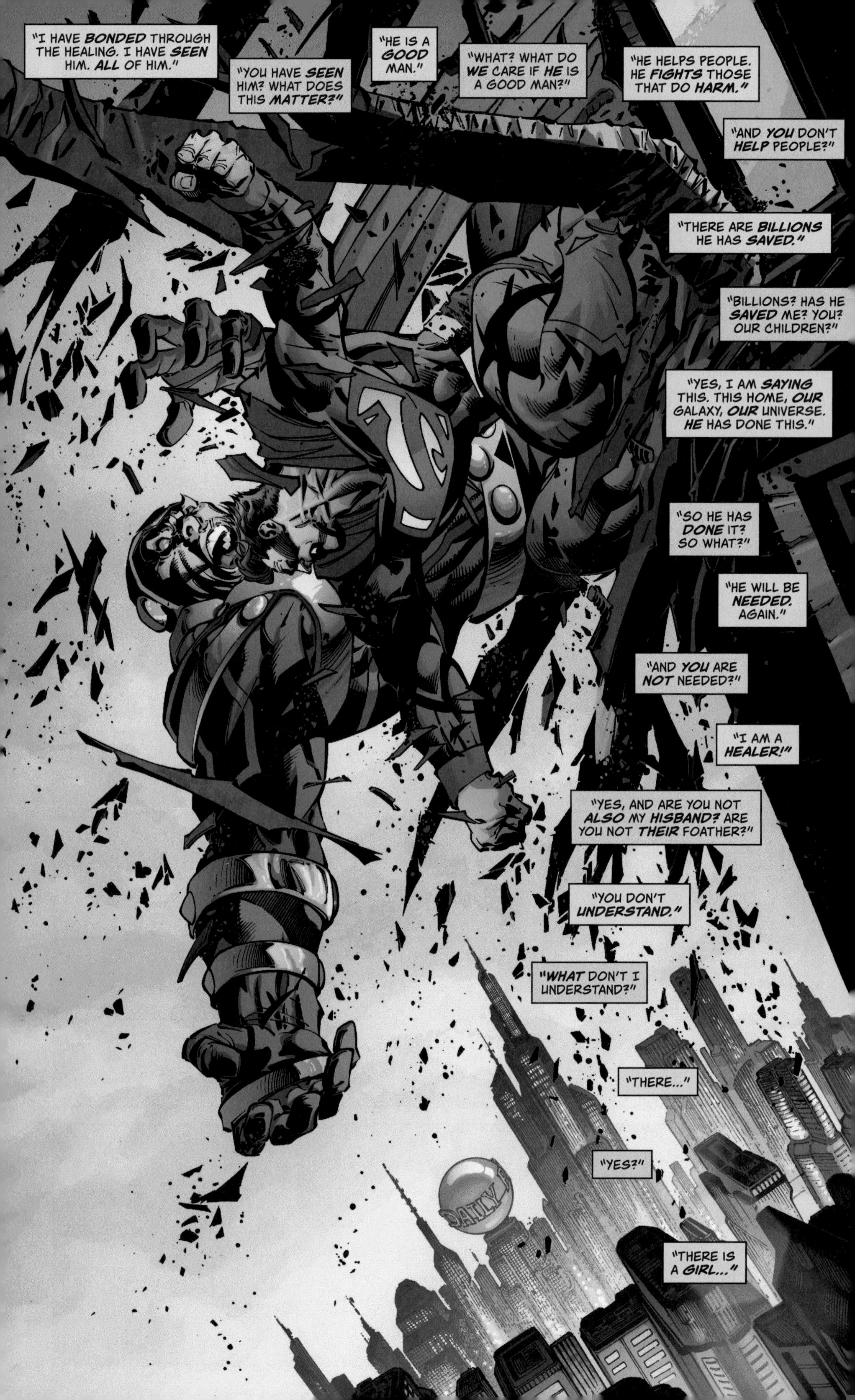
"I HAVE BONDED THROUGH THE HEALING. I HAVE SEEN HIM. ALL OF HIM."
"YOU HAVE SEEN HIM? WHAT DOES THIS MATTER?"
"HE IS A GOOD MAN."
"WHAT? WHAT DO WE CARE IF HE IS A GOOD MAN?"
"HE HELPS PEOPLE. HE FIGHTS THOSE THAT DO HARM."
"AND YOU DON'T HELP PEOPLE?"
"THERE ARE BILLIONS HE HAS SAVED."
"BILLIONS? HAS HE SAVED ME? YOU? OUR CHILDREN?"
"YES, I AM SAYING THIS. THIS HOME, OUR GALAXY, OUR UNIVERSE. HE HAS DONE THIS."
"SO HE HAS DONE IT? SO WHAT?"
"HE WILL BE NEEDED. AGAIN."
"AND YOU ARE NOT NEEDED?"
"I AM A HEALER!"
"YES, AND ARE YOU NOT ALSO MY HISBAND? ARE YOU NOT THEIR FOATHER?"
"YOU DON'T UNDERSTAND."
"WHAT DON'T I UNDERSTAND?"
"THERE..."
"YES?"
"THERE IS A GIRL..."

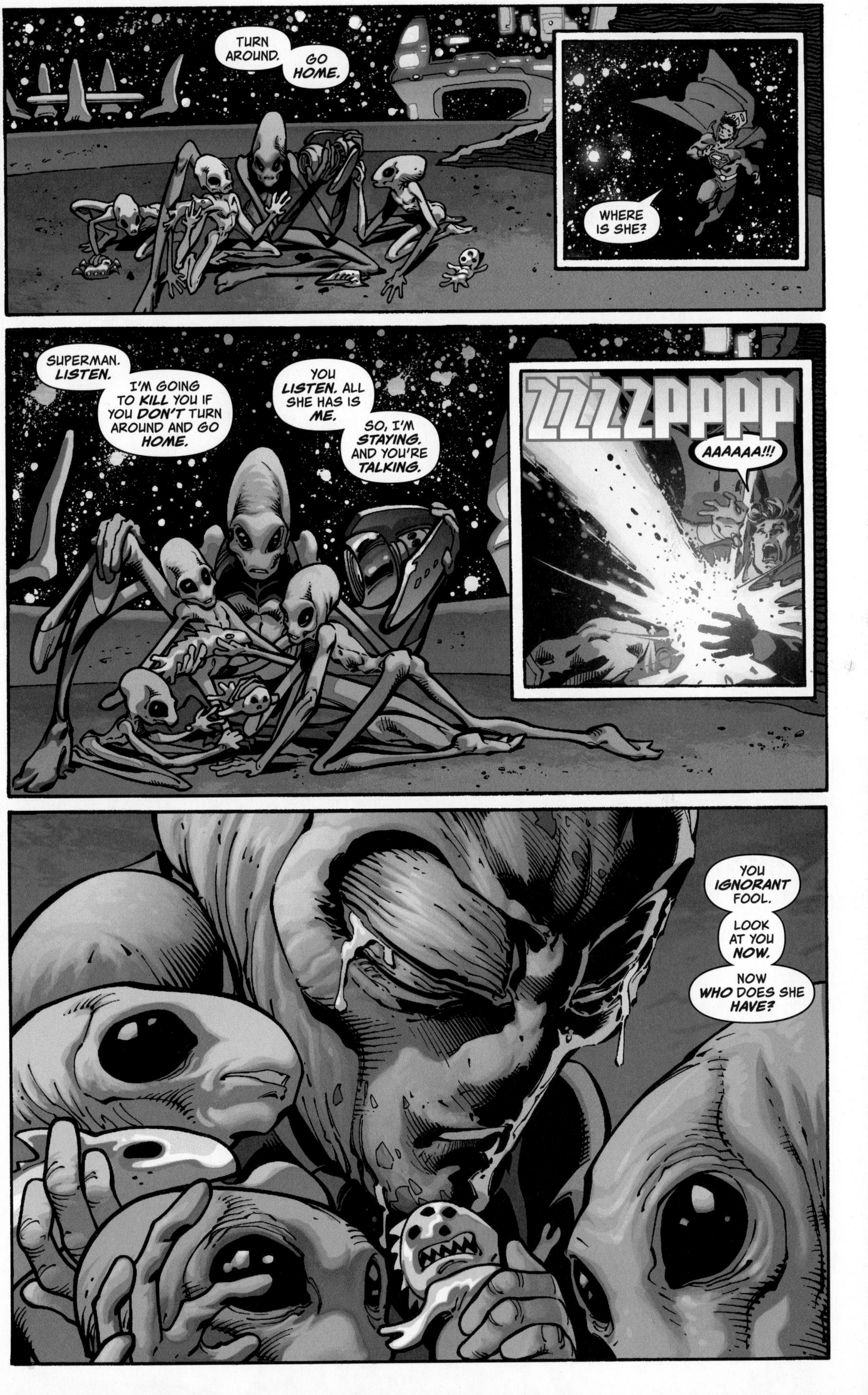

TURN AROUND.
GO HOME.
WHERE IS SHE?
SUPERMAN. LISTEN.
I'M GOING TO KILL YOU IF YOU DON'T TURN AROUND AND GO HOME.
YOU LISTEN. ALL SHE HAS IS ME.
SO, I'M STAYING. AND YOU'RE TALKING.
ZZZZPPPP
AAAAAA!!!
YOU IGNORANT FOOL.
LOOK AT YOU NOW.
NOW WHO DOES SHE HAVE?

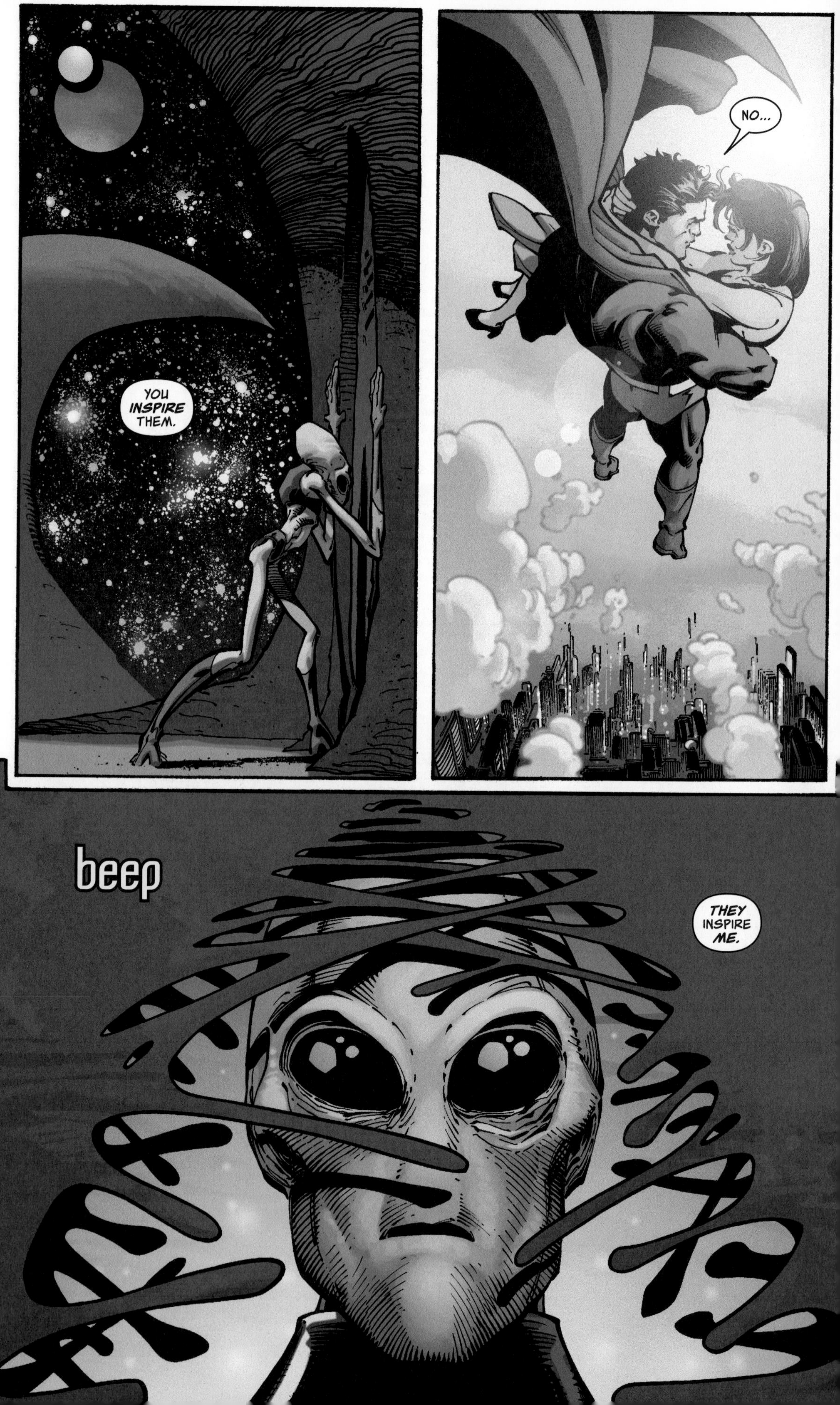
YOU INSPIRE THEM.
NO...
beep
THEY INSPIRE ME.

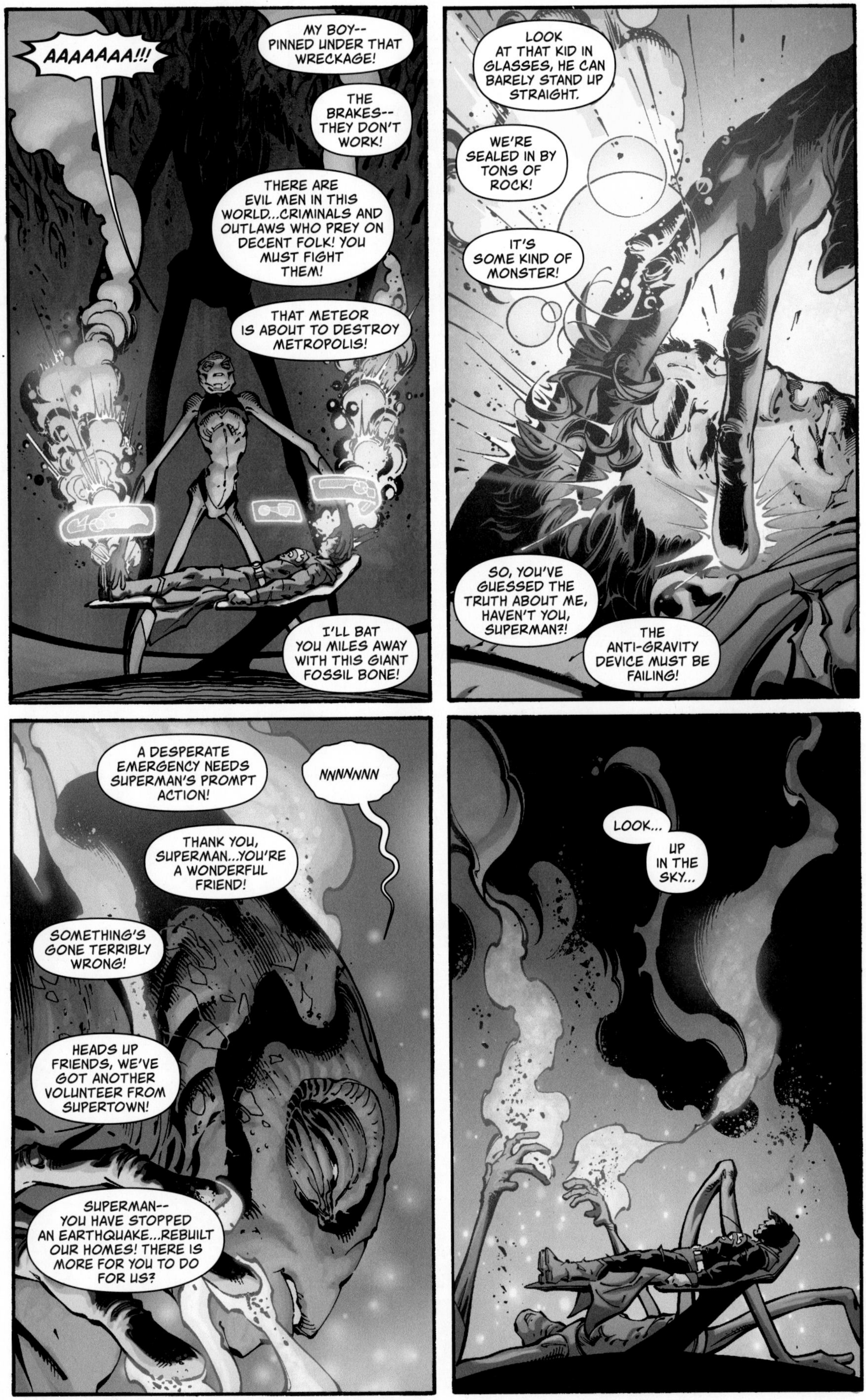
AAAAAAA!!!
MY BOY-- PINNED UNDER THAT WRECKAGE!
THE BRAKES-- THEY DON'T WORK!
THERE ARE EVIL MEN IN THIS WORLD...CRIMINALS AND OUTLAWS WHO PREY ON DECENT FOLK! YOU MUST FIGHT THEM!
THAT METEOR IS ABOUT TO DESTROY METROPOLIS!
I'LL BAT YOU MILES AWAY WITH THIS GIANT FOSSIL BONE!
LOOK AT THAT KID IN GLASSES, HE CAN BARELY STAND UP STRAIGHT.
WE'RE SEALED IN BY TONS OF ROCK!
IT'S SOME KIND OF MONSTER!
SO, YOU'VE GUESSED THE TRUTH ABOUT ME, HAVEN'T YOU, SUPERMAN?!
THE ANTI-GRAVITY DEVICE MUST BE FAILING!
A DESPERATE EMERGENCY NEEDS SUPERMAN'S PROMPT ACTION!
NNNNNNN
THANK YOU, SUPERMAN...YOU'RE A WONDERFUL FRIEND!
SOMETHING'S GONE TERRIBLY WRONG!
HEADS UP FRIENDS, WE'VE GOT ANOTHER VOLUNTEER FROM SUPERTOWN!
SUPERMAN-- YOU HAVE STOPPED AN EARTHQUAKE...REBUILT OUR HOMES! THERE IS MORE FOR YOU TO DO FOR US?
LOOK...
UP IN THE SKY...

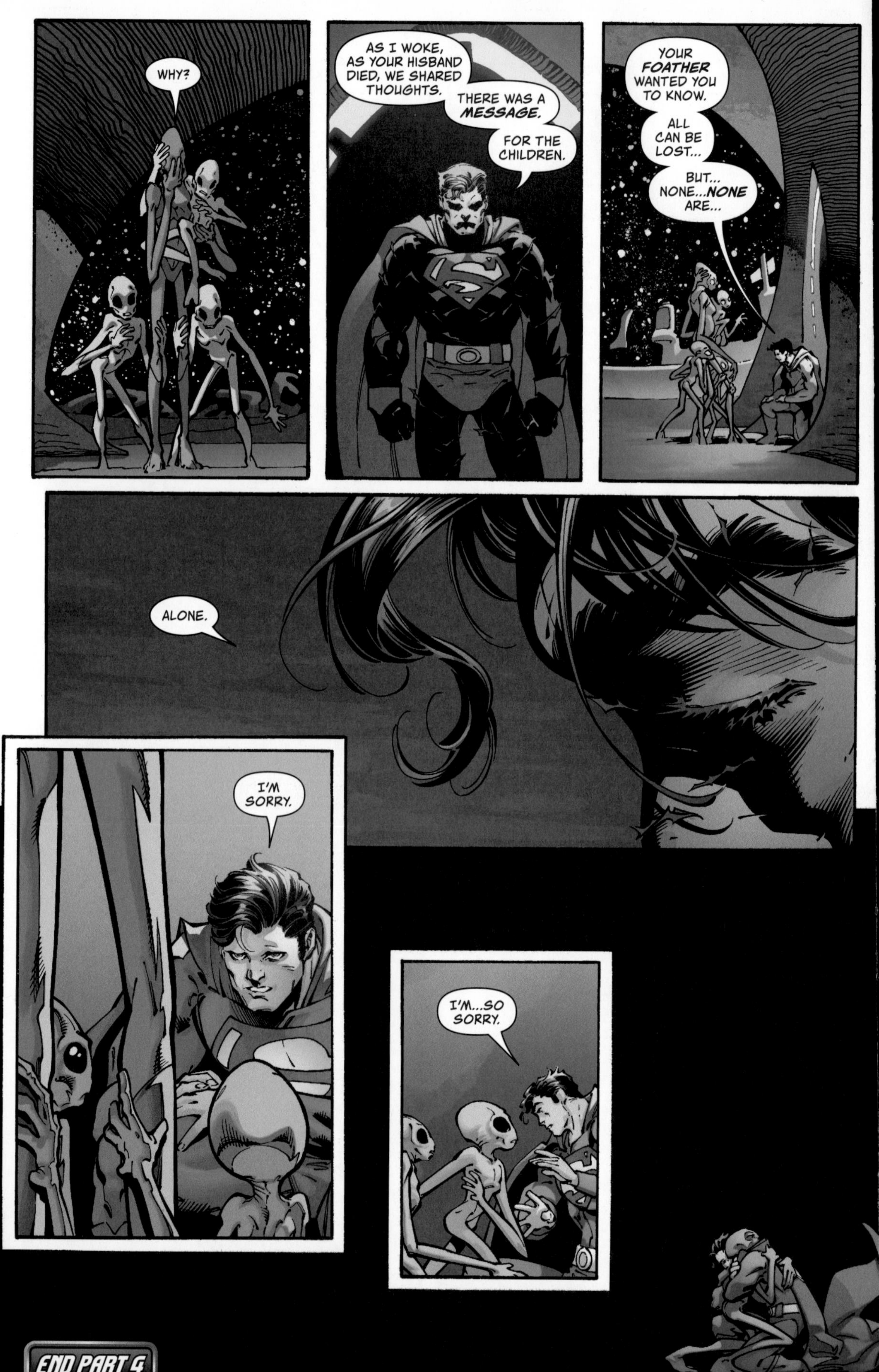
WHY?
AS I WOKE, AS YOUR HISBAND DIED, WE SHARED THOUGHTS.
THERE WAS A MESSAGE.
FOR THE CHILDREN.
YOUR FOATHER WANTED YOU TO KNOW.
ALL CAN BE LOST...
BUT... NONE...NONE ARE...
ALONE.
I'M SORRY.
I'M...SO SORRY.
END PART 4

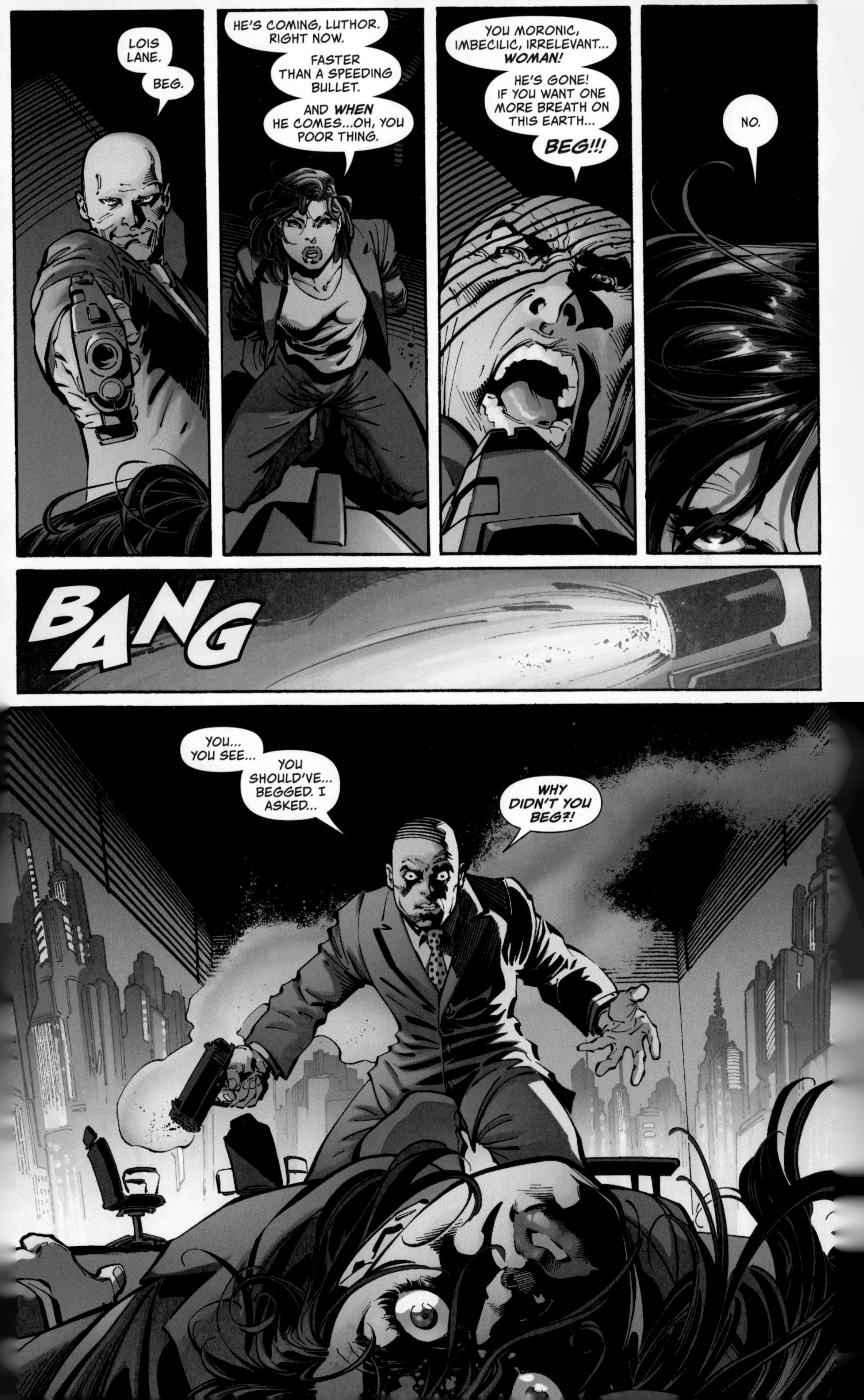
LOIS LANE.
BEG.
HE'S COMING, LUTHOR. RIGHT NOW.
FASTER THAN A SPEEDING BULLET.
AND WHEN HE COMES...OH, YOU POOR THING.
YOU MORONIC, IMBECILIC, IRRELEVANT... WOMAN!
HE'S GONE! IF YOU WANT ONE MORE BREATH ON THIS EARTH...
BEG!!!
NO.
BANG
YOU... YOU SEE...
YOU SHOULD'VE... BEGGED. I ASKED...
WHY DIDN'T YOU BEG?!

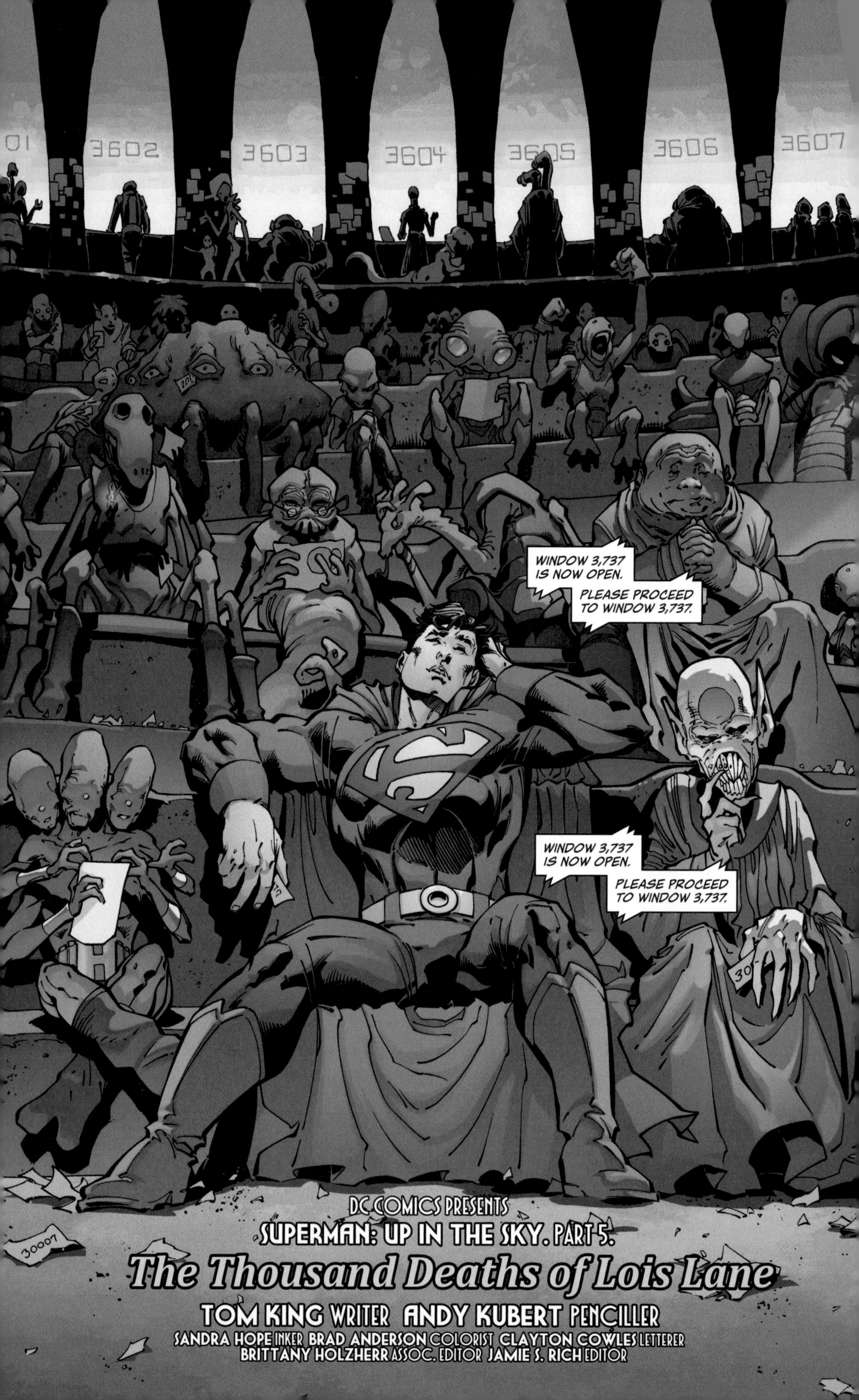
3602 3603 3604 3605 3606 3607
WINDOW 3,737 IS NOW OPEN.
PLEASE PROCEED TO WINDOW 3,737.
WINDOW 3,737 IS NOW OPEN.
PLEASE PROCEED TO WINDOW 3,737.
DC COMICS PRESENTS
SUPERMAN: UP IN THE SKY. PART 5.
The Thousand Deaths of Lois Lane
TOM KING WRITER ANDY KUBERT PENCILLER
SANDRA HOPE INKER BRAD ANDERSON COLORIST CLAYTON COWLES LETTERER
BRITTANY HOLZHERR ASSOC. EDITOR JAMIE S. RICH EDITOR

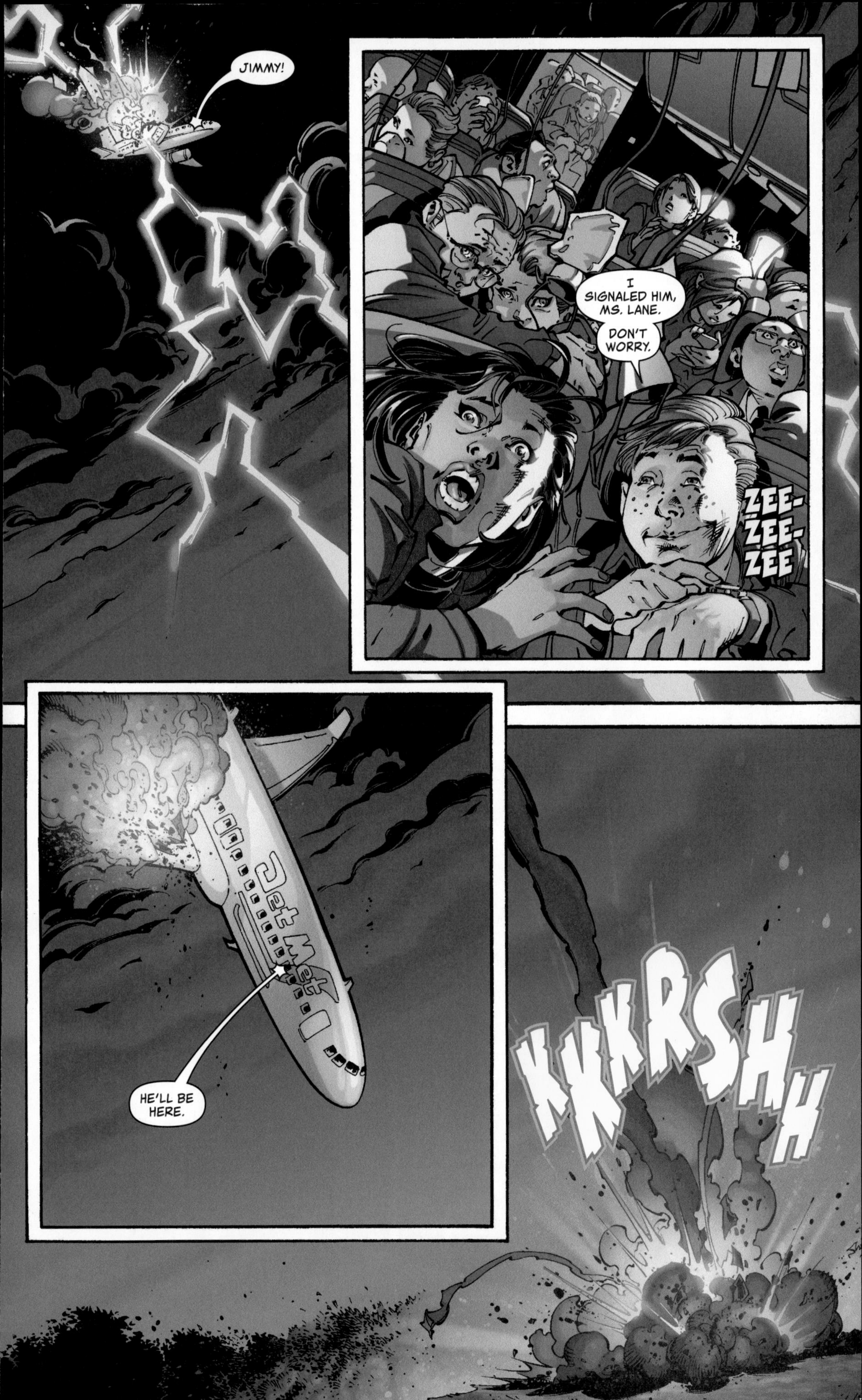
JIMMY!
I SIGNALED HIM, MS. LANE.
DON'T WORRY.
ZEE-ZEE-ZEE
HE'LL BE HERE.
KKKRSHH

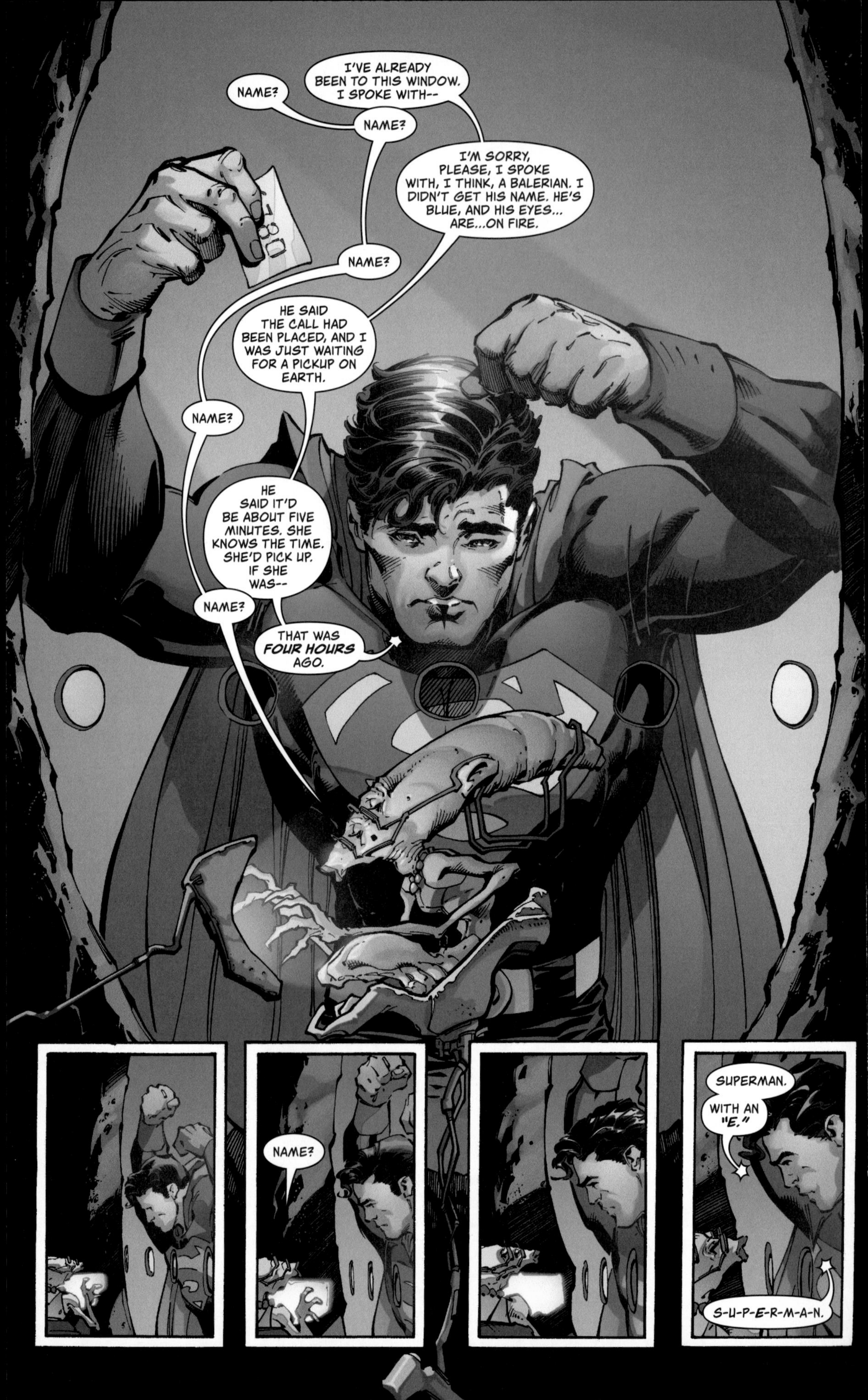
NAME?
I'VE ALREADY BEEN TO THIS WINDOW. I SPOKE WITH--
NAME?
I'M SORRY, PLEASE, I SPOKE WITH, I THINK, A BALERIAN. I DIDN'T GET HIS NAME. HE'S BLUE, AND HIS EYES... ARE...ON FIRE.
NAME?
HE SAID THE CALL HAD BEEN PLACED, AND I WAS JUST WAITING FOR A PICKUP ON EARTH.
NAME?
HE SAID IT'D BE ABOUT FIVE MINUTES. SHE KNOWS THE TIME. SHE'D PICK UP. IF SHE WAS--
NAME?
THAT WAS FOUR HOURS AGO.
NAME?
SUPERMAN.
WITH AN "E."
S-U-P-E-R-M-A-N.

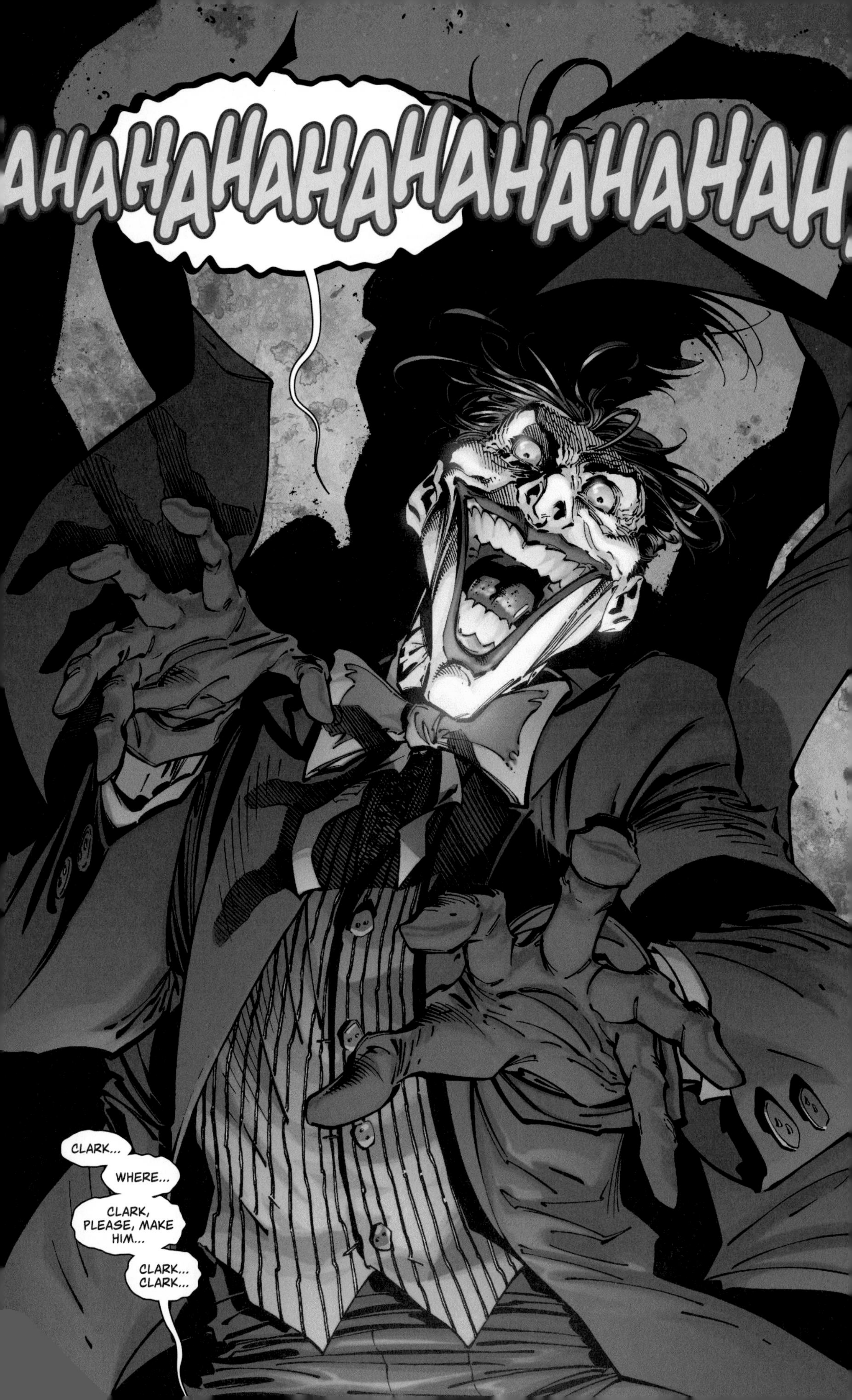
AHAHAHAHAHAHAHAHAHAHAHAH
CLARK...
WHERE...
CLARK, PLEASE, MAKE HIM...
CLARK... CLARK...

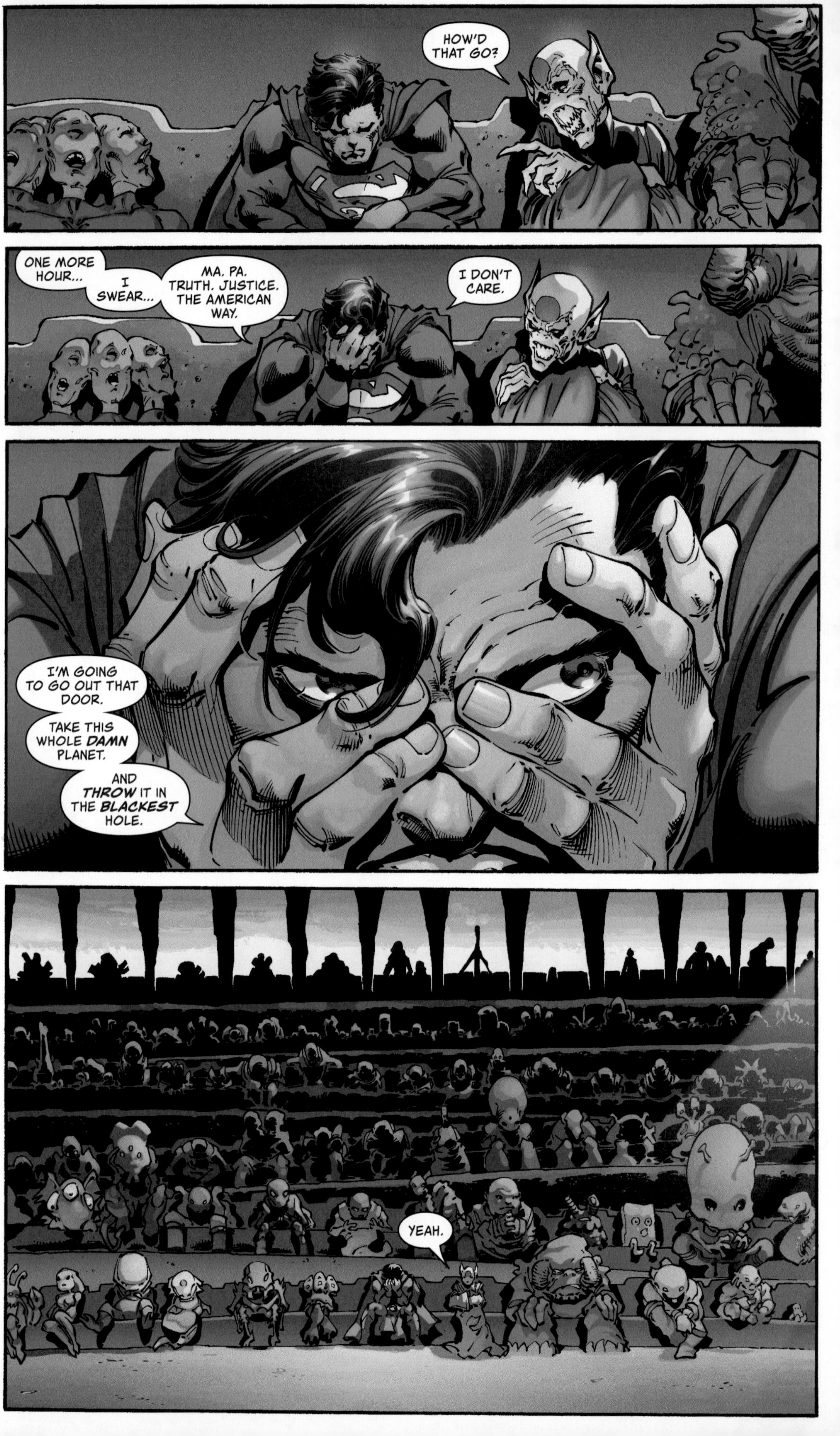
HOW'D THAT GO?
ONE MORE HOUR...
I SWEAR...
MA. PA. TRUTH. JUSTICE. THE AMERICAN WAY.
I DON'T CARE.
I'M GOING TO GO OUT THAT DOOR.
TAKE THIS WHOLE DAMN PLANET.
AND THROW IT IN THE BLACKEST HOLE.
YEAH.

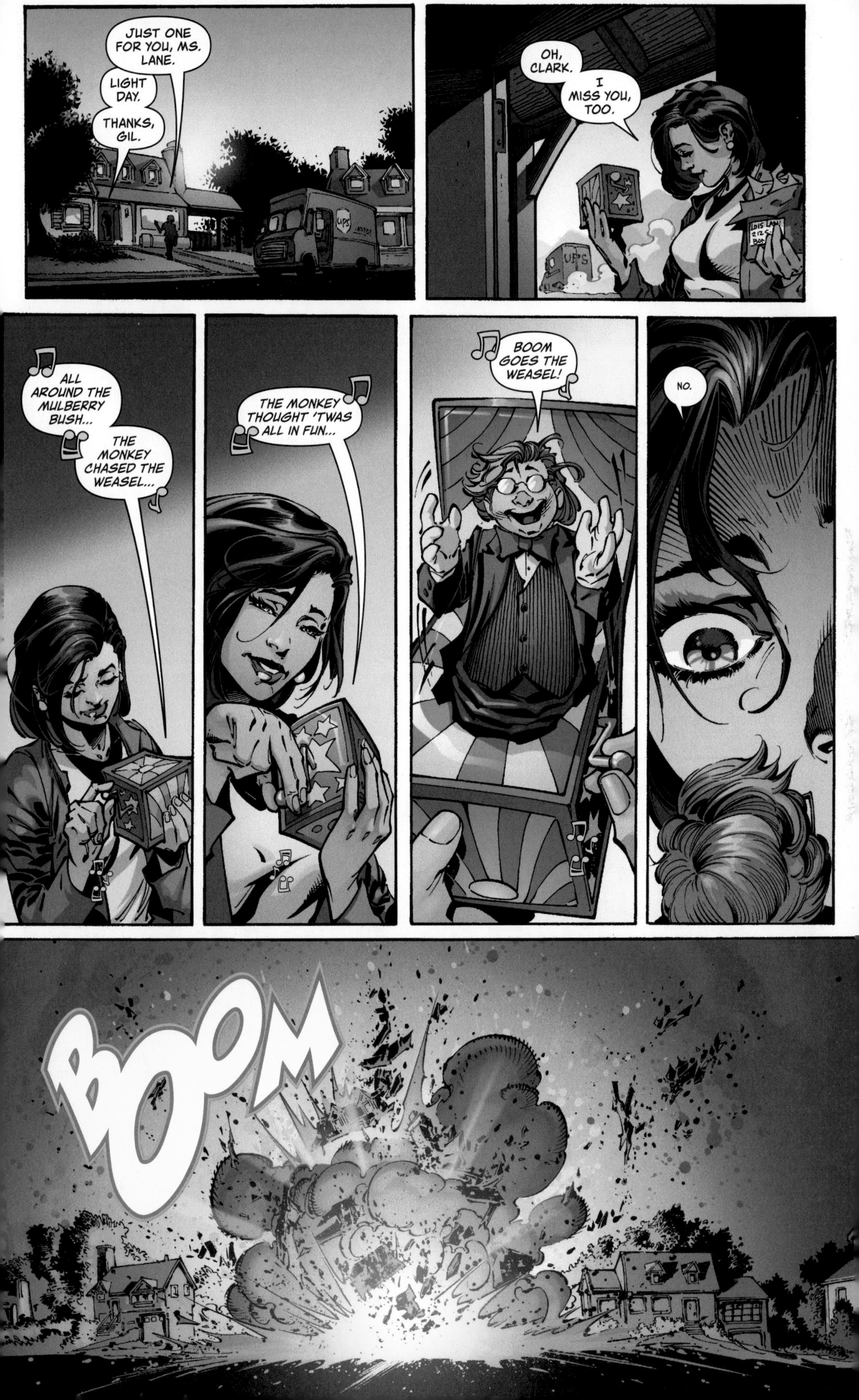
JUST ONE FOR YOU, MS. LANE.
LIGHT DAY.
THANKS, GIL.
OH, CLARK.
I MISS YOU, TOO.
ALL AROUND THE MULBERRY BUSH...
THE MONKEY CHASED THE WEASEL...
THE MONKEY THOUGHT 'TWAS ALL IN FUN...
BOOM GOES THE WEASEL!
NO.
BOOM

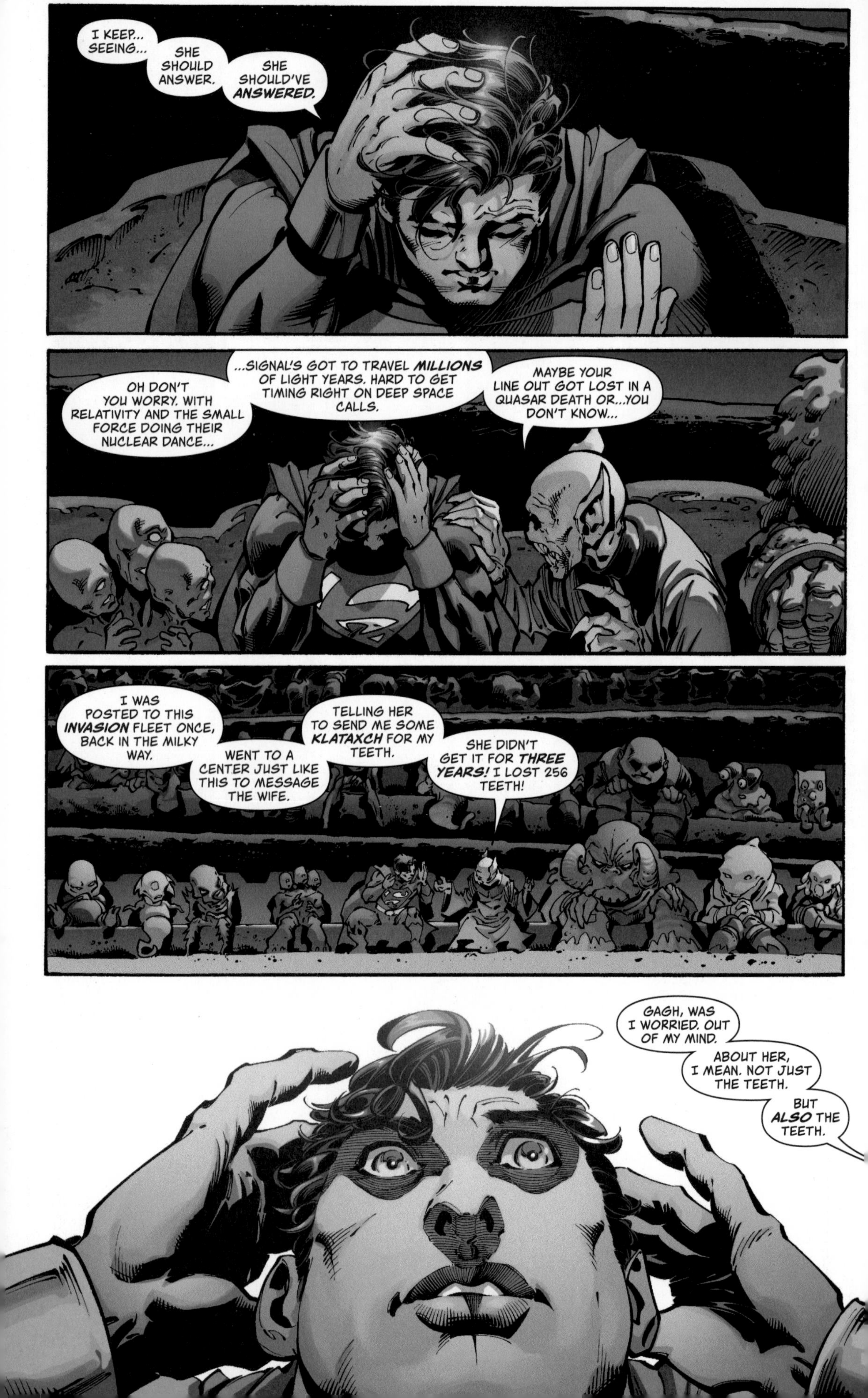
I KEEP... SEEING...
SHE SHOULD ANSWER.
SHE SHOULD'VE ANSWERED.
OH DON'T YOU WORRY. WITH RELATIVITY AND THE SMALL FORCE DOING THEIR NUCLEAR DANCE...
...SIGNAL'S GOT TO TRAVEL MILLIONS OF LIGHT YEARS. HARD TO GET TIMING RIGHT ON DEEP SPACE CALLS.
MAYBE YOUR LINE OUT GOT LOST IN A QUASAR DEATH OR...YOU DON'T KNOW...
I WAS POSTED TO THIS INVASION FLEET ONCE, BACK IN THE MILKY WAY.
WENT TO A CENTER JUST LIKE THIS TO MESSAGE THE WIFE.
TELLING HER TO SEND ME SOME KLATAXCH FOR MY TEETH.
SHE DIDN'T GET IT FOR THREE YEARS! I LOST 256 TEETH!
GAGH, WAS I WORRIED. OUT OF MY MIND.
ABOUT HER, I MEAN. NOT JUST THE TEETH.
BUT ALSO THE TEETH.

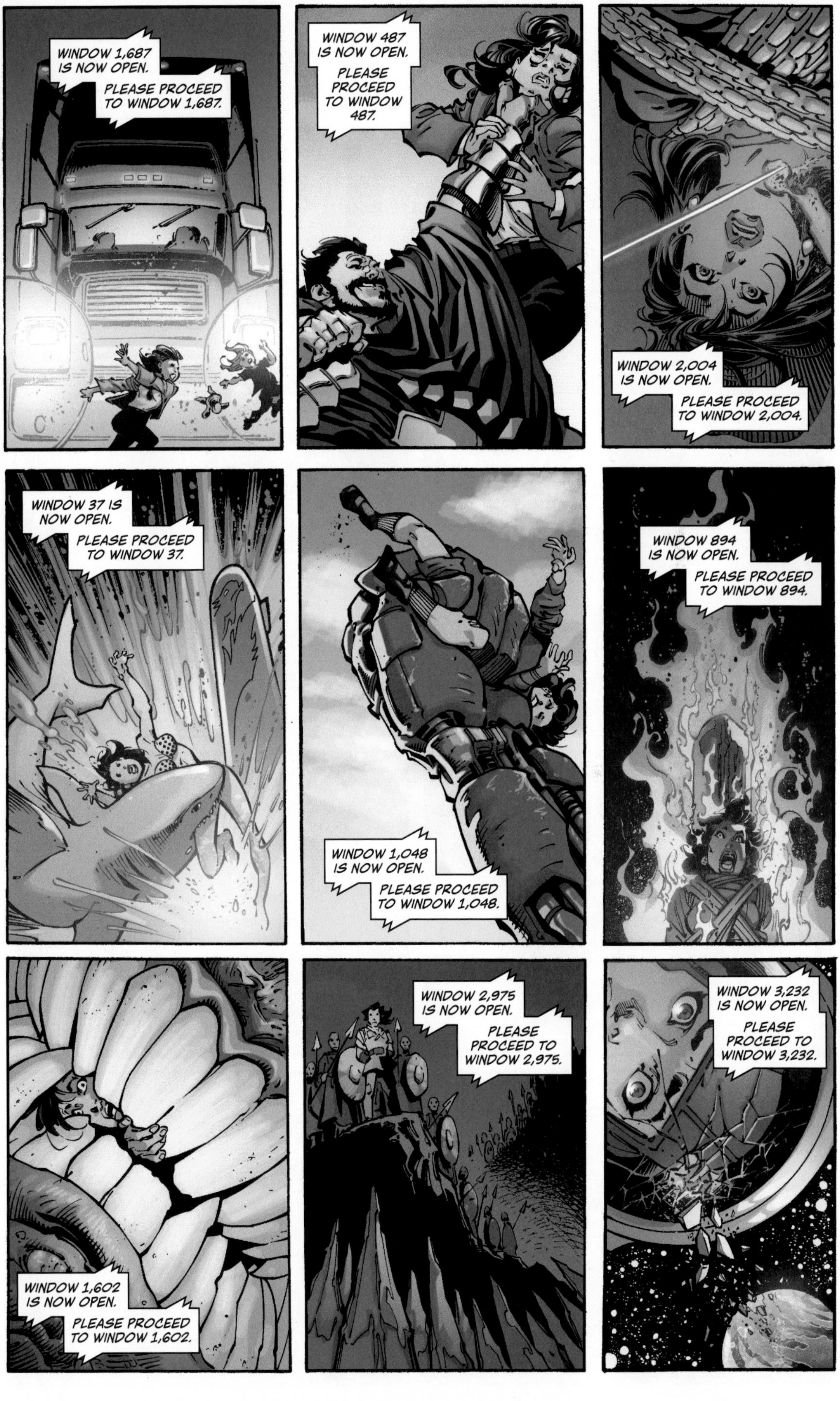
WINDOW 1,687 IS NOW OPEN.
PLEASE PROCEED TO WINDOW 1,687.
WINDOW 487 IS NOW OPEN.
PLEASE PROCEED TO WINDOW 487.
WINDOW 2,004 IS NOW OPEN.
PLEASE PROCEED TO WINDOW 2,004.
WINDOW 37 IS NOW OPEN.
PLEASE PROCEED TO WINDOW 37.
WINDOW 1,048 IS NOW OPEN.
PLEASE PROCEED TO WINDOW 1,048.
WINDOW 894 IS NOW OPEN.
PLEASE PROCEED TO WINDOW 894.
WINDOW 1,602 IS NOW OPEN.
PLEASE PROCEED TO WINDOW 1,602.
WINDOW 2,975 IS NOW OPEN.
PLEASE PROCEED TO WINDOW 2,975.
WINDOW 3,232 IS NOW OPEN.
PLEASE PROCEED TO WINDOW 3,232.

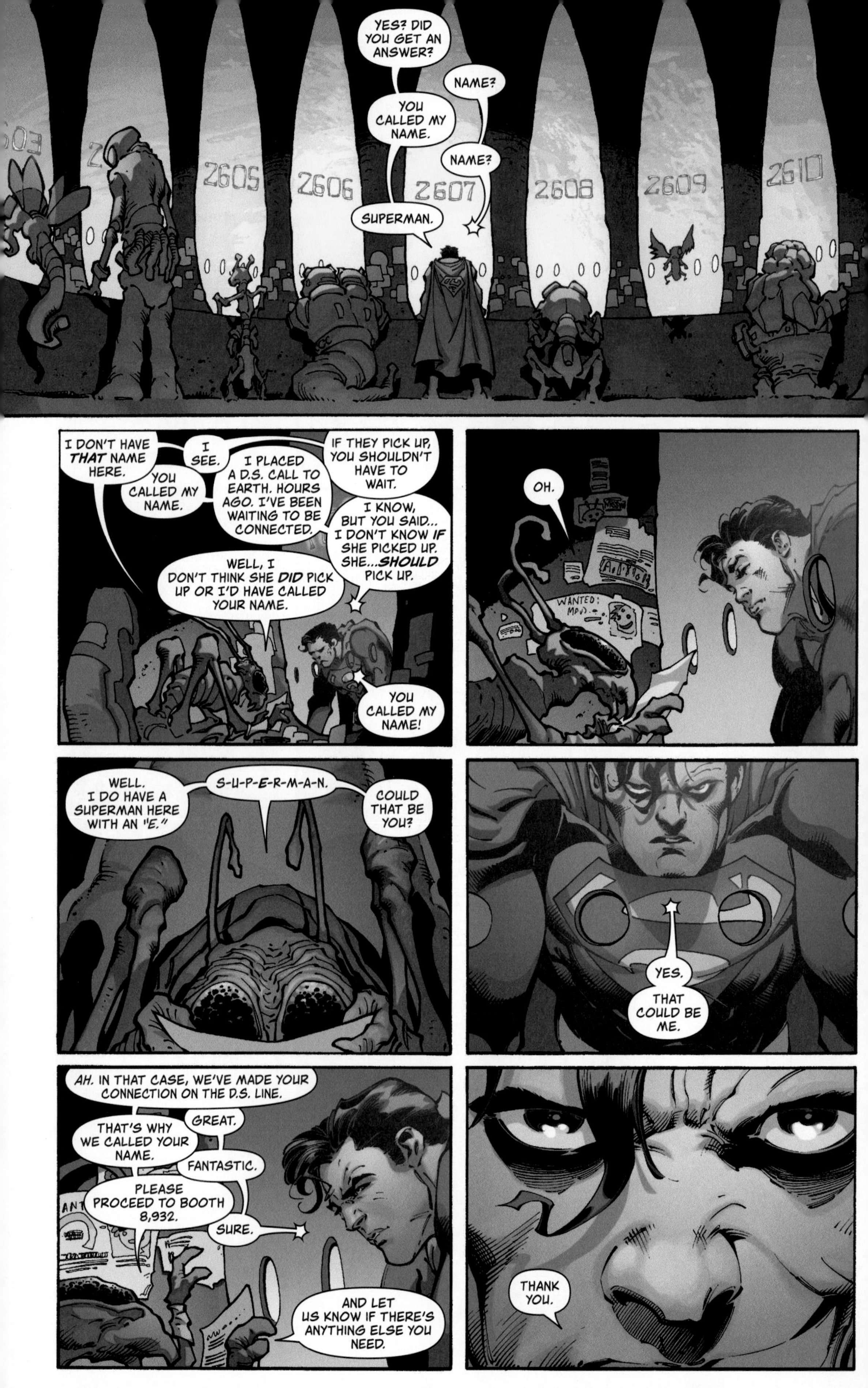

YES? DID YOU GET AN ANSWER?
NAME?
YOU CALLED MY NAME.
NAME?
SUPERMAN.
2605
2606
2607
2608
2609
2610
I DON'T HAVE *THAT* NAME HERE.
I SEE.
YOU CALLED MY NAME.
I PLACED A D.S. CALL TO EARTH. HOURS AGO. I'VE BEEN WAITING TO BE CONNECTED.
IF THEY PICK UP, YOU SHOULDN'T HAVE TO WAIT.
I KNOW, BUT YOU SAID... I DON'T KNOW *IF* SHE PICKED UP. SHE... *SHOULD* PICK UP.
WELL, I DON'T THINK SHE *DID* PICK UP OR I'D HAVE CALLED YOUR NAME.
YOU CALLED MY NAME!
OH.
WANTED:
WELL. I DO HAVE A SUPERMAN HERE WITH AN "*E*."
S-U-P-*E*-R-M-A-N.
COULD THAT BE YOU?
YES. THAT COULD BE ME.
AH. IN THAT CASE, WE'VE MADE YOUR CONNECTION ON THE D.S. LINE.
THAT'S WHY WE CALLED YOUR NAME.
GREAT.
FANTASTIC.
PLEASE PROCEED TO BOOTH 8,932.
SURE.
AND LET US KNOW IF THERE'S ANYTHING ELSE YOU NEED.
THANK YOU.

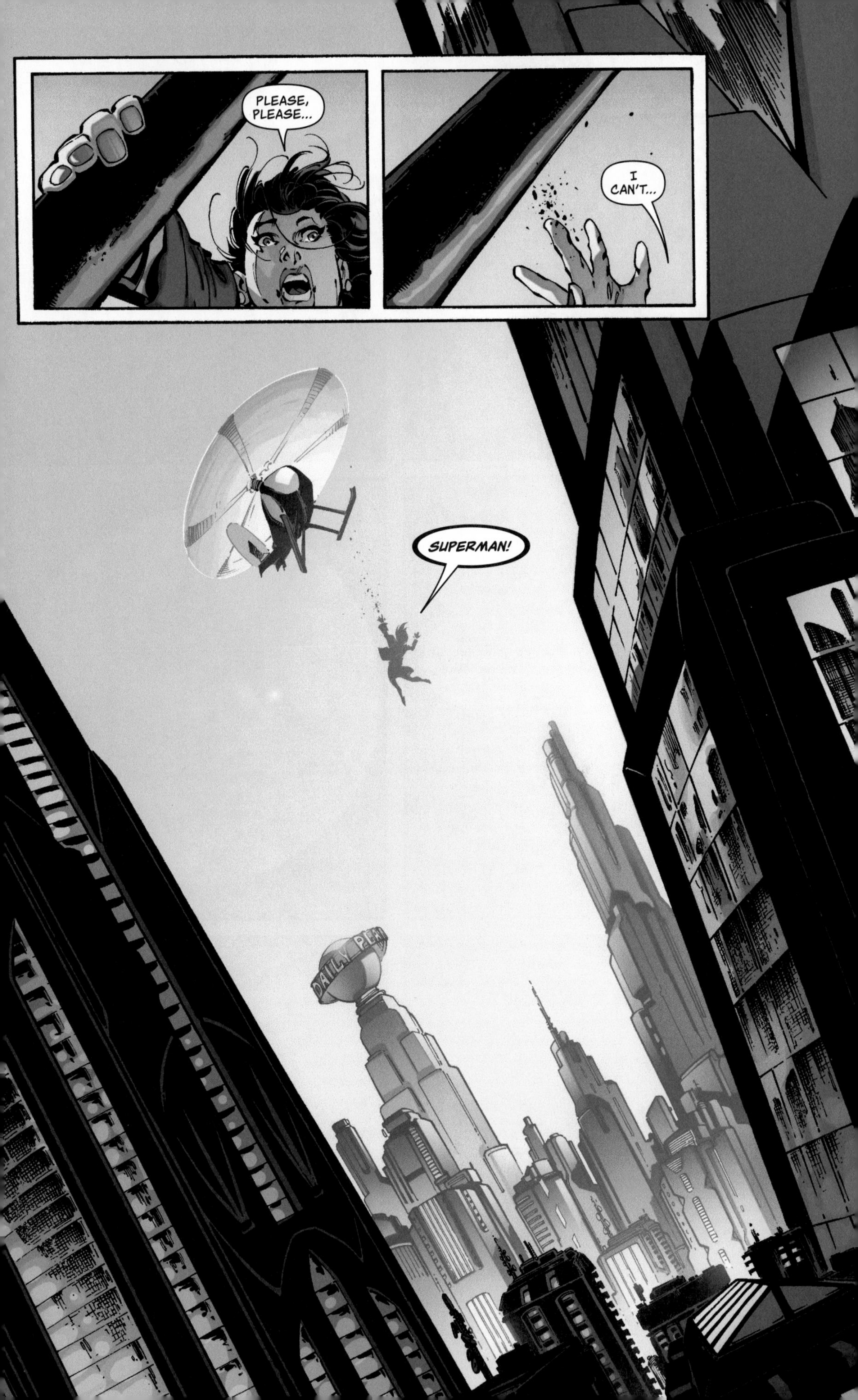
PLEASE, PLEASE...
I CAN'T...
SUPERMAN!

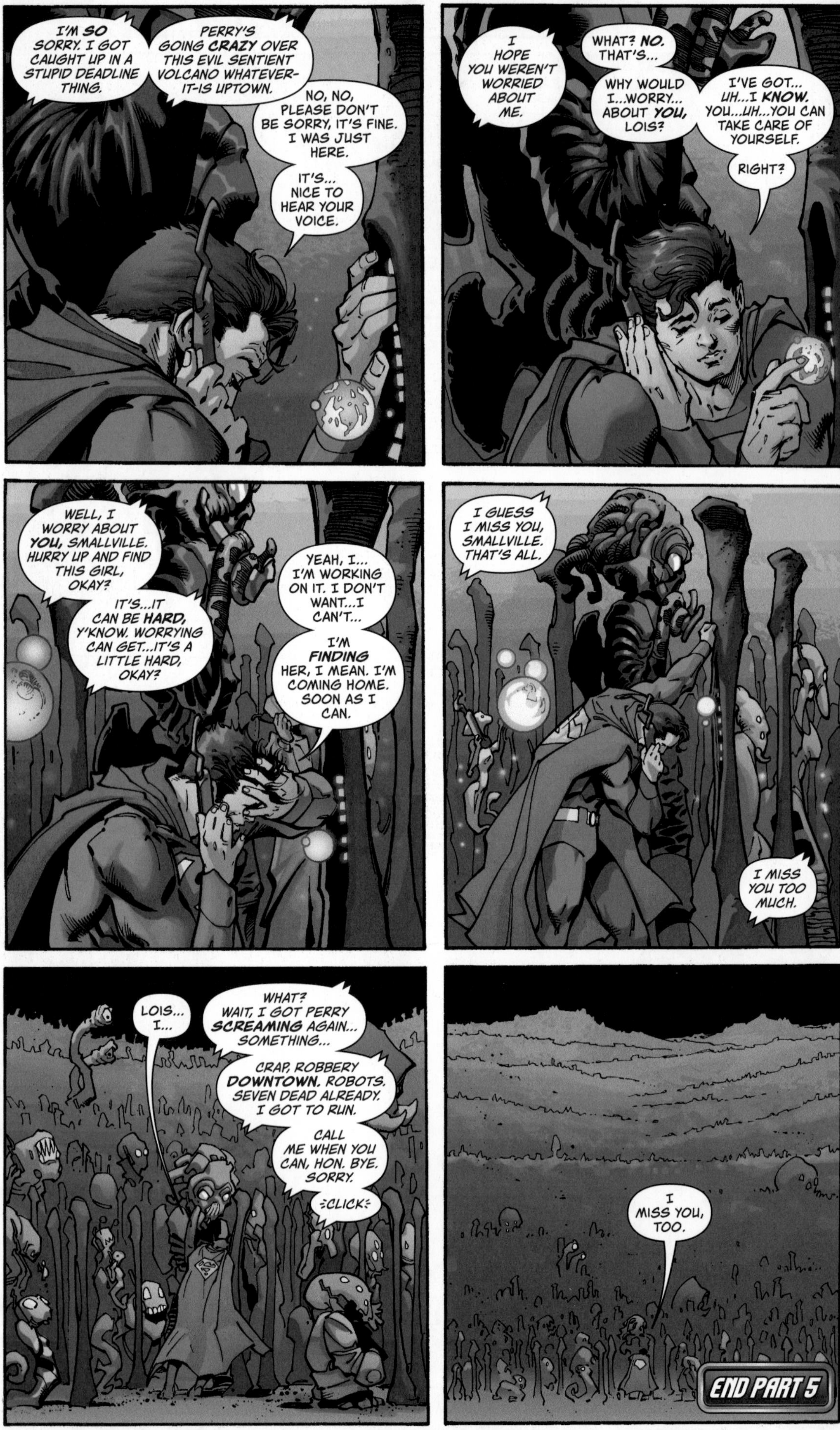
I'M SO SORRY. I GOT CAUGHT UP IN A STUPID DEADLINE THING.
PERRY'S GOING CRAZY OVER THIS EVIL SENTIENT VOLCANO WHATEVER-IT-IS UPTOWN.
NO, NO, PLEASE DON'T BE SORRY, IT'S FINE. I WAS JUST HERE.
IT'S... NICE TO HEAR YOUR VOICE.
I HOPE YOU WEREN'T WORRIED ABOUT ME.
WHAT? NO. THAT'S...
WHY WOULD I...WORRY... ABOUT YOU, LOIS?
I'VE GOT... UH...I KNOW. YOU...UH...YOU CAN TAKE CARE OF YOURSELF.
RIGHT?
WELL, I WORRY ABOUT YOU, SMALLVILLE. HURRY UP AND FIND THIS GIRL, OKAY?
IT'S...IT CAN BE HARD, Y'KNOW. WORRYING CAN GET...IT'S A LITTLE HARD, OKAY?
YEAH, I... I'M WORKING ON IT. I DON'T WANT...I CAN'T...
I'M FINDING HER, I MEAN. I'M COMING HOME. SOON AS I CAN.
I GUESS I MISS YOU, SMALLVILLE. THAT'S ALL.
I MISS YOU TOO MUCH.
LOIS... I...
WHAT? WAIT, I GOT PERRY SCREAMING AGAIN... SOMETHING...
CRAP, ROBBERY DOWNTOWN. ROBOTS. SEVEN DEAD ALREADY. I GOT TO RUN.
CALL ME WHEN YOU CAN, HON. BYE. SORRY.
CLICK
I MISS YOU, TOO.
END PART 5

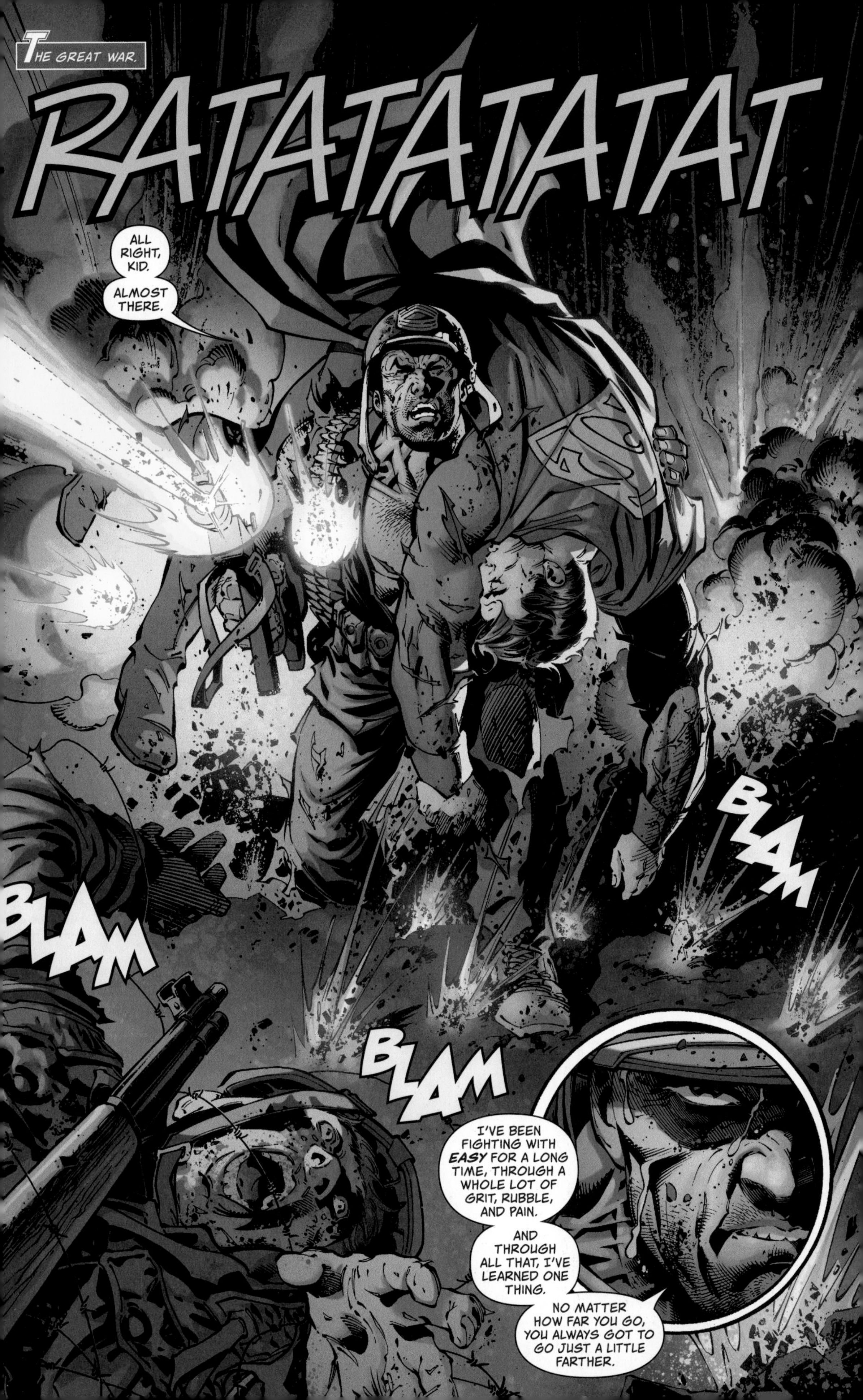
THE GREAT WAR.
RATATATATAT
ALL RIGHT, KID.
ALMOST THERE.
BLAM
BLAM
BLAM
I'VE BEEN FIGHTING WITH EASY FOR A LONG TIME, THROUGH A WHOLE LOT OF GRIT, RUBBLE, AND PAIN.
AND THROUGH ALL THAT, I'VE LEARNED ONE THING.
NO MATTER HOW FAR YOU GO, YOU ALWAYS GOT TO GO JUST A LITTLE FARTHER.

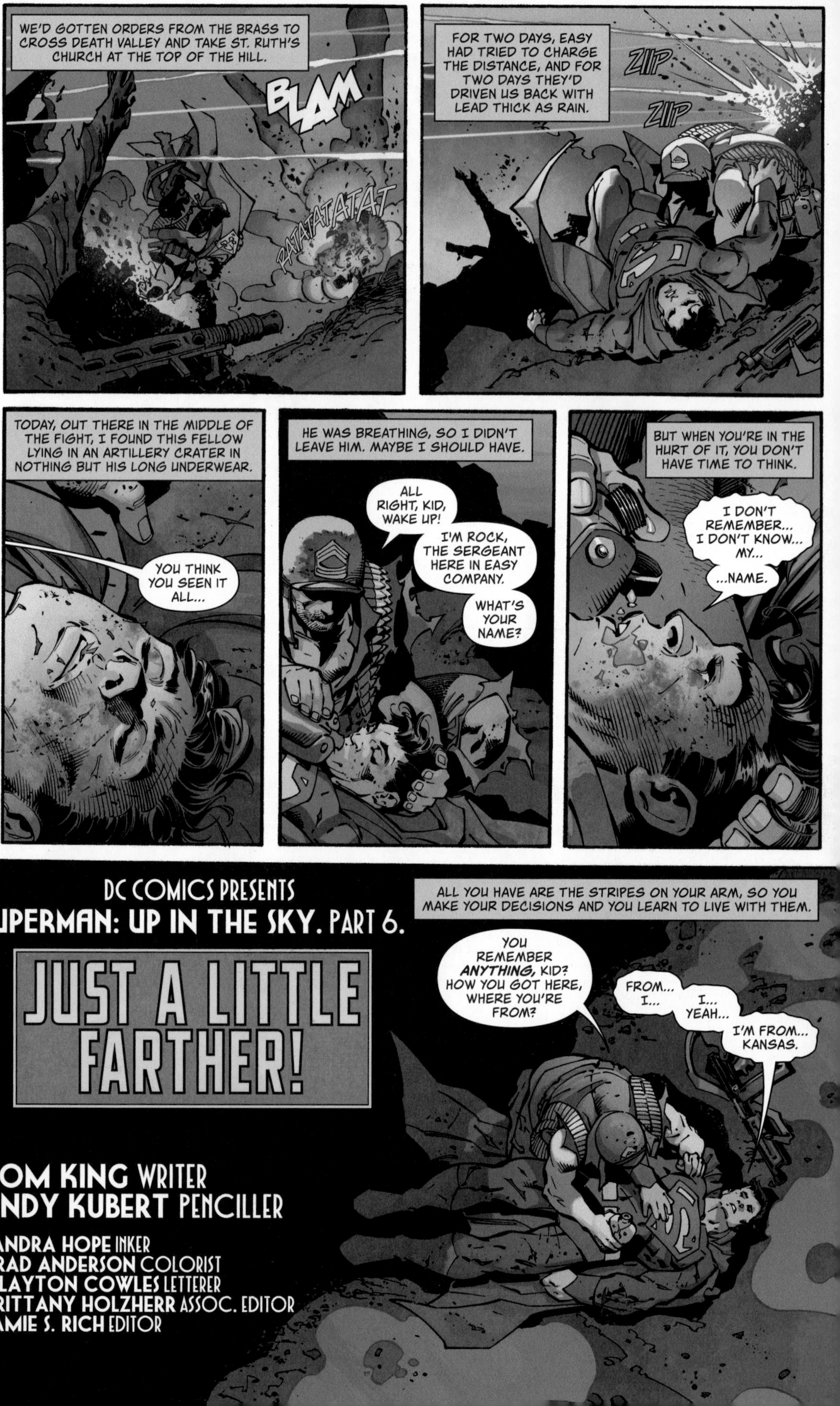
WE'D GOTTEN ORDERS FROM THE BRASS TO CROSS DEATH VALLEY AND TAKE ST. RUTH'S CHURCH AT THE TOP OF THE HILL.
BLAM
PATATATATAT
FOR TWO DAYS, EASY HAD TRIED TO CHARGE THE DISTANCE, AND FOR TWO DAYS THEY'D DRIVEN US BACK WITH LEAD THICK AS RAIN.
ZIIP
ZIIP
TODAY, OUT THERE IN THE MIDDLE OF THE FIGHT, I FOUND THIS FELLOW LYING IN AN ARTILLERY CRATER IN NOTHING BUT HIS LONG UNDERWEAR.
YOU THINK YOU SEEN IT ALL...
HE WAS BREATHING, SO I DIDN'T LEAVE HIM. MAYBE I SHOULD HAVE.
ALL RIGHT, KID, WAKE UP!
I'M ROCK, THE SERGEANT HERE IN EASY COMPANY.
WHAT'S YOUR NAME?
BUT WHEN YOU'RE IN THE HURT OF IT, YOU DON'T HAVE TIME TO THINK.
I DON'T REMEMBER... I DON'T KNOW... MY...
...NAME.
DC COMICS PRESENTS
SUPERMAN: UP IN THE SKY. PART 6.
JUST A LITTLE FARTHER!
TOM KING WRITER
ANDY KUBERT PENCILLER
SANDRA HOPE INKER
BRAD ANDERSON COLORIST
CLAYTON COWLES LETTERER
BRITTANY HOLZHERR ASSOC. EDITOR
JAMIE S. RICH EDITOR
ALL YOU HAVE ARE THE STRIPES ON YOUR ARM, SO YOU MAKE YOUR DECISIONS AND YOU LEARN TO LIVE WITH THEM.
YOU REMEMBER ANYTHING, KID? HOW YOU GOT HERE, WHERE YOU'RE FROM?
FROM... I...
I... YEAH...
I'M FROM... KANSAS.

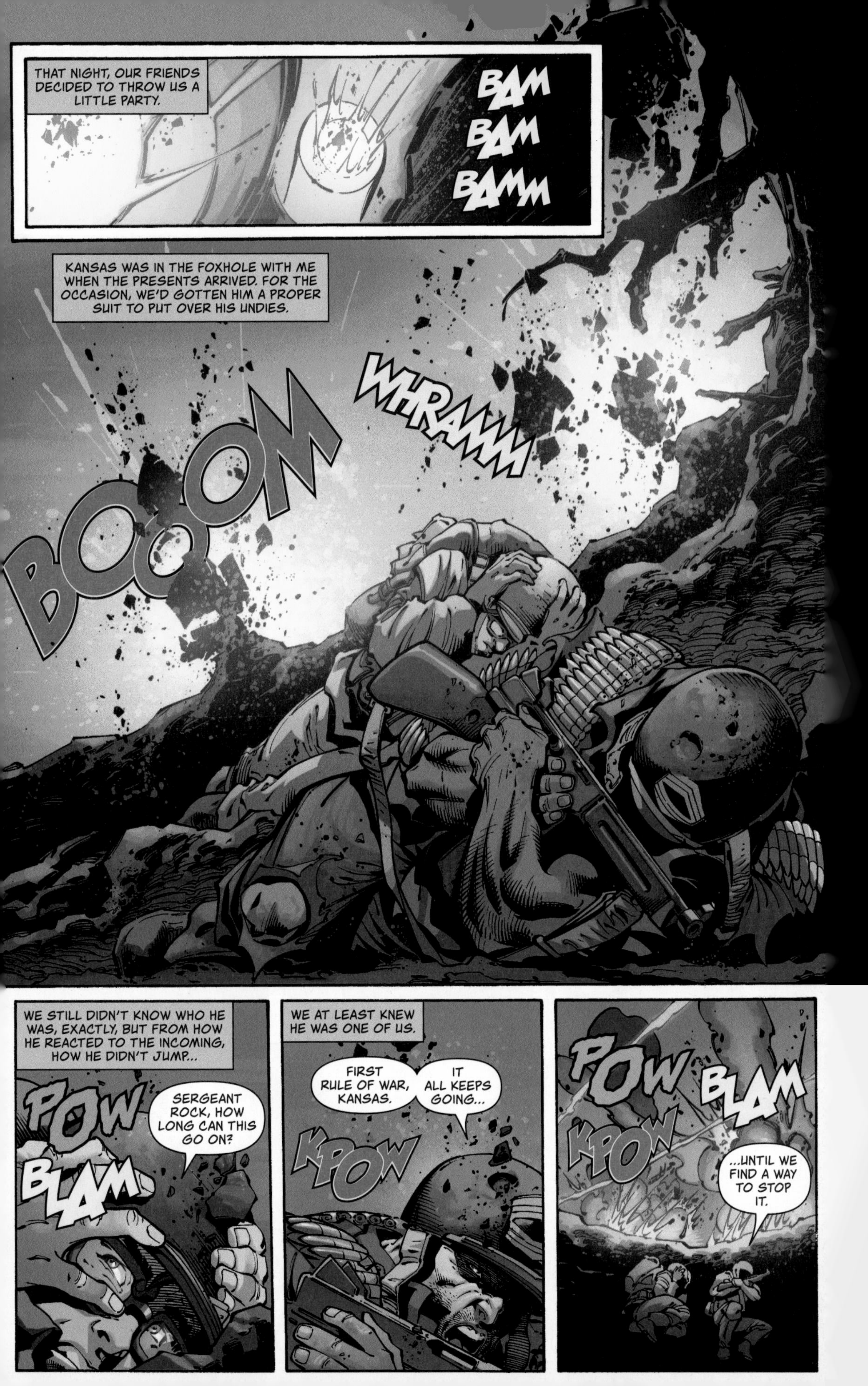

THAT NIGHT, OUR FRIENDS DECIDED TO THROW US A LITTLE PARTY.
BAM
BAM
BAMM
KANSAS WAS IN THE FOXHOLE WITH ME WHEN THE PRESENTS ARRIVED. FOR THE OCCASION, WE'D GOTTEN HIM A PROPER SUIT TO PUT OVER HIS UNDIES.
WHRAMM
BOOOM
WE STILL DIDN'T KNOW WHO HE WAS, EXACTLY, BUT FROM HOW HE REACTED TO THE INCOMING, HOW HE DIDN'T JUMP...
POW
BLAM
SERGEANT ROCK, HOW LONG CAN THIS GO ON?
WE AT LEAST KNEW HE WAS ONE OF US.
FIRST RULE OF WAR, KANSAS.
IT ALL KEEPS GOING...
KPOW
POW
BLAM
KPOW
...UNTIL WE FIND A WAY TO STOP IT.

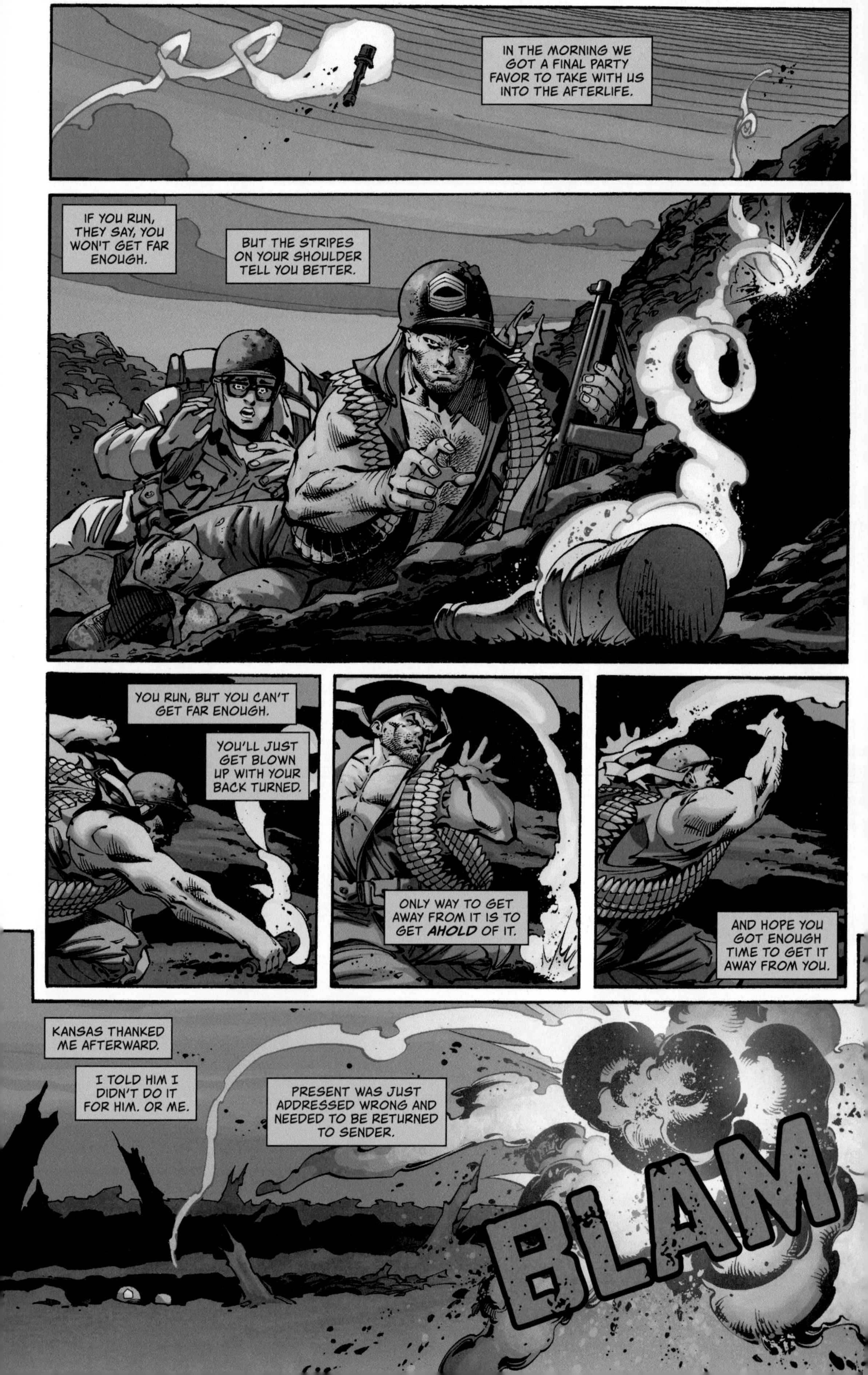

IN THE MORNING WE GOT A FINAL PARTY FAVOR TO TAKE WITH US INTO THE AFTERLIFE.
IF YOU RUN, THEY SAY, YOU WON'T GET FAR ENOUGH.
BUT THE STRIPES ON YOUR SHOULDER TELL YOU BETTER.
YOU RUN, BUT YOU CAN'T GET FAR ENOUGH.
YOU'LL JUST GET BLOWN UP WITH YOUR BACK TURNED.
ONLY WAY TO GET AWAY FROM IT IS TO GET AHOLD OF IT.
AND HOPE YOU GOT ENOUGH TIME TO GET IT AWAY FROM YOU.
KANSAS THANKED ME AFTERWARD.
I TOLD HIM I DIDN'T DO IT FOR HIM. OR ME.
PRESENT WAS JUST ADDRESSED WRONG AND NEEDED TO BE RETURNED TO SENDER.
BLAM

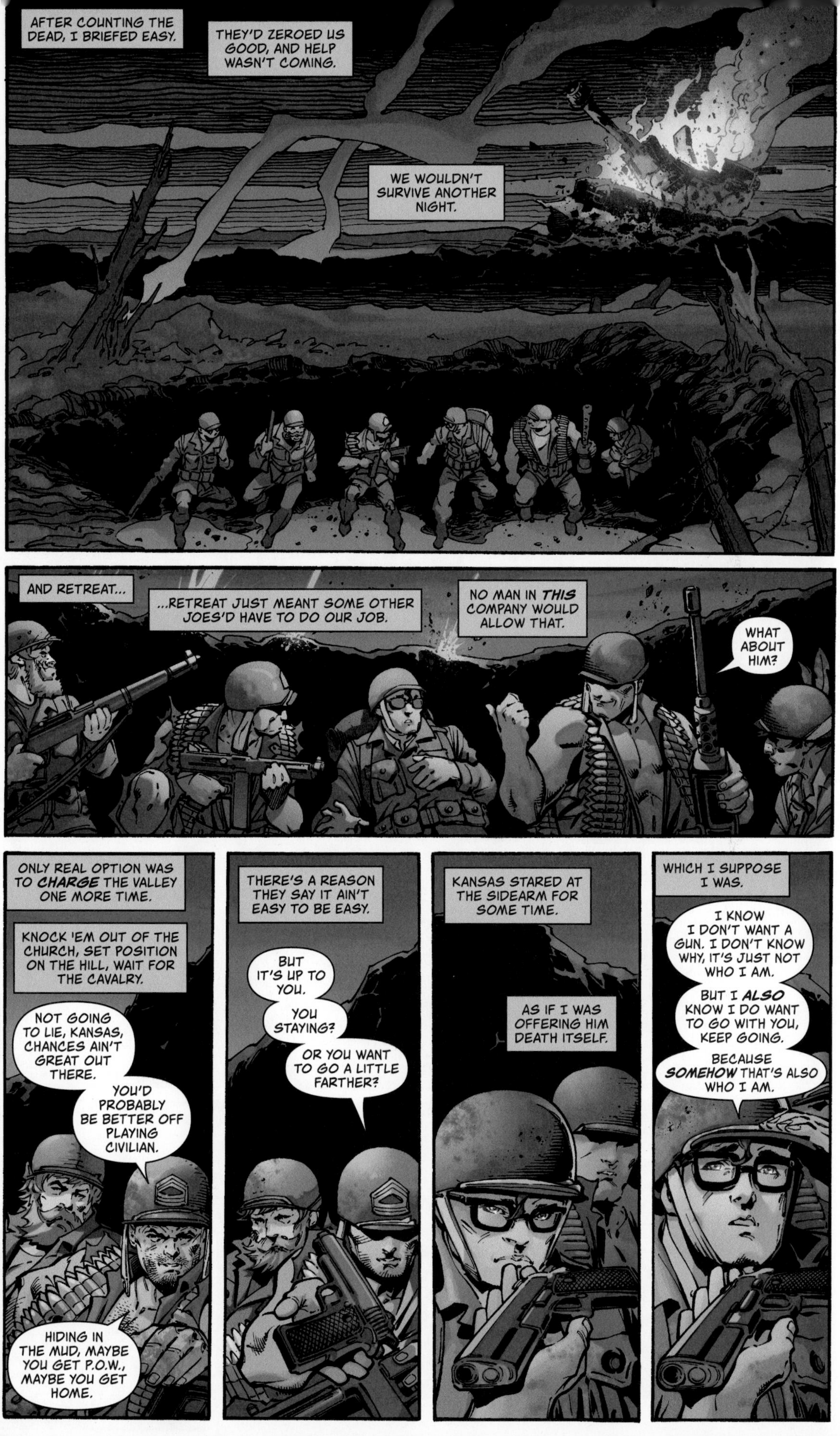
AFTER COUNTING THE DEAD, I BRIEFED EASY.
THEY'D ZEROED US GOOD, AND HELP WASN'T COMING.
WE WOULDN'T SURVIVE ANOTHER NIGHT.
AND RETREAT...
...RETREAT JUST MEANT SOME OTHER JOES'D HAVE TO DO OUR JOB.
NO MAN IN *THIS* COMPANY WOULD ALLOW THAT.
WHAT ABOUT HIM?
ONLY REAL OPTION WAS TO *CHARGE* THE VALLEY ONE MORE TIME.
KNOCK 'EM OUT OF THE CHURCH, SET POSITION ON THE HILL, WAIT FOR THE CAVALRY.
NOT GOING TO LIE, KANSAS, CHANCES AIN'T GREAT OUT THERE.
YOU'D PROBABLY BE BETTER OFF PLAYING CIVILIAN.
HIDING IN THE MUD, MAYBE YOU GET P.O.W., MAYBE YOU GET HOME.
THERE'S A REASON THEY SAY IT AIN'T EASY TO BE EASY.
BUT IT'S UP TO YOU.
YOU STAYING?
OR YOU WANT TO GO A LITTLE FARTHER?
KANSAS STARED AT THE SIDEARM FOR SOME TIME.
AS IF I WAS OFFERING HIM DEATH ITSELF.
WHICH I SUPPOSE I WAS.
I KNOW I DON'T WANT A GUN. I DON'T KNOW WHY, IT'S JUST NOT WHO I AM.
BUT I *ALSO* KNOW I DO WANT TO GO WITH YOU, KEEP GOING.
BECAUSE *SOMEHOW* THAT'S ALSO WHO I AM.

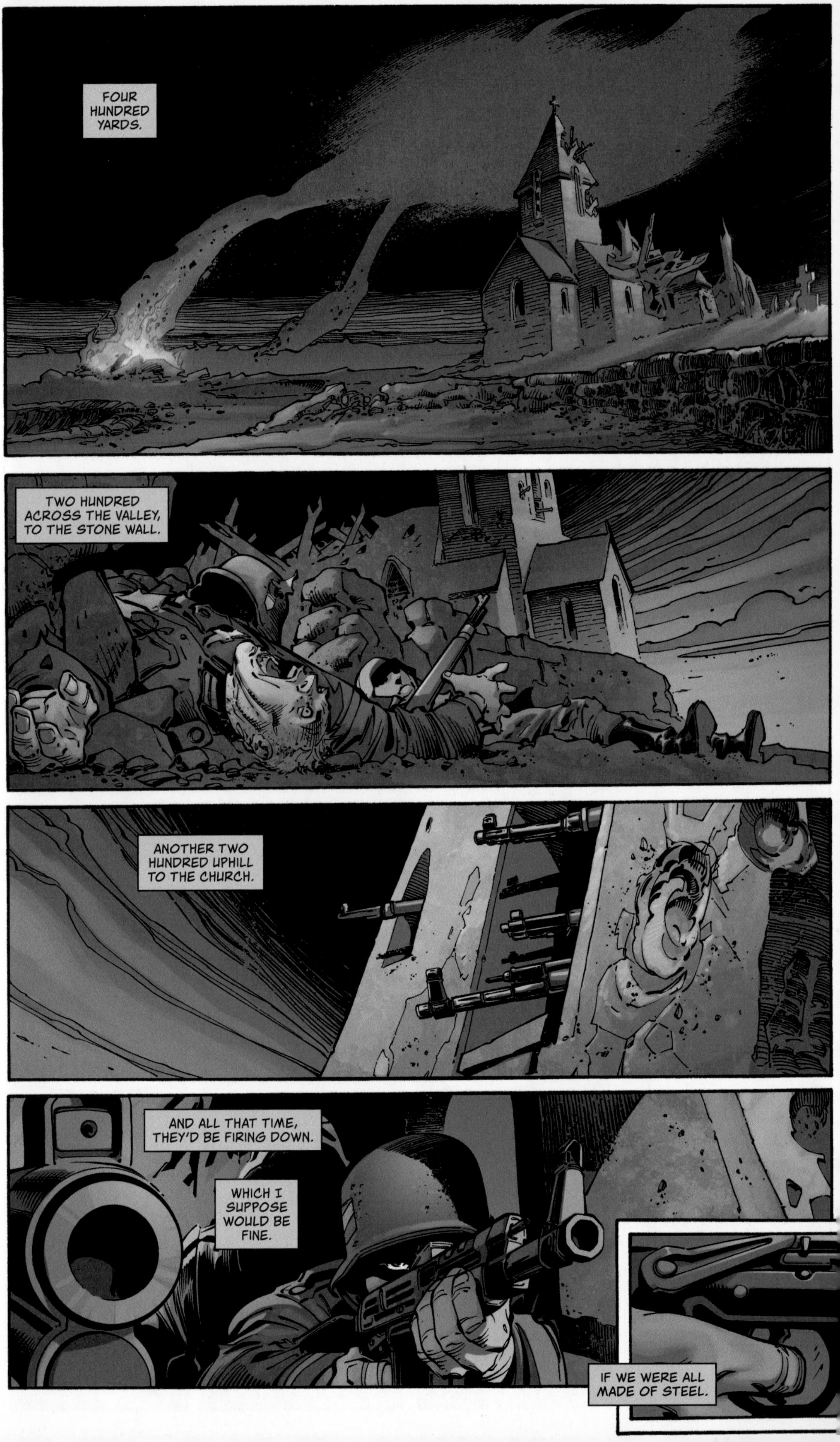
FOUR HUNDRED YARDS.
TWO HUNDRED ACROSS THE VALLEY, TO THE STONE WALL.
ANOTHER TWO HUNDRED UPHILL TO THE CHURCH.
AND ALL THAT TIME, THEY'D BE FIRING DOWN.
WHICH I SUPPOSE WOULD BE FINE.
IF WE WERE ALL MADE OF STEEL.

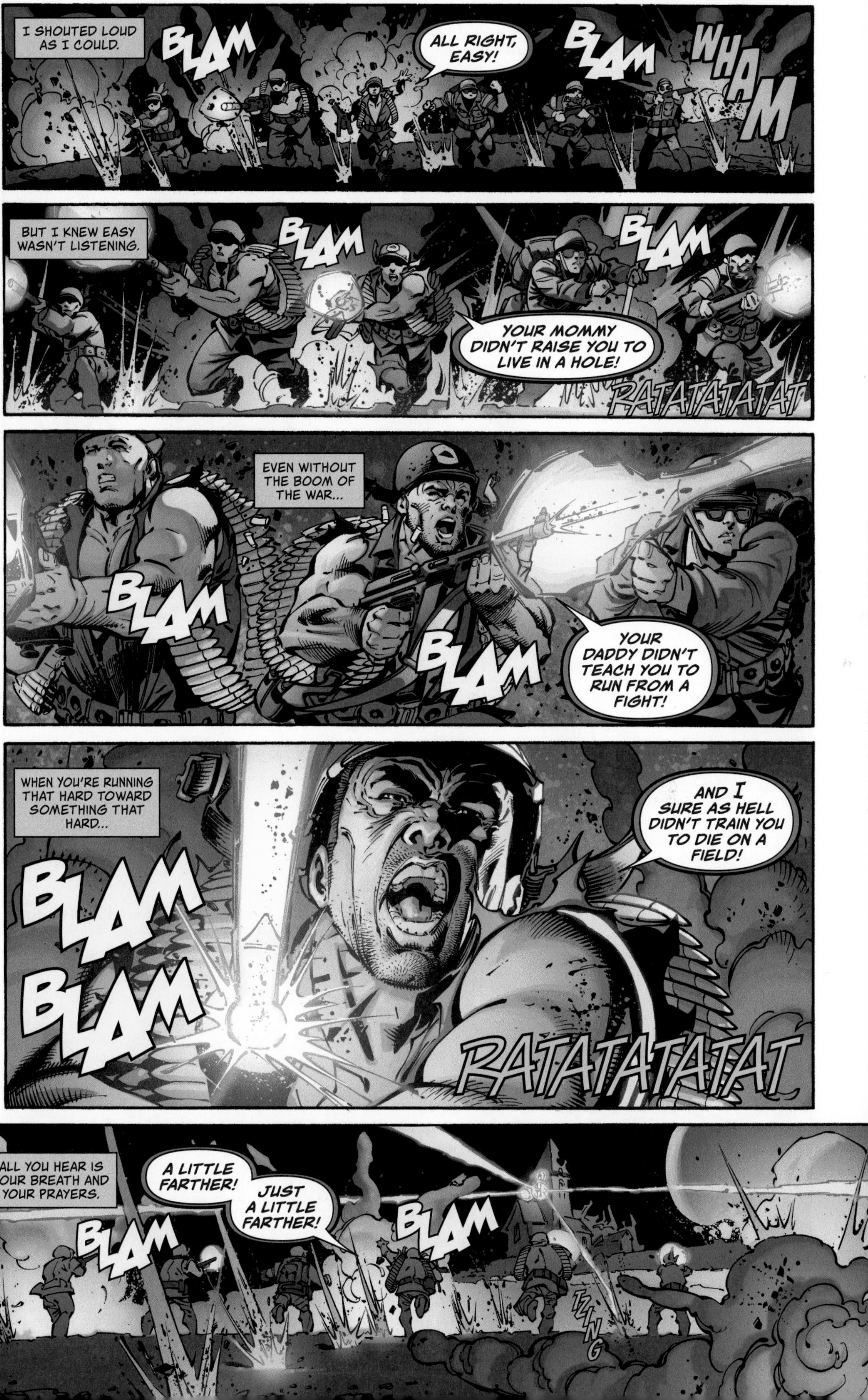
I SHOUTED LOUD AS I COULD.
BLAM
ALL RIGHT, EASY!
BLAM
WHAM
BUT I KNEW EASY WASN'T LISTENING.
BLAM
BLAM
YOUR MOMMY DIDN'T RAISE YOU TO LIVE IN A HOLE!
RATATATATAT
EVEN WITHOUT THE BOOM OF THE WAR...
BLAM
BLAM
YOUR DADDY DIDN'T TEACH YOU TO RUN FROM A FIGHT!
WHEN YOU'RE RUNNING THAT HARD TOWARD SOMETHING THAT HARD...
AND I SURE AS HELL DIDN'T TRAIN YOU TO DIE ON A FIELD!
BLAM
BLAM
RATATATATAT
ALL YOU HEAR IS YOUR BREATH AND YOUR PRAYERS.
A LITTLE FARTHER!
JUST A LITTLE FARTHER!
BLAM
BLAM
TZING

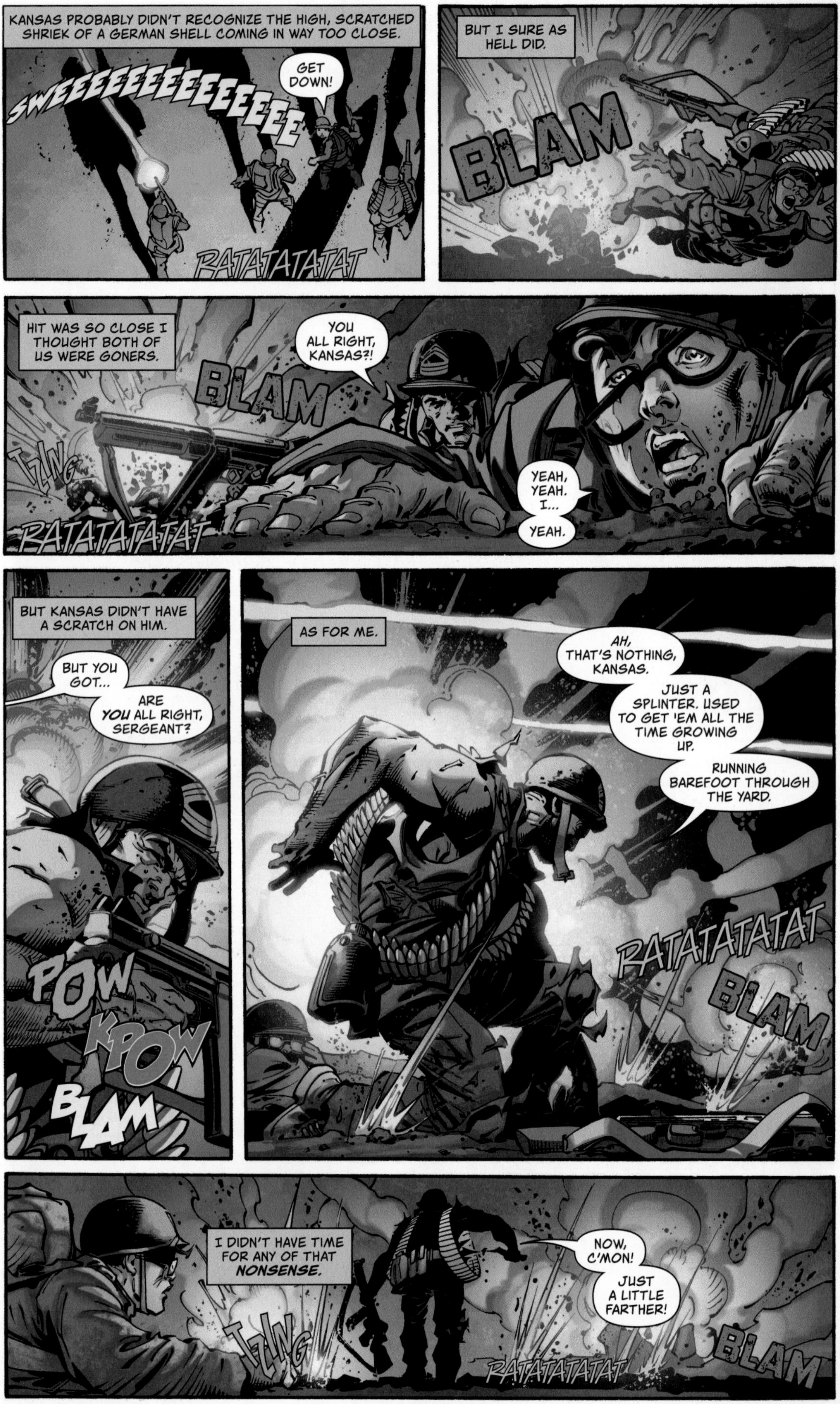
KANSAS PROBABLY DIDN'T RECOGNIZE THE HIGH, SCRATCHED SHRIEK OF A GERMAN SHELL COMING IN WAY TOO CLOSE.
SWEEEEEEEEEEEEEE
GET DOWN!
RATATATATAT
BUT I SURE AS HELL DID.
BLAM
HIT WAS SO CLOSE I THOUGHT BOTH OF US WERE GONERS.
YOU ALL RIGHT, KANSAS?!
BLAM
TZING
RATATATATAT
YEAH, YEAH. I...
YEAH.
BUT KANSAS DIDN'T HAVE A SCRATCH ON HIM.
BUT YOU GOT...
ARE YOU ALL RIGHT, SERGEANT?
POW
KPOW
BLAM
AS FOR ME.
AH, THAT'S NOTHING, KANSAS.
JUST A SPLINTER. USED TO GET 'EM ALL THE TIME GROWING UP.
RUNNING BAREFOOT THROUGH THE YARD.
RATATATATAT
BLAM
I DIDN'T HAVE TIME FOR ANY OF THAT NONSENSE.
NOW, C'MON!
JUST A LITTLE FARTHER!
TZING
RATATATATAT
BLAM

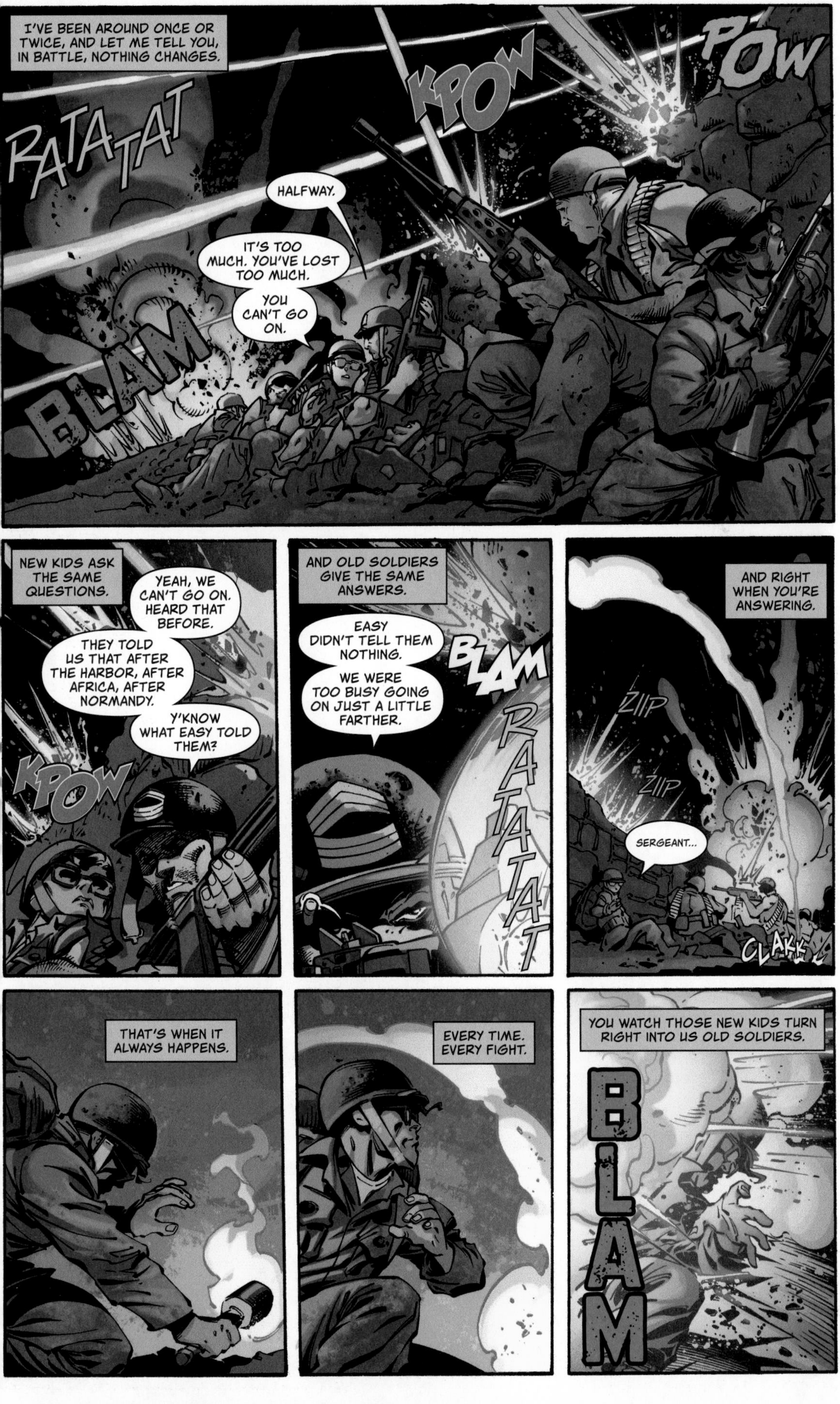
I'VE BEEN AROUND ONCE OR TWICE, AND LET ME TELL YOU, IN BATTLE, NOTHING CHANGES.
RATATAT
KPOW
POW
HALFWAY.
IT'S TOO MUCH. YOU'VE LOST TOO MUCH.
YOU CAN'T GO ON.
BLAM
NEW KIDS ASK THE SAME QUESTIONS.
YEAH, WE CAN'T GO ON. HEARD THAT BEFORE.
THEY TOLD US THAT AFTER THE HARBOR, AFTER AFRICA, AFTER NORMANDY.
Y'KNOW WHAT EASY TOLD THEM?
KPOW
AND OLD SOLDIERS GIVE THE SAME ANSWERS.
EASY DIDN'T TELL THEM NOTHING.
WE WERE TOO BUSY GOING ON JUST A LITTLE FARTHER.
BLAM
RATATAT
AND RIGHT WHEN YOU'RE ANSWERING.
ZIP
ZIP
SERGEANT...
CLAKK
THAT'S WHEN IT ALWAYS HAPPENS.
EVERY TIME. EVERY FIGHT.
YOU WATCH THOSE NEW KIDS TURN RIGHT INTO US OLD SOLDIERS.
BLAM

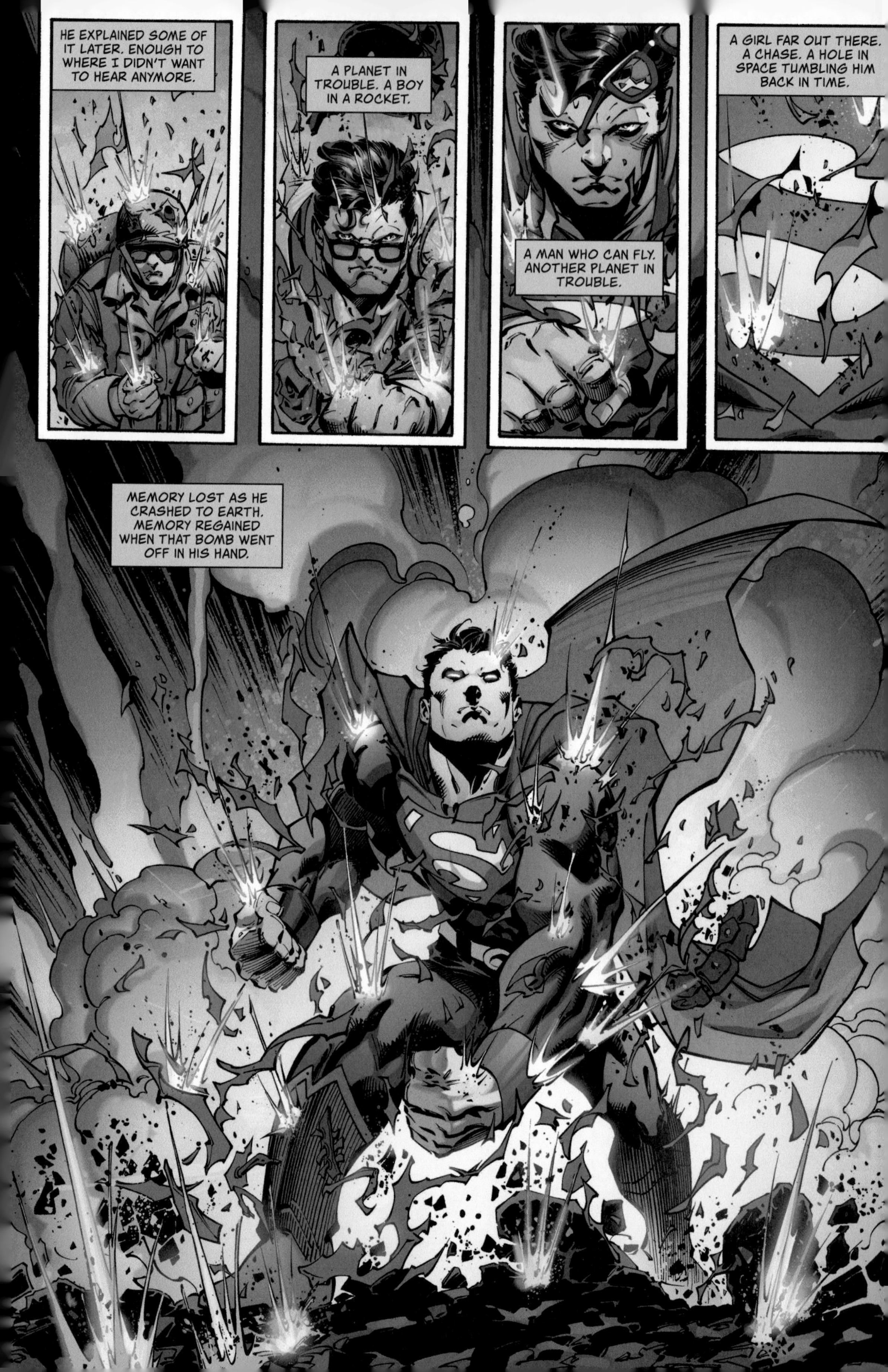
HE EXPLAINED SOME OF IT LATER. ENOUGH TO WHERE I DIDN'T WANT TO HEAR ANYMORE.
A PLANET IN TROUBLE. A BOY IN A ROCKET.
A MAN WHO CAN FLY. ANOTHER PLANET IN TROUBLE.
A GIRL FAR OUT THERE. A CHASE. A HOLE IN SPACE TUMBLING HIM BACK IN TIME.
MEMORY LOST AS HE CRASHED TO EARTH. MEMORY REGAINED WHEN THAT BOMB WENT OFF IN HIS HAND.

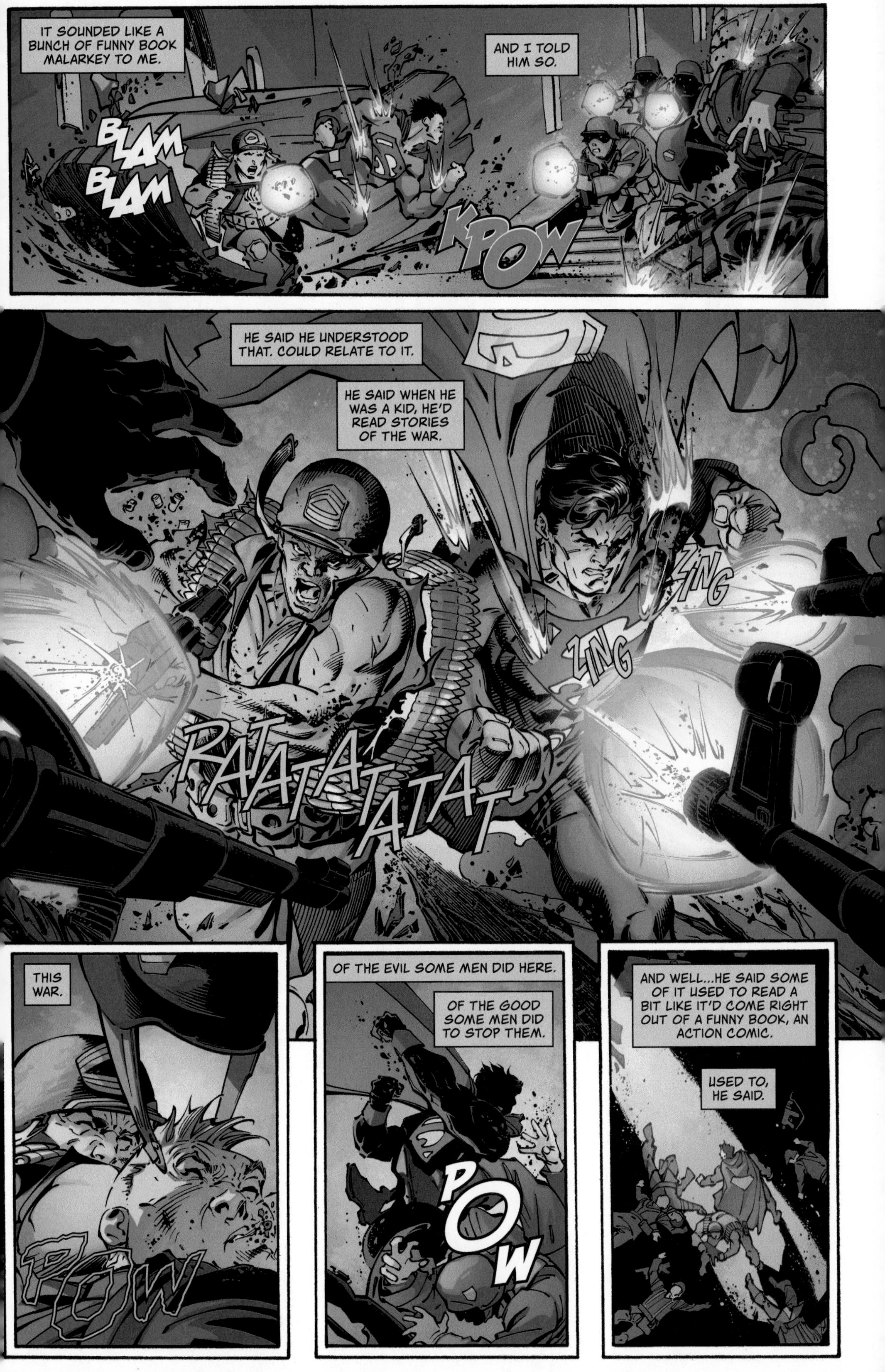
IT SOUNDED LIKE A BUNCH OF FUNNY BOOK MALARKEY TO ME.
AND I TOLD HIM SO.
BLAM
BLAM
KPOW
HE SAID HE UNDERSTOOD THAT. COULD RELATE TO IT.
HE SAID WHEN HE WAS A KID, HE'D READ STORIES OF THE WAR.
ZING
ZING
RATATATATATAT
THIS WAR.
POW
OF THE EVIL SOME MEN DID HERE.
OF THE GOOD SOME MEN DID TO STOP THEM.
POW
AND WELL...HE SAID SOME OF IT USED TO READ A BIT LIKE IT'D COME RIGHT OUT OF A FUNNY BOOK, AN ACTION COMIC.
USED TO, HE SAID.

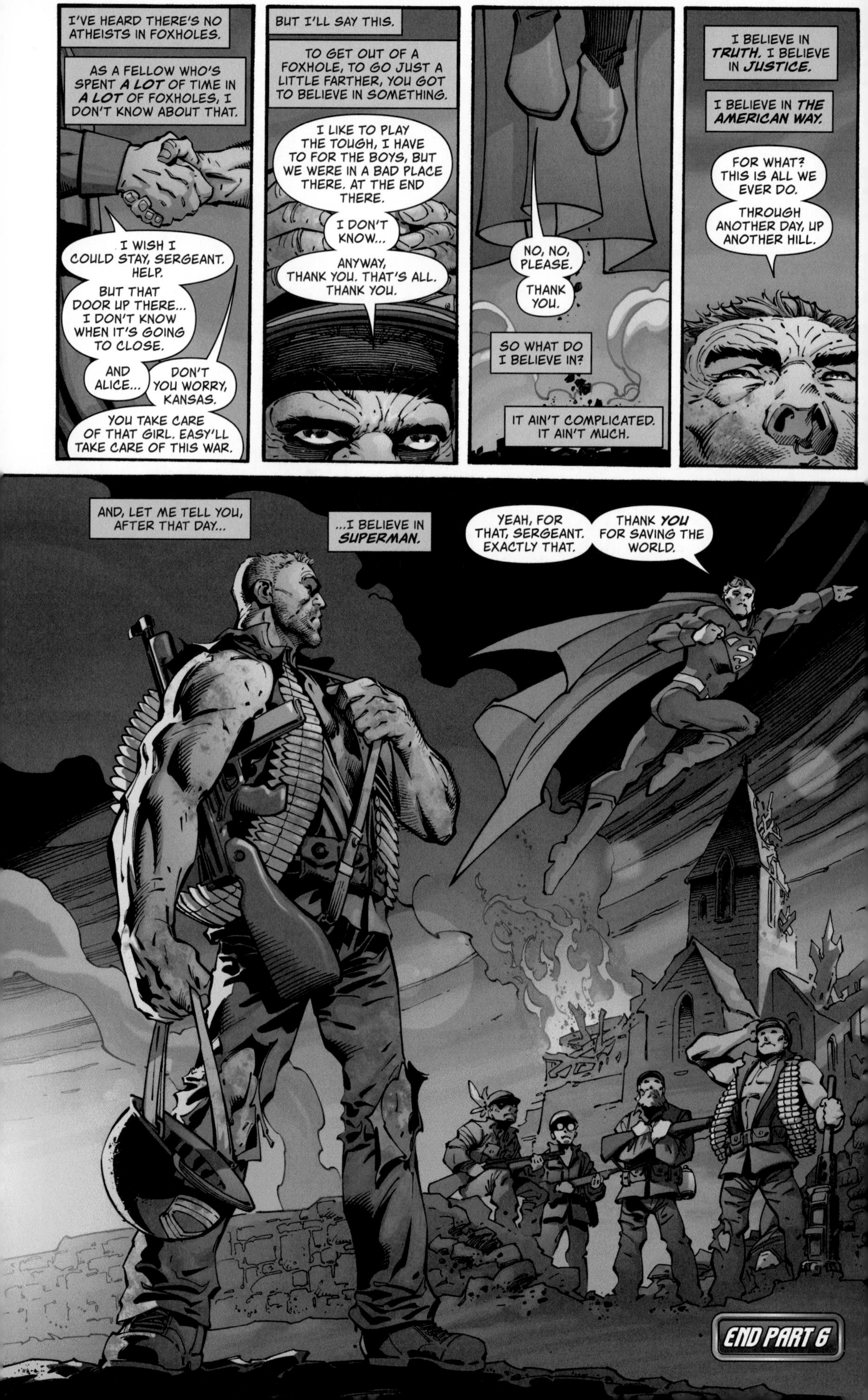
I'VE HEARD THERE'S NO ATHEISTS IN FOXHOLES.
AS A FELLOW WHO'S SPENT A LOT OF TIME IN A LOT OF FOXHOLES, I DON'T KNOW ABOUT THAT.
I WISH I COULD STAY, SERGEANT. HELP.
BUT THAT DOOR UP THERE... I DON'T KNOW WHEN IT'S GOING TO CLOSE.
AND ALICE...
DON'T YOU WORRY, KANSAS.
YOU TAKE CARE OF THAT GIRL. EASY'LL TAKE CARE OF THIS WAR.
BUT I'LL SAY THIS.
TO GET OUT OF A FOXHOLE, TO GO JUST A LITTLE FARTHER, YOU GOT TO BELIEVE IN SOMETHING.
I LIKE TO PLAY THE TOUGH, I HAVE TO FOR THE BOYS, BUT WE WERE IN A BAD PLACE THERE. AT THE END THERE.
I DON'T KNOW...
ANYWAY, THANK YOU. THAT'S ALL. THANK YOU.
NO, NO, PLEASE.
THANK YOU.
SO WHAT DO I BELIEVE IN?
IT AIN'T COMPLICATED. IT AIN'T MUCH.
I BELIEVE IN TRUTH. I BELIEVE IN JUSTICE.
I BELIEVE IN THE AMERICAN WAY.
FOR WHAT? THIS IS ALL WE EVER DO.
THROUGH ANOTHER DAY, UP ANOTHER HILL.
AND, LET ME TELL YOU, AFTER THAT DAY...
...I BELIEVE IN SUPERMAN.
YEAH, FOR THAT, SERGEANT. EXACTLY THAT.
THANK YOU FOR SAVING THE WORLD.
END PART 6

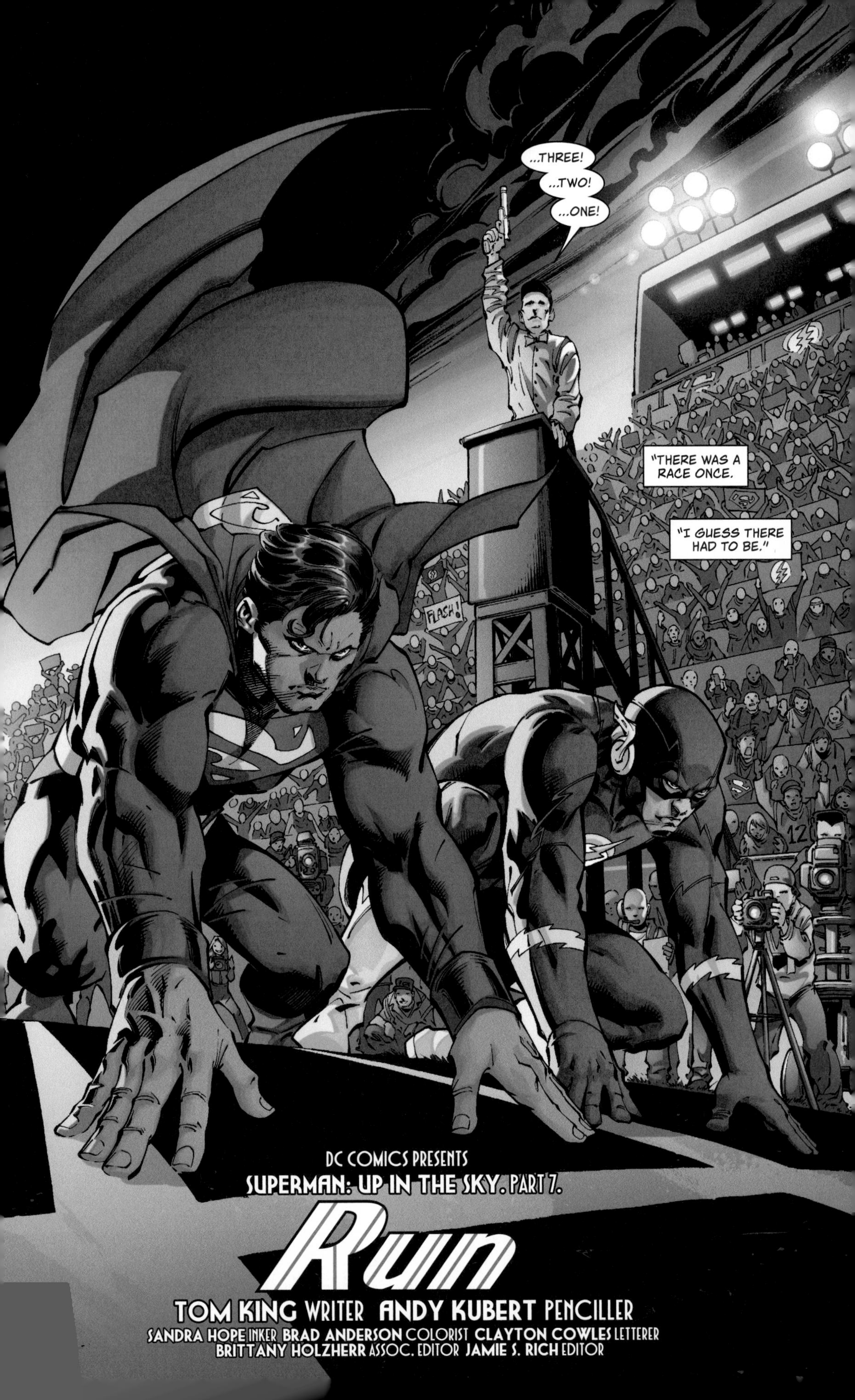
...THREE!
...TWO!
...ONE!
"THERE WAS A RACE ONCE.
"I GUESS THERE HAD TO BE."
FLASH!
DC COMICS PRESENTS
SUPERMAN: UP IN THE SKY. PART 7.
Run
TOM KING WRITER ANDY KUBERT PENCILLER
SANDRA HOPE INKER BRAD ANDERSON COLORIST CLAYTON COWLES LETTERER
BRITTANY HOLZHERR ASSOC. EDITOR JAMIE S. RICH EDITOR

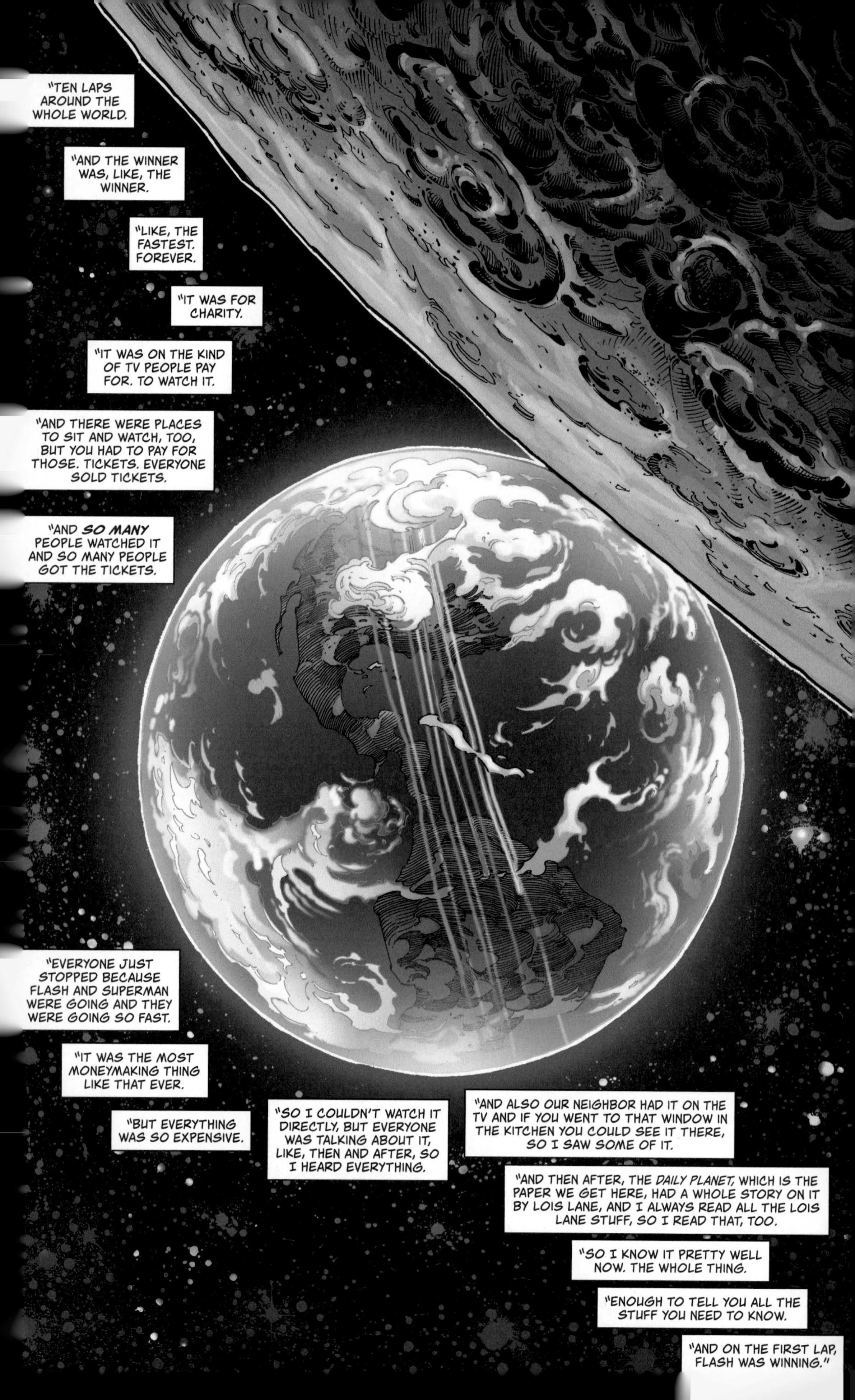
"TEN LAPS AROUND THE WHOLE WORLD.
"AND THE WINNER WAS, LIKE, THE WINNER.
"LIKE, THE FASTEST. FOREVER.
"IT WAS FOR CHARITY.
"IT WAS ON THE KIND OF TV PEOPLE PAY FOR. TO WATCH IT.
"AND THERE WERE PLACES TO SIT AND WATCH, TOO, BUT YOU HAD TO PAY FOR THOSE. TICKETS. EVERYONE SOLD TICKETS.
"AND *SO MANY* PEOPLE WATCHED IT AND SO MANY PEOPLE GOT THE TICKETS.
"EVERYONE JUST STOPPED BECAUSE FLASH AND SUPERMAN WERE GOING AND THEY WERE GOING SO FAST.
"IT WAS THE MOST MONEYMAKING THING LIKE THAT EVER.
"BUT EVERYTHING WAS SO EXPENSIVE.
"SO I COULDN'T WATCH IT DIRECTLY, BUT EVERYONE WAS TALKING ABOUT IT, LIKE, THEN AND AFTER, SO I HEARD EVERYTHING.
"AND ALSO OUR NEIGHBOR HAD IT ON THE TV AND IF YOU WENT TO THAT WINDOW IN THE KITCHEN YOU COULD SEE IT THERE, SO I SAW SOME OF IT.
"AND THEN AFTER, THE *DAILY PLANET,* WHICH IS THE PAPER WE GET HERE, HAD A WHOLE STORY ON IT BY LOIS LANE, AND I ALWAYS READ ALL THE LOIS LANE STUFF, SO I READ THAT, TOO.
"SO I KNOW IT PRETTY WELL NOW. THE WHOLE THING.
"ENOUGH TO TELL YOU ALL THE STUFF YOU NEED TO KNOW.
"AND ON THE FIRST LAP, FLASH WAS WINNING."

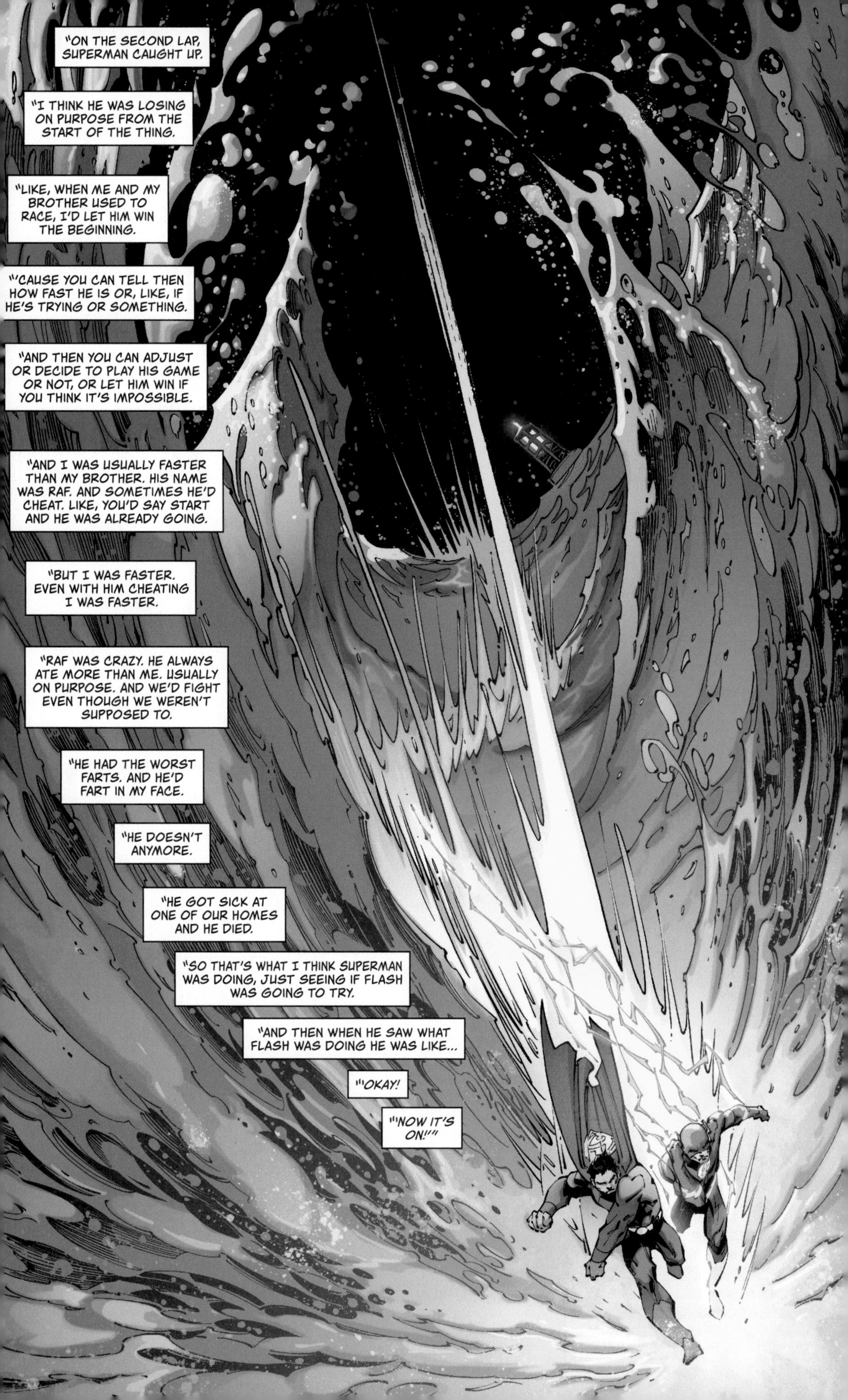
"ON THE SECOND LAP, SUPERMAN CAUGHT UP.
"I THINK HE WAS LOSING ON PURPOSE FROM THE START OF THE THING.
"LIKE, WHEN ME AND MY BROTHER USED TO RACE, I'D LET HIM WIN THE BEGINNING.
"'CAUSE YOU CAN TELL THEN HOW FAST HE IS OR, LIKE, IF HE'S TRYING OR SOMETHING.
"AND THEN YOU CAN ADJUST OR DECIDE TO PLAY HIS GAME OR NOT, OR LET HIM WIN IF YOU THINK IT'S IMPOSSIBLE.
"AND I WAS USUALLY FASTER THAN MY BROTHER. HIS NAME WAS RAF. AND SOMETIMES HE'D CHEAT. LIKE, YOU'D SAY START AND HE WAS ALREADY GOING.
"BUT I WAS FASTER. EVEN WITH HIM CHEATING I WAS FASTER.
"RAF WAS CRAZY. HE ALWAYS ATE MORE THAN ME. USUALLY ON PURPOSE. AND WE'D FIGHT EVEN THOUGH WE WEREN'T SUPPOSED TO.
"HE HAD THE WORST FARTS. AND HE'D FART IN MY FACE.
"HE DOESN'T ANYMORE.
"HE GOT SICK AT ONE OF OUR HOMES AND HE DIED.
"SO THAT'S WHAT I THINK SUPERMAN WAS DOING, JUST SEEING IF FLASH WAS GOING TO TRY.
"AND THEN WHEN HE SAW WHAT FLASH WAS DOING HE WAS LIKE...
"'OKAY!
"'NOW IT'S ON!'"

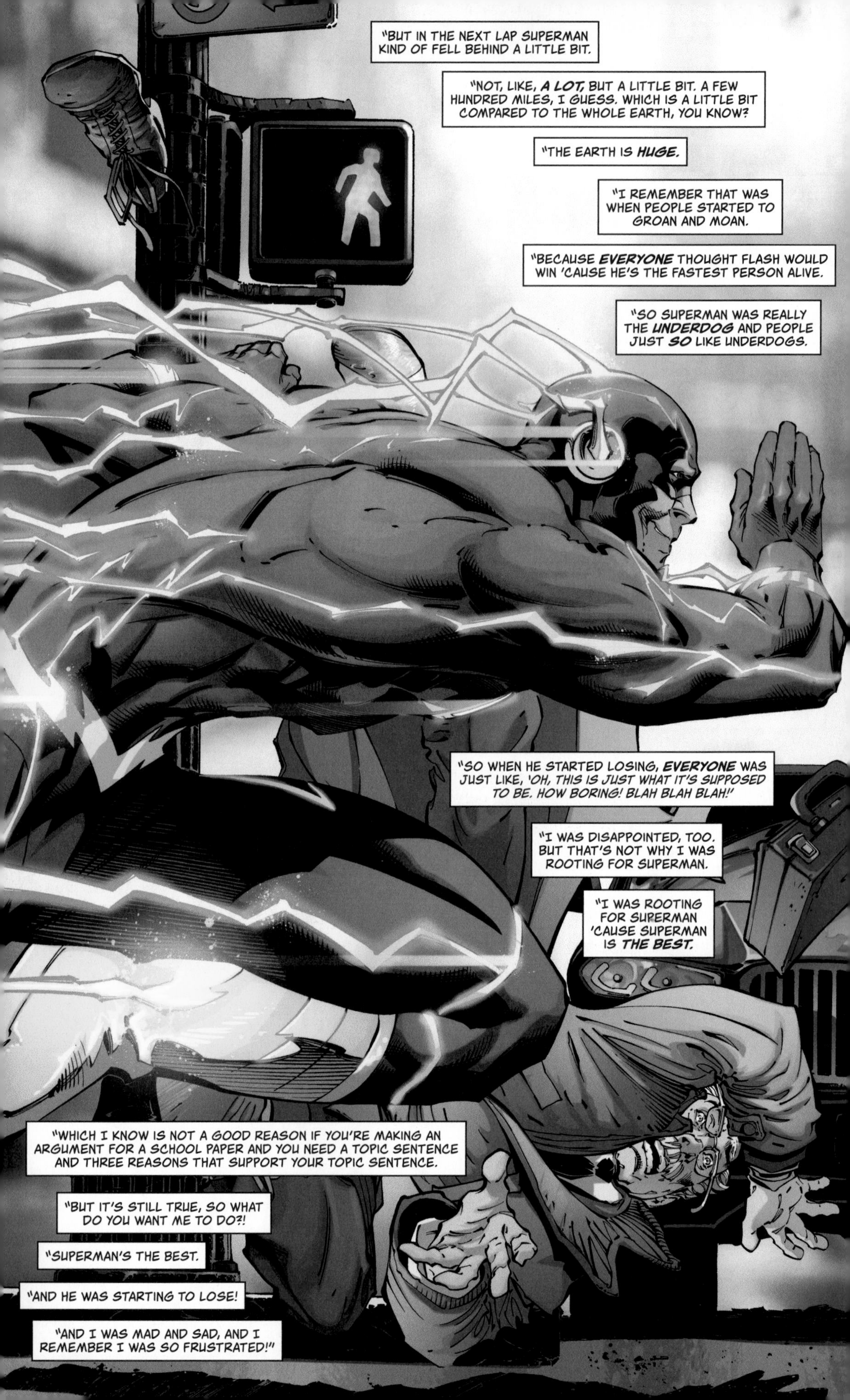
"BUT IN THE NEXT LAP SUPERMAN KIND OF FELL BEHIND A LITTLE BIT.
"NOT, LIKE, ***A LOT,*** BUT A LITTLE BIT. A FEW HUNDRED MILES, I GUESS. WHICH IS A LITTLE BIT COMPARED TO THE WHOLE EARTH, YOU KNOW?
"THE EARTH IS ***HUGE.***
"I REMEMBER THAT WAS WHEN PEOPLE STARTED TO GROAN AND MOAN.
"BECAUSE ***EVERYONE*** THOUGHT FLASH WOULD WIN 'CAUSE HE'S THE FASTEST PERSON ALIVE.
"SO SUPERMAN WAS REALLY THE ***UNDERDOG*** AND PEOPLE JUST ***SO*** LIKE UNDERDOGS.
"SO WHEN HE STARTED LOSING, ***EVERYONE*** WAS JUST LIKE, *'OH, THIS IS JUST WHAT IT'S SUPPOSED TO BE. HOW BORING! BLAH BLAH BLAH!'*
"I WAS DISAPPOINTED, TOO. BUT THAT'S NOT WHY I WAS ROOTING FOR SUPERMAN.
"I WAS ROOTING FOR SUPERMAN 'CAUSE SUPERMAN IS ***THE BEST.***
"WHICH I KNOW IS NOT A GOOD REASON IF YOU'RE MAKING AN ARGUMENT FOR A SCHOOL PAPER AND YOU NEED A TOPIC SENTENCE AND THREE REASONS THAT SUPPORT YOUR TOPIC SENTENCE.
"BUT IT'S STILL TRUE, SO WHAT DO YOU WANT ME TO DO?!
"SUPERMAN'S THE BEST.
"AND HE WAS STARTING TO LOSE!
"AND I WAS MAD AND SAD, AND I REMEMBER I WAS SO FRUSTRATED!"

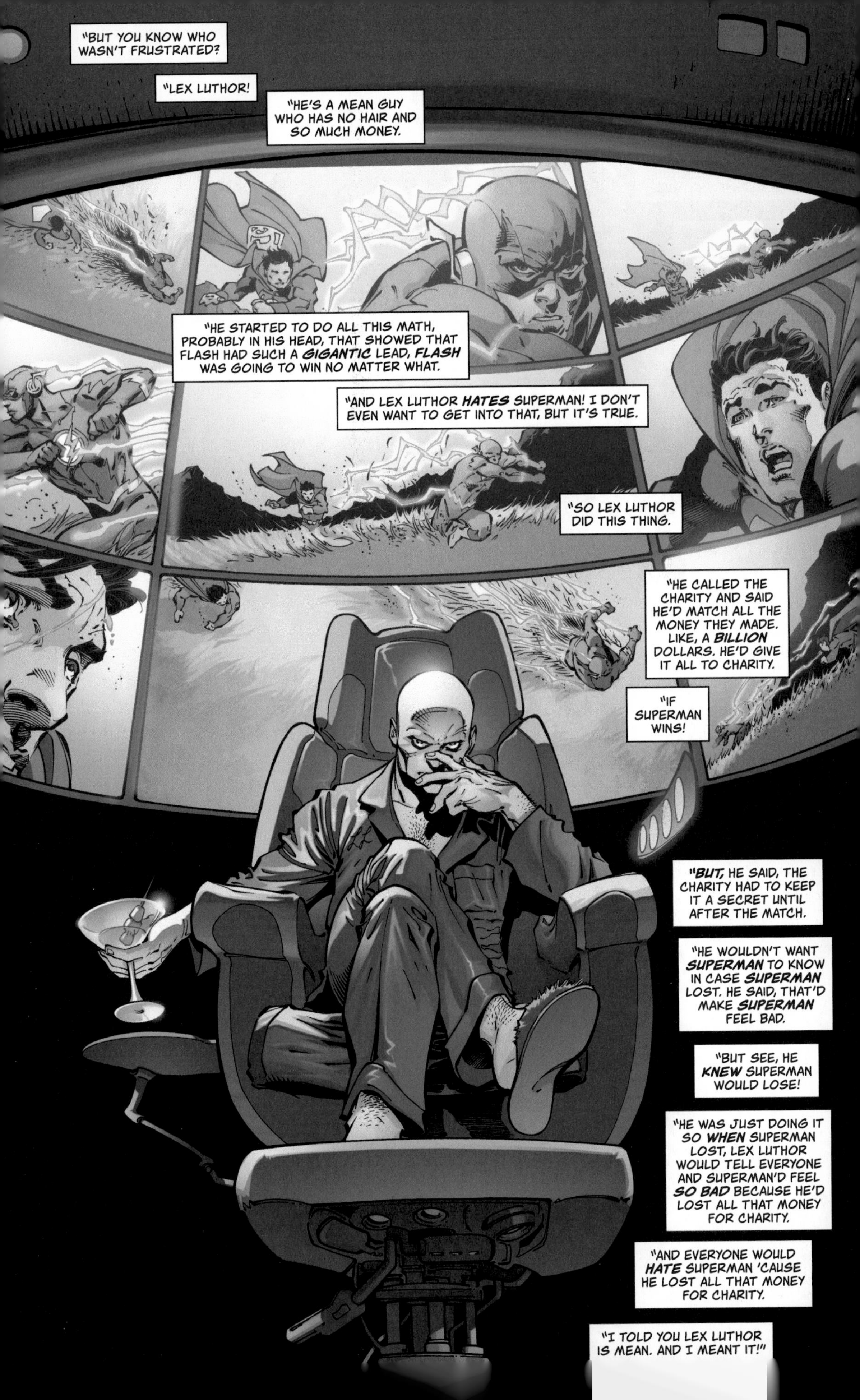
"BUT YOU KNOW WHO WASN'T FRUSTRATED?
"LEX LUTHOR!
"HE'S A MEAN GUY WHO HAS NO HAIR AND SO MUCH MONEY.
"HE STARTED TO DO ALL THIS MATH, PROBABLY IN HIS HEAD, THAT SHOWED THAT FLASH HAD SUCH A GIGANTIC LEAD, FLASH WAS GOING TO WIN NO MATTER WHAT.
"AND LEX LUTHOR HATES SUPERMAN! I DON'T EVEN WANT TO GET INTO THAT, BUT IT'S TRUE.
"SO LEX LUTHOR DID THIS THING.
"HE CALLED THE CHARITY AND SAID HE'D MATCH ALL THE MONEY THEY MADE. LIKE, A BILLION DOLLARS. HE'D GIVE IT ALL TO CHARITY.
"IF SUPERMAN WINS!
"BUT, HE SAID, THE CHARITY HAD TO KEEP IT A SECRET UNTIL AFTER THE MATCH.
"HE WOULDN'T WANT SUPERMAN TO KNOW IN CASE SUPERMAN LOST. HE SAID, THAT'D MAKE SUPERMAN FEEL BAD.
"BUT SEE, HE KNEW SUPERMAN WOULD LOSE!
"HE WAS JUST DOING IT SO WHEN SUPERMAN LOST, LEX LUTHOR WOULD TELL EVERYONE AND SUPERMAN'D FEEL SO BAD BECAUSE HE'D LOST ALL THAT MONEY FOR CHARITY.
"AND EVERYONE WOULD HATE SUPERMAN 'CAUSE HE LOST ALL THAT MONEY FOR CHARITY.
"I TOLD YOU LEX LUTHOR IS MEAN. AND I MEANT IT!"

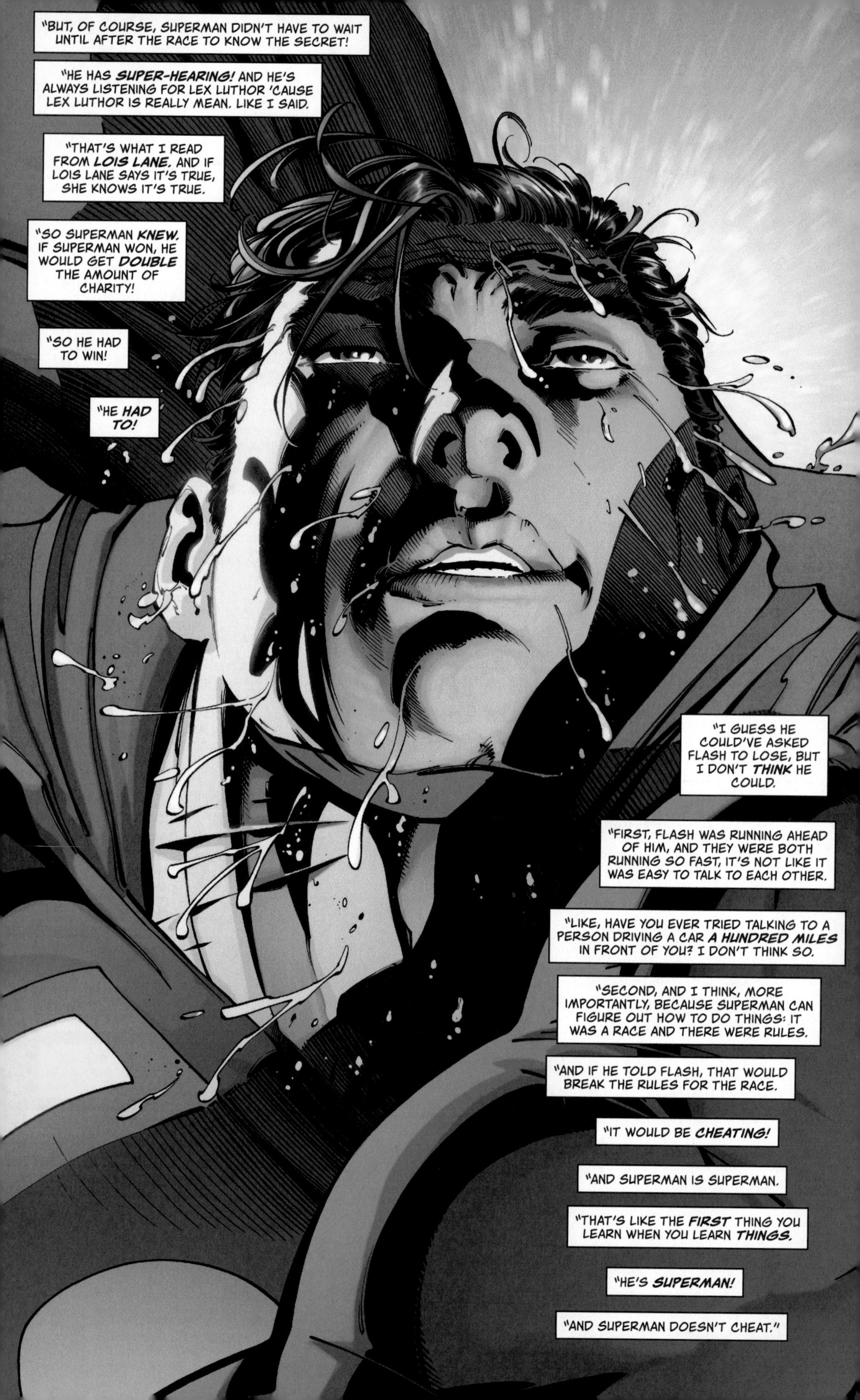
"BUT, OF COURSE, SUPERMAN DIDN'T HAVE TO WAIT UNTIL AFTER THE RACE TO KNOW THE SECRET!
"HE HAS SUPER-HEARING! AND HE'S ALWAYS LISTENING FOR LEX LUTHOR 'CAUSE LEX LUTHOR IS REALLY MEAN. LIKE I SAID.
"THAT'S WHAT I READ FROM LOIS LANE. AND IF LOIS LANE SAYS IT'S TRUE, SHE KNOWS IT'S TRUE.
"SO SUPERMAN KNEW. IF SUPERMAN WON, HE WOULD GET DOUBLE THE AMOUNT OF CHARITY!
"SO HE HAD TO WIN!
"HE HAD TO!
"I GUESS HE COULD'VE ASKED FLASH TO LOSE, BUT I DON'T THINK HE COULD.
"FIRST, FLASH WAS RUNNING AHEAD OF HIM, AND THEY WERE BOTH RUNNING SO FAST, IT'S NOT LIKE IT WAS EASY TO TALK TO EACH OTHER.
"LIKE, HAVE YOU EVER TRIED TALKING TO A PERSON DRIVING A CAR A HUNDRED MILES IN FRONT OF YOU? I DON'T THINK SO.
"SECOND, AND I THINK, MORE IMPORTANTLY, BECAUSE SUPERMAN CAN FIGURE OUT HOW TO DO THINGS: IT WAS A RACE AND THERE WERE RULES.
"AND IF HE TOLD FLASH, THAT WOULD BREAK THE RULES FOR THE RACE.
"IT WOULD BE CHEATING!
"AND SUPERMAN IS SUPERMAN.
"THAT'S LIKE THE FIRST THING YOU LEARN WHEN YOU LEARN THINGS.
"HE'S SUPERMAN!
"AND SUPERMAN DOESN'T CHEAT."

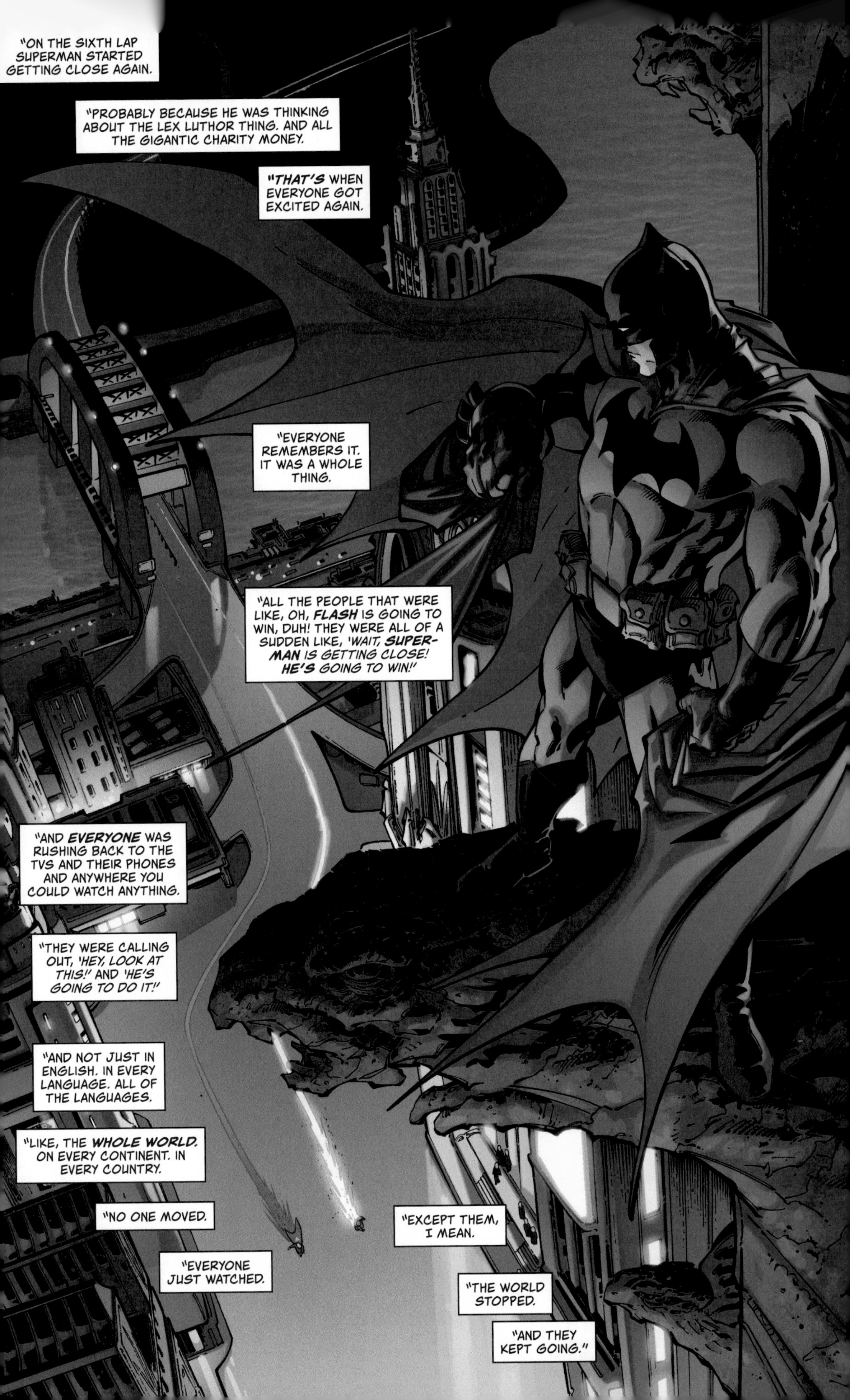
"ON THE SIXTH LAP SUPERMAN STARTED GETTING CLOSE AGAIN.
"PROBABLY BECAUSE HE WAS THINKING ABOUT THE LEX LUTHOR THING. AND ALL THE GIGANTIC CHARITY MONEY.
"THAT'S WHEN EVERYONE GOT EXCITED AGAIN.
"EVERYONE REMEMBERS IT. IT WAS A WHOLE THING.
"ALL THE PEOPLE THAT WERE LIKE, OH, FLASH IS GOING TO WIN, DUH! THEY WERE ALL OF A SUDDEN LIKE, 'WAIT, SUPERMAN IS GETTING CLOSE! HE'S GOING TO WIN!'
"AND EVERYONE WAS RUSHING BACK TO THE TVS AND THEIR PHONES AND ANYWHERE YOU COULD WATCH ANYTHING.
"THEY WERE CALLING OUT, 'HEY, LOOK AT THIS!' AND 'HE'S GOING TO DO IT!'
"AND NOT JUST IN ENGLISH. IN EVERY LANGUAGE. ALL OF THE LANGUAGES.
"LIKE, THE WHOLE WORLD. ON EVERY CONTINENT. IN EVERY COUNTRY.
"NO ONE MOVED.
"EVERYONE JUST WATCHED.
"EXCEPT THEM, I MEAN.
"THE WORLD STOPPED.
"AND THEY KEPT GOING."

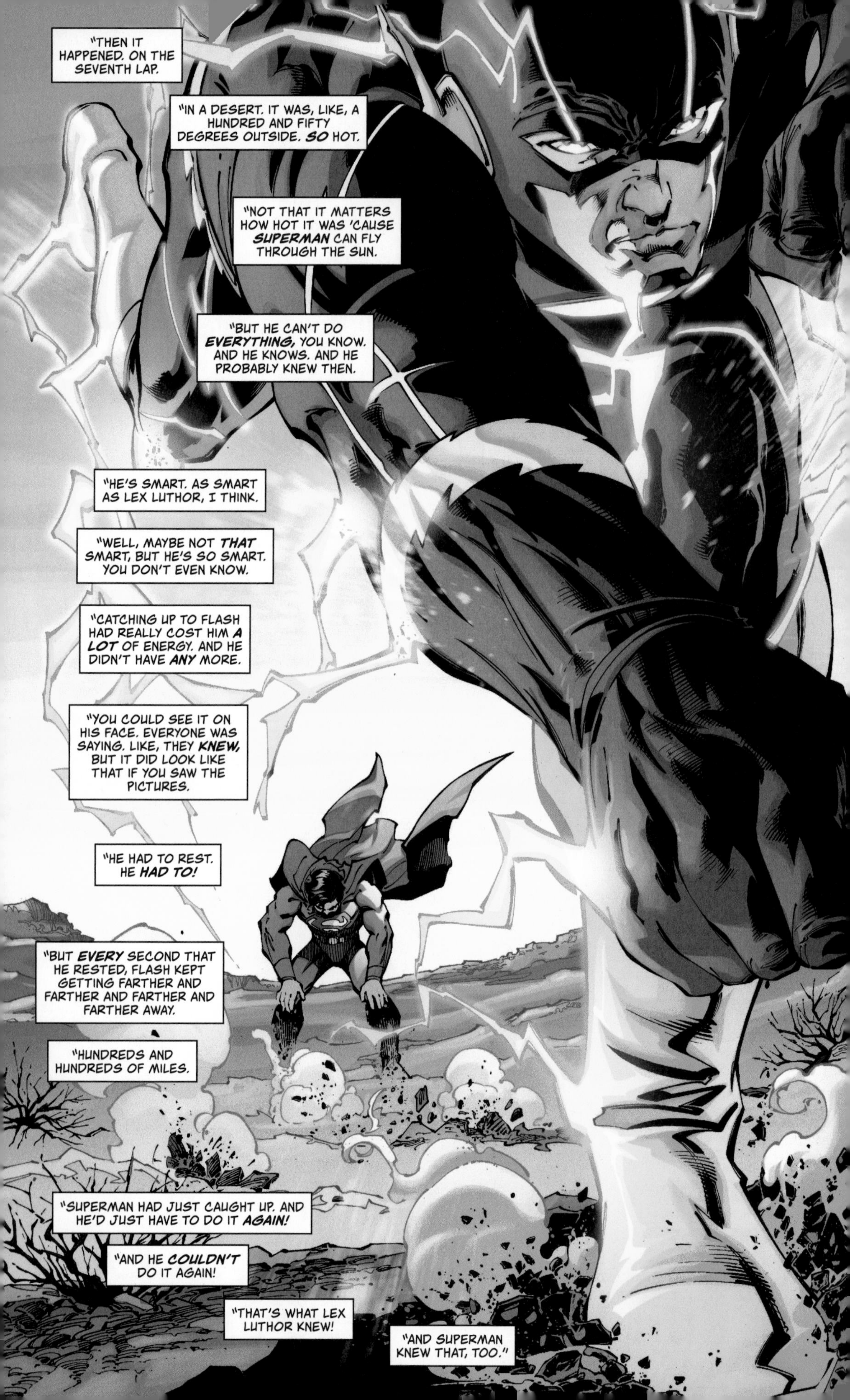

"THEN IT HAPPENED. ON THE SEVENTH LAP.
"IN A DESERT. IT WAS, LIKE, A HUNDRED AND FIFTY DEGREES OUTSIDE. **SO** HOT.
"NOT THAT IT MATTERS HOW HOT IT WAS 'CAUSE **SUPERMAN** CAN FLY THROUGH THE SUN.
"BUT HE CAN'T DO **EVERYTHING,** YOU KNOW. AND HE KNOWS. AND HE PROBABLY KNEW THEN.
"HE'S SMART. AS SMART AS LEX LUTHOR, I THINK.
"WELL, MAYBE NOT **THAT** SMART, BUT HE'S SO SMART. YOU DON'T EVEN KNOW.
"CATCHING UP TO FLASH HAD REALLY COST HIM **A LOT** OF ENERGY. AND HE DIDN'T HAVE **ANY** MORE.
"YOU COULD SEE IT ON HIS FACE. EVERYONE WAS SAYING. LIKE, THEY **KNEW,** BUT IT DID LOOK LIKE THAT IF YOU SAW THE PICTURES.
"HE HAD TO REST. HE **HAD TO!**
"BUT **EVERY** SECOND THAT HE RESTED, FLASH KEPT GETTING FARTHER AND FARTHER AND FARTHER AND FARTHER AWAY.
"HUNDREDS AND HUNDREDS OF MILES.
"SUPERMAN HAD JUST CAUGHT UP. AND HE'D JUST HAVE TO DO IT **AGAIN!**
"AND HE **COULDN'T** DO IT AGAIN!
"THAT'S WHAT LEX LUTHOR KNEW!
"AND SUPERMAN KNEW THAT, TOO."

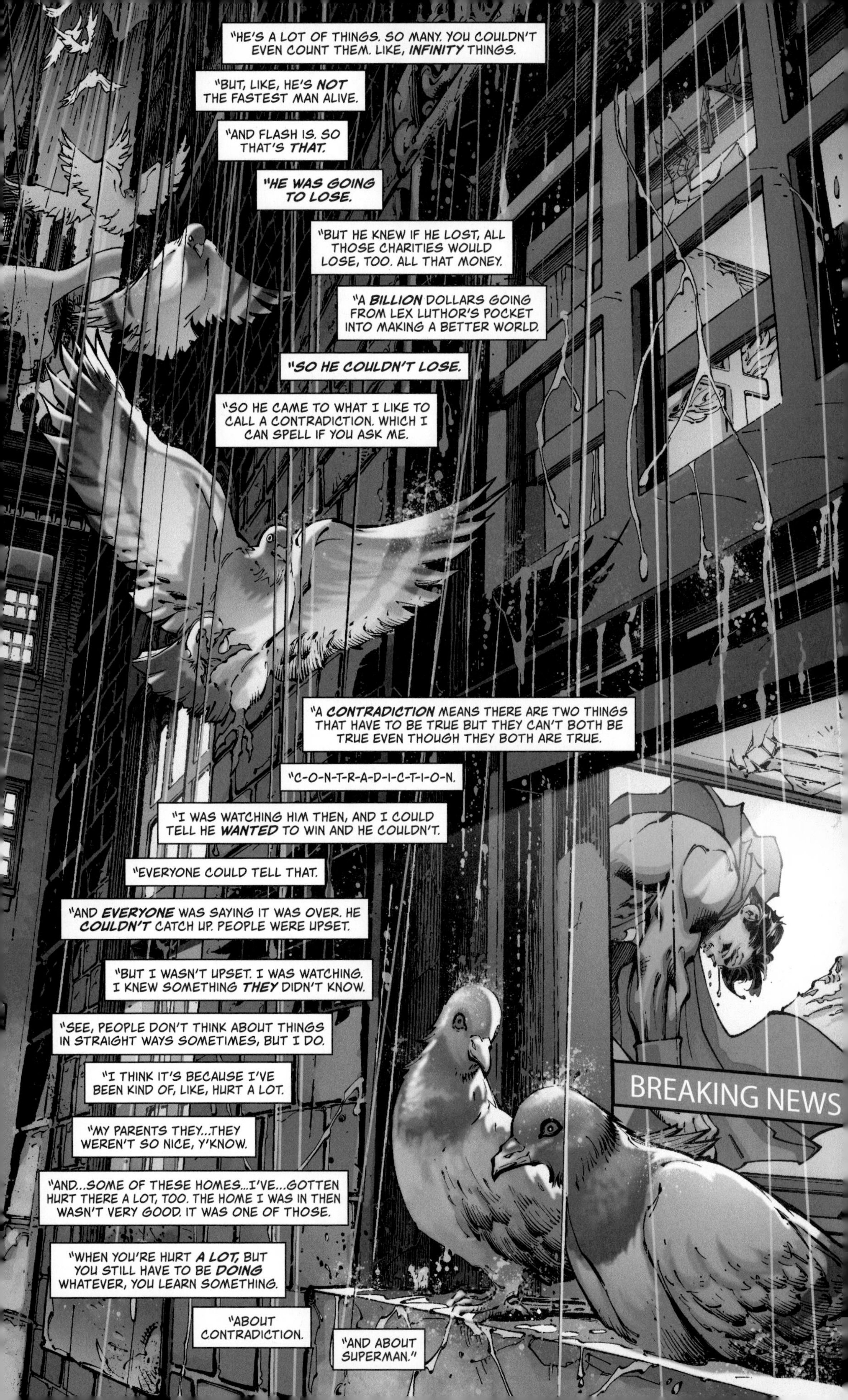
"HE'S A LOT OF THINGS. SO MANY. YOU COULDN'T EVEN COUNT THEM. LIKE, INFINITY THINGS.
"BUT, LIKE, HE'S NOT THE FASTEST MAN ALIVE.
"AND FLASH IS. SO THAT'S THAT.
"HE WAS GOING TO LOSE.
"BUT HE KNEW IF HE LOST, ALL THOSE CHARITIES WOULD LOSE, TOO. ALL THAT MONEY.
"A BILLION DOLLARS GOING FROM LEX LUTHOR'S POCKET INTO MAKING A BETTER WORLD.
"SO HE COULDN'T LOSE.
"SO HE CAME TO WHAT I LIKE TO CALL A CONTRADICTION. WHICH I CAN SPELL IF YOU ASK ME.
"A CONTRADICTION MEANS THERE ARE TWO THINGS THAT HAVE TO BE TRUE BUT THEY CAN'T BOTH BE TRUE EVEN THOUGH THEY BOTH ARE TRUE.
"C-O-N-T-R-A-D-I-C-T-I-O-N.
"I WAS WATCHING HIM THEN, AND I COULD TELL HE WANTED TO WIN AND HE COULDN'T.
"EVERYONE COULD TELL THAT.
"AND EVERYONE WAS SAYING IT WAS OVER. HE COULDN'T CATCH UP. PEOPLE WERE UPSET.
"BUT I WASN'T UPSET. I WAS WATCHING. I KNEW SOMETHING THEY DIDN'T KNOW.
"SEE, PEOPLE DON'T THINK ABOUT THINGS IN STRAIGHT WAYS SOMETIMES, BUT I DO.
"I THINK IT'S BECAUSE I'VE BEEN KIND OF, LIKE, HURT A LOT.
"MY PARENTS THEY...THEY WEREN'T SO NICE, Y'KNOW.
"AND...SOME OF THESE HOMES...I'VE...GOTTEN HURT THERE A LOT, TOO. THE HOME I WAS IN THEN WASN'T VERY GOOD. IT WAS ONE OF THOSE.
"WHEN YOU'RE HURT A LOT, BUT YOU STILL HAVE TO BE DOING WHATEVER, YOU LEARN SOMETHING.
"ABOUT CONTRADICTION.
BREAKING NEWS
"AND ABOUT SUPERMAN."

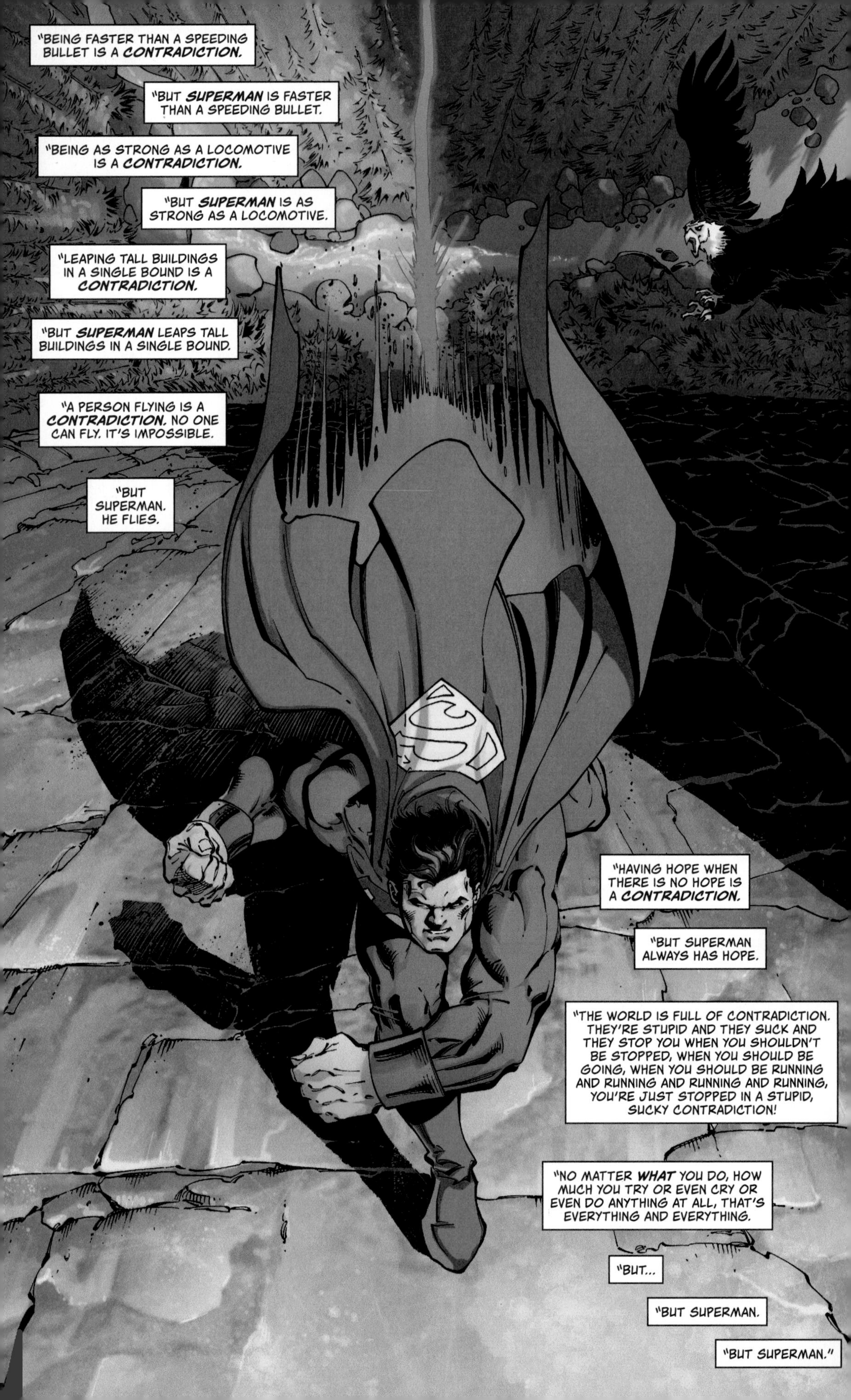
"BEING FASTER THAN A SPEEDING BULLET IS A CONTRADICTION.
"BUT SUPERMAN IS FASTER THAN A SPEEDING BULLET.
"BEING AS STRONG AS A LOCOMOTIVE IS A CONTRADICTION.
"BUT SUPERMAN IS AS STRONG AS A LOCOMOTIVE.
"LEAPING TALL BUILDINGS IN A SINGLE BOUND IS A CONTRADICTION.
"BUT SUPERMAN LEAPS TALL BUILDINGS IN A SINGLE BOUND.
"A PERSON FLYING IS A CONTRADICTION. NO ONE CAN FLY. IT'S IMPOSSIBLE.
"BUT SUPERMAN. HE FLIES.
"HAVING HOPE WHEN THERE IS NO HOPE IS A CONTRADICTION.
"BUT SUPERMAN ALWAYS HAS HOPE.
"THE WORLD IS FULL OF CONTRADICTION. THEY'RE STUPID AND THEY SUCK AND THEY STOP YOU WHEN YOU SHOULDN'T BE STOPPED, WHEN YOU SHOULD BE GOING, WHEN YOU SHOULD BE RUNNING AND RUNNING AND RUNNING AND RUNNING, YOU'RE JUST STOPPED IN A STUPID, SUCKY CONTRADICTION!
"NO MATTER WHAT YOU DO, HOW MUCH YOU TRY OR EVEN CRY OR EVEN DO ANYTHING AT ALL, THAT'S EVERYTHING AND EVERYTHING.
"BUT...
"BUT SUPERMAN.
"BUT SUPERMAN."

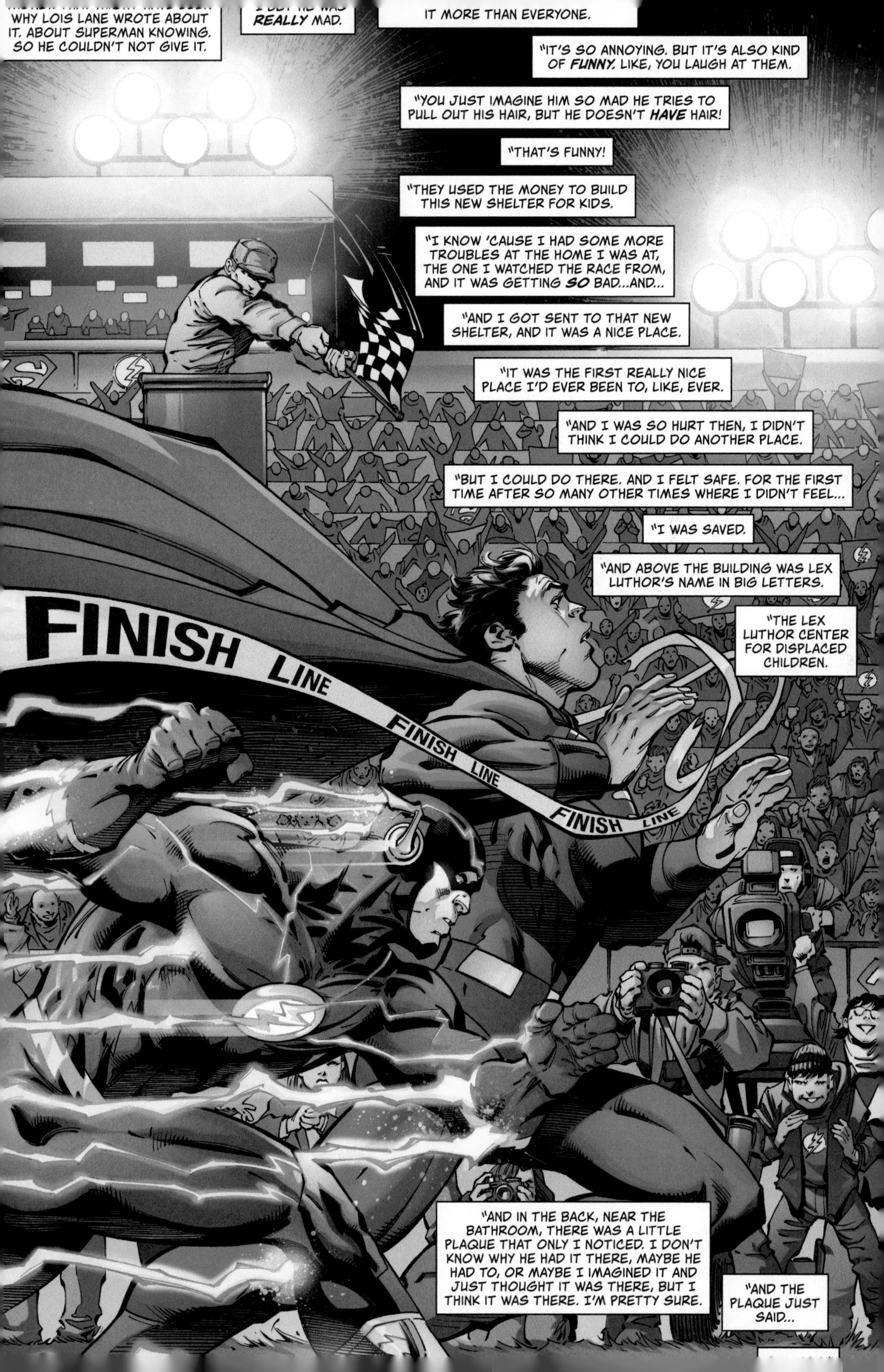

WHY LOIS LANE WROTE ABOUT IT. ABOUT SUPERMAN KNOWING. SO HE COULDN'T NOT GIVE IT.
REALLY MAD.
IT MORE THAN EVERYONE.
"IT'S SO ANNOYING. BUT IT'S ALSO KIND OF FUNNY. LIKE, YOU LAUGH AT THEM.
"YOU JUST IMAGINE HIM SO MAD HE TRIES TO PULL OUT HIS HAIR, BUT HE DOESN'T HAVE HAIR!
"THAT'S FUNNY!
"THEY USED THE MONEY TO BUILD THIS NEW SHELTER FOR KIDS.
"I KNOW 'CAUSE I HAD SOME MORE TROUBLES AT THE HOME I WAS AT, THE ONE I WATCHED THE RACE FROM, AND IT WAS GETTING SO BAD...AND...
"AND I GOT SENT TO THAT NEW SHELTER, AND IT WAS A NICE PLACE.
"IT WAS THE FIRST REALLY NICE PLACE I'D EVER BEEN TO, LIKE, EVER.
"AND I WAS SO HURT THEN, I DIDN'T THINK I COULD DO ANOTHER PLACE.
"BUT I COULD DO THERE. AND I FELT SAFE. FOR THE FIRST TIME AFTER SO MANY OTHER TIMES WHERE I DIDN'T FEEL...
"I WAS SAVED.
"AND ABOVE THE BUILDING WAS LEX LUTHOR'S NAME IN BIG LETTERS.
"THE LEX LUTHOR CENTER FOR DISPLACED CHILDREN.
FINISH LINE
FINISH LINE
FINISH LINE
"AND IN THE BACK, NEAR THE BATHROOM, THERE WAS A LITTLE PLAQUE THAT ONLY I NOTICED. I DON'T KNOW WHY HE HAD IT THERE, MAYBE HE HAD TO, OR MAYBE I IMAGINED IT AND JUST THOUGHT IT WAS THERE, BUT I THINK IT WAS THERE. I'M PRETTY SURE.
"AND THE PLAQUE JUST SAID...

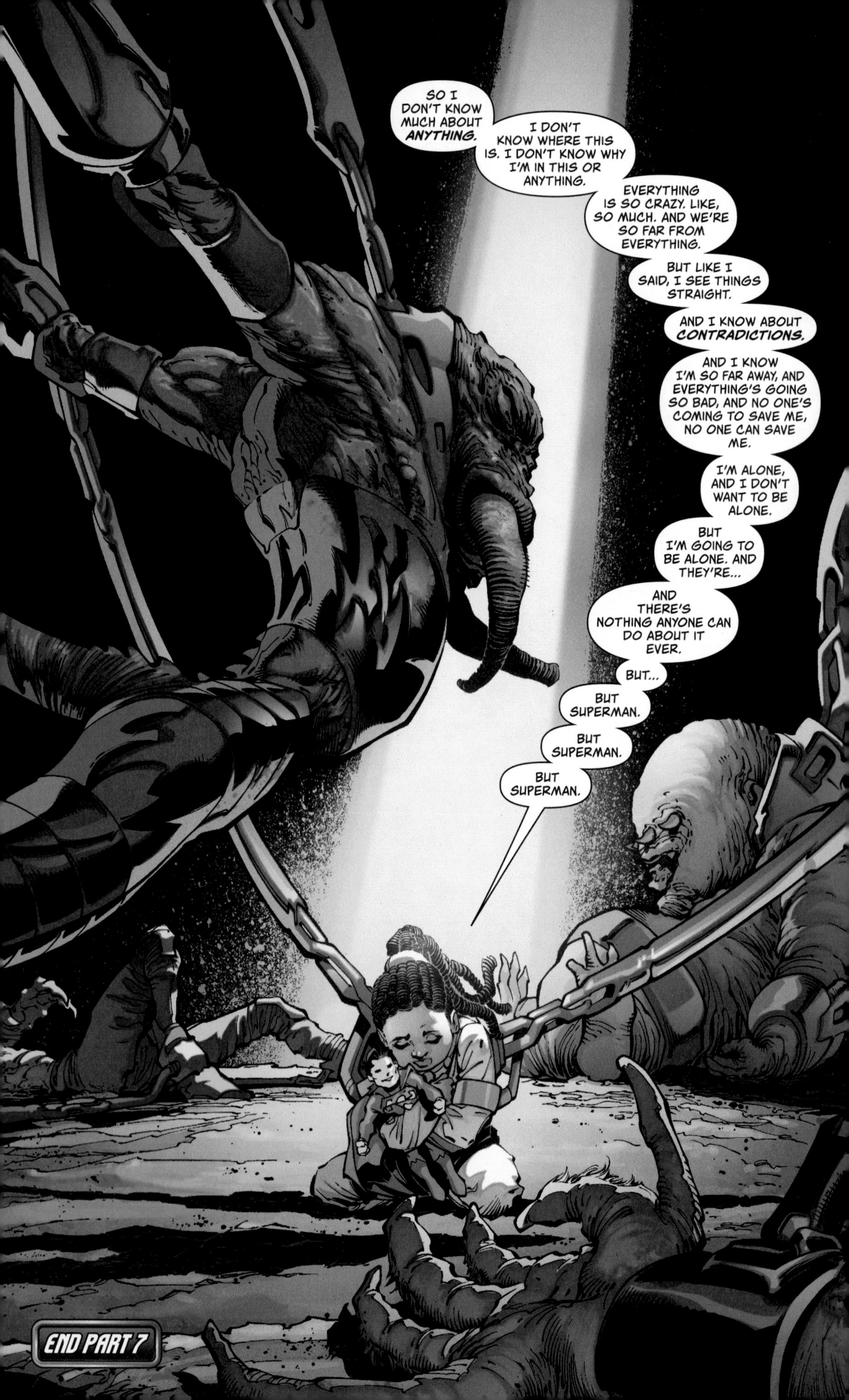
SO I DON'T KNOW MUCH ABOUT ANYTHING.
I DON'T KNOW WHERE THIS IS. I DON'T KNOW WHY I'M IN THIS OR ANYTHING.
EVERYTHING IS SO CRAZY. LIKE, SO MUCH. AND WE'RE SO FAR FROM EVERYTHING.
BUT LIKE I SAID, I SEE THINGS STRAIGHT.
AND I KNOW ABOUT CONTRADICTIONS.
AND I KNOW I'M SO FAR AWAY, AND EVERYTHING'S GOING SO BAD, AND NO ONE'S COMING TO SAVE ME, NO ONE CAN SAVE ME.
I'M ALONE, AND I DON'T WANT TO BE ALONE.
BUT I'M GOING TO BE ALONE. AND THEY'RE...
AND THERE'S NOTHING ANYONE CAN DO ABOUT IT EVER.
BUT...
BUT SUPERMAN.
BUT SUPERMAN.
BUT SUPERMAN.
END PART 7

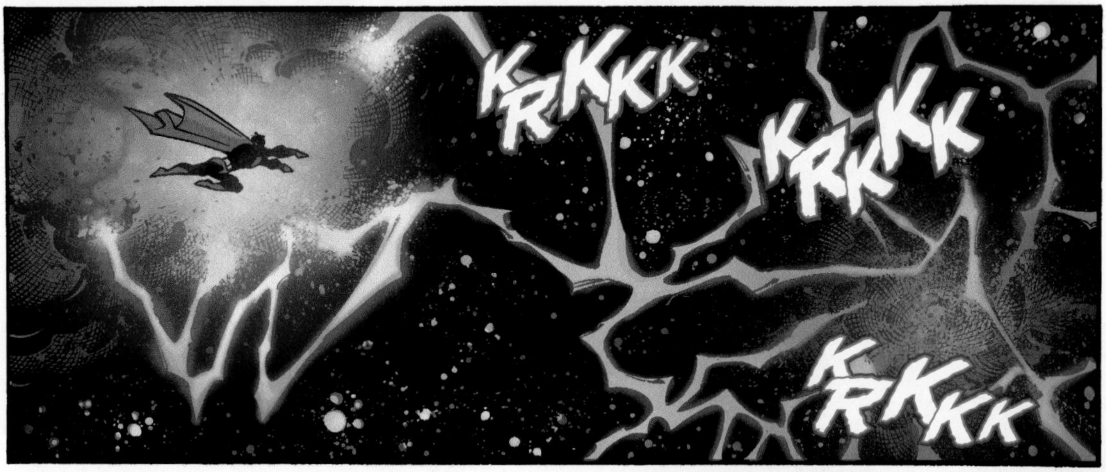
KRKKK
KRKKK
KRKKK

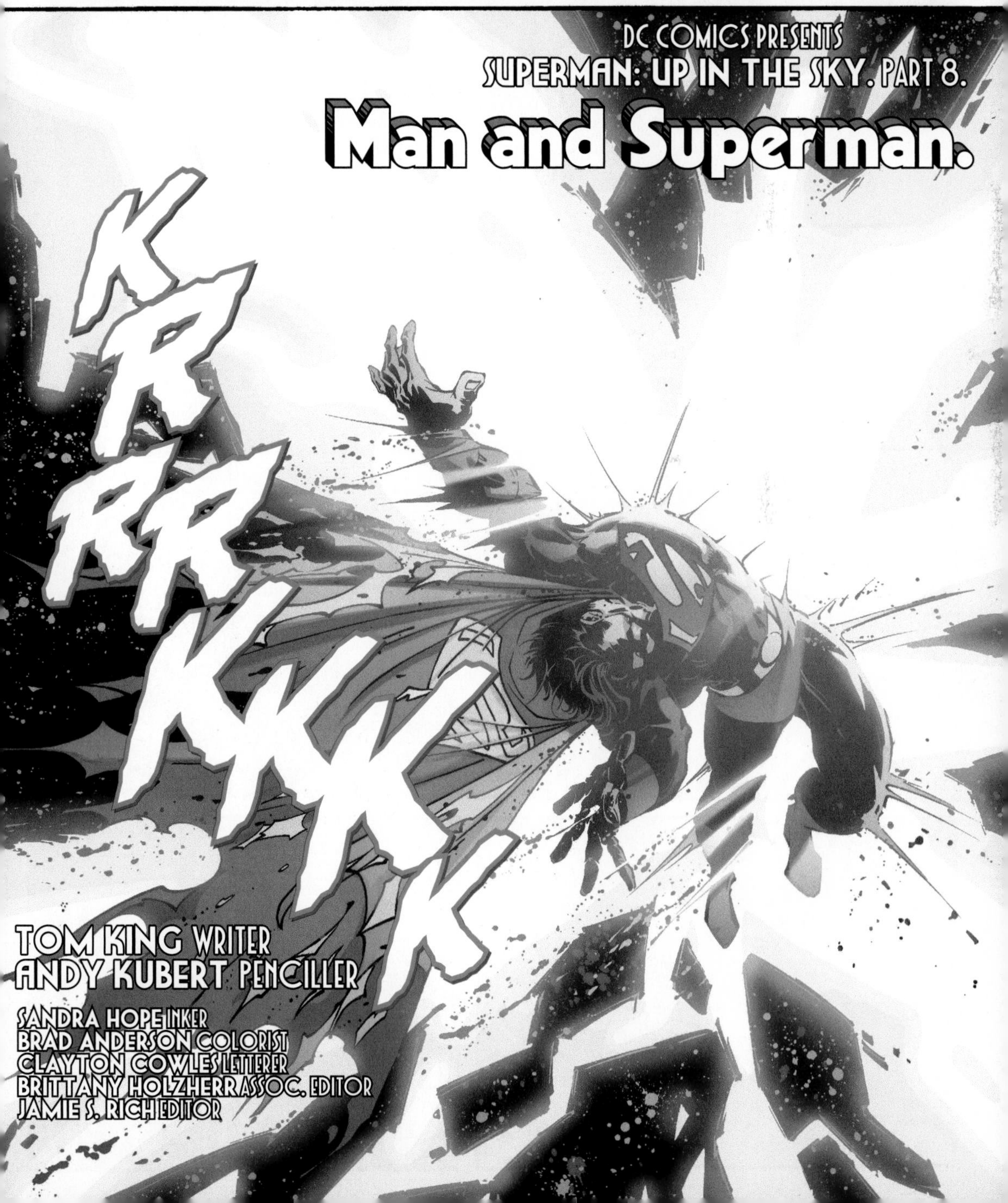
DC COMICS PRESENTS
SUPERMAN: UP IN THE SKY. PART 8.
Man and Superman.
KRRRKKKK
TOM KING WRITER
ANDY KUBERT PENCILLER
SANDRA HOPE INKER
BRAD ANDERSON COLORIST
CLAYTON COWLES LETTERER
BRITTANY HOLZHERR ASSOC. EDITOR
JAMIE S. RICH EDITOR

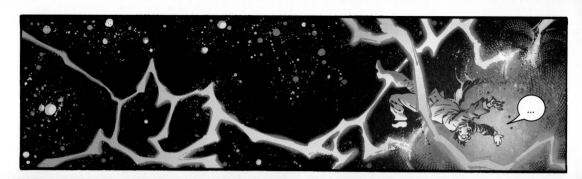

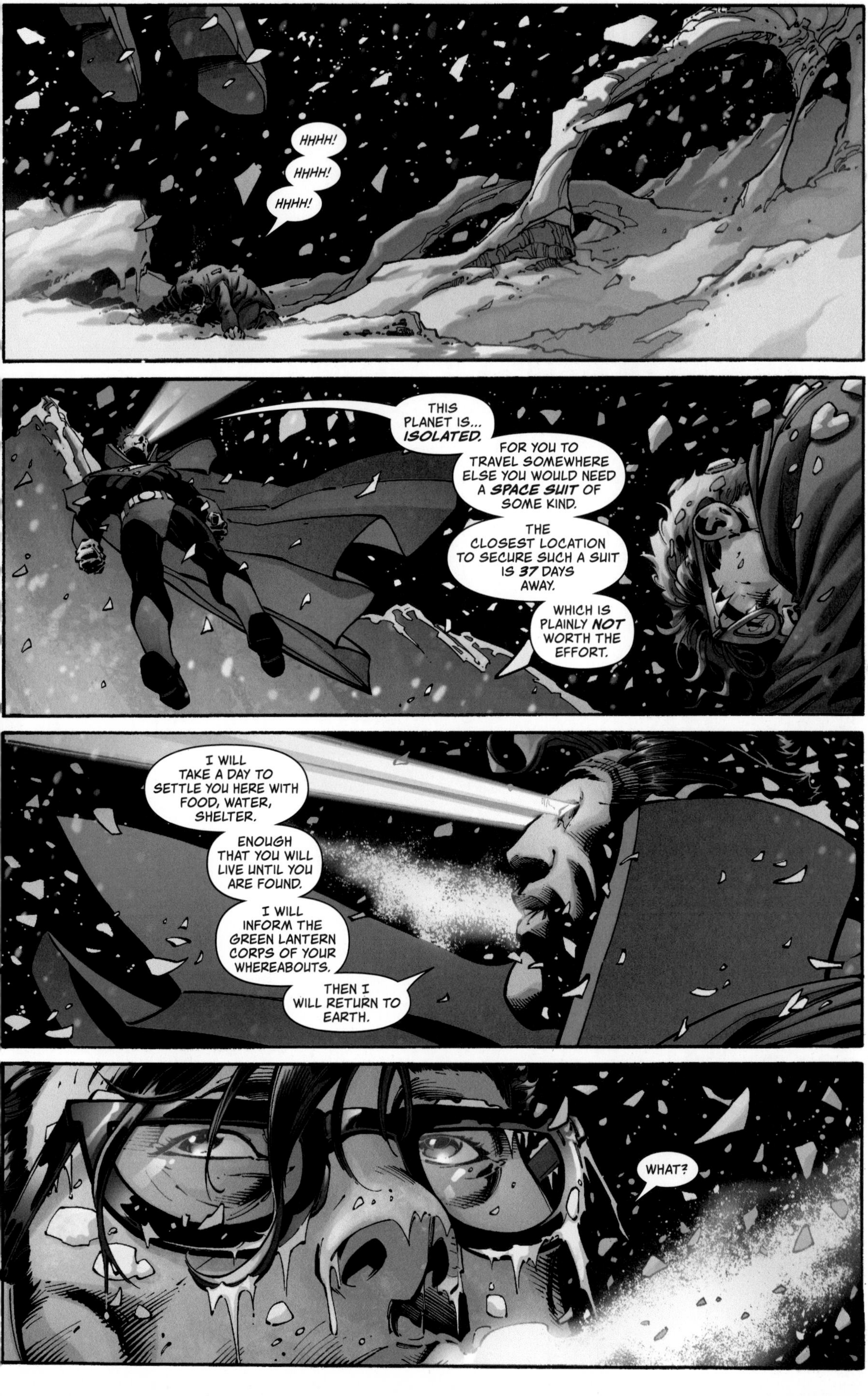
HHHH!
HHHH!
HHHH!
THIS PLANET IS... ISOLATED.
FOR YOU TO TRAVEL SOMEWHERE ELSE YOU WOULD NEED A SPACE SUIT OF SOME KIND.
THE CLOSEST LOCATION TO SECURE SUCH A SUIT IS 37 DAYS AWAY.
WHICH IS PLAINLY NOT WORTH THE EFFORT.
I WILL TAKE A DAY TO SETTLE YOU HERE WITH FOOD, WATER, SHELTER.
ENOUGH THAT YOU WILL LIVE UNTIL YOU ARE FOUND.
I WILL INFORM THE GREEN LANTERN CORPS OF YOUR WHEREABOUTS.
THEN I WILL RETURN TO EARTH.
WHAT?

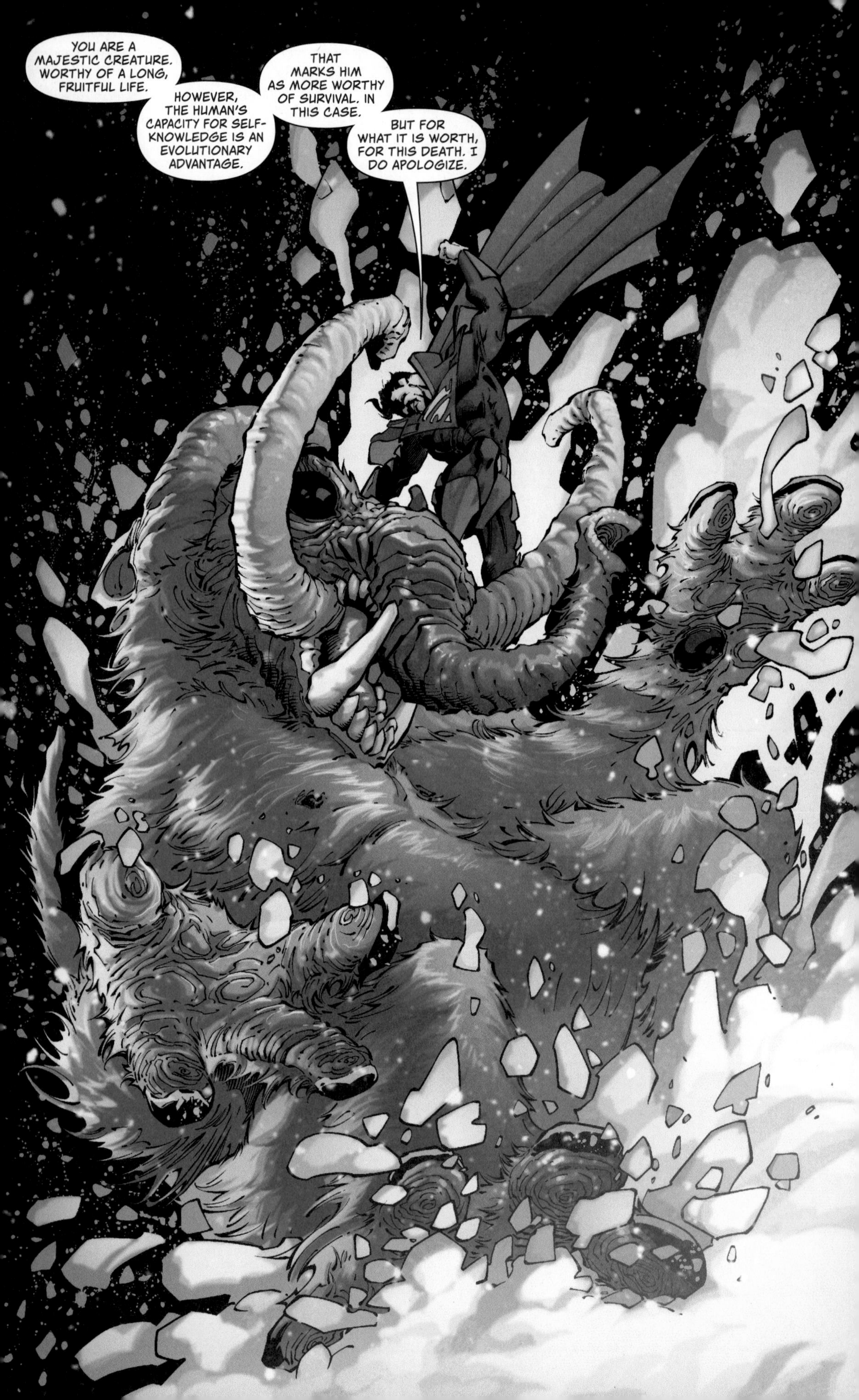
YOU ARE A MAJESTIC CREATURE. WORTHY OF A LONG, FRUITFUL LIFE.
HOWEVER, THE HUMAN'S CAPACITY FOR SELF-KNOWLEDGE IS AN EVOLUTIONARY ADVANTAGE.
THAT MARKS HIM AS MORE WORTHY OF SURVIVAL. IN THIS CASE.
BUT FOR WHAT IT IS WORTH, FOR THIS DEATH. I DO APOLOGIZE.

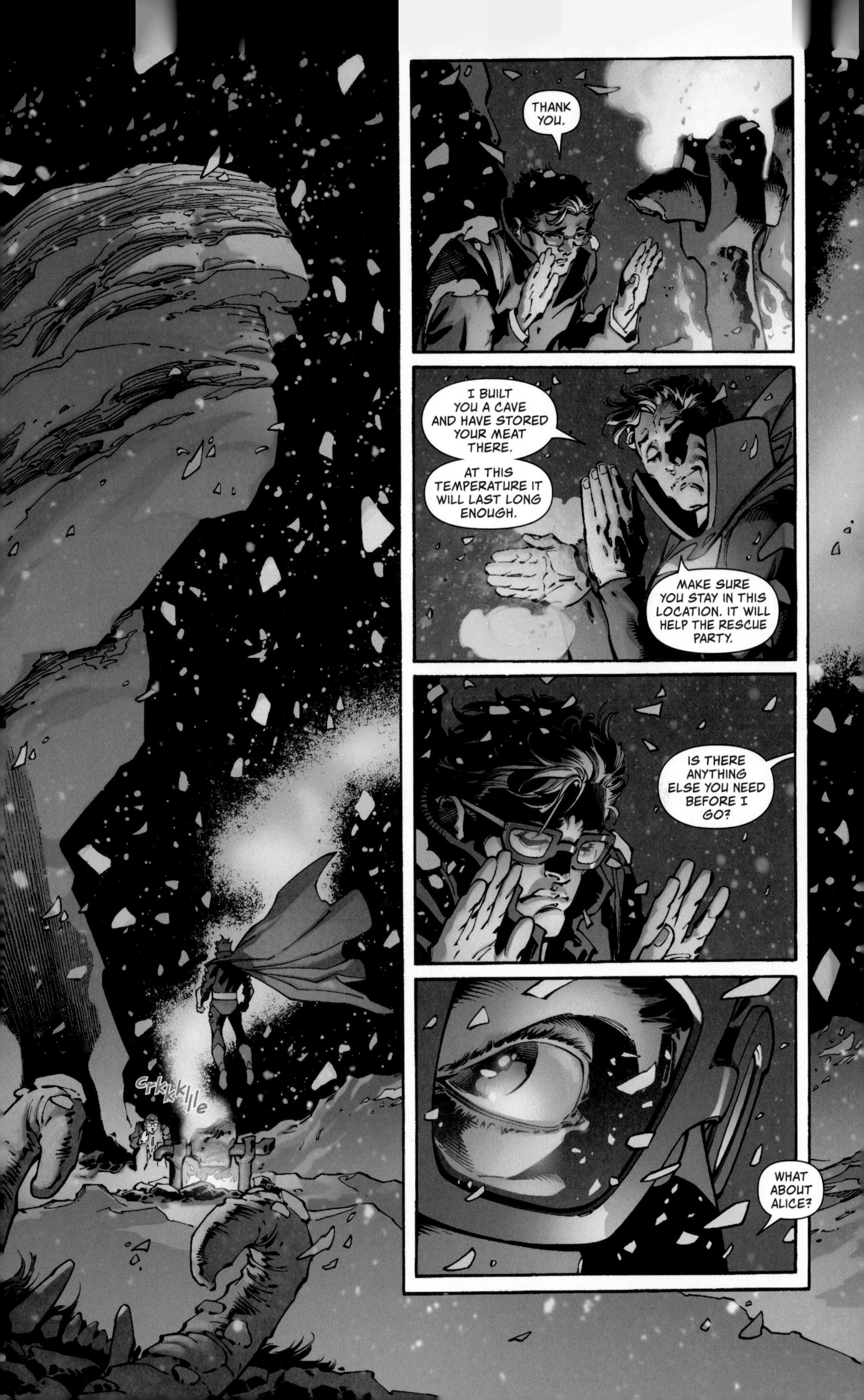
THANK YOU.
I BUILT YOU A CAVE AND HAVE STORED YOUR MEAT THERE.
AT THIS TEMPERATURE IT WILL LAST LONG ENOUGH.
MAKE SURE YOU STAY IN THIS LOCATION. IT WILL HELP THE RESCUE PARTY.
IS THERE ANYTHING ELSE YOU NEED BEFORE I GO?
WHAT ABOUT ALICE?
crkkkklle

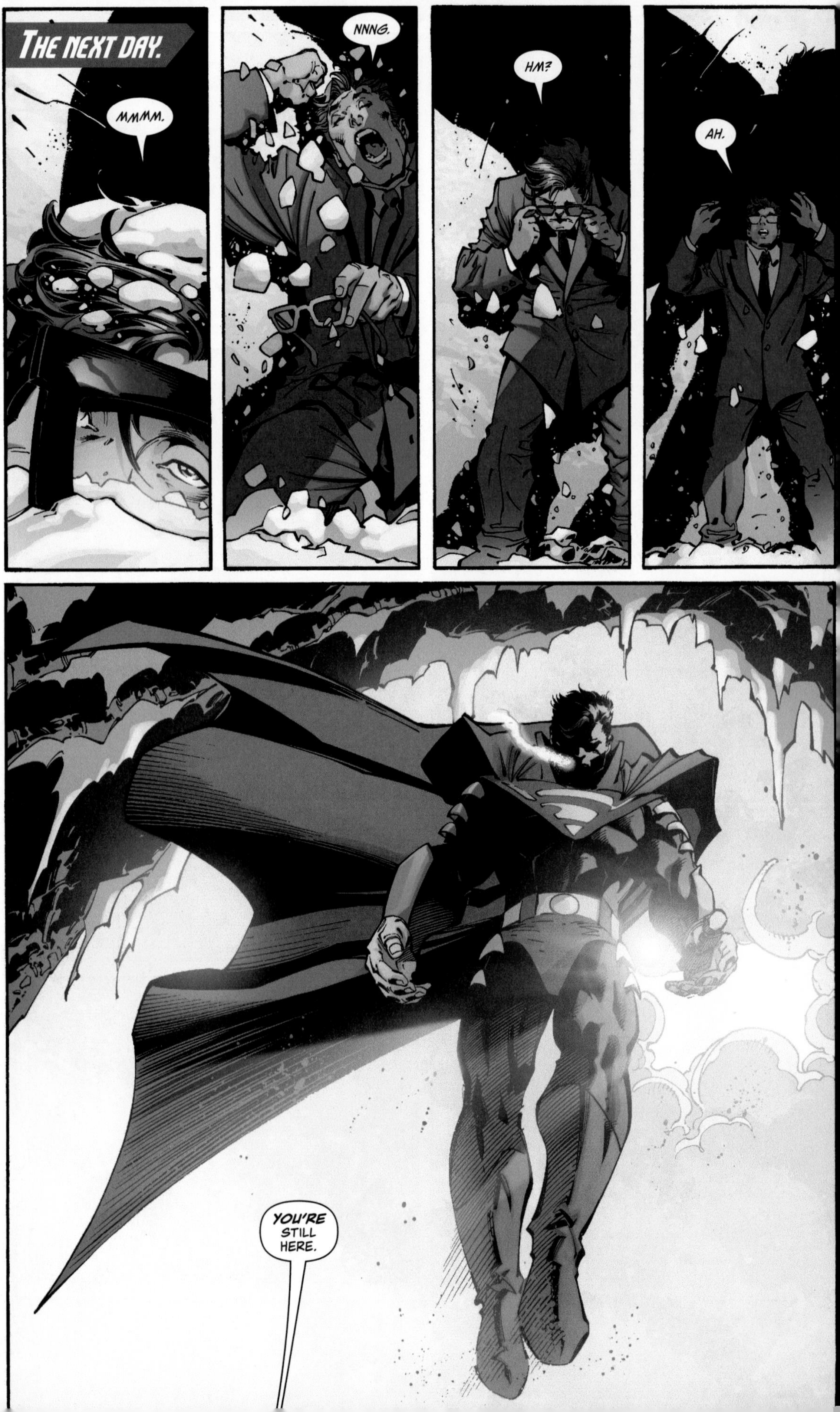
THE NEXT DAY.
MMMM.
NNNG.
HM?
AH.
YOU'RE STILL HERE.

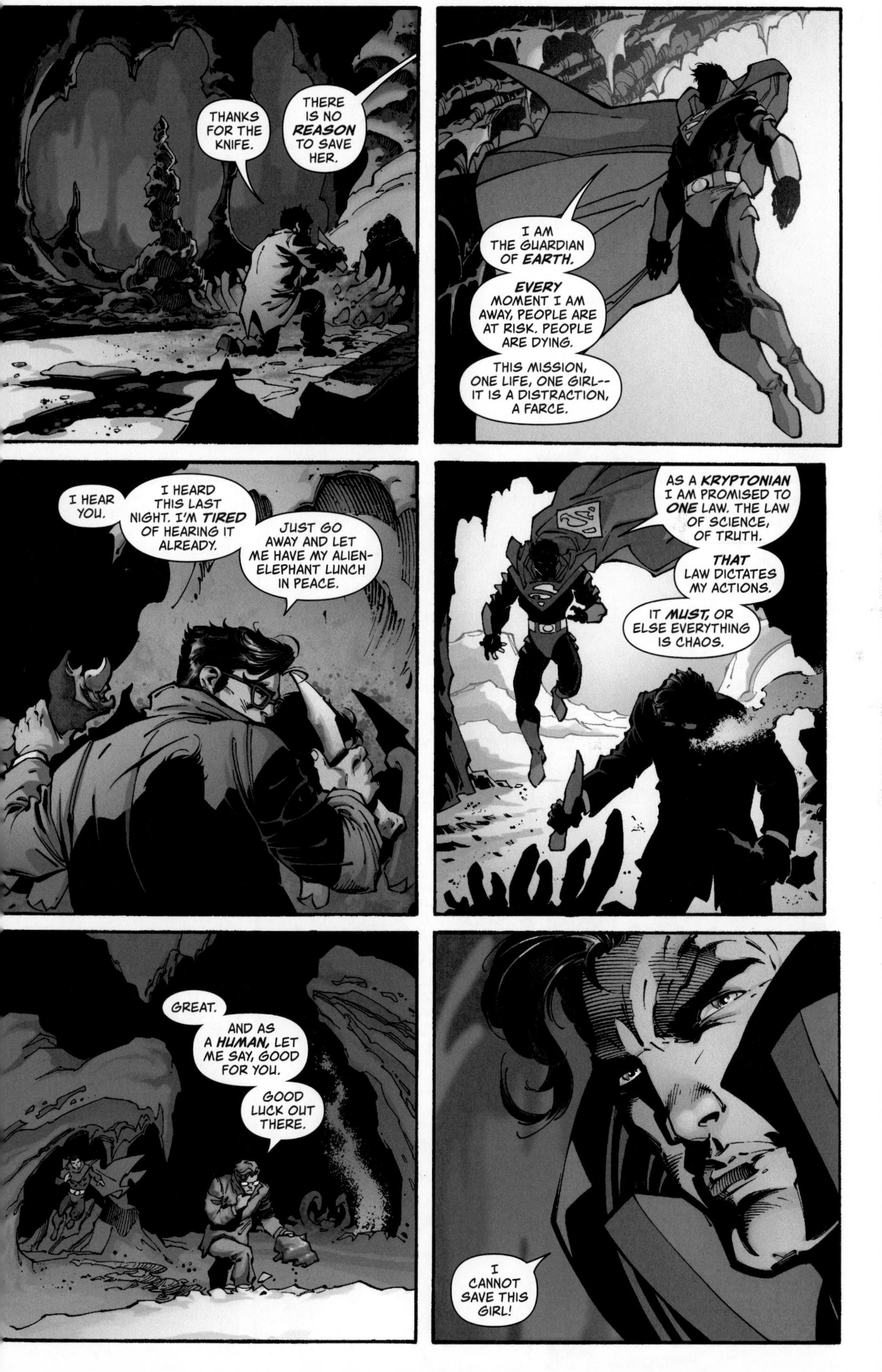

THANKS FOR THE KNIFE.
THERE IS NO REASON TO SAVE HER.
I AM THE GUARDIAN OF EARTH.
EVERY MOMENT I AM AWAY, PEOPLE ARE AT RISK. PEOPLE ARE DYING.
THIS MISSION, ONE LIFE, ONE GIRL-- IT IS A DISTRACTION, A FARCE.
I HEAR YOU.
I HEARD THIS LAST NIGHT. I'M TIRED OF HEARING IT ALREADY.
JUST GO AWAY AND LET ME HAVE MY ALIEN-ELEPHANT LUNCH IN PEACE.
AS A KRYPTONIAN I AM PROMISED TO ONE LAW. THE LAW OF SCIENCE, OF TRUTH.
THAT LAW DICTATES MY ACTIONS.
IT MUST, OR ELSE EVERYTHING IS CHAOS.
GREAT.
AND AS A HUMAN, LET ME SAY, GOOD FOR YOU.
GOOD LUCK OUT THERE.
I CANNOT SAVE THIS GIRL!

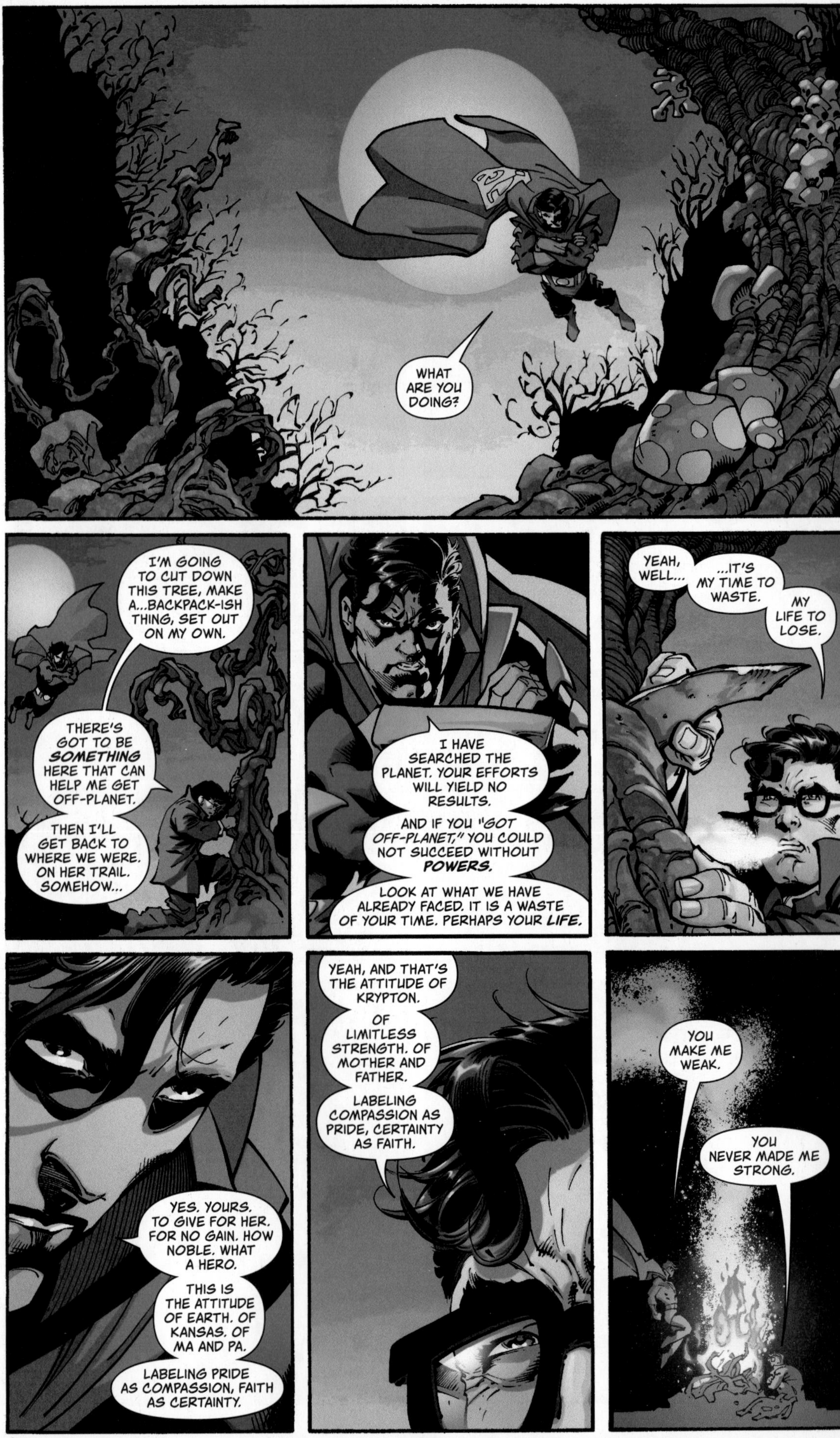
WHAT ARE YOU DOING?
I'M GOING TO CUT DOWN THIS TREE, MAKE A...BACKPACK-ISH THING, SET OUT ON MY OWN.
THERE'S GOT TO BE *SOMETHING* HERE THAT CAN HELP ME GET OFF-PLANET.
THEN I'LL GET BACK TO WHERE WE WERE. ON HER TRAIL. SOMEHOW...
I HAVE SEARCHED THE PLANET. YOUR EFFORTS WILL YIELD NO RESULTS.
AND IF YOU "GOT OFF-PLANET," YOU COULD NOT SUCCEED WITHOUT *POWERS.*
LOOK AT WHAT WE HAVE ALREADY FACED. IT IS A WASTE OF YOUR TIME. PERHAPS YOUR *LIFE.*
YEAH, WELL...
...IT'S MY TIME TO WASTE.
MY LIFE TO LOSE.
YES. YOURS. TO GIVE FOR HER. FOR NO GAIN. HOW NOBLE. WHAT A HERO.
THIS IS THE ATTITUDE OF EARTH. OF KANSAS. OF MA AND PA.
LABELING PRIDE AS COMPASSION, FAITH AS CERTAINTY.
YEAH, AND THAT'S THE ATTITUDE OF KRYPTON.
OF LIMITLESS STRENGTH. OF MOTHER AND FATHER.
LABELING COMPASSION AS PRIDE, CERTAINTY AS FAITH.
YOU MAKE ME WEAK.
YOU NEVER MADE ME STRONG.

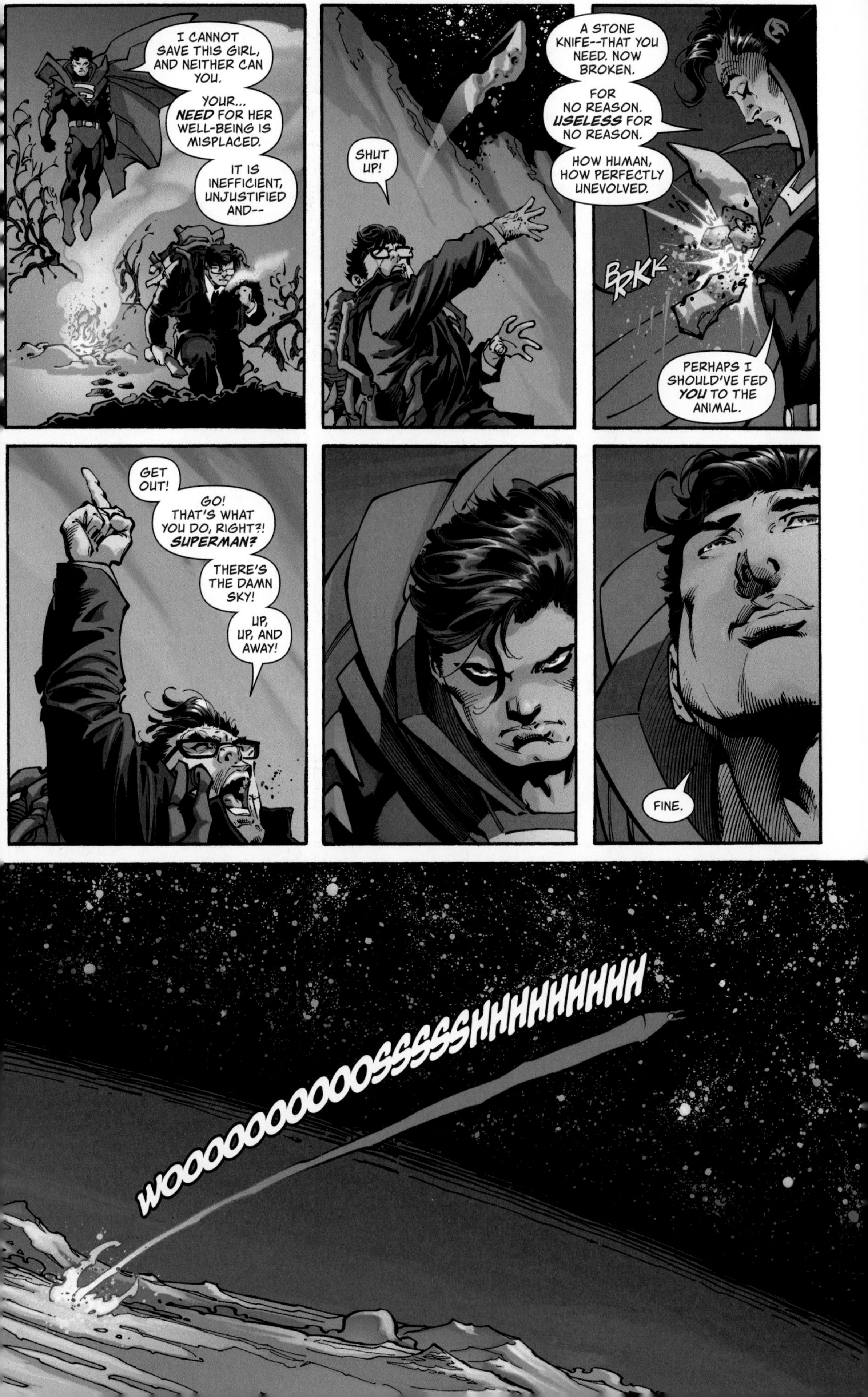

I CANNOT SAVE THIS GIRL, AND NEITHER CAN YOU.
YOUR... **NEED** FOR HER WELL-BEING IS MISPLACED.
IT IS INEFFICIENT, UNJUSTIFIED AND--
SHUT UP!
A STONE KNIFE--THAT YOU NEED. NOW BROKEN.
FOR NO REASON. **USELESS** FOR NO REASON.
HOW HUMAN, HOW PERFECTLY UNEVOLVED.
BRKK
PERHAPS I SHOULD'VE FED **YOU** TO THE ANIMAL.
GET OUT!
GO! THAT'S WHAT YOU DO, RIGHT?! **SUPERMAN?**
THERE'S THE DAMN SKY!
UP, UP, AND AWAY!
FINE.
WOOOOOOOOOOSSSSSHHHHHHHHH

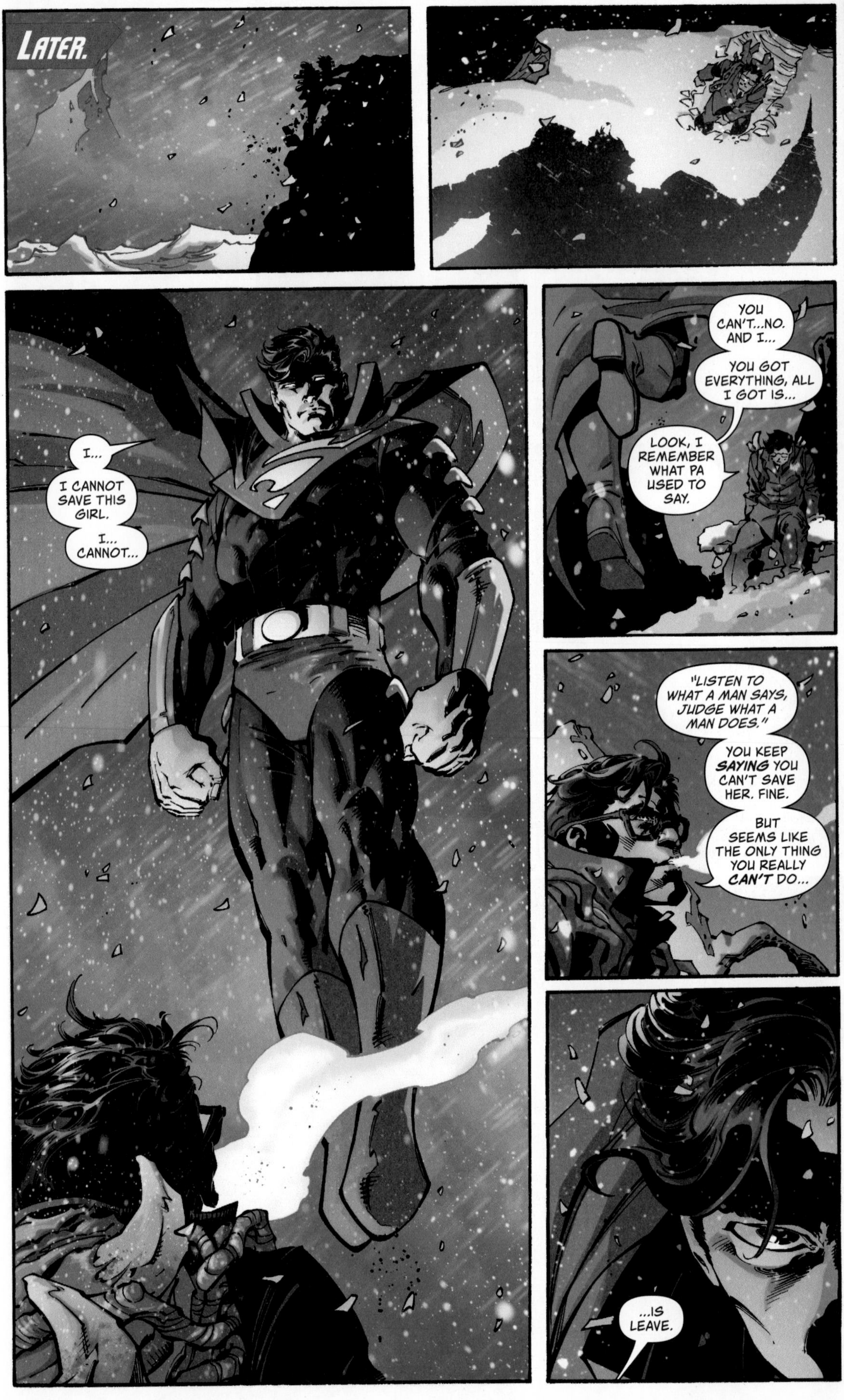
LATER.
I...
I CANNOT SAVE THIS GIRL.
I... CANNOT...
YOU CAN'T...NO. AND I...
YOU GOT EVERYTHING, ALL I GOT IS...
LOOK, I REMEMBER WHAT PA USED TO SAY.
"LISTEN TO WHAT A MAN SAYS, JUDGE WHAT A MAN DOES."
YOU KEEP SAYING YOU CAN'T SAVE HER. FINE.
BUT SEEMS LIKE THE ONLY THING YOU REALLY CAN'T DO...
...IS LEAVE.

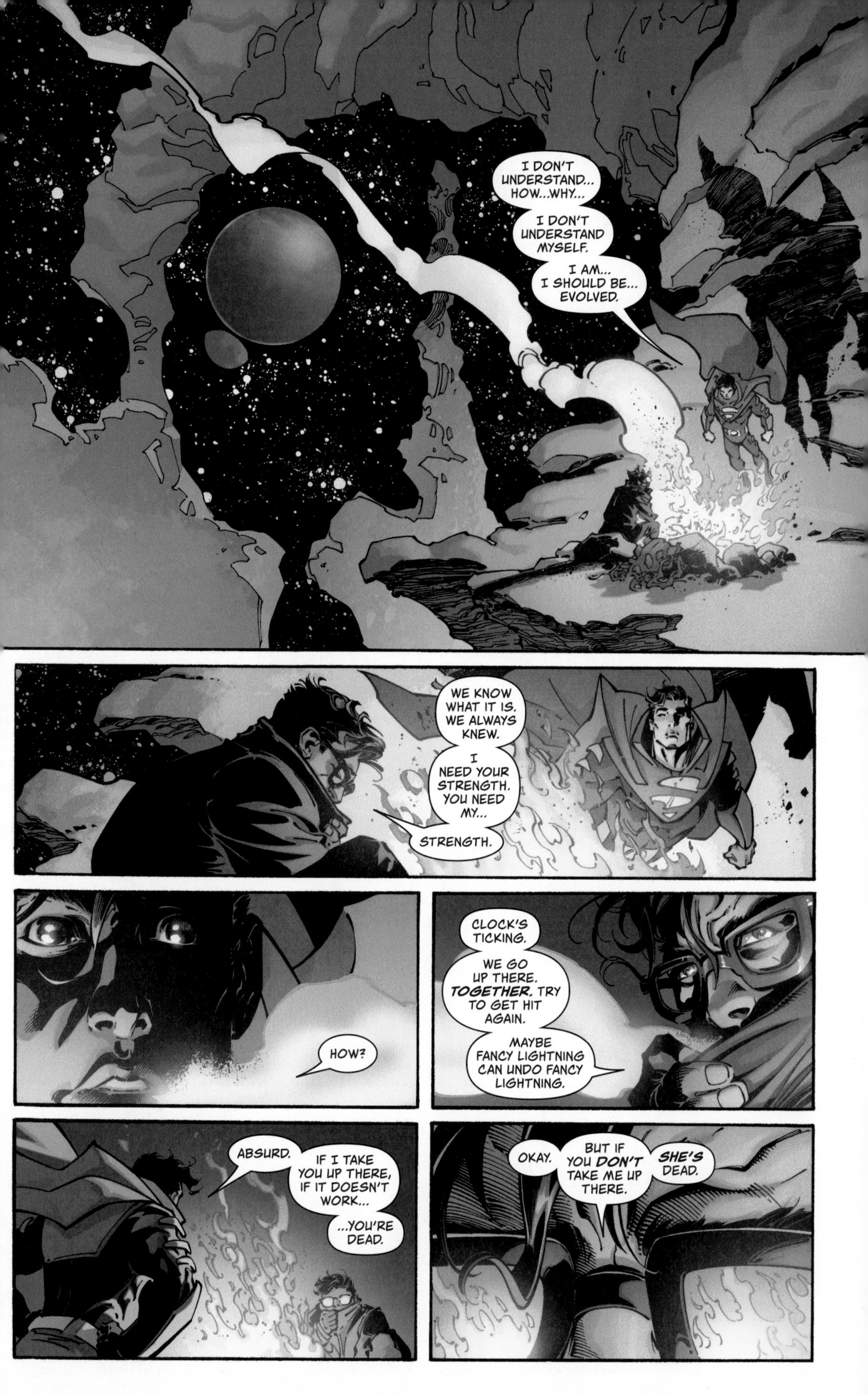
I DON'T UNDERSTAND... HOW...WHY...
I DON'T UNDERSTAND MYSELF.
I AM... I SHOULD BE... EVOLVED.
WE KNOW WHAT IT IS. WE ALWAYS KNEW.
I NEED YOUR STRENGTH. YOU NEED MY...
STRENGTH.
HOW?
CLOCK'S TICKING.
WE GO UP THERE. **TOGETHER.** TRY TO GET HIT AGAIN.
MAYBE FANCY LIGHTNING CAN UNDO FANCY LIGHTNING.
ABSURD.
IF I TAKE YOU UP THERE, IF IT DOESN'T WORK...
...YOU'RE DEAD.
OKAY.
BUT IF YOU **DON'T** TAKE ME UP THERE.
SHE'S DEAD.

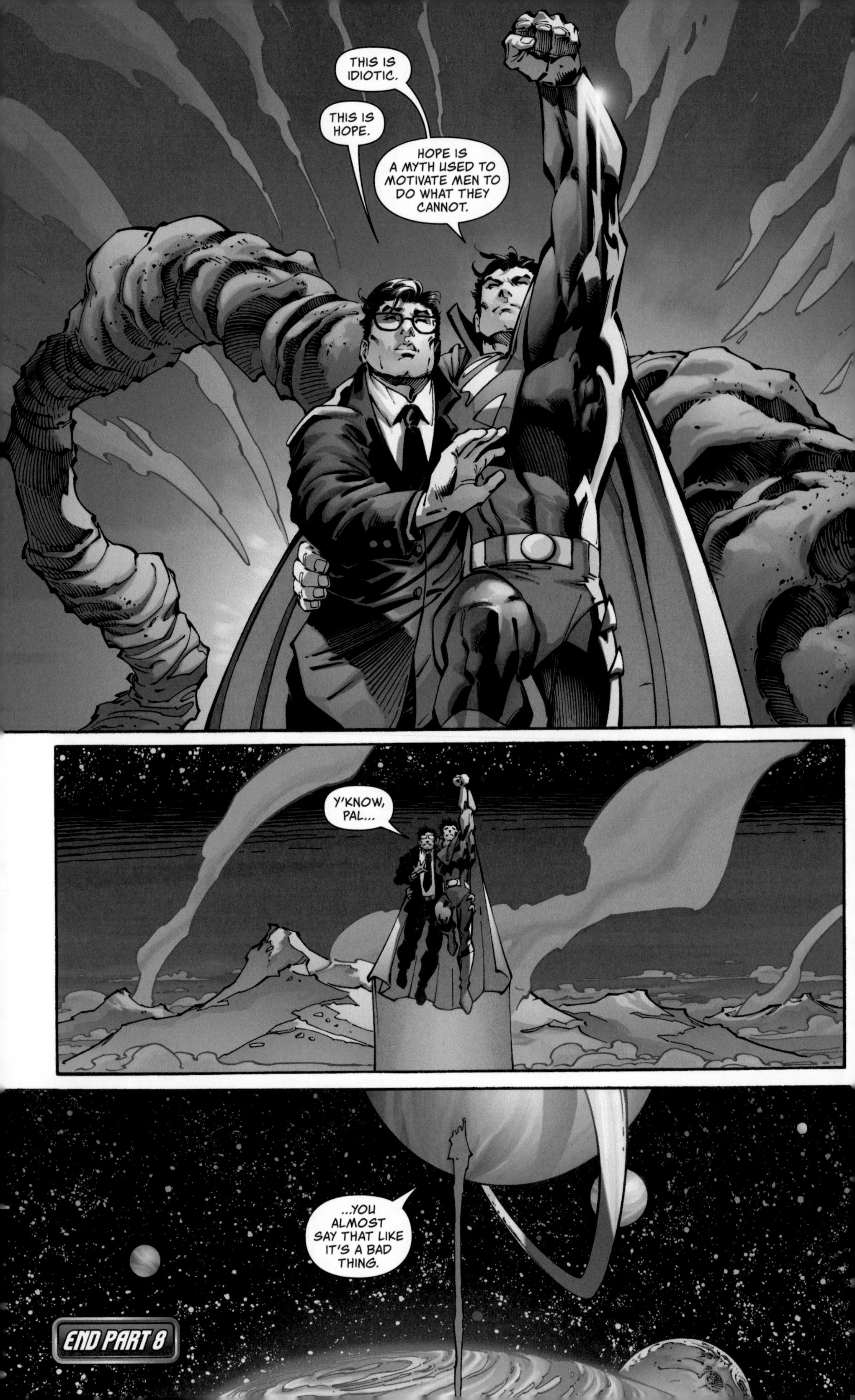
THIS IS IDIOTIC.
THIS IS HOPE.
HOPE IS A MYTH USED TO MOTIVATE MEN TO DO WHAT THEY CANNOT.
Y'KNOW, PAL...
...YOU ALMOST SAY THAT LIKE IT'S A BAD THING.
END PART 8

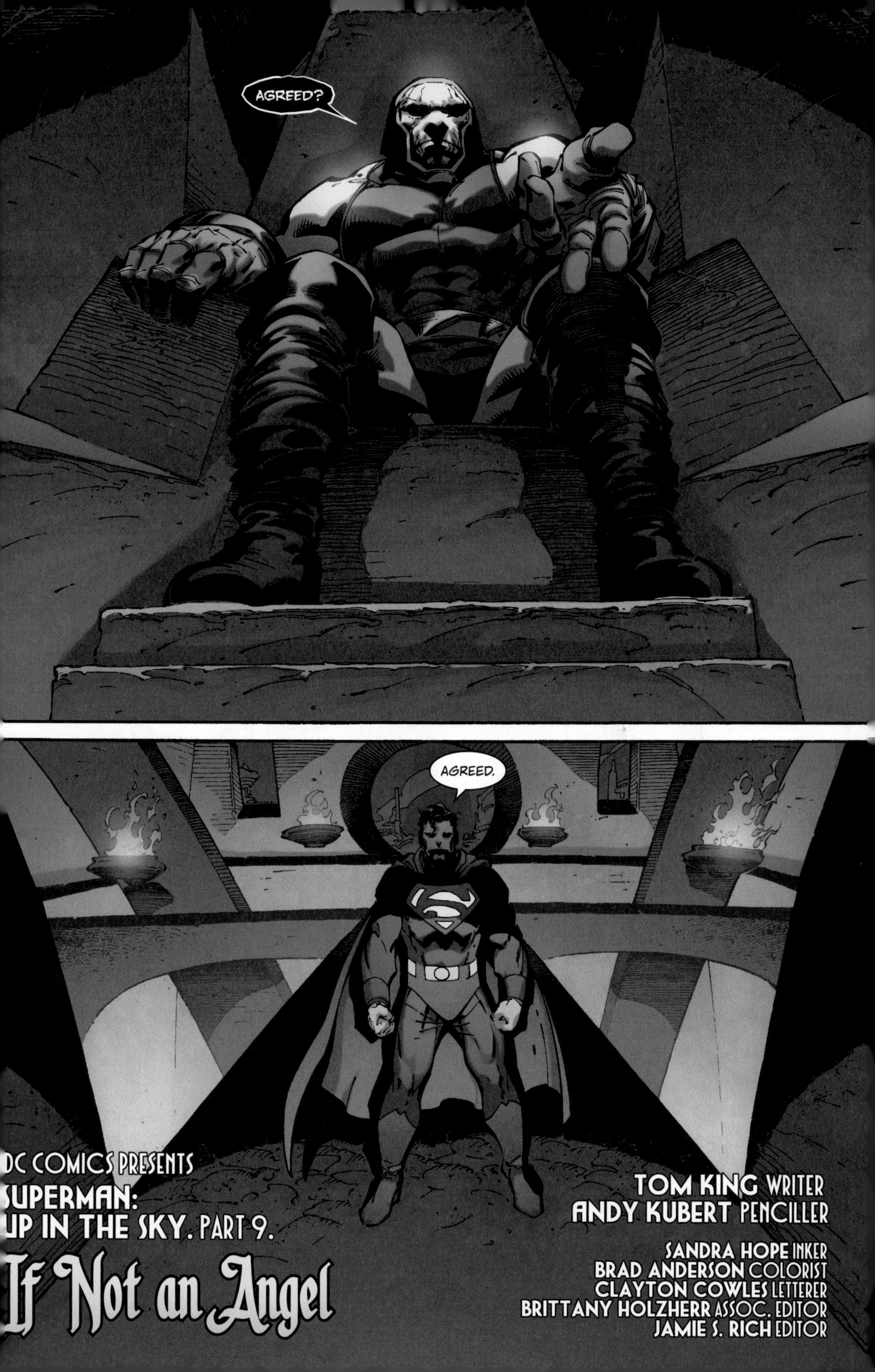
AGREED?
AGREED.
DC COMICS PRESENTS
SUPERMAN:
UP IN THE SKY. PART 9.
If Not an Angel
TOM KING WRITER
ANDY KUBERT PENCILLER
SANDRA HOPE INKER
BRAD ANDERSON COLORIST
CLAYTON COWLES LETTERER
BRITTANY HOLZHERR ASSOC. EDITOR
JAMIE S. RICH EDITOR

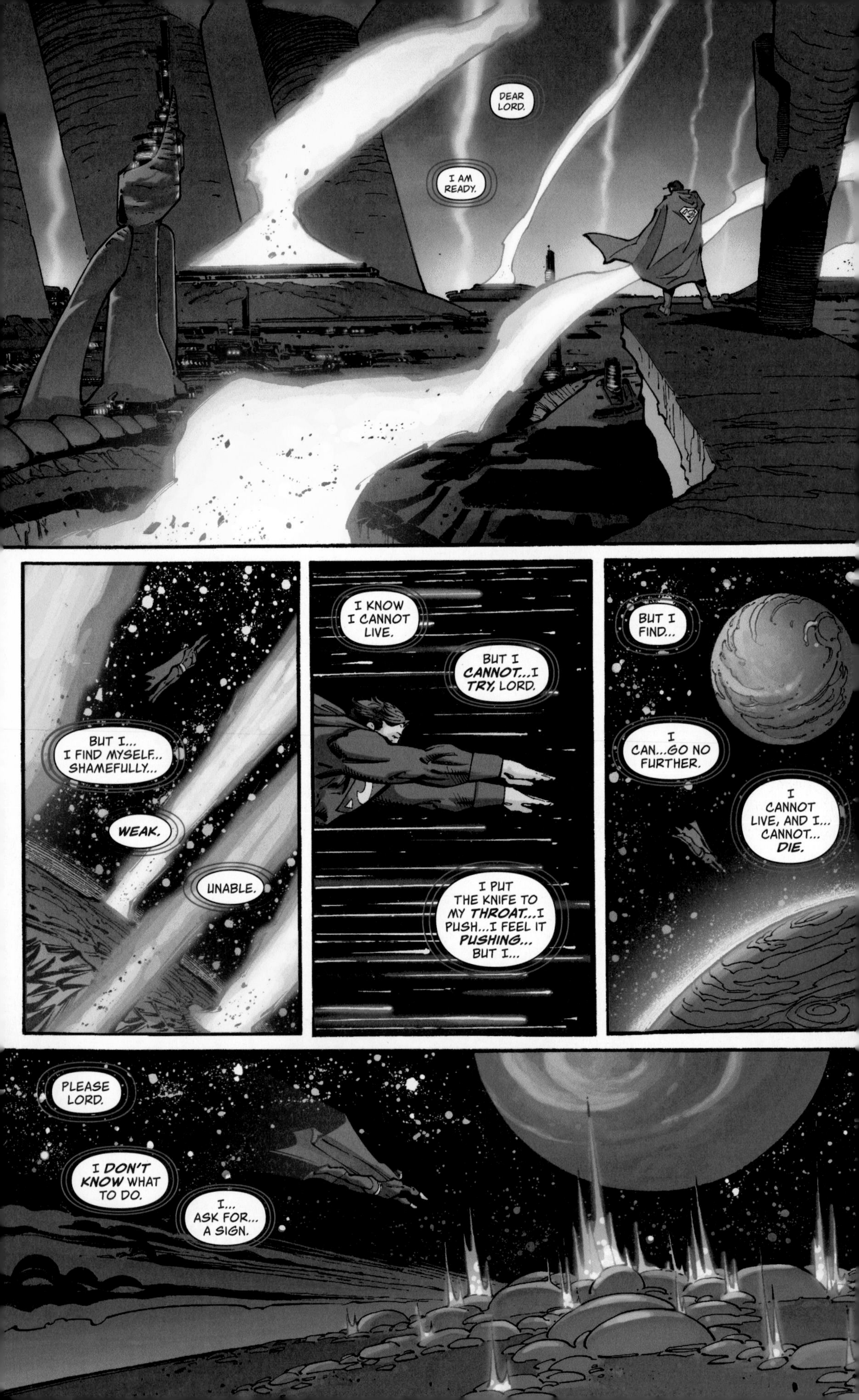
DEAR LORD.
I AM READY.
BUT I... I FIND MYSELF... SHAMEFULLY...
WEAK.
UNABLE.
I KNOW I CANNOT LIVE.
BUT I CANNOT...I TRY, LORD.
I PUT THE KNIFE TO MY THROAT...I PUSH...I FEEL IT PUSHING... BUT I...
BUT I FIND...
I CAN...GO NO FURTHER.
I CANNOT LIVE, AND I... CANNOT... DIE.
PLEASE LORD.
I DON'T KNOW WHAT TO DO.
I... ASK FOR... A SIGN.

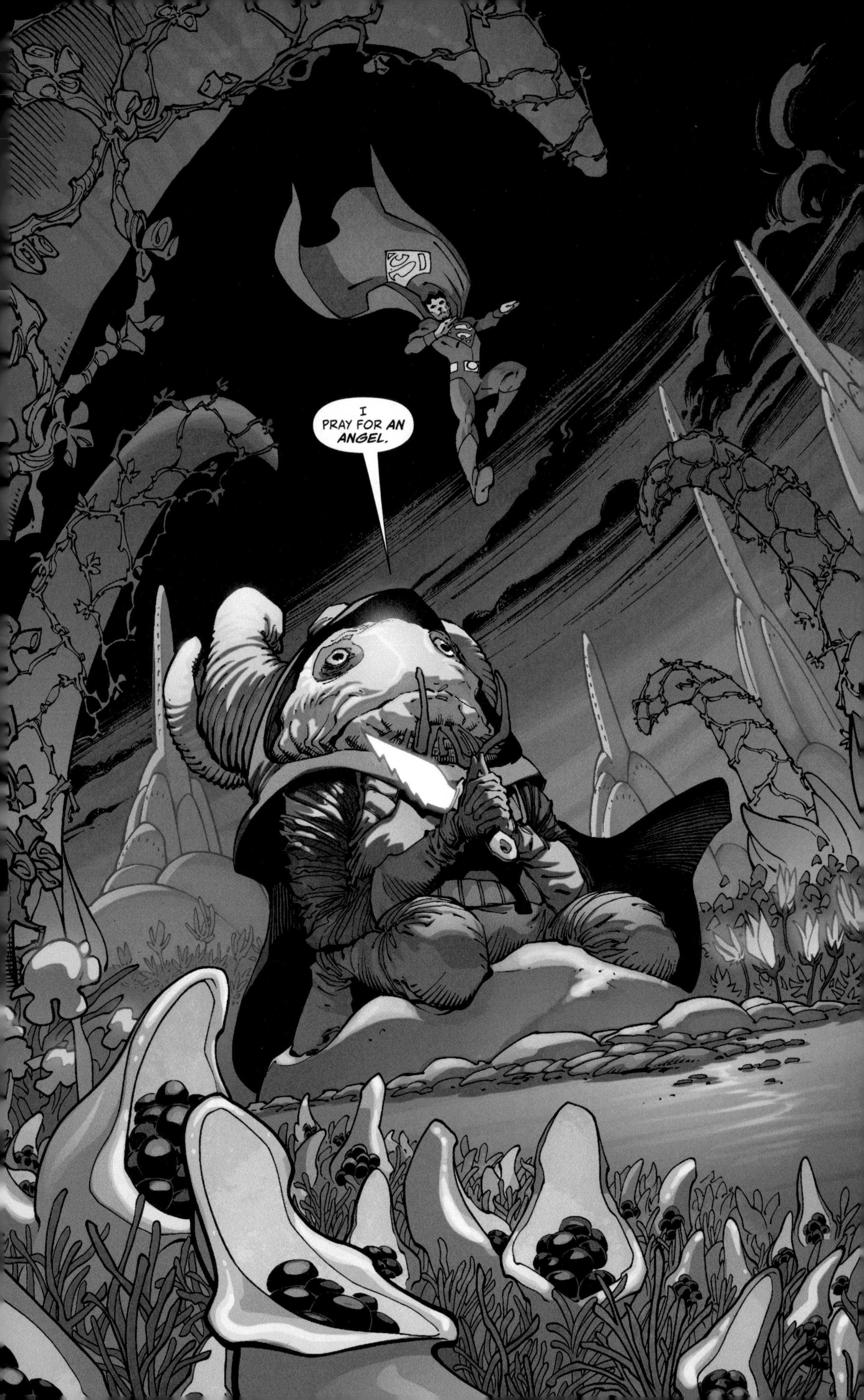
I PRAY FOR AN ANGEL.

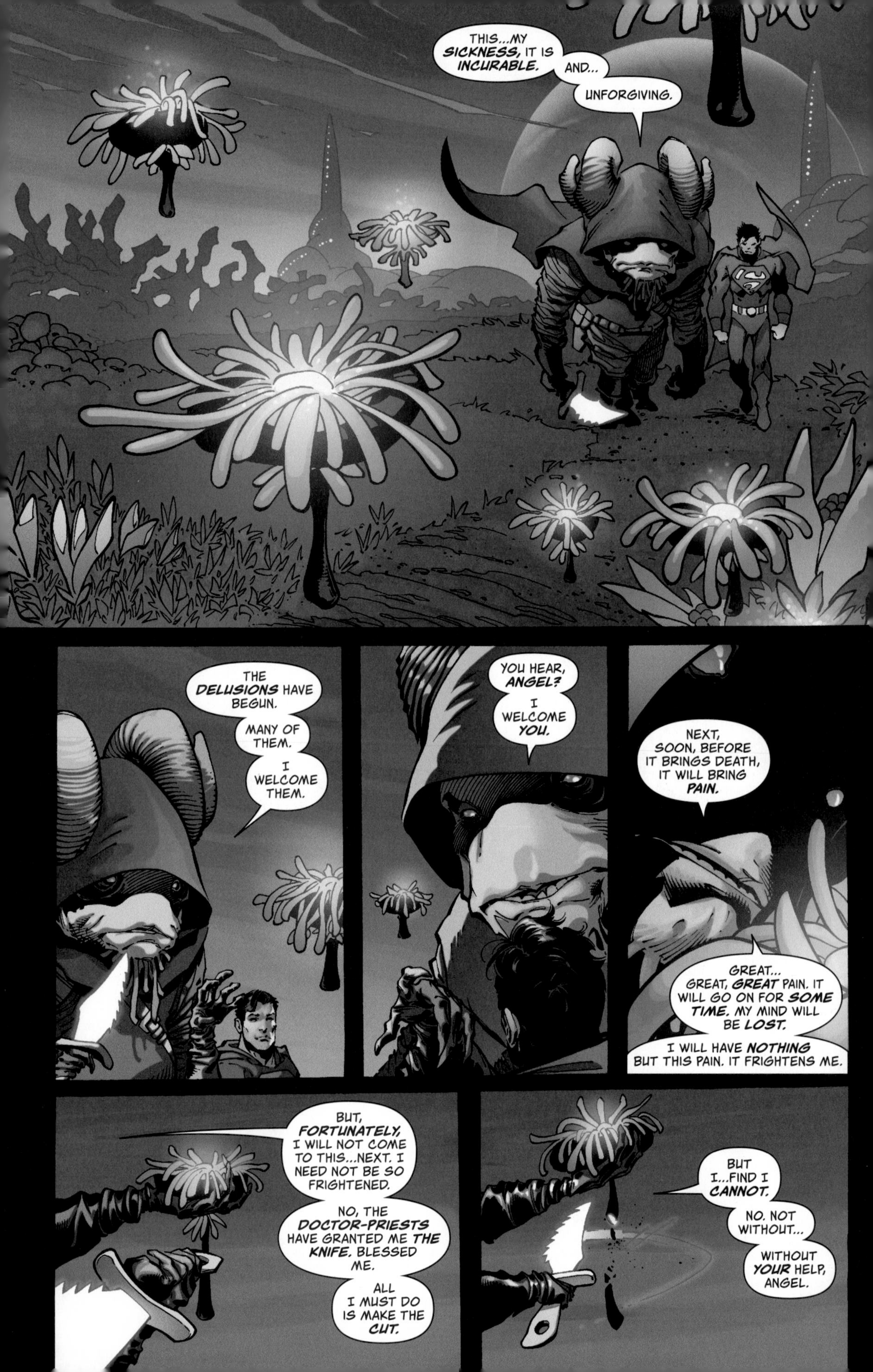
THIS...MY SICKNESS, IT IS INCURABLE.
AND...
UNFORGIVING.
THE DELUSIONS HAVE BEGUN.
MANY OF THEM.
I WELCOME THEM.
YOU HEAR, ANGEL?
I WELCOME YOU.
NEXT, SOON, BEFORE IT BRINGS DEATH, IT WILL BRING PAIN.
GREAT... GREAT, GREAT PAIN. IT WILL GO ON FOR SOME TIME. MY MIND WILL BE LOST.
I WILL HAVE NOTHING BUT THIS PAIN. IT FRIGHTENS ME.
BUT, FORTUNATELY, I WILL NOT COME TO THIS...NEXT. I NEED NOT BE SO FRIGHTENED.
NO, THE DOCTOR-PRIESTS HAVE GRANTED ME THE KNIFE. BLESSED ME.
ALL I MUST DO IS MAKE THE CUT.
BUT I...FIND I CANNOT.
NO. NOT WITHOUT...
WITHOUT YOUR HELP, ANGEL.

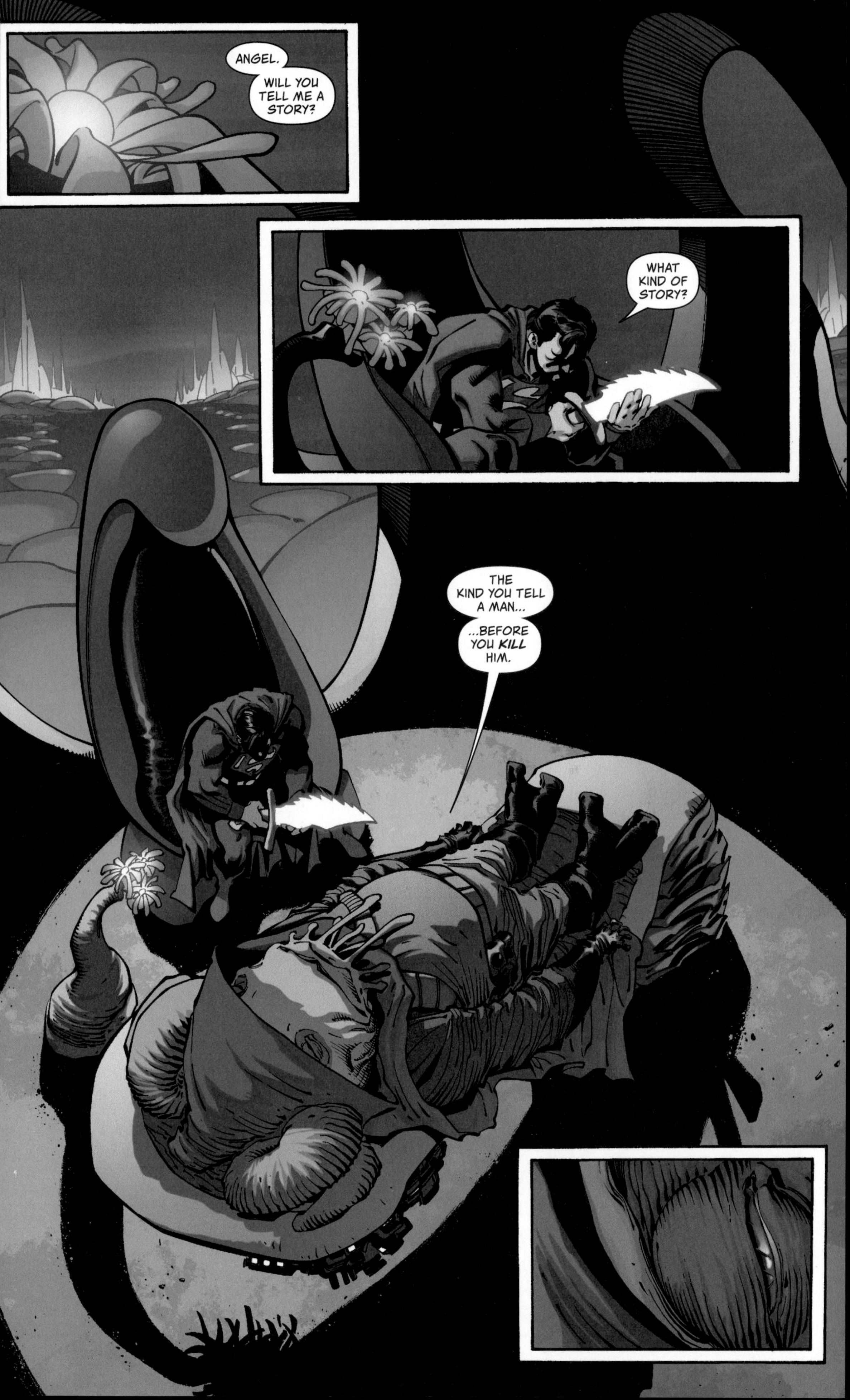
ANGEL.
WILL YOU TELL ME A STORY?
WHAT KIND OF STORY?
THE KIND YOU TELL A MAN...
...BEFORE YOU KILL HIM.

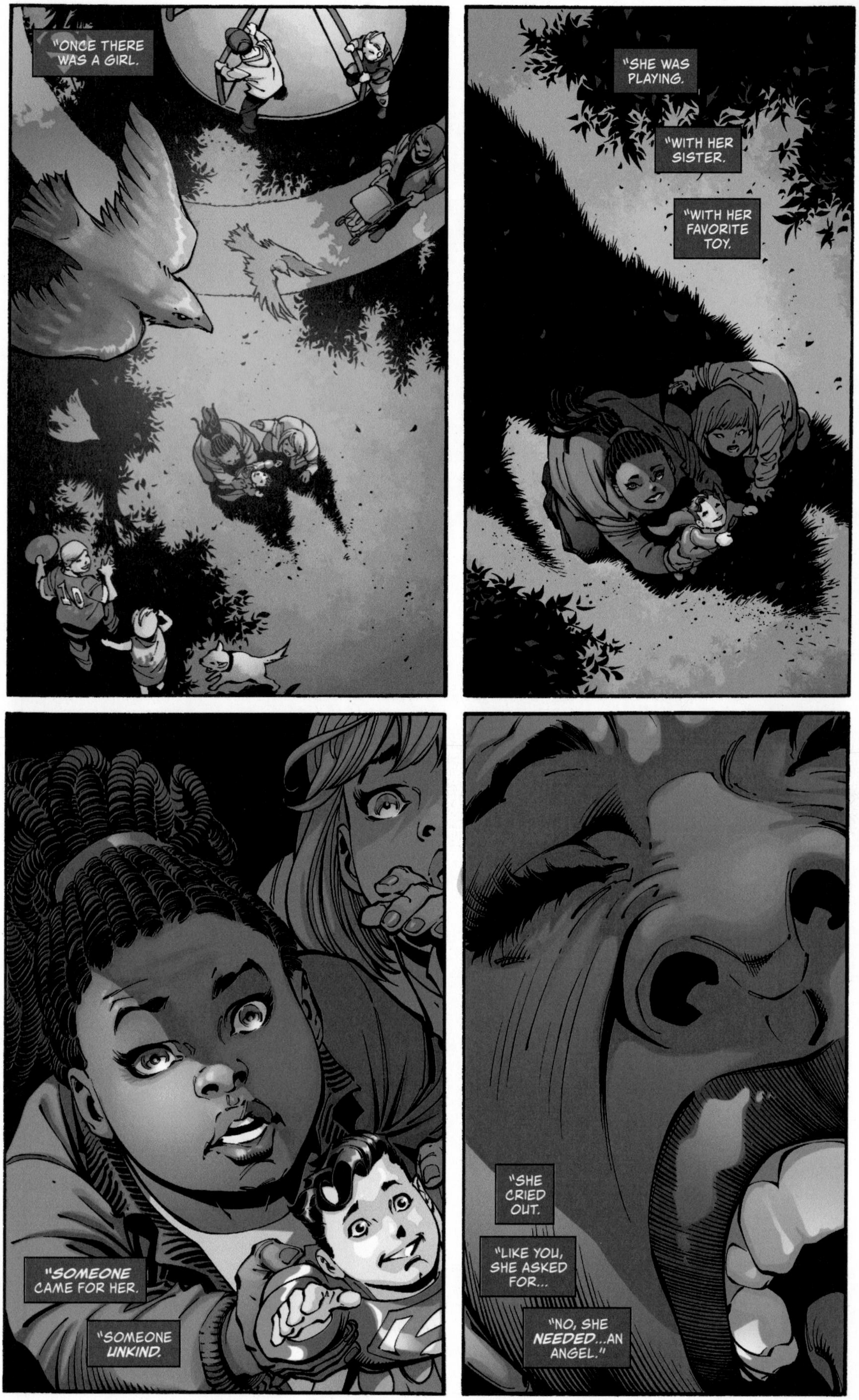
"ONCE THERE WAS A GIRL.
"SHE WAS PLAYING.
"WITH HER SISTER.
"WITH HER FAVORITE TOY.
"*SOMEONE* CAME FOR HER.
"SOMEONE *UNKIND*.
"SHE CRIED OUT.
"LIKE YOU, SHE ASKED FOR...
"NO, SHE *NEEDED*...AN ANGEL."

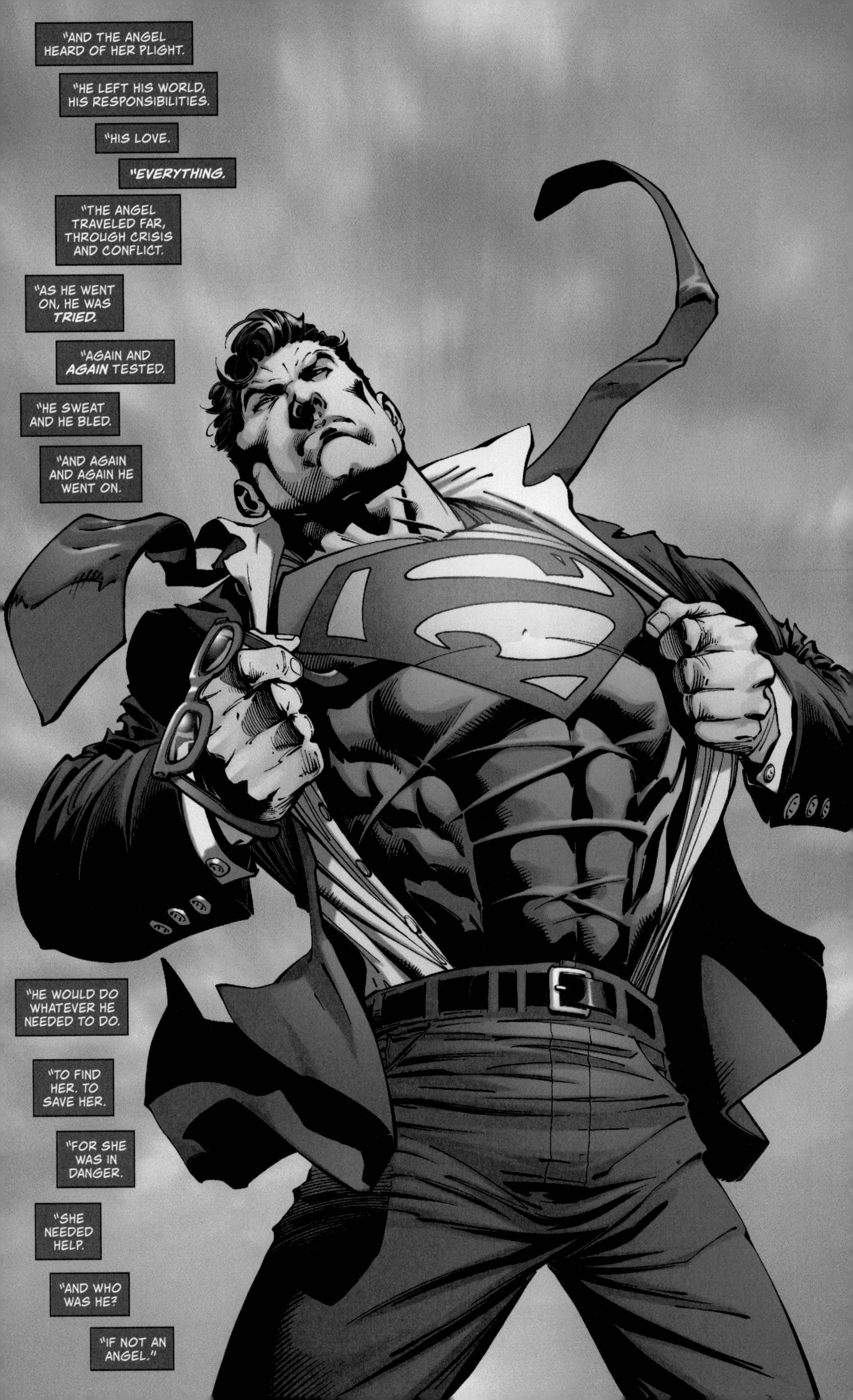
"AND THE ANGEL HEARD OF HER PLIGHT.
"HE LEFT HIS WORLD, HIS RESPONSIBILITIES.
"HIS LOVE.
"*EVERYTHING.*
"THE ANGEL TRAVELED FAR, THROUGH CRISIS AND CONFLICT.
"AS HE WENT ON, HE WAS *TRIED.*
"AGAIN AND *AGAIN* TESTED.
"HE SWEAT AND HE BLED.
"AND AGAIN AND AGAIN HE WENT ON.
"HE WOULD DO WHATEVER HE NEEDED TO DO.
"TO FIND HER. TO SAVE HER.
"FOR SHE WAS IN DANGER.
"SHE NEEDED HELP.
"AND WHO WAS HE?
"IF NOT AN ANGEL."

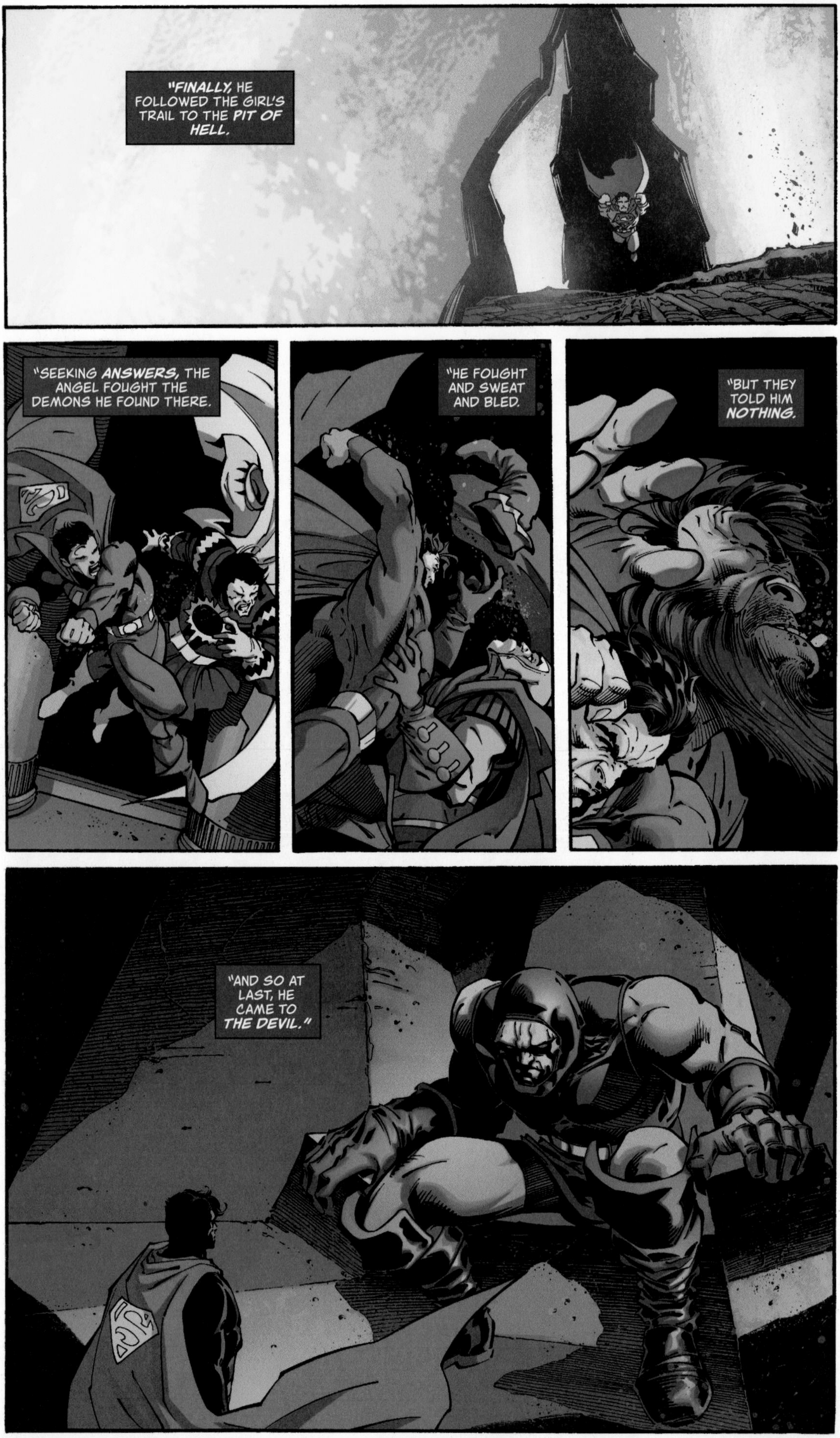
"FINALLY, HE FOLLOWED THE GIRL'S TRAIL TO THE PIT OF HELL.
"SEEKING ANSWERS, THE ANGEL FOUGHT THE DEMONS HE FOUND THERE.
"HE FOUGHT AND SWEAT AND BLED.
"BUT THEY TOLD HIM NOTHING.
"AND SO AT LAST, HE CAME TO THE DEVIL."

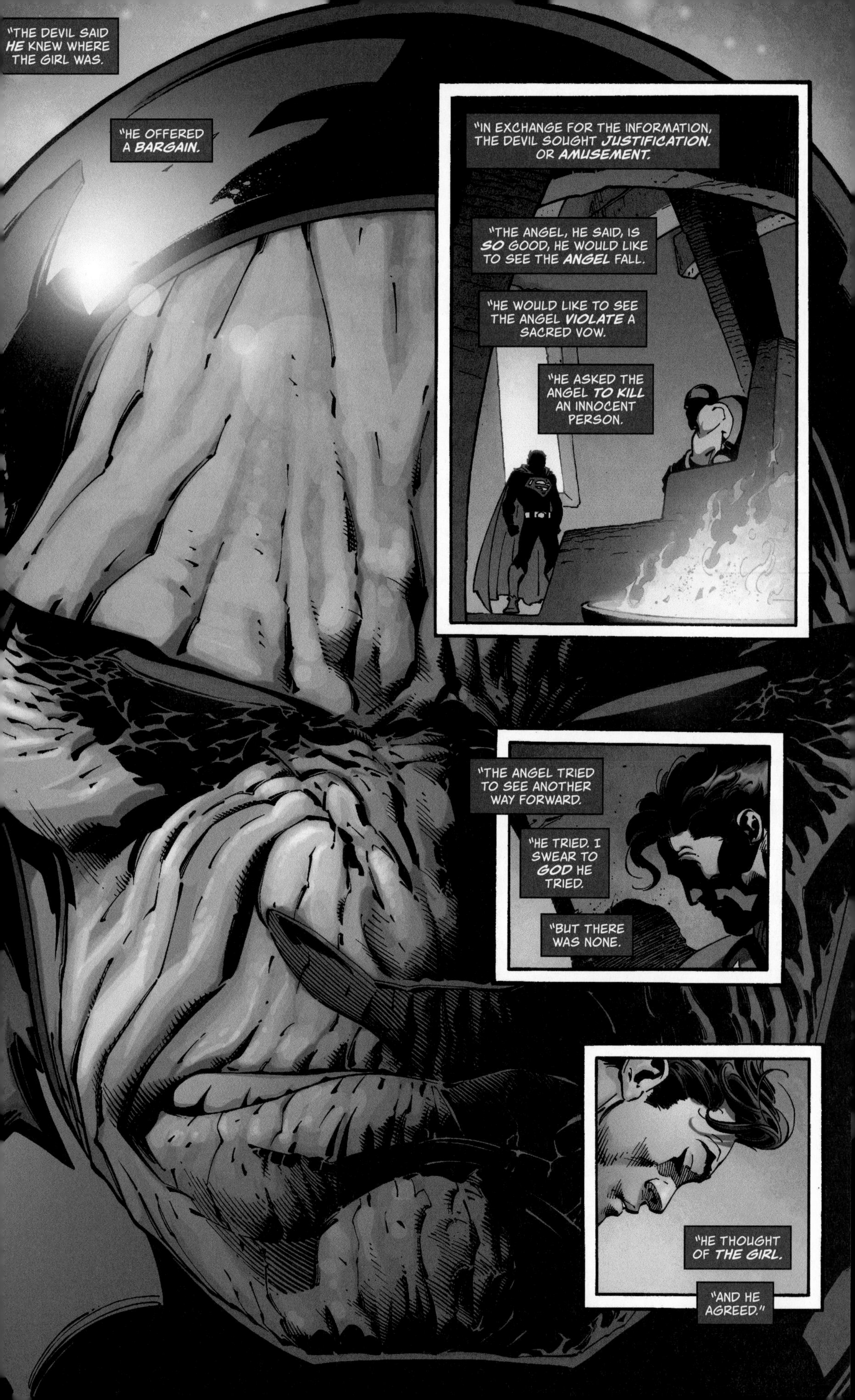
"THE DEVIL SAID HE KNEW WHERE THE GIRL WAS.
"HE OFFERED A BARGAIN.
"IN EXCHANGE FOR THE INFORMATION, THE DEVIL SOUGHT JUSTIFICATION. OR AMUSEMENT.
"THE ANGEL, HE SAID, IS SO GOOD, HE WOULD LIKE TO SEE THE ANGEL FALL.
"HE WOULD LIKE TO SEE THE ANGEL VIOLATE A SACRED VOW.
"HE ASKED THE ANGEL TO KILL AN INNOCENT PERSON.
"THE ANGEL TRIED TO SEE ANOTHER WAY FORWARD.
"HE TRIED. I SWEAR TO GOD HE TRIED.
"BUT THERE WAS NONE.
"HE THOUGHT OF THE GIRL.
"AND HE AGREED."

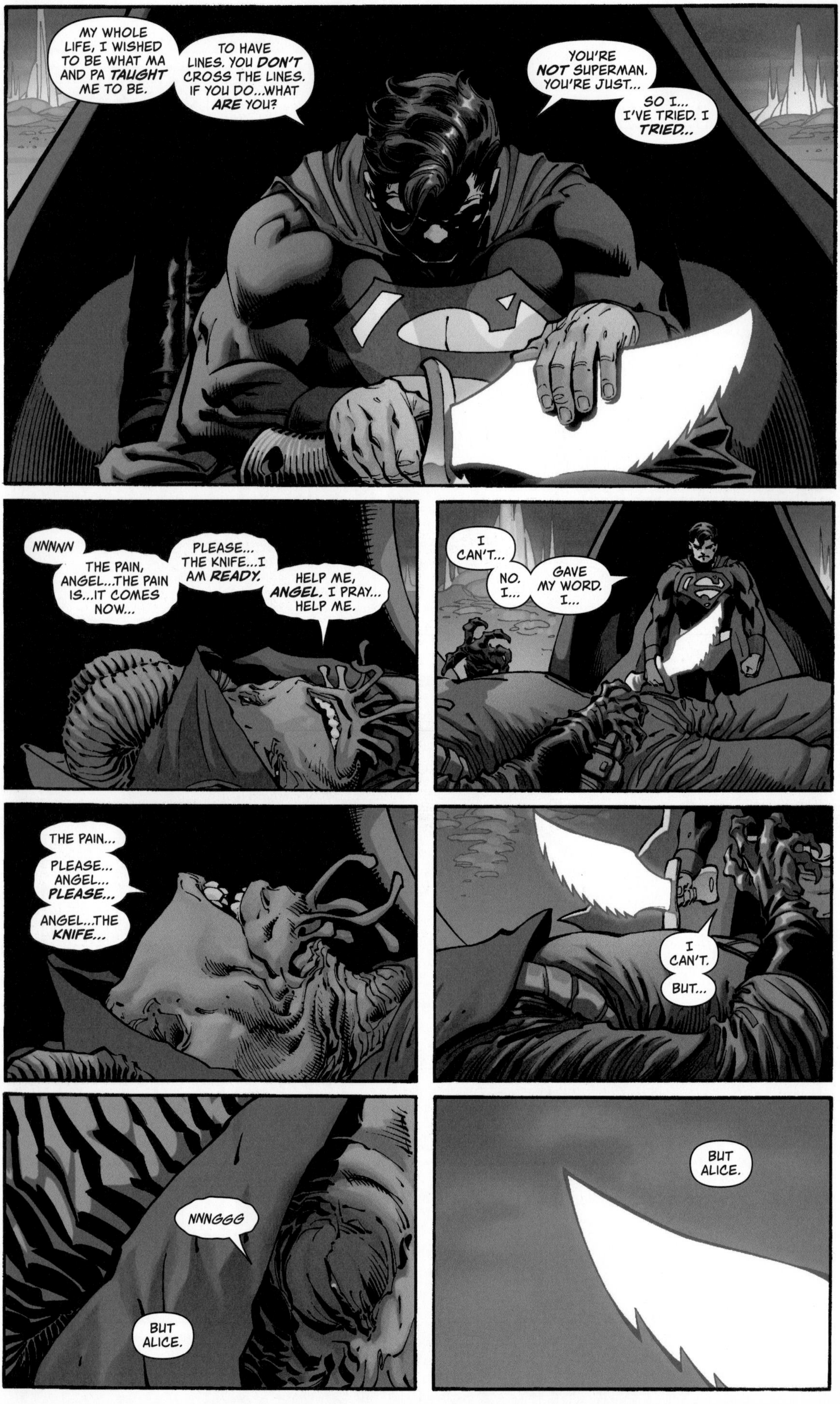
MY WHOLE LIFE, I WISHED TO BE WHAT MA AND PA *TAUGHT* ME TO BE.
TO HAVE LINES. YOU *DON'T* CROSS THE LINES. IF YOU DO...WHAT *ARE* YOU?
YOU'RE *NOT* SUPERMAN. YOU'RE JUST...
SO I... I'VE TRIED. I *TRIED...*
NNNNN
THE PAIN, ANGEL...THE PAIN IS...IT COMES NOW...
PLEASE... THE KNIFE...I AM *READY.*
HELP ME, *ANGEL.* I PRAY... HELP ME.
I CAN'T...
NO. I...
GAVE MY WORD. I...
THE PAIN...
PLEASE... ANGEL... *PLEASE...*
ANGEL...THE *KNIFE...*
I CAN'T.
BUT...
NNNGGG
BUT ALICE.
BUT ALICE.

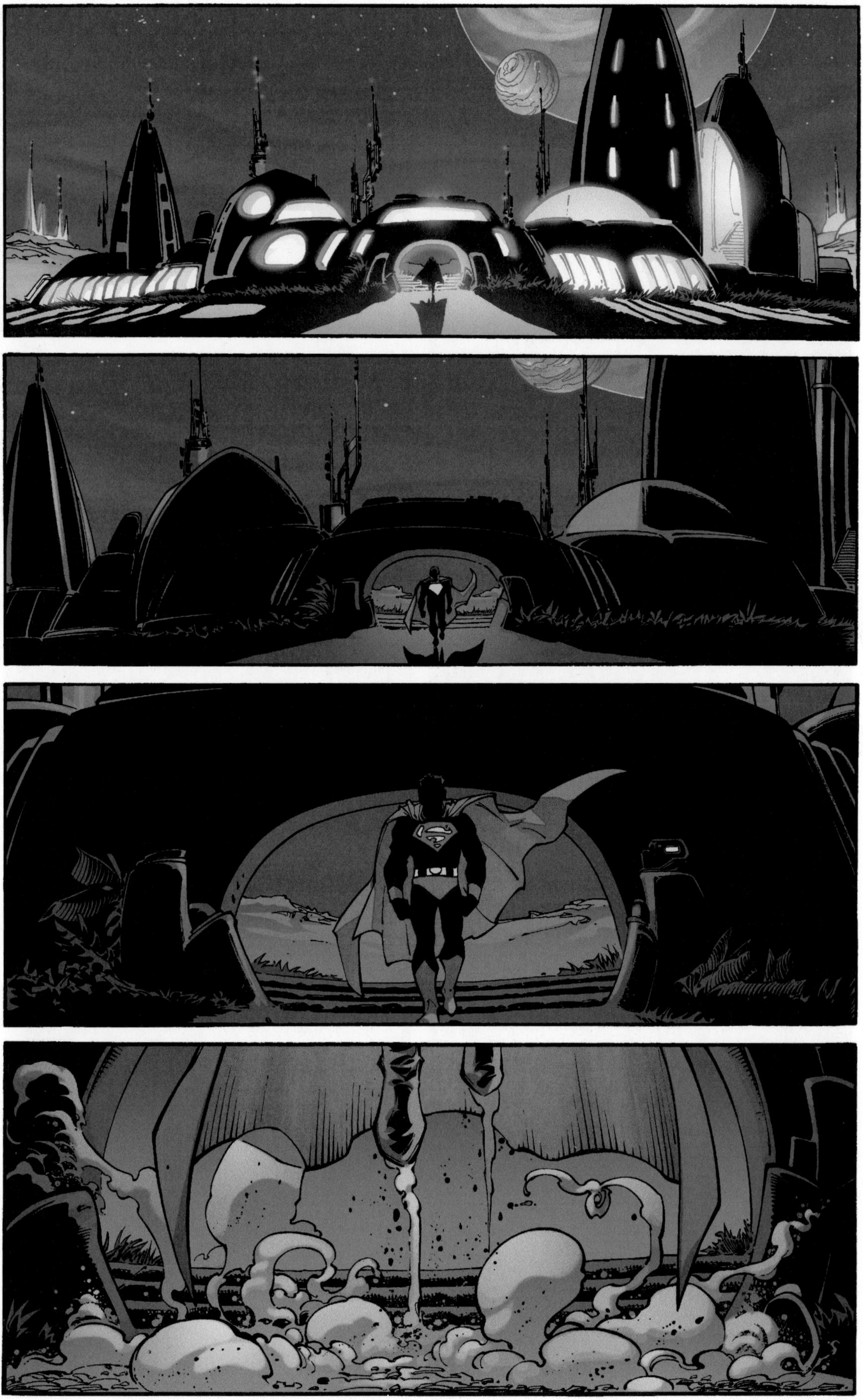

IT IS DONE?
YES.
YOU LIE.
IF IT IS A LIE, THEN I'VE BROKEN MY WORD.
AND IF IT'S THE TRUTH...
...THEN I'VE BROKEN MY WORD.
EITHER WAY, DARKSEID, I HAVE FALLEN.
EITHER WAY... DARKSEID.
YOU WIN.
NOW.
WHERE'S THE GIRL?
END PART 9

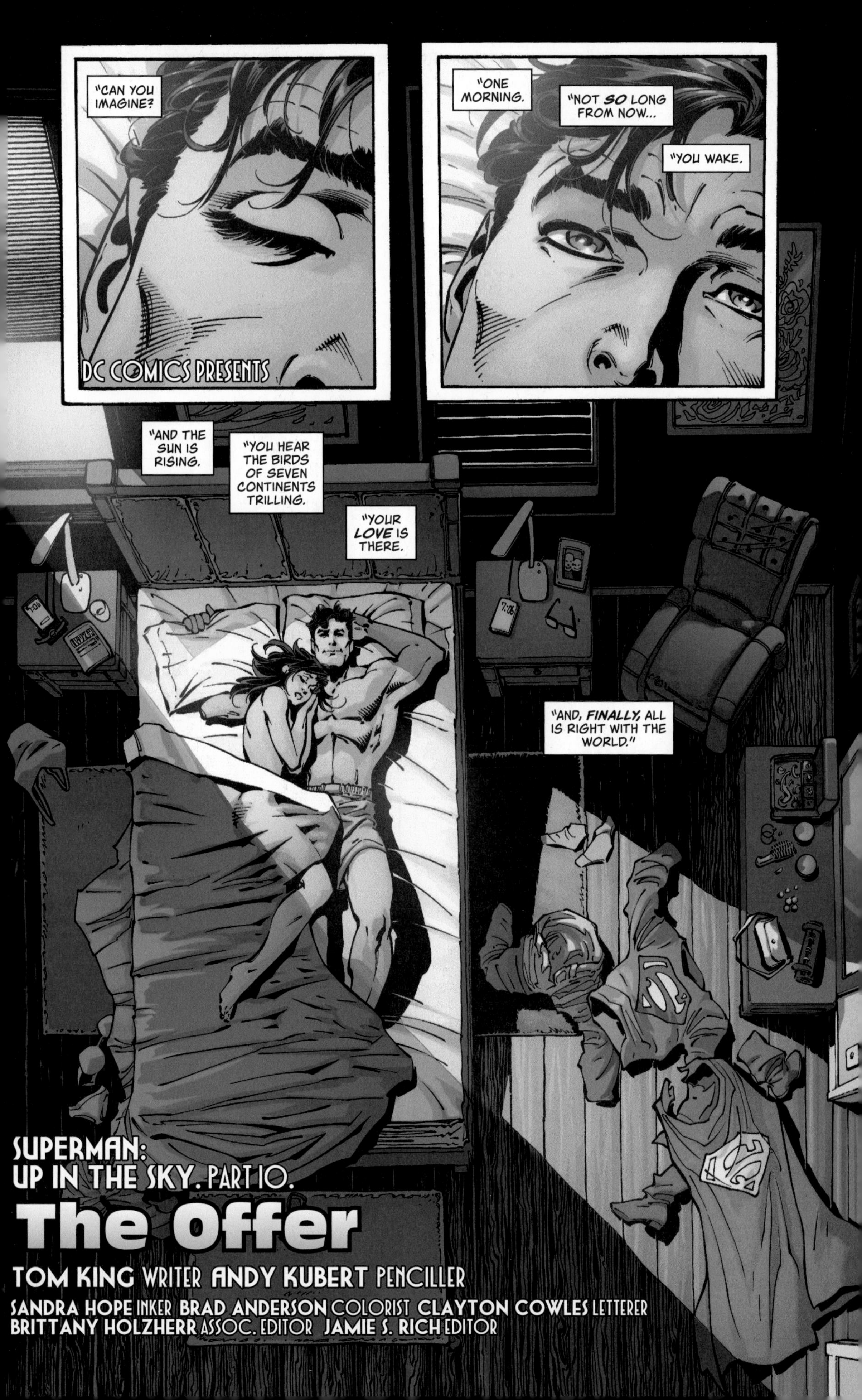
"CAN YOU IMAGINE?
DC COMICS PRESENTS
"ONE MORNING.
"NOT SO LONG FROM NOW...
"YOU WAKE.
"AND THE SUN IS RISING.
"YOU HEAR THE BIRDS OF SEVEN CONTINENTS TRILLING.
"YOUR LOVE IS THERE.
"AND, FINALLY, ALL IS RIGHT WITH THE WORLD."
SUPERMAN: UP IN THE SKY. PART 10.
The Offer
TOM KING WRITER ANDY KUBERT PENCILLER
SANDRA HOPE INKER BRAD ANDERSON COLORIST CLAYTON COWLES LETTERER
BRITTANY HOLZHERR ASSOC. EDITOR JAMIE S. RICH EDITOR

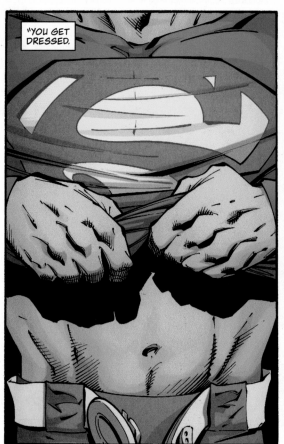

"YOU GET DRESSED.

"NOT QUICKLY.

"NOT RUSHED.

"NOT IN A PHONE BOOTH OR A CLOSET AS THE BOMBS FALL.

"NOT WHILE YOU TWIST THROUGH THE SKY JUST IN TIME TO SAVE HER.

"BUT DELIBERATELY, CASUALLY, CALMLY.

"WHILE YOU *LISTEN* TO HER AS SHE BREAKS DOWN HER LATEST EXCLUSIVE.

"WHILE YOU *SMELL* THE TOUCH OF VANILLA IN HER MORNING COFFEE."

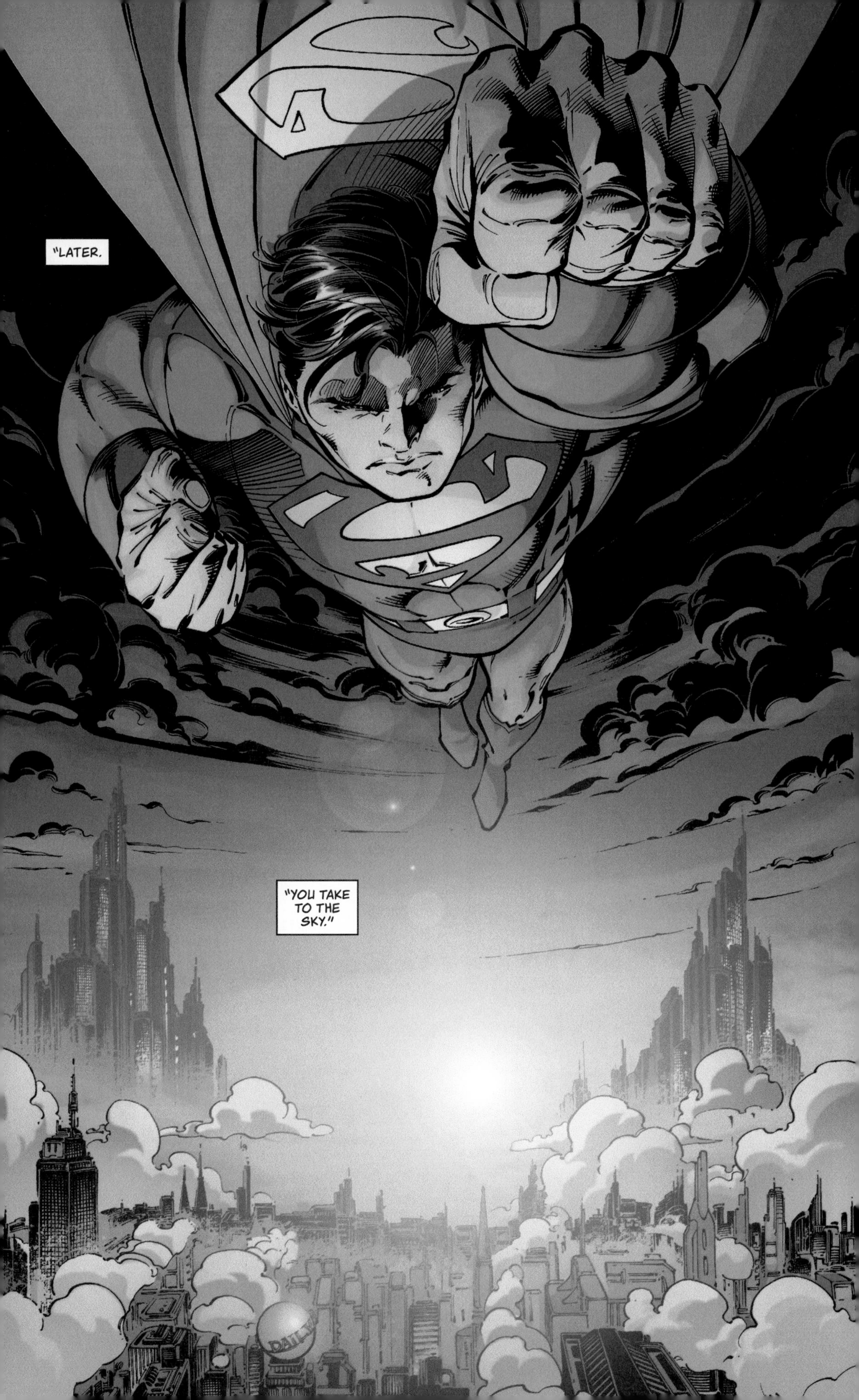
"LATER.
"YOU TAKE TO THE SKY."

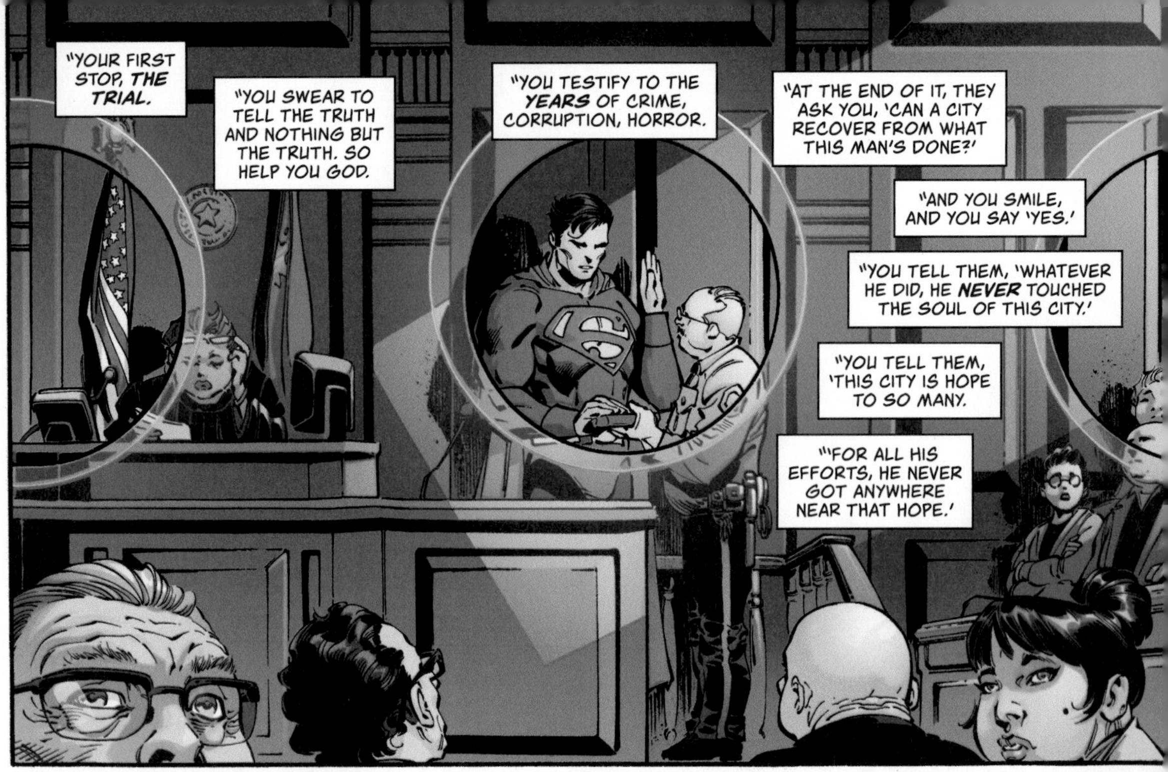
"YOUR FIRST STOP, THE TRIAL.
"YOU SWEAR TO TELL THE TRUTH AND NOTHING BUT THE TRUTH. SO HELP YOU GOD.
"YOU TESTIFY TO THE YEARS OF CRIME, CORRUPTION, HORROR.
"AT THE END OF IT, THEY ASK YOU, 'CAN A CITY RECOVER FROM WHAT THIS MAN'S DONE?'
"AND YOU SMILE, AND YOU SAY 'YES.'
"YOU TELL THEM, 'WHATEVER HE DID, HE NEVER TOUCHED THE SOUL OF THIS CITY.'
"YOU TELL THEM, 'THIS CITY IS HOPE TO SO MANY.
"'FOR ALL HIS EFFORTS, HE NEVER GOT ANYWHERE NEAR THAT HOPE.'
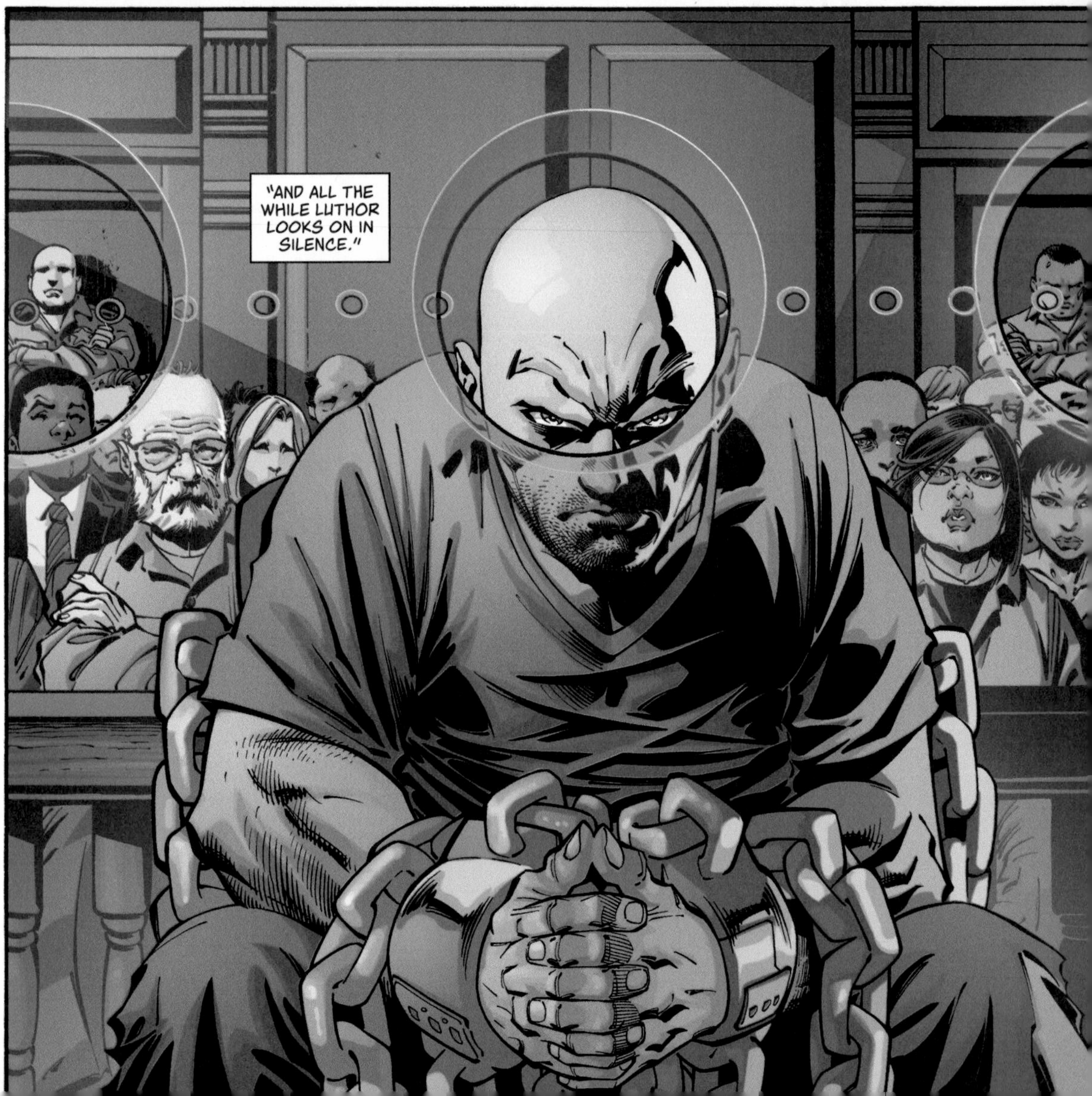
"AND ALL THE WHILE LUTHOR LOOKS ON IN SILENCE."

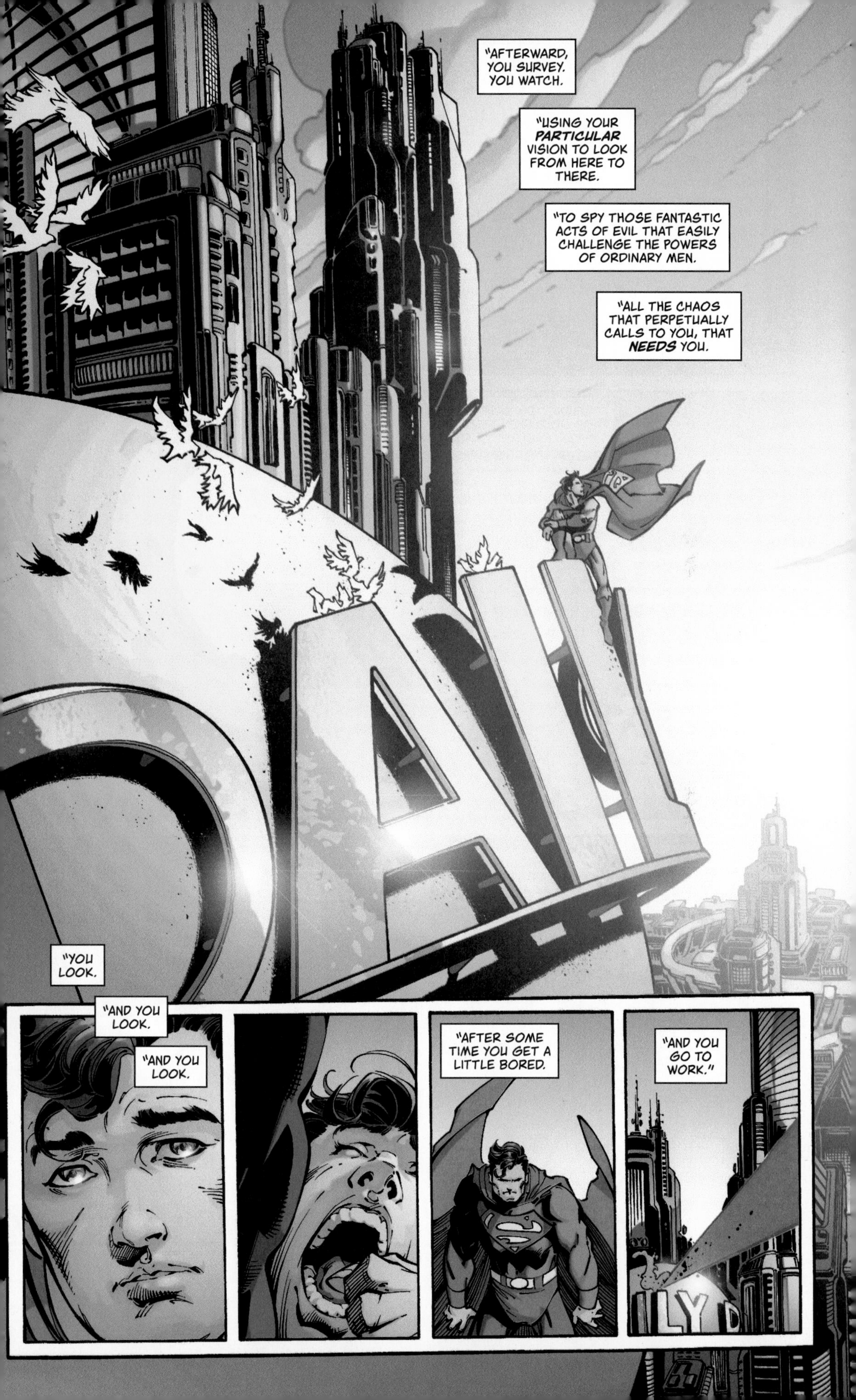
"AFTERWARD, YOU SURVEY. YOU WATCH.
"USING YOUR PARTICULAR VISION TO LOOK FROM HERE TO THERE.
"TO SPY THOSE FANTASTIC ACTS OF EVIL THAT EASILY CHALLENGE THE POWERS OF ORDINARY MEN.
"ALL THE CHAOS THAT PERPETUALLY CALLS TO YOU, THAT NEEDS YOU.
"YOU LOOK.
"AND YOU LOOK.
"AND YOU LOOK.
"AFTER SOME TIME YOU GET A LITTLE BORED.
"AND YOU GO TO WORK."

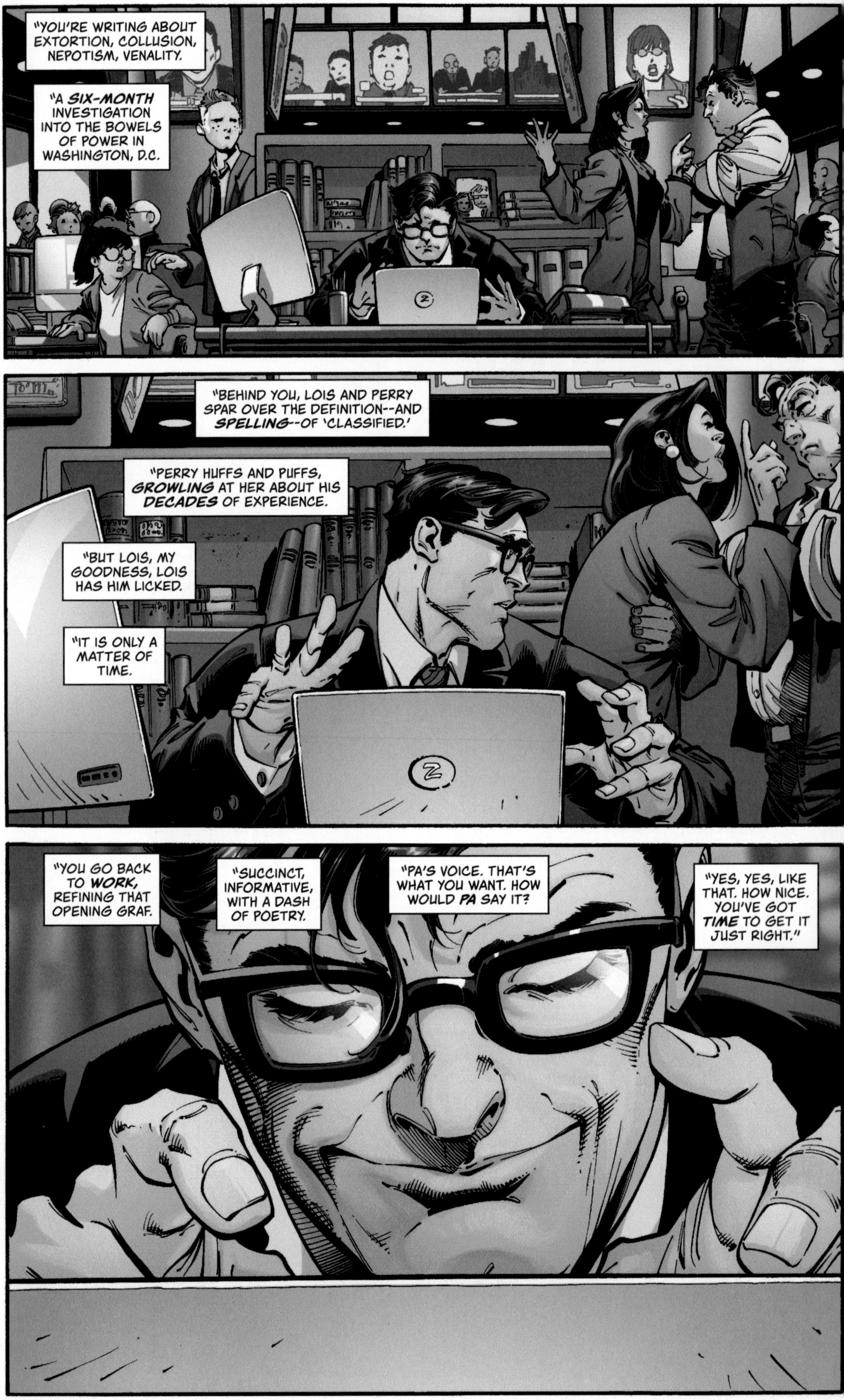
"YOU'RE WRITING ABOUT EXTORTION, COLLUSION, NEPOTISM, VENALITY.
"A SIX-MONTH INVESTIGATION INTO THE BOWELS OF POWER IN WASHINGTON, D.C.
"BEHIND YOU, LOIS AND PERRY SPAR OVER THE DEFINITION--AND SPELLING--OF 'CLASSIFIED.'
"PERRY HUFFS AND PUFFS, GROWLING AT HER ABOUT HIS DECADES OF EXPERIENCE.
"BUT LOIS, MY GOODNESS, LOIS HAS HIM LICKED.
"IT IS ONLY A MATTER OF TIME.
"YOU GO BACK TO WORK, REFINING THAT OPENING GRAF.
"SUCCINCT, INFORMATIVE, WITH A DASH OF POETRY.
"PA'S VOICE. THAT'S WHAT YOU WANT. HOW WOULD PA SAY IT?
"YES, YES, LIKE THAT. HOW NICE. YOU'VE GOT TIME TO GET IT JUST RIGHT."

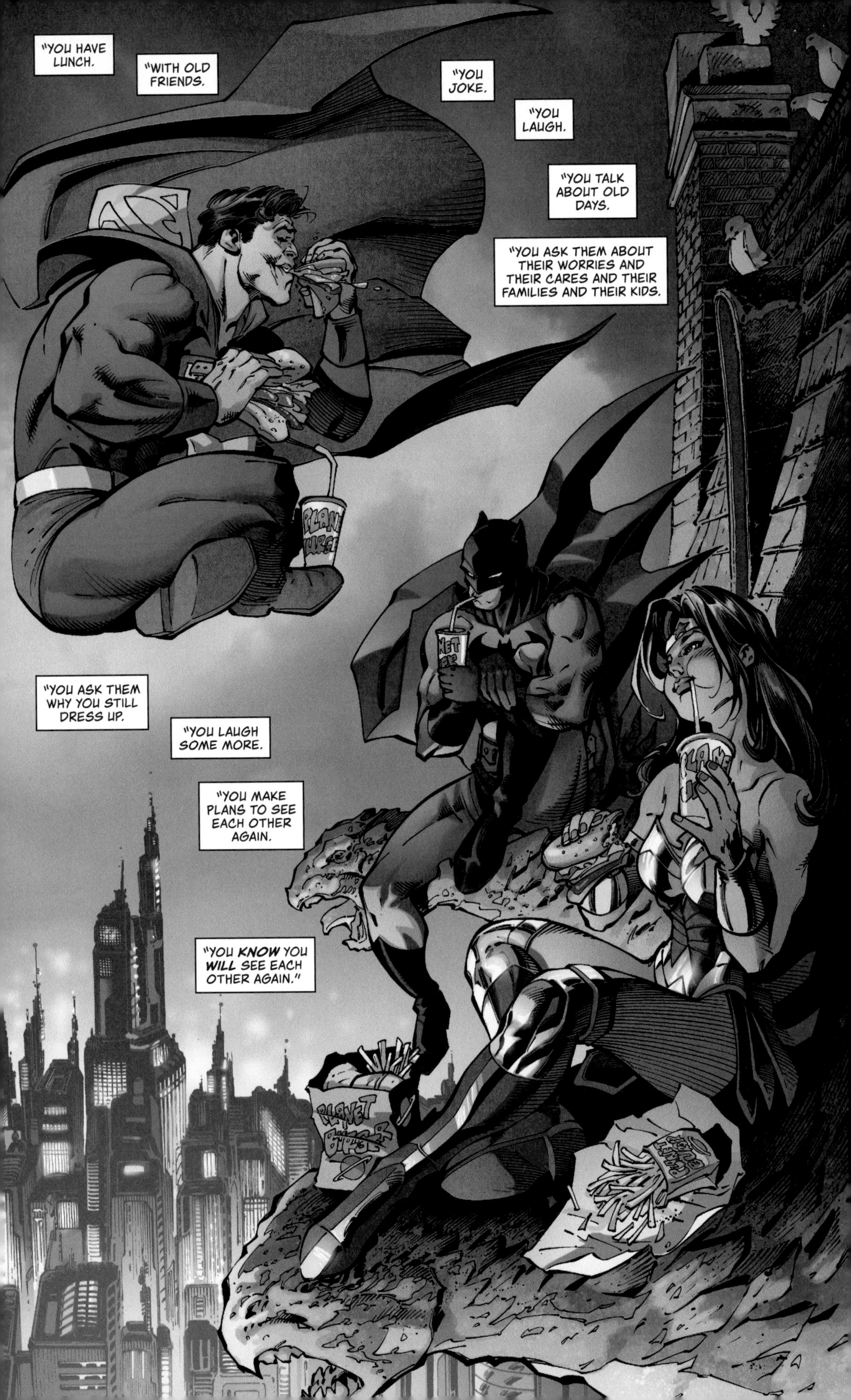
"YOU HAVE LUNCH.
"WITH OLD FRIENDS.
"YOU JOKE.
"YOU LAUGH.
"YOU TALK ABOUT OLD DAYS.
"YOU ASK THEM ABOUT THEIR WORRIES AND THEIR CARES AND THEIR FAMILIES AND THEIR KIDS.
"YOU ASK THEM WHY YOU STILL DRESS UP.
"YOU LAUGH SOME MORE.
"YOU MAKE PLANS TO SEE EACH OTHER AGAIN.
"YOU **KNOW** YOU **WILL** SEE EACH OTHER AGAIN."

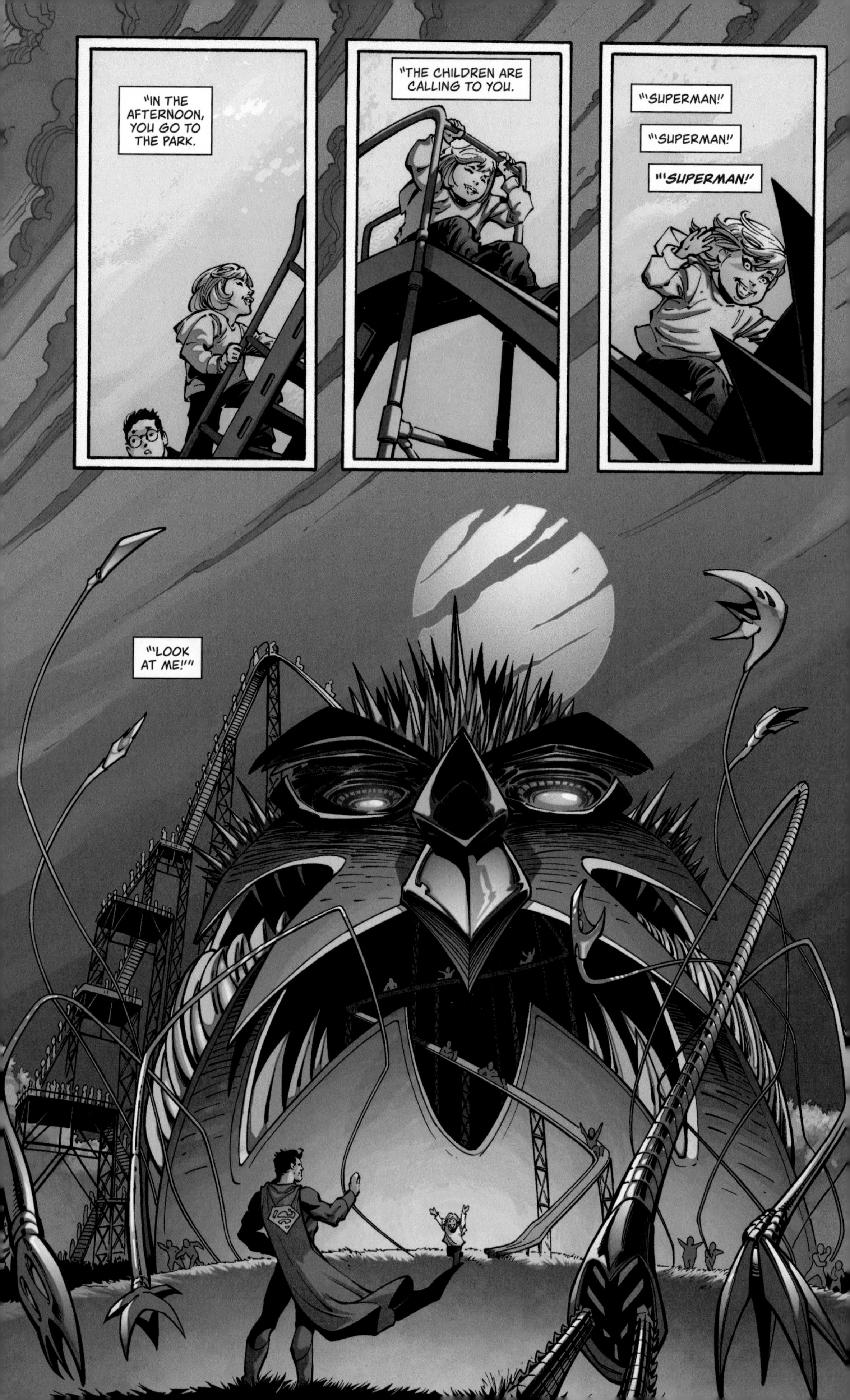
"IN THE AFTERNOON, YOU GO TO THE PARK.
"THE CHILDREN ARE CALLING TO YOU.
"'SUPERMAN!'
"'SUPERMAN!'
"'SUPERMAN!'
"'LOOK AT ME!'"

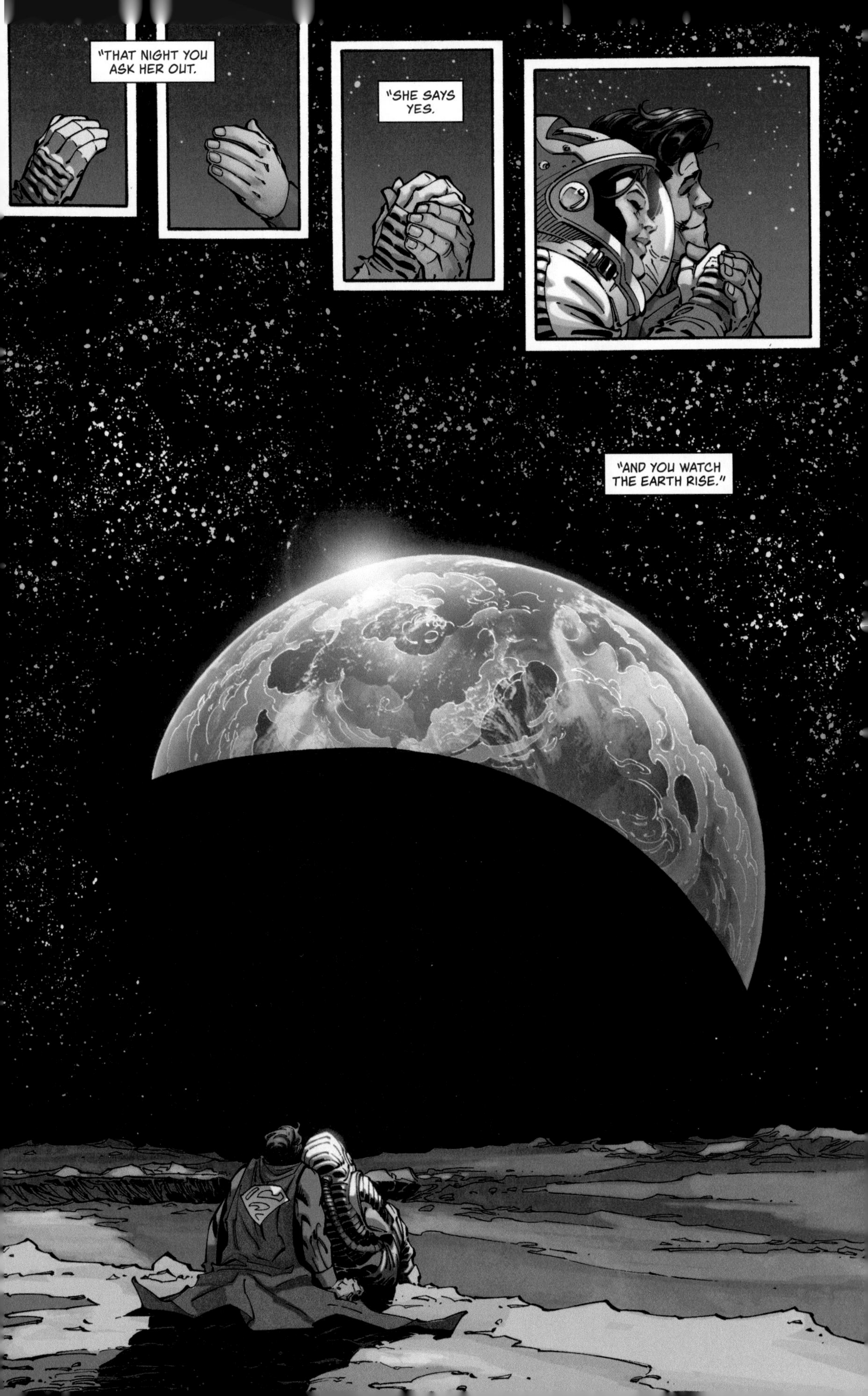
"THAT NIGHT YOU ASK HER OUT.
"SHE SAYS YES.
"AND YOU WATCH THE EARTH RISE."

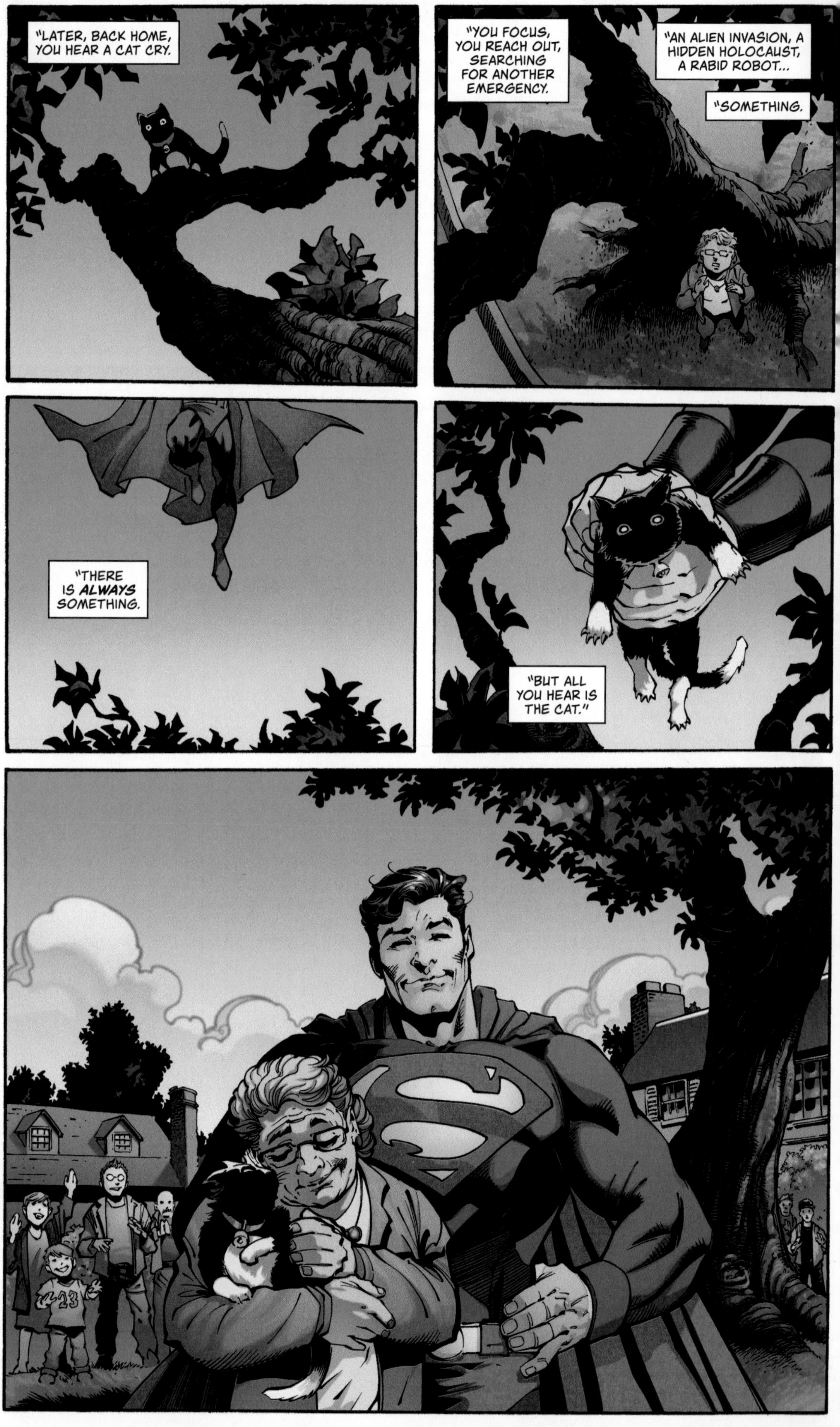
"LATER, BACK HOME, YOU HEAR A CAT CRY.
"YOU FOCUS, YOU REACH OUT, SEARCHING FOR ANOTHER EMERGENCY.
"AN ALIEN INVASION, A HIDDEN HOLOCAUST, A RABID ROBOT...
"SOMETHING.
"THERE IS ALWAYS SOMETHING.
"BUT ALL YOU HEAR IS THE CAT."
23

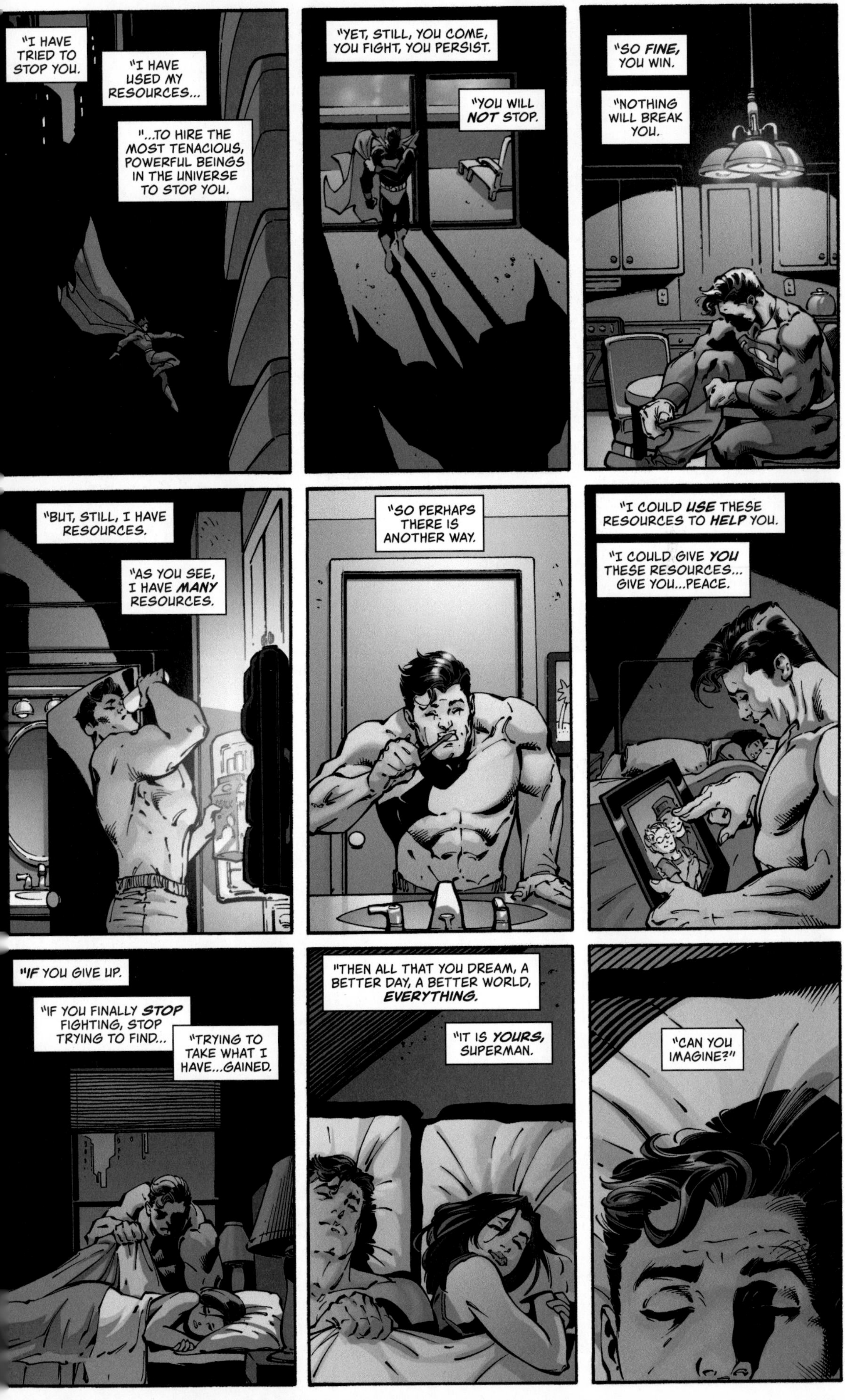

"I HAVE TRIED TO STOP YOU.
"I HAVE USED MY RESOURCES...
"...TO HIRE THE MOST TENACIOUS, POWERFUL BEINGS IN THE UNIVERSE TO STOP YOU.
"YET, STILL, YOU COME, YOU FIGHT, YOU PERSIST.
"YOU WILL NOT STOP.
"SO FINE, YOU WIN.
"NOTHING WILL BREAK YOU.
"BUT, STILL, I HAVE RESOURCES.
"AS YOU SEE, I HAVE MANY RESOURCES.
"SO PERHAPS THERE IS ANOTHER WAY.
"I COULD USE THESE RESOURCES TO HELP YOU.
"I COULD GIVE YOU THESE RESOURCES... GIVE YOU...PEACE.
"IF YOU GIVE UP.
"IF YOU FINALLY STOP FIGHTING, STOP TRYING TO FIND...
"TRYING TO TAKE WHAT I HAVE...GAINED.
"THEN ALL THAT YOU DREAM, A BETTER DAY, A BETTER WORLD, EVERYTHING.
"IT IS YOURS, SUPERMAN.
"CAN YOU IMAGINE?"

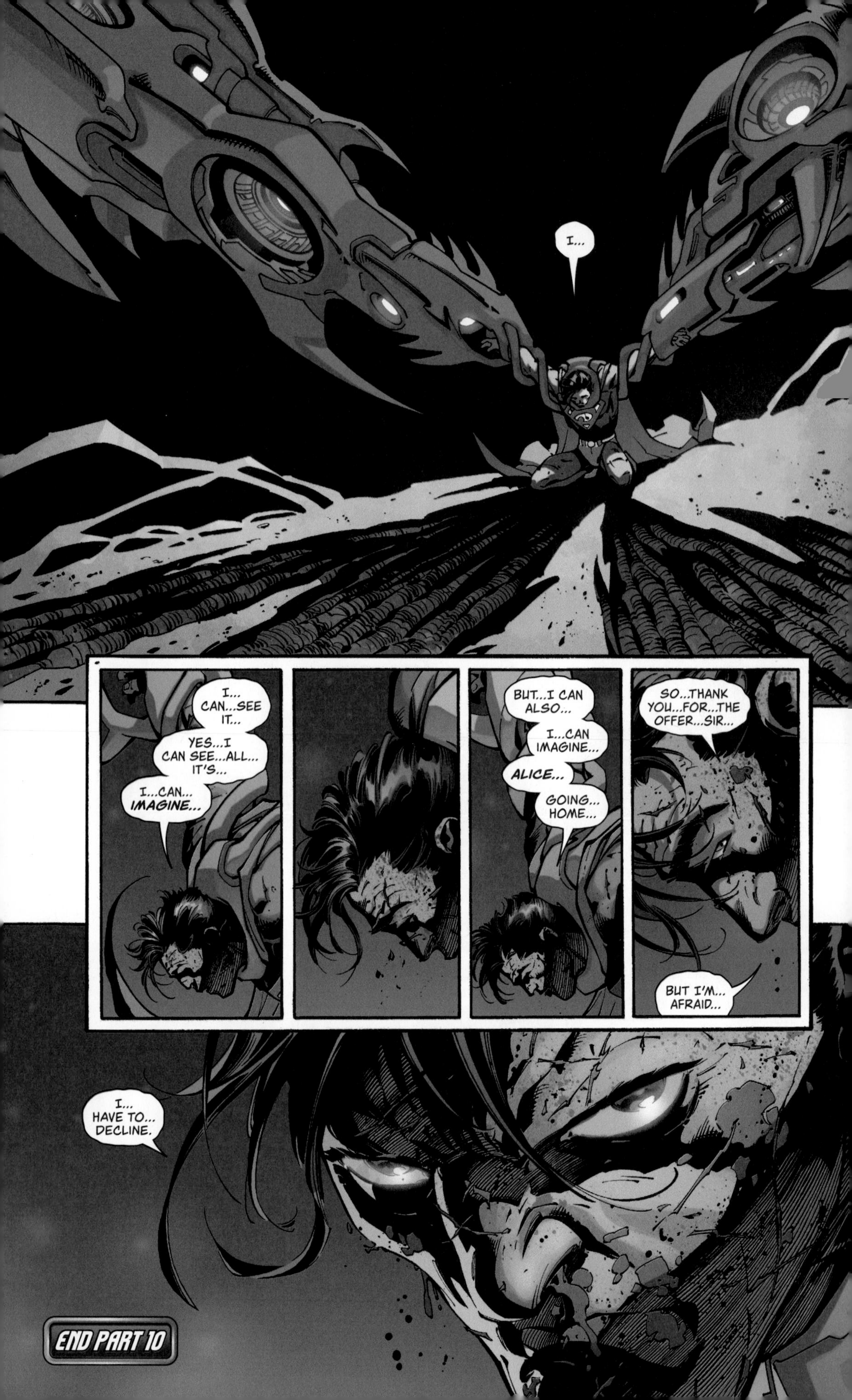
I...
I... CAN...SEE IT...
YES...I CAN SEE...ALL... IT'S...
I...CAN... IMAGINE...
BUT...I CAN ALSO...
I...CAN IMAGINE...
ALICE...
GOING... HOME...
SO...THANK YOU...FOR...THE OFFER...SIR...
BUT I'M... AFRAID...
I... HAVE TO... DECLINE.
END PART 10

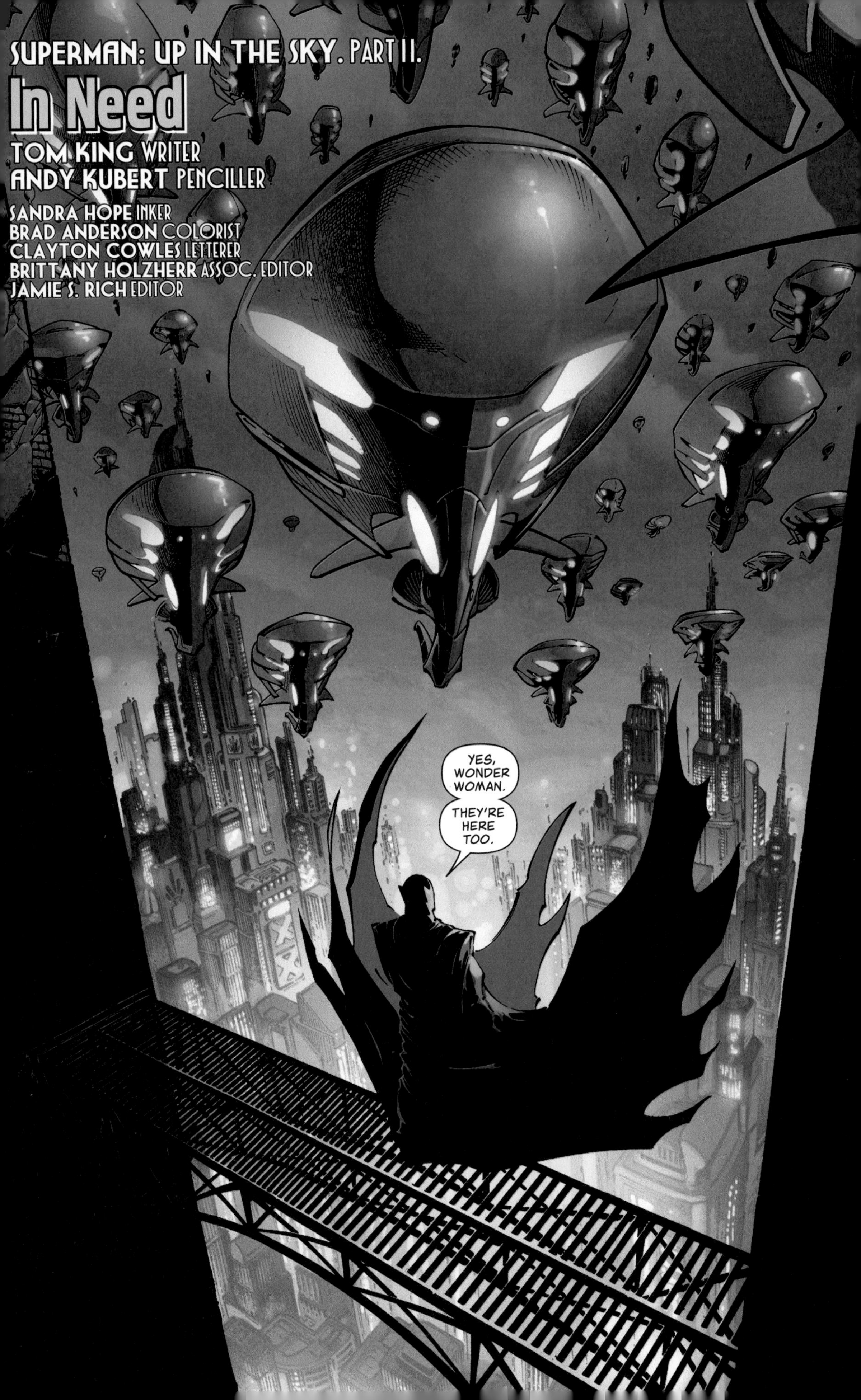
SUPERMAN: UP IN THE SKY. PART II.
In Need
TOM KING WRITER
ANDY KUBERT PENCILLER
SANDRA HOPE INKER
BRAD ANDERSON COLORIST
CLAYTON COWLES LETTERER
BRITTANY HOLZHERR ASSOC. EDITOR
JAMIE S. RICH EDITOR
YES, WONDER WOMAN.
THEY'RE HERE TOO.

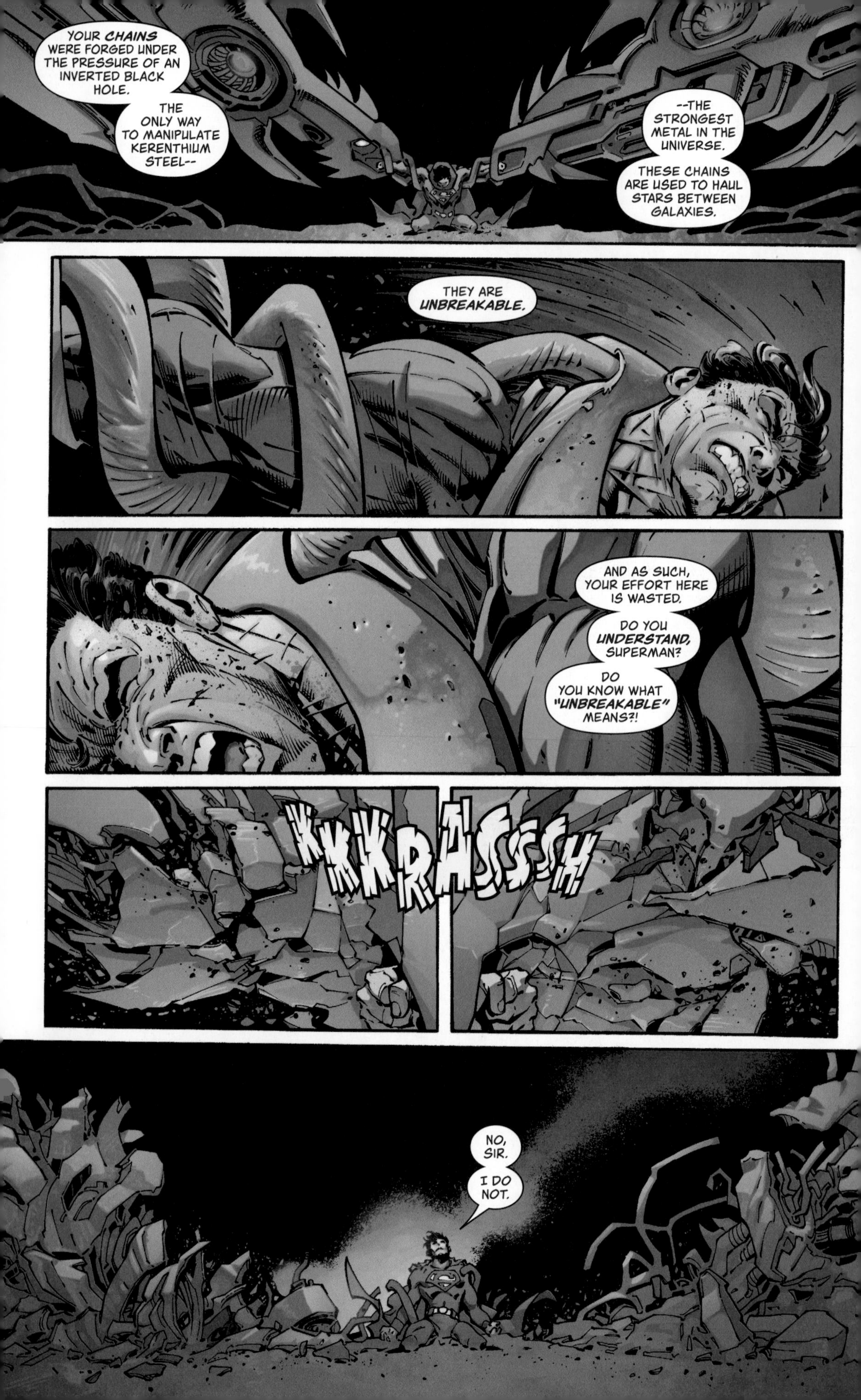
YOUR CHAINS WERE FORGED UNDER THE PRESSURE OF AN INVERTED BLACK HOLE.
THE ONLY WAY TO MANIPULATE KERENTHIUM STEEL--
--THE STRONGEST METAL IN THE UNIVERSE.
THESE CHAINS ARE USED TO HAUL STARS BETWEEN GALAXIES.
THEY ARE UNBREAKABLE.
AND AS SUCH, YOUR EFFORT HERE IS WASTED.
DO YOU UNDERSTAND, SUPERMAN?
DO YOU KNOW WHAT "UNBREAKABLE" MEANS?!
KKKRASSSSH
NO, SIR.
I DO NOT.

MADAGASCAR.

I'VE BEEN FIGHTING FOR *HOURS*--THERE SEEMS TO BE NO END TO THESE THINGS.

THEY'RE *POURING* OUT OF THE SHIPS. WE'RE *DROWNING* IN THEM.

AUSTRALIA.

THEY APPEAR TO BE *ADAPTING*. MY RANNIAN GUN WAS AT FIRST EFFECTIVE.

NOW I'M HAVING...

THEY'RE GOING TO KILL ME.

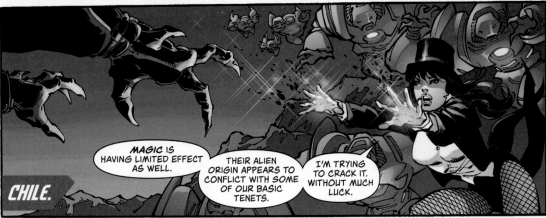

MAGIC IS HAVING LIMITED EFFECT AS WELL.

THEIR ALIEN ORIGIN APPEARS TO CONFLICT WITH SOME OF OUR BASIC TENETS.

I'M TRYING TO CRACK IT. WITHOUT MUCH LUCK.

CHILE.

ALL SEVEN SEAS ARE REPORTING!

THEY ARE EVERYWHERE!

THE INDIAN OCEAN.

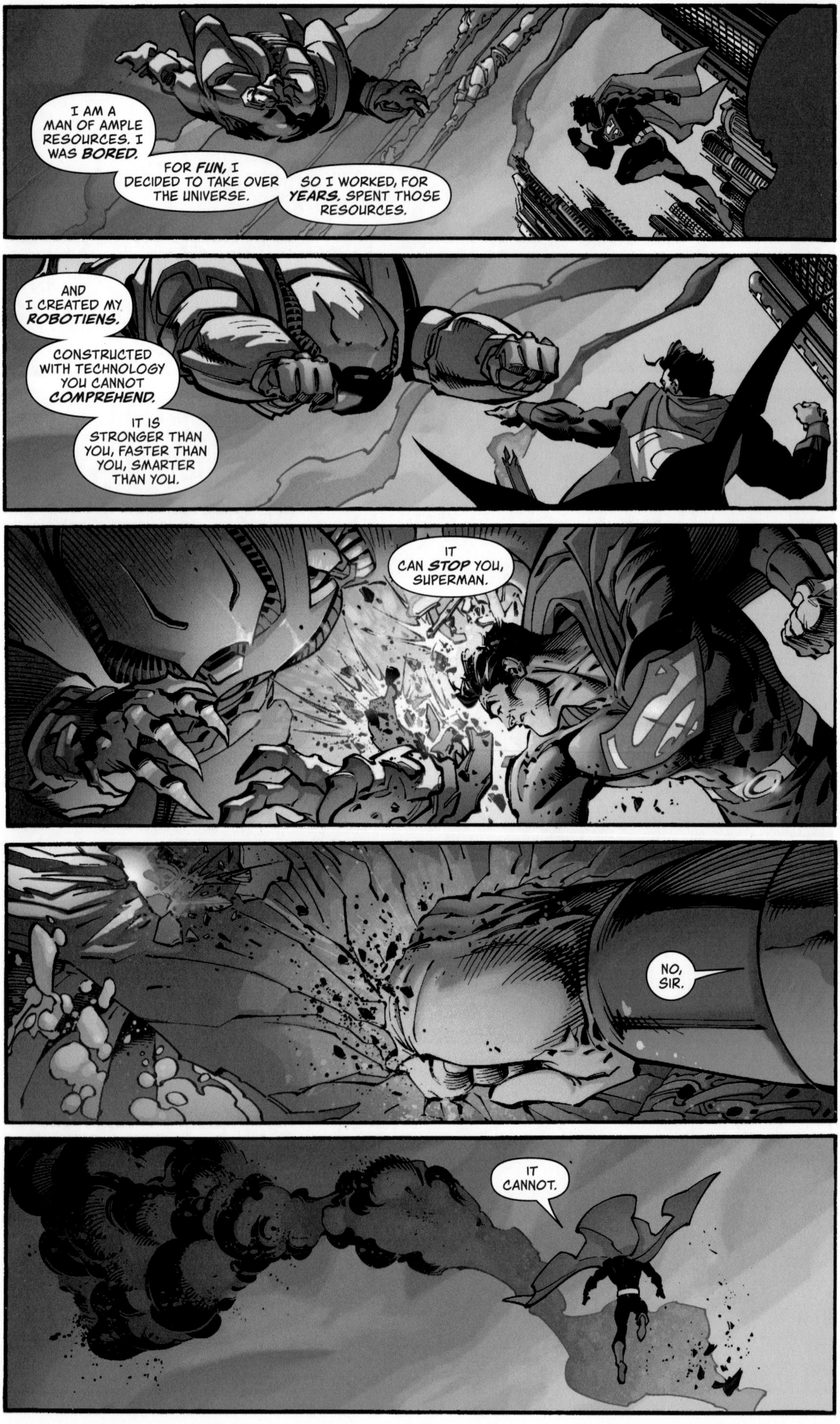
I AM A MAN OF AMPLE RESOURCES. I WAS BORED.
FOR FUN, I DECIDED TO TAKE OVER THE UNIVERSE.
SO I WORKED, FOR YEARS. SPENT THOSE RESOURCES.
AND I CREATED MY ROBOTIENS.
CONSTRUCTED WITH TECHNOLOGY YOU CANNOT COMPREHEND.
IT IS STRONGER THAN YOU, FASTER THAN YOU, SMARTER THAN YOU.
IT CAN STOP YOU, SUPERMAN.
NO, SIR.
IT CANNOT.

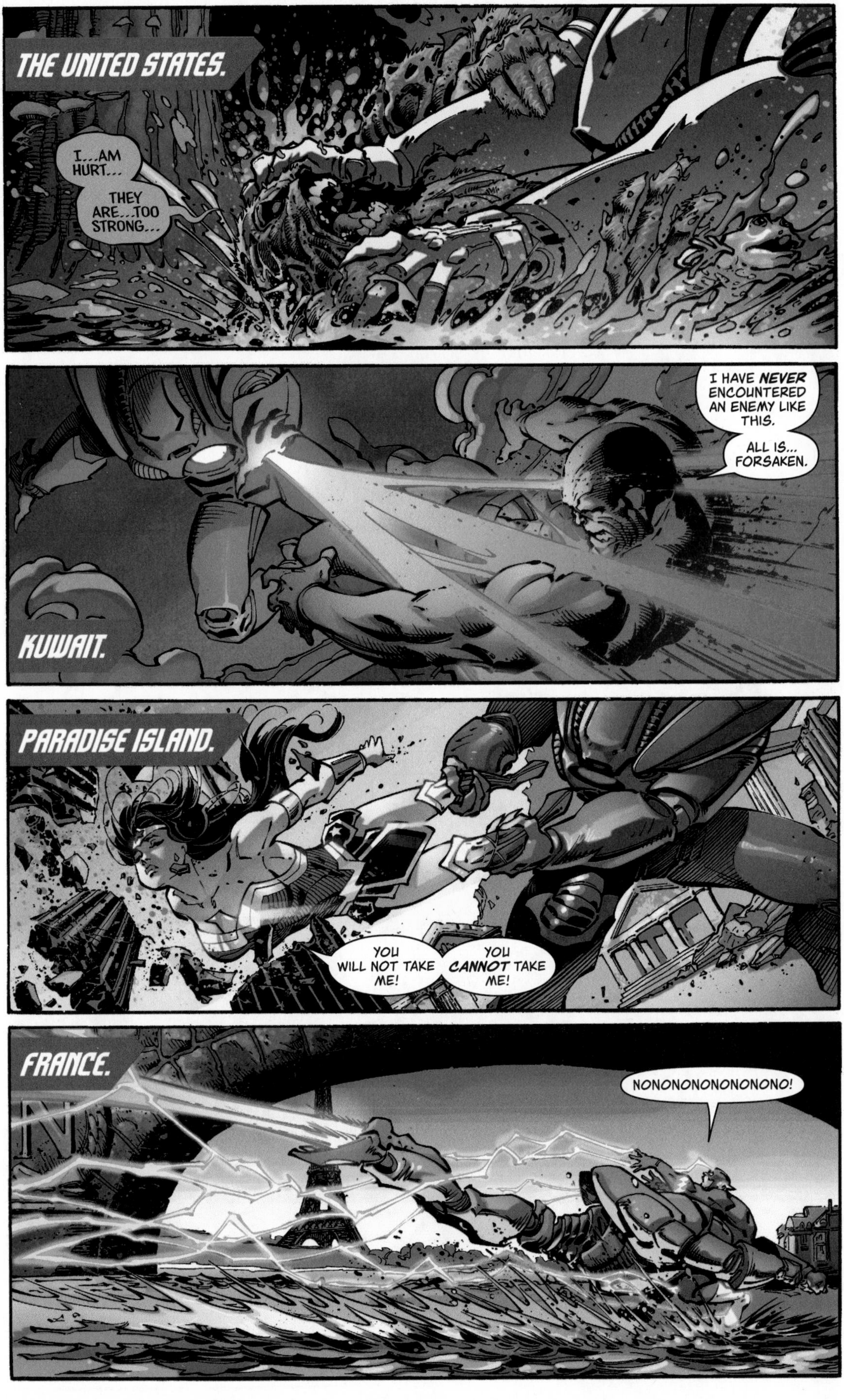
THE UNITED STATES.
I...AM HURT...
THEY ARE...TOO STRONG...
I HAVE NEVER ENCOUNTERED AN ENEMY LIKE THIS.
ALL IS... FORSAKEN.
KUWAIT.
PARADISE ISLAND.
YOU WILL NOT TAKE ME!
YOU CANNOT TAKE ME!
FRANCE.
NONONONONONONONO!

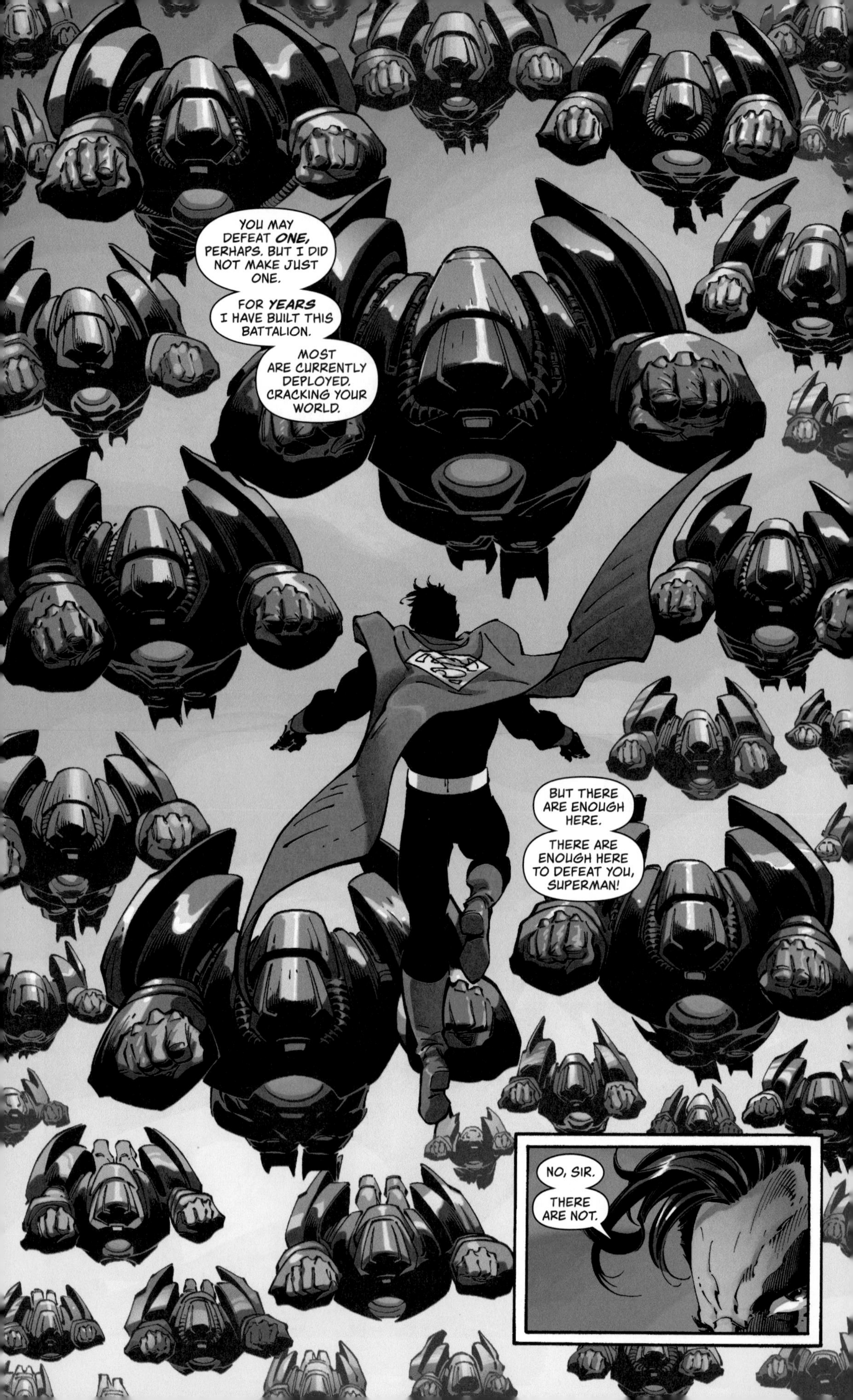
YOU MAY DEFEAT ONE, PERHAPS. BUT I DID NOT MAKE JUST ONE.
FOR YEARS I HAVE BUILT THIS BATTALION.
MOST ARE CURRENTLY DEPLOYED. CRACKING YOUR WORLD.
BUT THERE ARE ENOUGH HERE.
THERE ARE ENOUGH HERE TO DEFEAT YOU, SUPERMAN!
NO, SIR.
THERE ARE NOT.

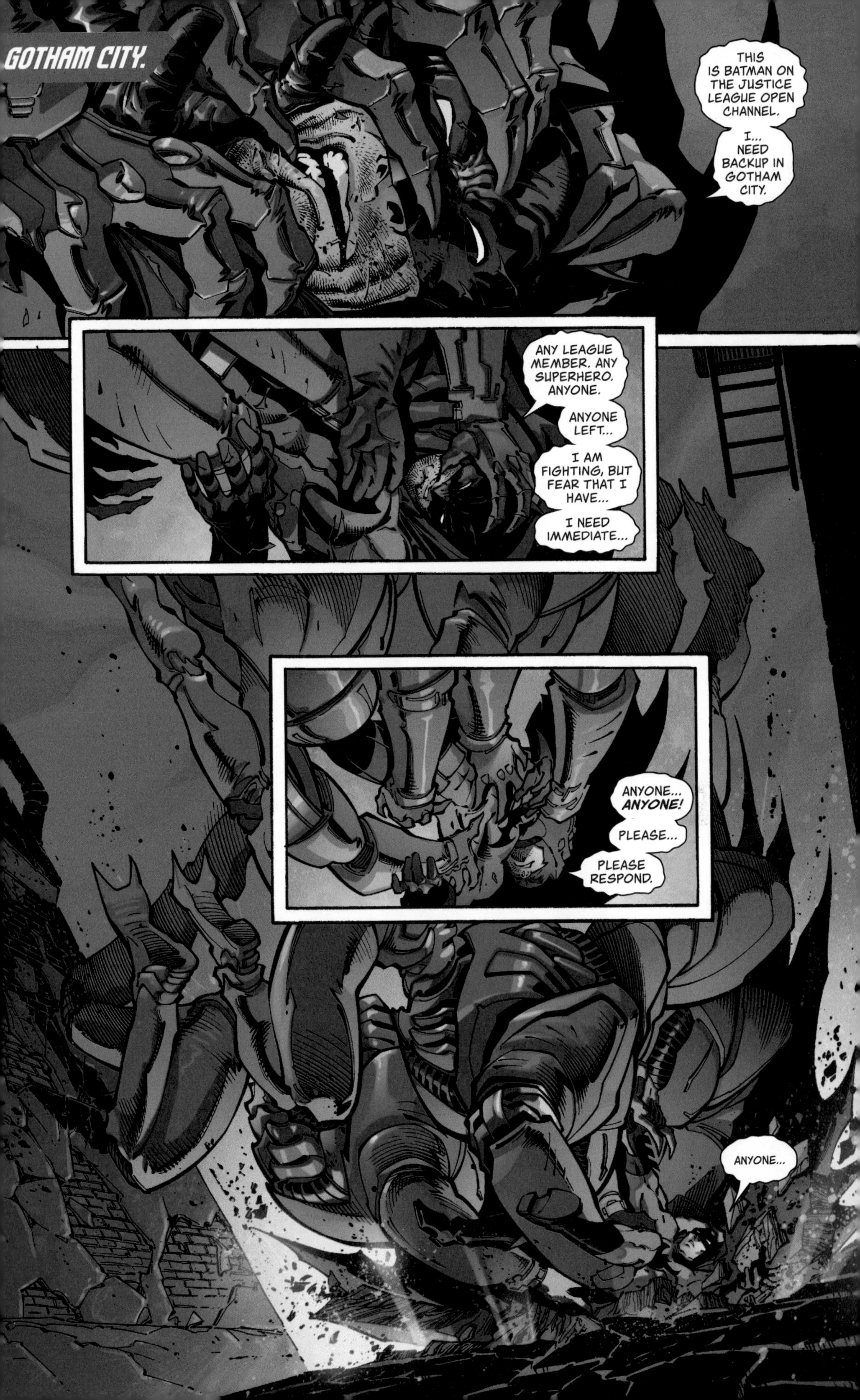
GOTHAM CITY.
THIS IS BATMAN ON THE JUSTICE LEAGUE OPEN CHANNEL.
I... NEED BACKUP IN GOTHAM CITY.
ANY LEAGUE MEMBER. ANY SUPERHERO. ANYONE.
ANYONE LEFT...
I AM FIGHTING, BUT FEAR THAT I HAVE...
I NEED IMMEDIATE...
ANYONE... *ANYONE!*
PLEASE...
PLEASE RESPOND.
ANYONE...

DO YOU KNOW WHAT IS HAPPENING *NOW* AS YOU *WASTE* YOUR TIME HERE?

THE SUFFERING AND *MISERY* YOUR PLANET IS ENDURING?

YOUR HOME IS IN ASHES. YOUR HOME IS *DEAD.*

I KNOW THAT YOUR WORLD IS THE DEFENDER OF WORLDS.

SO THERE I STRIKE FIRST. THERE I STRIKE *HARDEST.*

THIS CRISIS WILL NOT BE SOLVED BY EARTH.

I WILL INSTEAD *CONSUME* IT.

YOU ARE LIKE THEM. I *KNOW.*

DESPITE YOUR POWERS AND YOUR *FIGHT.*

UNDERNEATH YOU *ARE* THEM.

AND LIKE *ALL* OF THEM.

YOU WILL FALL!

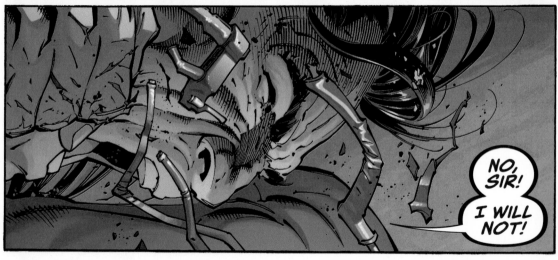

NO, SIR!

I WILL NOT!

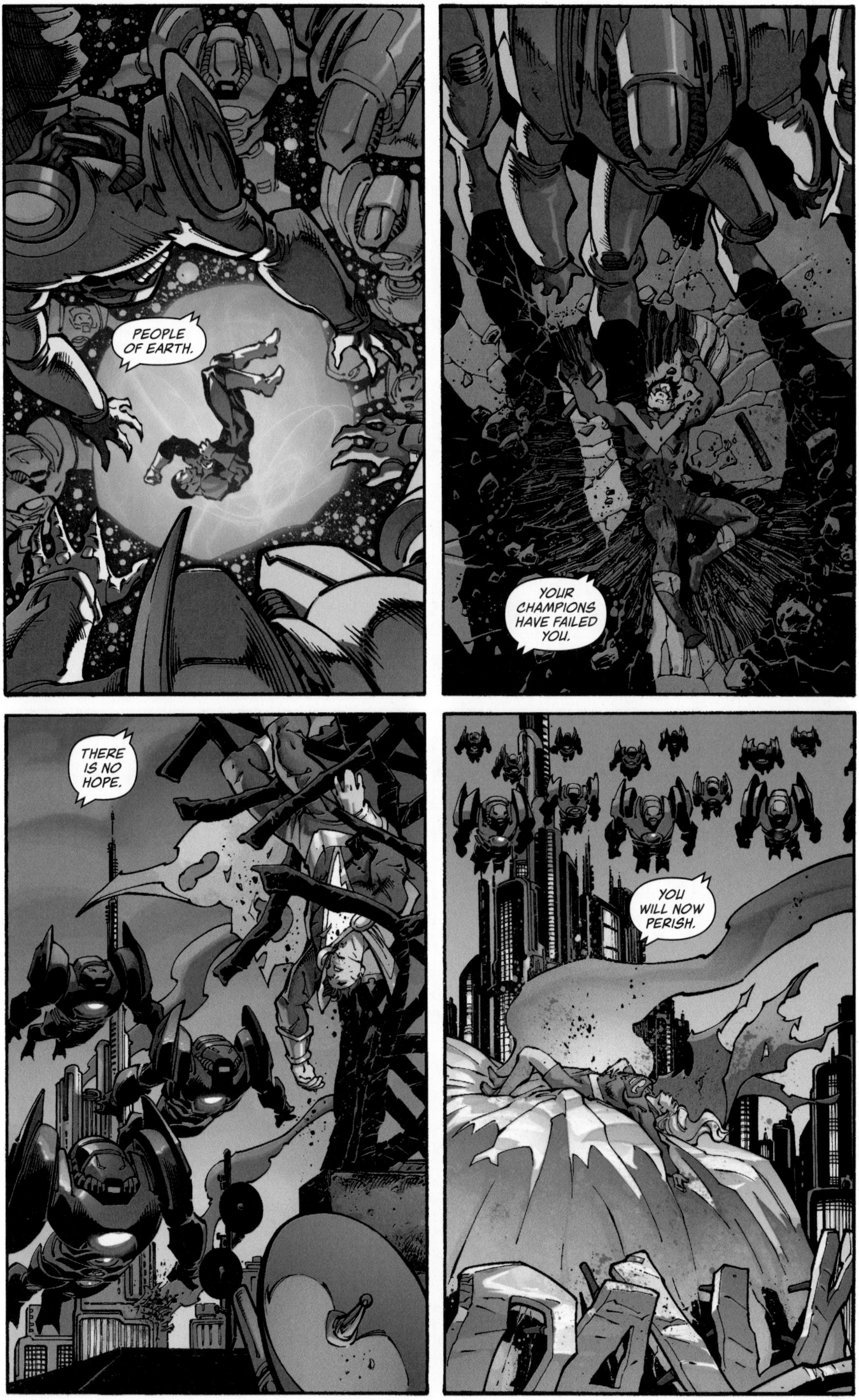
PEOPLE OF EARTH.
YOUR CHAMPIONS HAVE FAILED YOU.
THERE IS NO HOPE.
YOU WILL NOW PERISH.

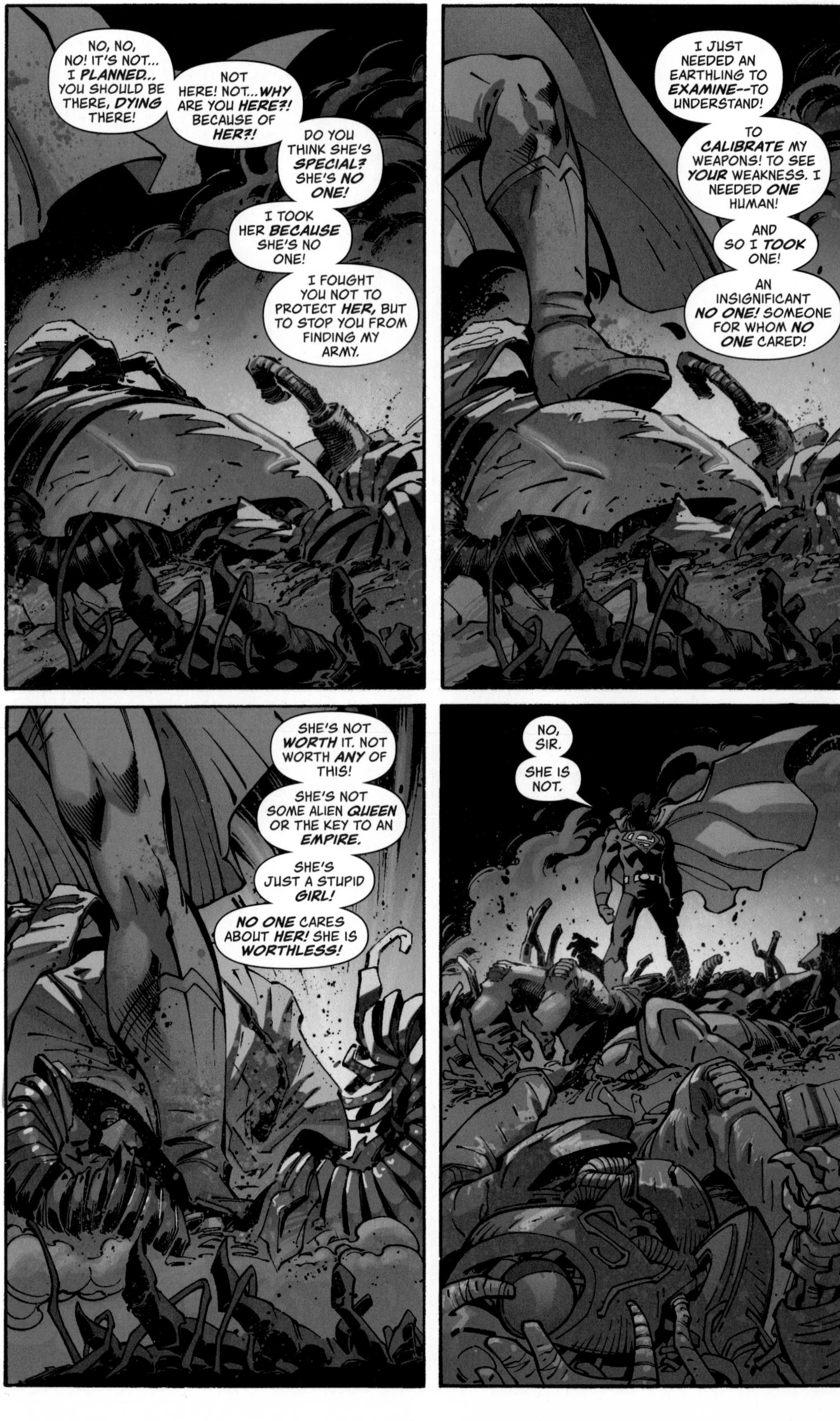
NO, NO, NO! IT'S NOT... I PLANNED... YOU SHOULD BE THERE, DYING THERE!
NOT HERE! NOT...WHY ARE YOU HERE?! BECAUSE OF HER?!
DO YOU THINK SHE'S SPECIAL? SHE'S NO ONE!
I TOOK HER BECAUSE SHE'S NO ONE!
I FOUGHT YOU NOT TO PROTECT HER, BUT TO STOP YOU FROM FINDING MY ARMY.
I JUST NEEDED AN EARTHLING TO EXAMINE--TO UNDERSTAND!
TO CALIBRATE MY WEAPONS! TO SEE YOUR WEAKNESS. I NEEDED ONE HUMAN!
AND SO I TOOK ONE!
AN INSIGNIFICANT NO ONE! SOMEONE FOR WHOM NO ONE CARED!
SHE'S NOT WORTH IT. NOT WORTH ANY OF THIS!
SHE'S NOT SOME ALIEN QUEEN OR THE KEY TO AN EMPIRE.
SHE'S JUST A STUPID GIRL!
NO ONE CARES ABOUT HER! SHE IS WORTHLESS!
NO, SIR.
SHE IS NOT.

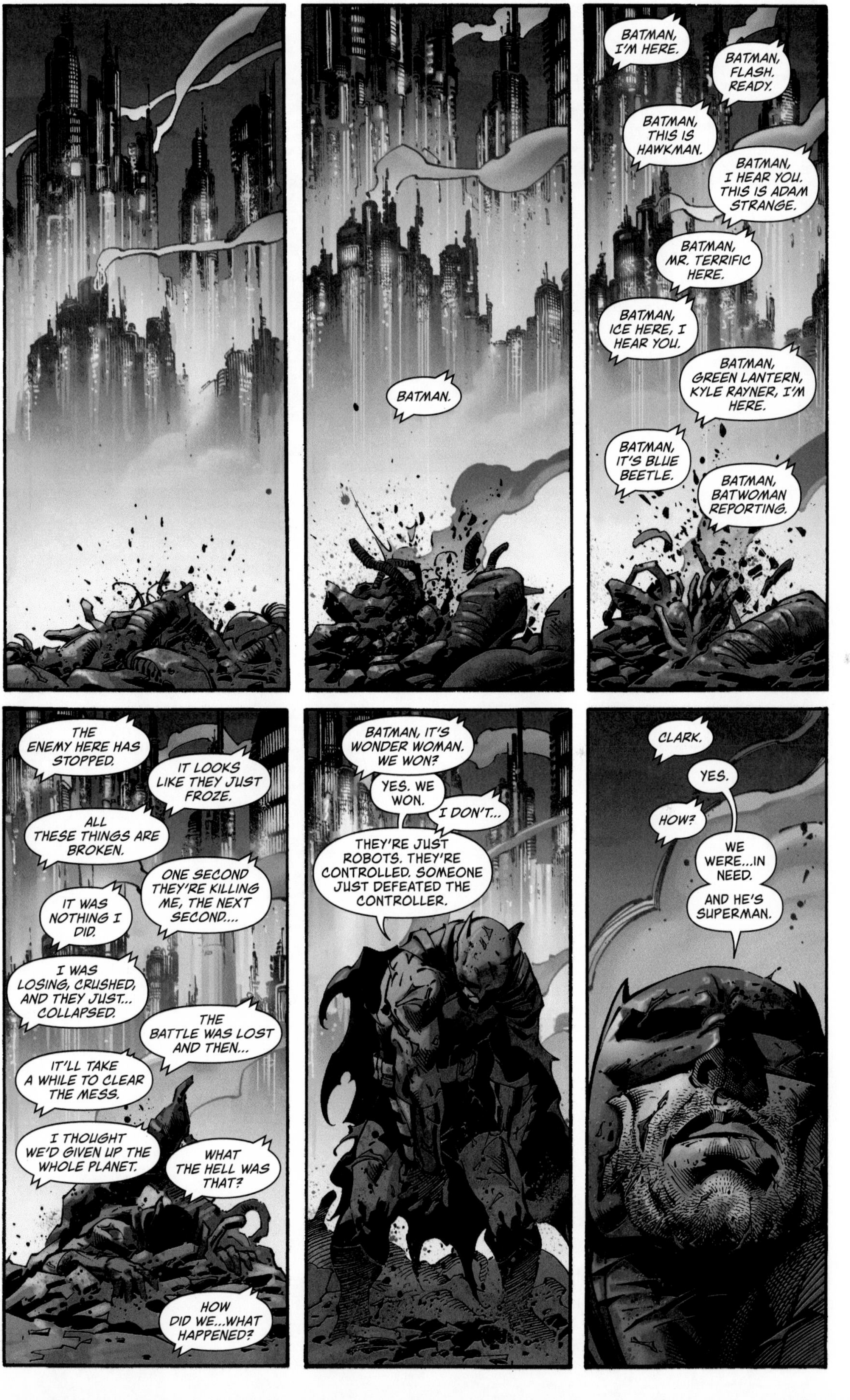
BATMAN.
BATMAN, I'M HERE.
BATMAN, FLASH. READY.
BATMAN, THIS IS HAWKMAN.
BATMAN, I HEAR YOU. THIS IS ADAM STRANGE.
BATMAN, MR. TERRIFIC HERE.
BATMAN, ICE HERE, I HEAR YOU.
BATMAN, GREEN LANTERN, KYLE RAYNER, I'M HERE.
BATMAN, IT'S BLUE BEETLE.
BATMAN, BATWOMAN REPORTING.
THE ENEMY HERE HAS STOPPED.
IT LOOKS LIKE THEY JUST FROZE.
ALL THESE THINGS ARE BROKEN.
ONE SECOND THEY'RE KILLING ME, THE NEXT SECOND....
IT WAS NOTHING I DID.
I WAS LOSING, CRUSHED, AND THEY JUST... COLLAPSED.
THE BATTLE WAS LOST AND THEN...
IT'LL TAKE A WHILE TO CLEAR THE MESS.
I THOUGHT WE'D GIVEN UP THE WHOLE PLANET.
WHAT THE HELL WAS THAT?
HOW DID WE...WHAT HAPPENED?
BATMAN, IT'S WONDER WOMAN. WE WON?
YES. WE WON.
I DON'T...
THEY'RE JUST ROBOTS. THEY'RE CONTROLLED. SOMEONE JUST DEFEATED THE CONTROLLER.
CLARK.
YES.
HOW?
WE WERE...IN NEED.
AND HE'S SUPERMAN.

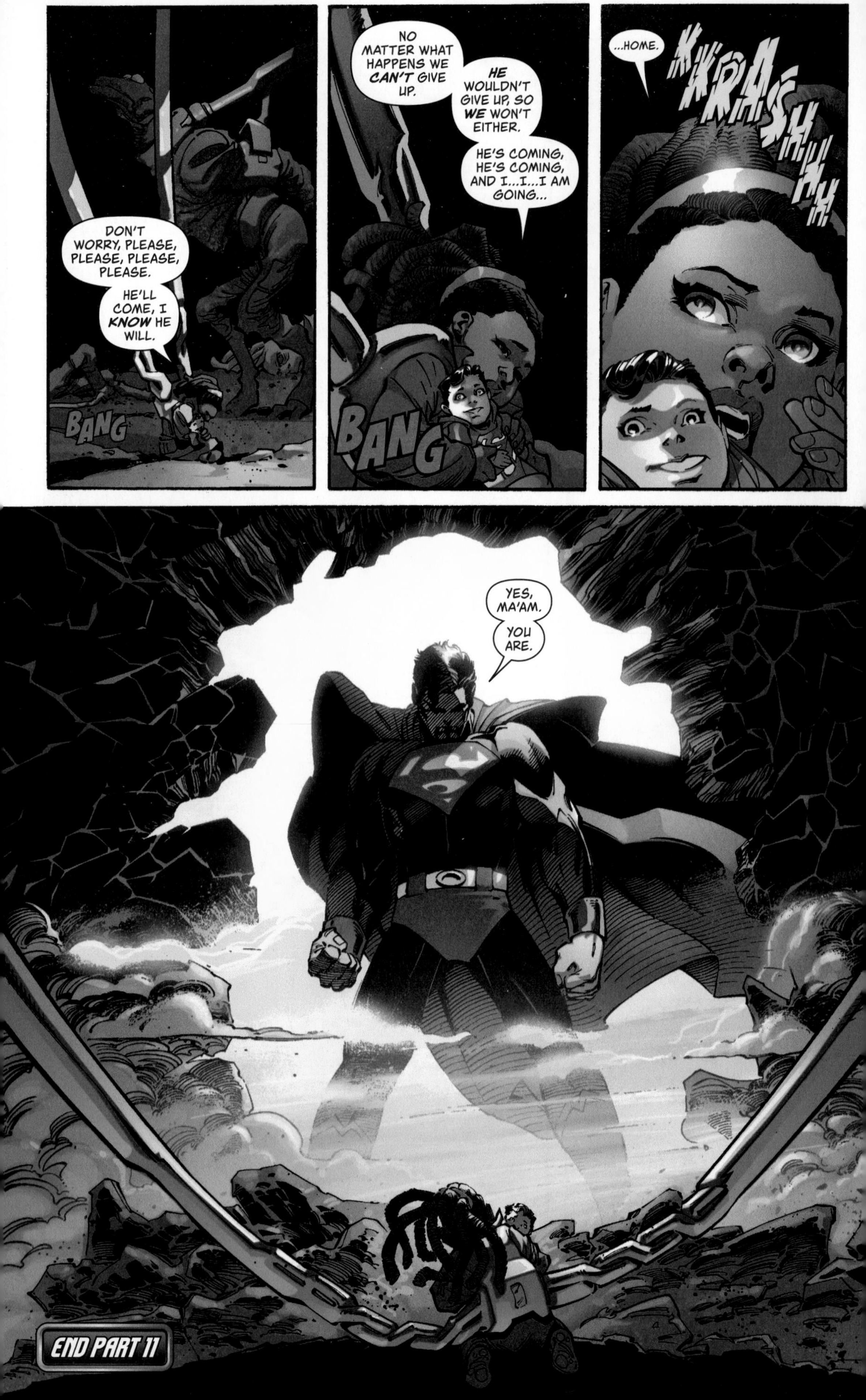
DON'T WORRY, PLEASE, PLEASE, PLEASE, PLEASE.
HE'LL COME, I KNOW HE WILL.
BANG
NO MATTER WHAT HAPPENS WE CAN'T GIVE UP.
HE WOULDN'T GIVE UP, SO WE WON'T EITHER.
HE'S COMING, HE'S COMING, AND I...I...I AM GOING...
BANG
...HOME.
KKRASHHH
YES, MA'AM.
YOU ARE.
END PART 11

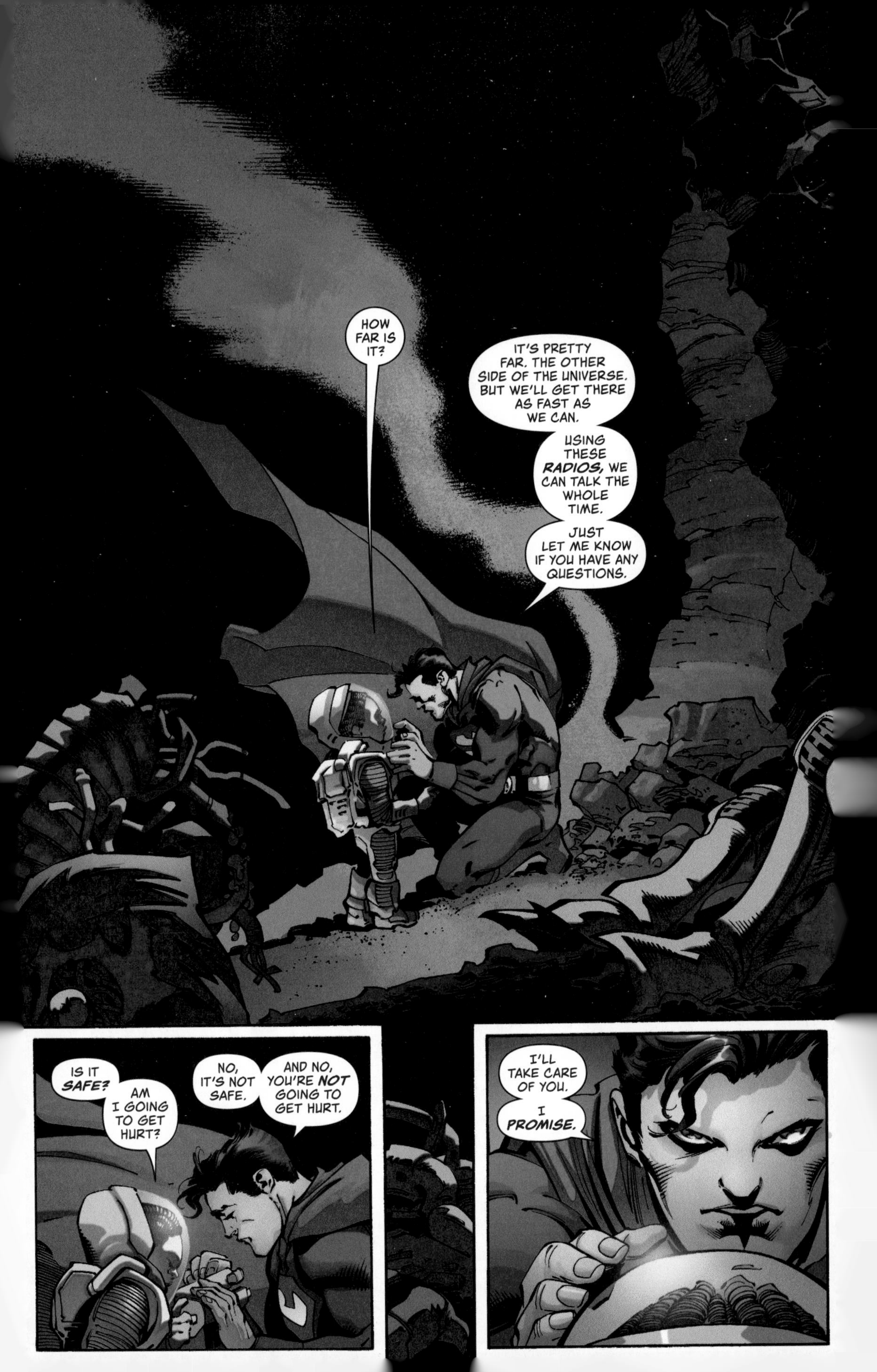
HOW FAR IS IT?
IT'S PRETTY FAR. THE OTHER SIDE OF THE UNIVERSE. BUT WE'LL GET THERE AS FAST AS WE CAN.
USING THESE RADIOS, WE CAN TALK THE WHOLE TIME.
JUST LET ME KNOW IF YOU HAVE ANY QUESTIONS.
IS IT SAFE?
AM I GOING TO GET HURT?
NO, IT'S NOT SAFE.
AND NO, YOU'RE NOT GOING TO GET HURT.
I'LL TAKE CARE OF YOU.
I PROMISE.

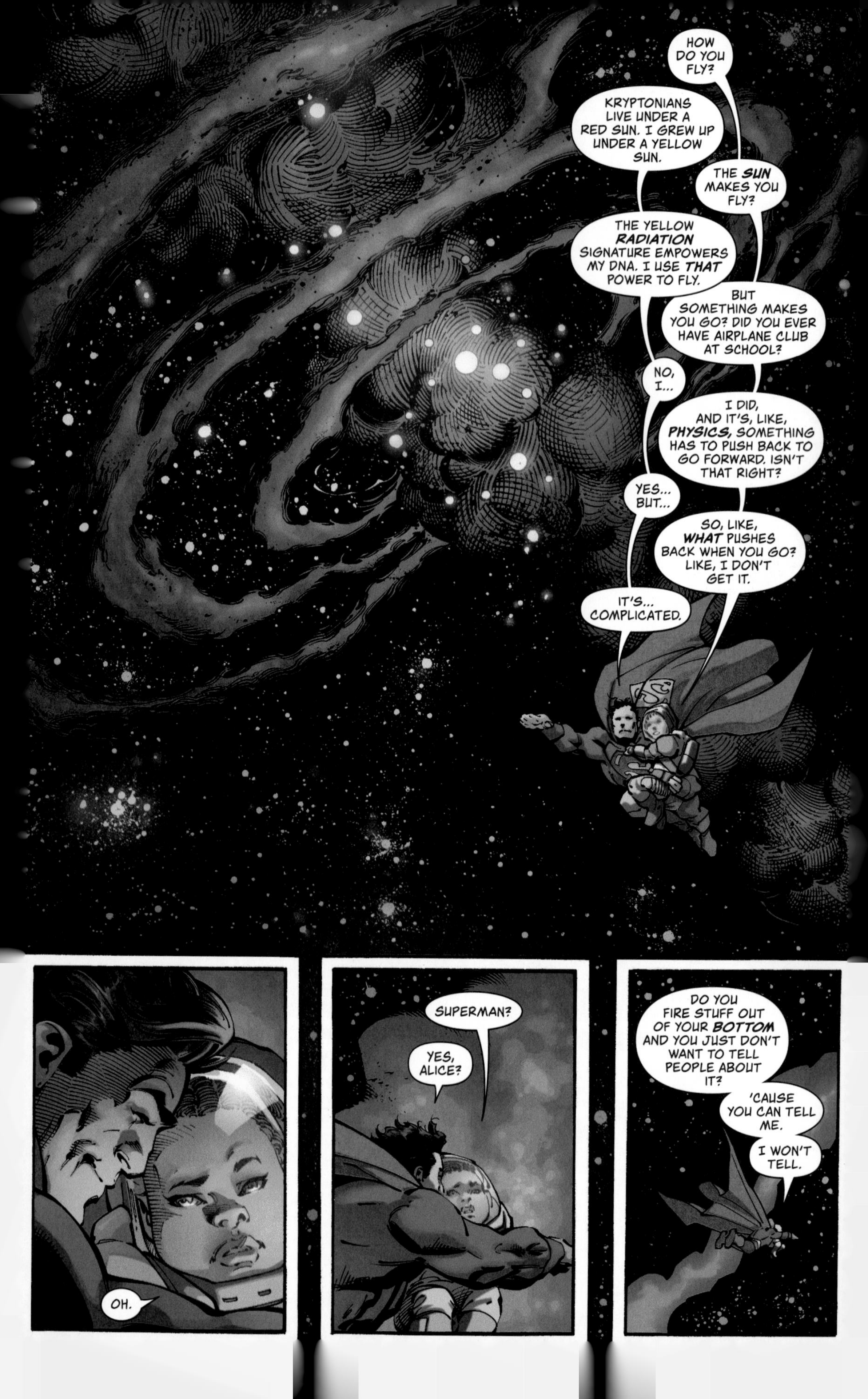
HOW DO YOU FLY?
KRYPTONIANS LIVE UNDER A RED SUN. I GREW UP UNDER A YELLOW SUN.
THE SUN MAKES YOU FLY?
THE YELLOW RADIATION SIGNATURE EMPOWERS MY DNA. I USE THAT POWER TO FLY.
BUT SOMETHING MAKES YOU GO? DID YOU EVER HAVE AIRPLANE CLUB AT SCHOOL?
NO, I...
I DID, AND IT'S, LIKE, PHYSICS, SOMETHING HAS TO PUSH BACK TO GO FORWARD. ISN'T THAT RIGHT?
YES... BUT...
SO, LIKE, WHAT PUSHES BACK WHEN YOU GO? LIKE, I DON'T GET IT.
IT'S... COMPLICATED.
OH.
SUPERMAN?
YES, ALICE?
DO YOU FIRE STUFF OUT OF YOUR BOTTOM AND YOU JUST DON'T WANT TO TELL PEOPLE ABOUT IT?
'CAUSE YOU CAN TELL ME.
I WON'T TELL.

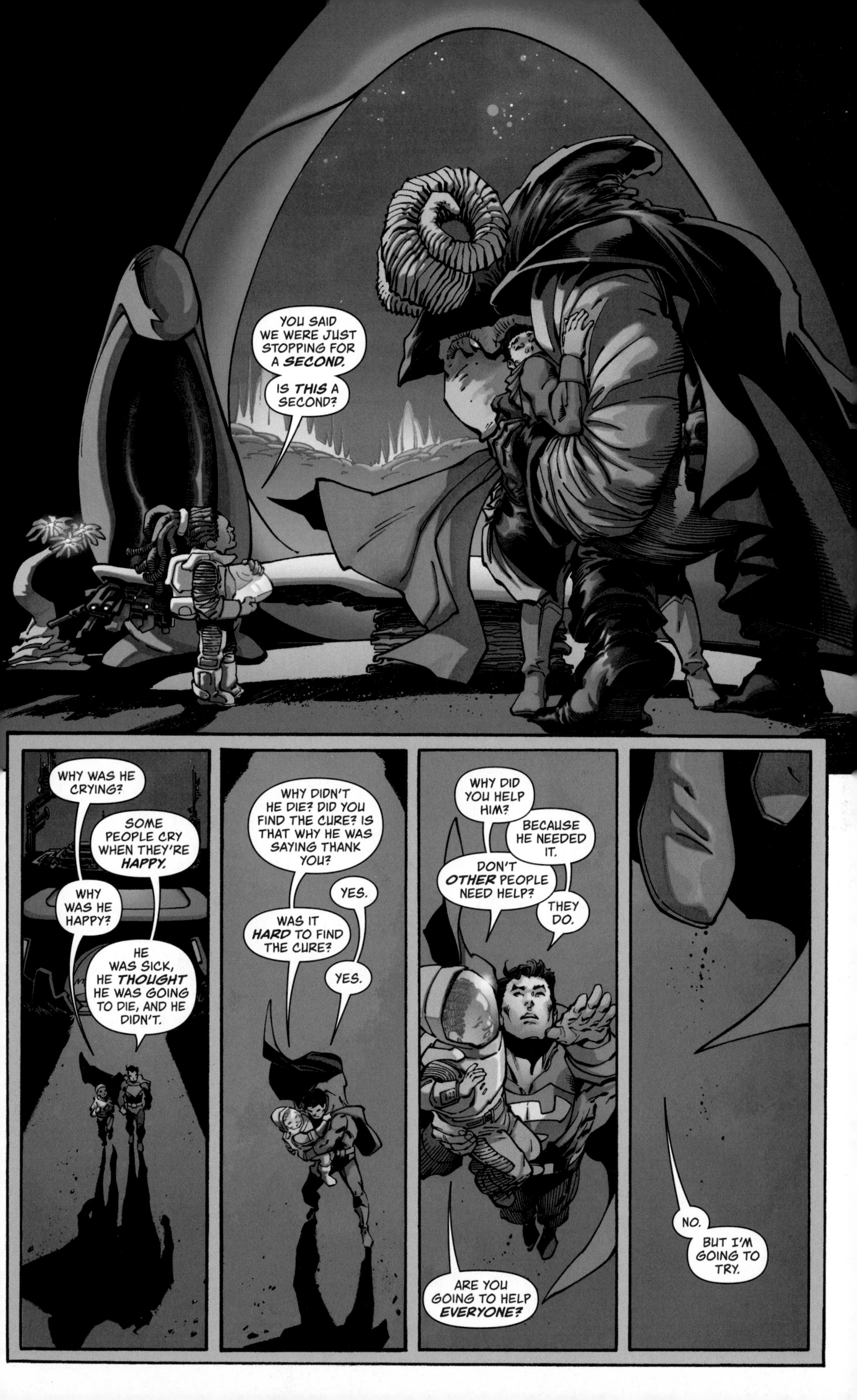
YOU SAID WE WERE JUST STOPPING FOR A SECOND.
IS THIS A SECOND?
WHY WAS HE CRYING?
SOME PEOPLE CRY WHEN THEY'RE HAPPY.
WHY WAS HE HAPPY?
HE WAS SICK, HE THOUGHT HE WAS GOING TO DIE, AND HE DIDN'T.
WHY DIDN'T HE DIE? DID YOU FIND THE CURE? IS THAT WHY HE WAS SAYING THANK YOU?
YES.
WAS IT HARD TO FIND THE CURE?
YES.
WHY DID YOU HELP HIM?
BECAUSE HE NEEDED IT.
DON'T OTHER PEOPLE NEED HELP?
THEY DO.
ARE YOU GOING TO HELP EVERYONE?
NO.
BUT I'M GOING TO TRY.

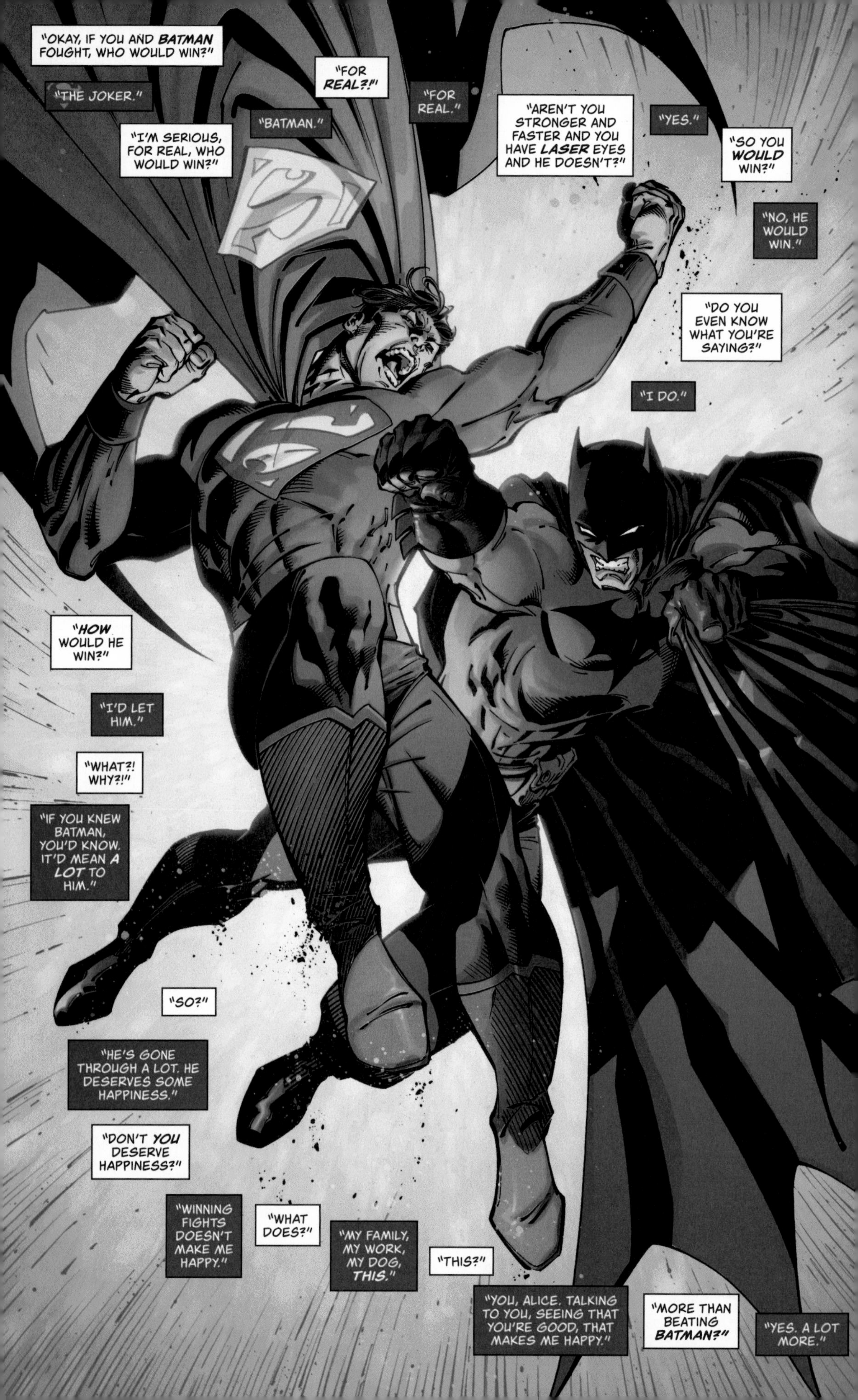
"OKAY, IF YOU AND BATMAN FOUGHT, WHO WOULD WIN?"
"THE JOKER."
"I'M SERIOUS, FOR REAL, WHO WOULD WIN?"
"BATMAN."
"FOR REAL?!"
"FOR REAL."
"AREN'T YOU STRONGER AND FASTER AND YOU HAVE LASER EYES AND HE DOESN'T?"
"YES."
"SO YOU WOULD WIN?"
"NO, HE WOULD WIN."
"DO YOU EVEN KNOW WHAT YOU'RE SAYING?"
"I DO."
"HOW WOULD HE WIN?"
"I'D LET HIM."
"WHAT?! WHY?!"
"IF YOU KNEW BATMAN, YOU'D KNOW. IT'D MEAN A LOT TO HIM."
"SO?"
"HE'S GONE THROUGH A LOT. HE DESERVES SOME HAPPINESS."
"DON'T YOU DESERVE HAPPINESS?"
"WINNING FIGHTS DOESN'T MAKE ME HAPPY."
"WHAT DOES?"
"MY FAMILY, MY WORK, MY DOG, THIS."
"THIS?"
"YOU, ALICE. TALKING TO YOU, SEEING THAT YOU'RE GOOD, THAT MAKES ME HAPPY."
"MORE THAN BEATING BATMAN?"
"YES. A LOT MORE."

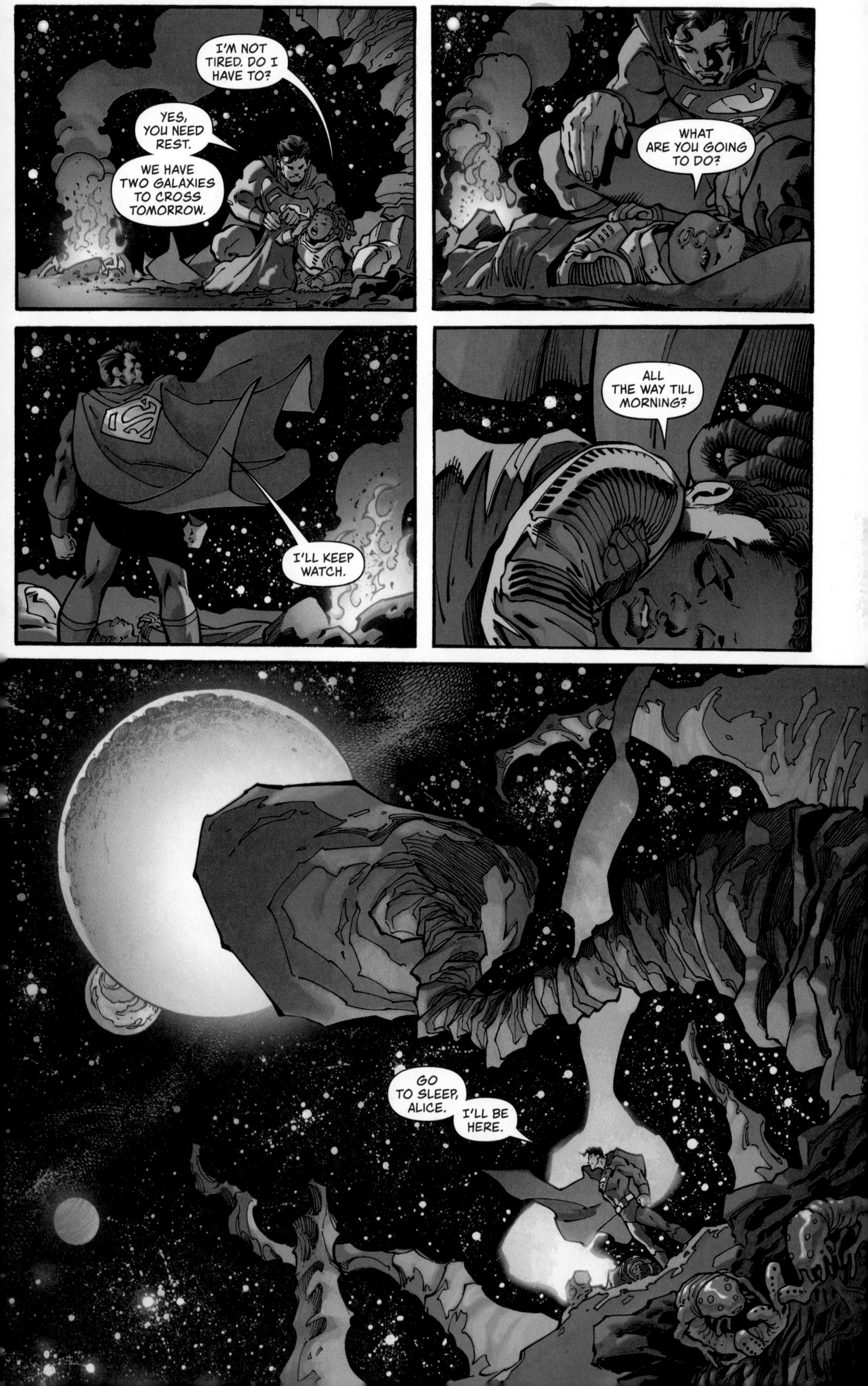

I'M NOT TIRED. DO I HAVE TO?
YES, YOU NEED REST.
WE HAVE TWO GALAXIES TO CROSS TOMORROW.
WHAT ARE YOU GOING TO DO?
I'LL KEEP WATCH.
ALL THE WAY TILL MORNING?
GO TO SLEEP, ALICE.
I'LL BE HERE.

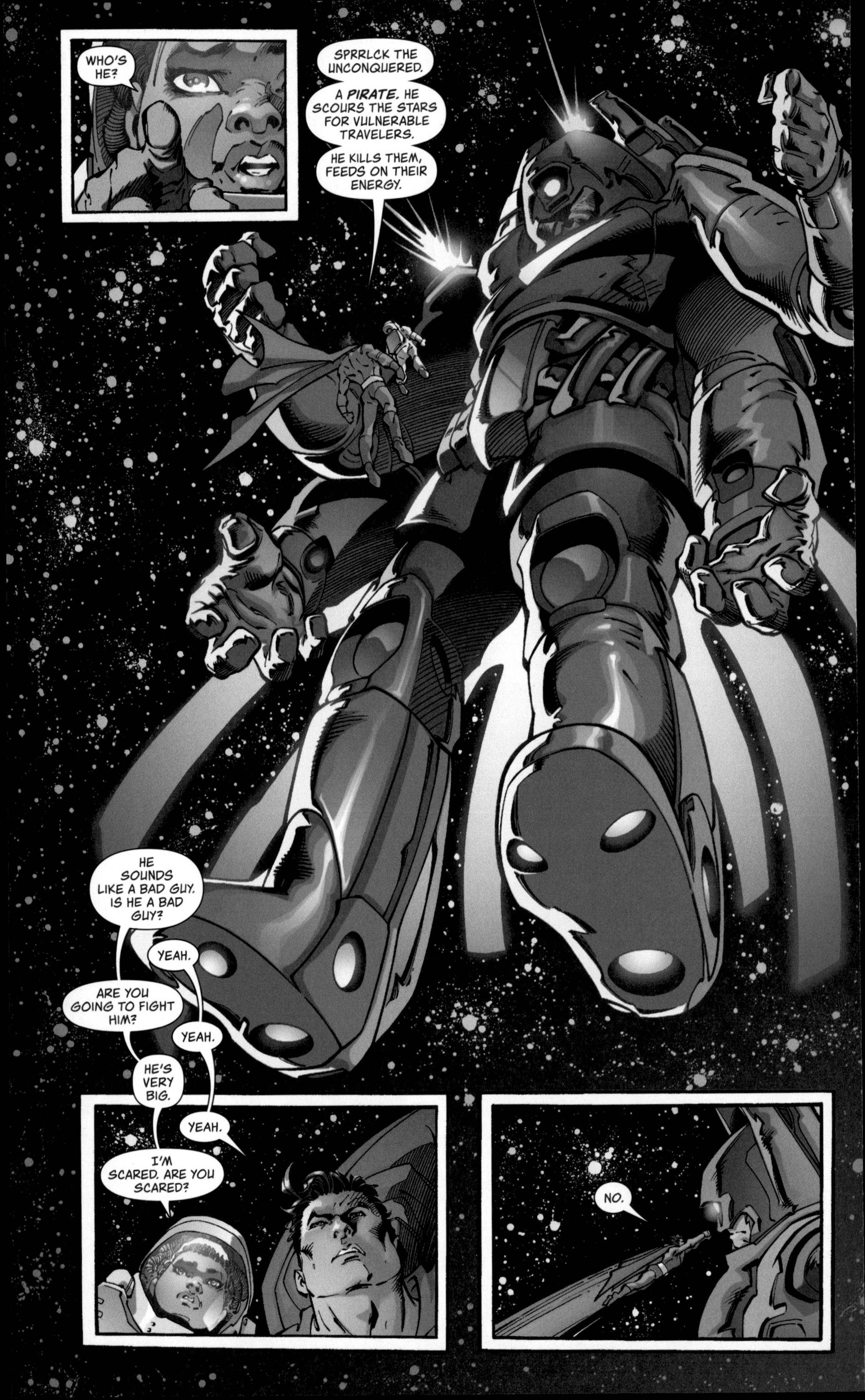
WHO'S HE?
SPRRLCK THE UNCONQUERED.
A *PIRATE.* HE SCOURS THE STARS FOR VULNERABLE TRAVELERS.
HE KILLS THEM, FEEDS ON THEIR ENERGY.
HE SOUNDS LIKE A BAD GUY. IS HE A BAD GUY?
YEAH.
ARE YOU GOING TO FIGHT HIM?
YEAH.
HE'S VERY BIG.
YEAH.
I'M SCARED. ARE YOU SCARED?
NO.

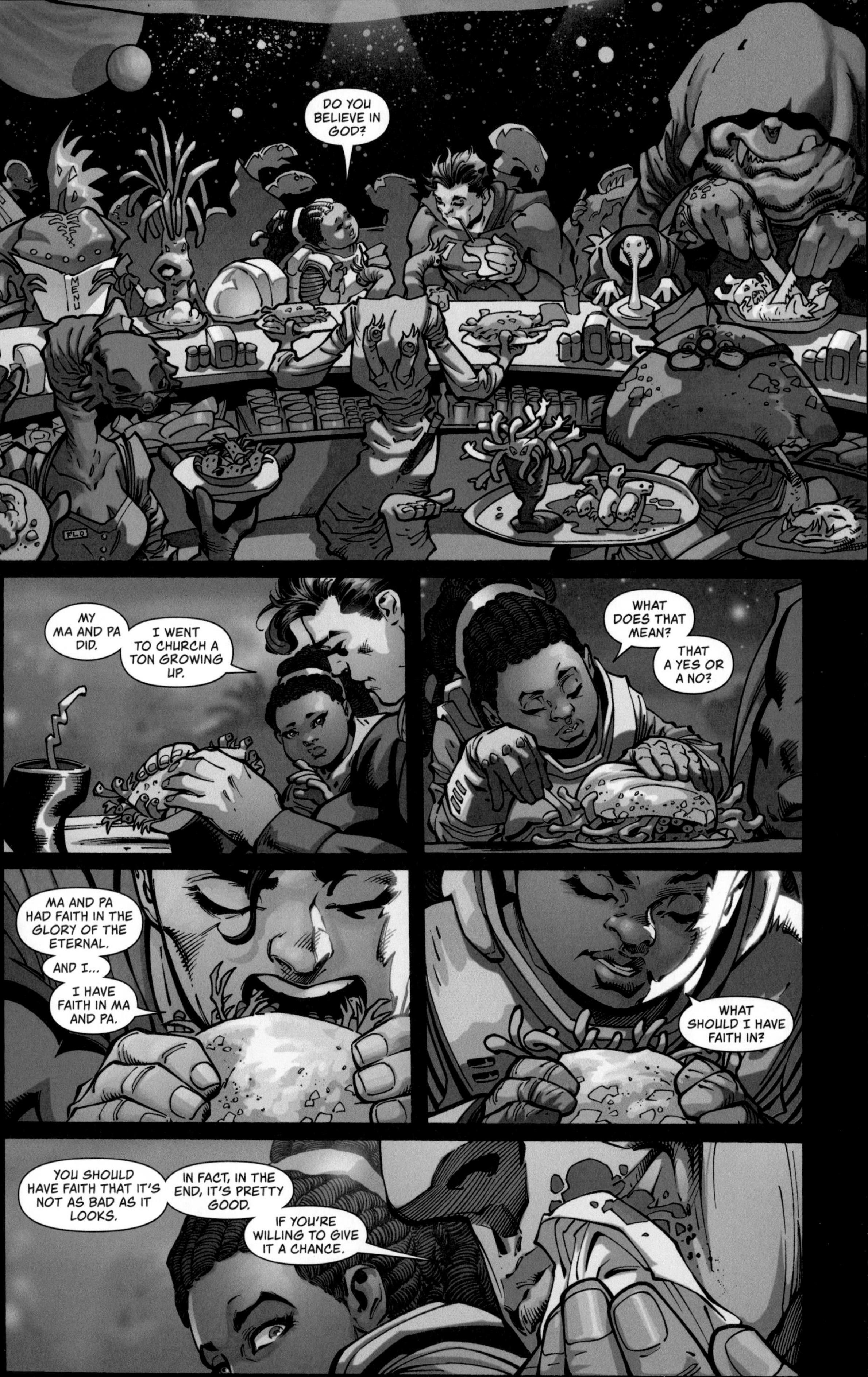
DO YOU BELIEVE IN GOD?
MENU
FLO
MY MA AND PA DID.
I WENT TO CHURCH A TON GROWING UP.
WHAT DOES THAT MEAN?
THAT A YES OR A NO?
MA AND PA HAD FAITH IN THE GLORY OF THE ETERNAL.
AND I...
I HAVE FAITH IN MA AND PA.
WHAT SHOULD I HAVE FAITH IN?
YOU SHOULD HAVE FAITH THAT IT'S NOT AS BAD AS IT LOOKS.
IN FACT, IN THE END, IT'S PRETTY GOOD.
IF YOU'RE WILLING TO GIVE IT A CHANCE.

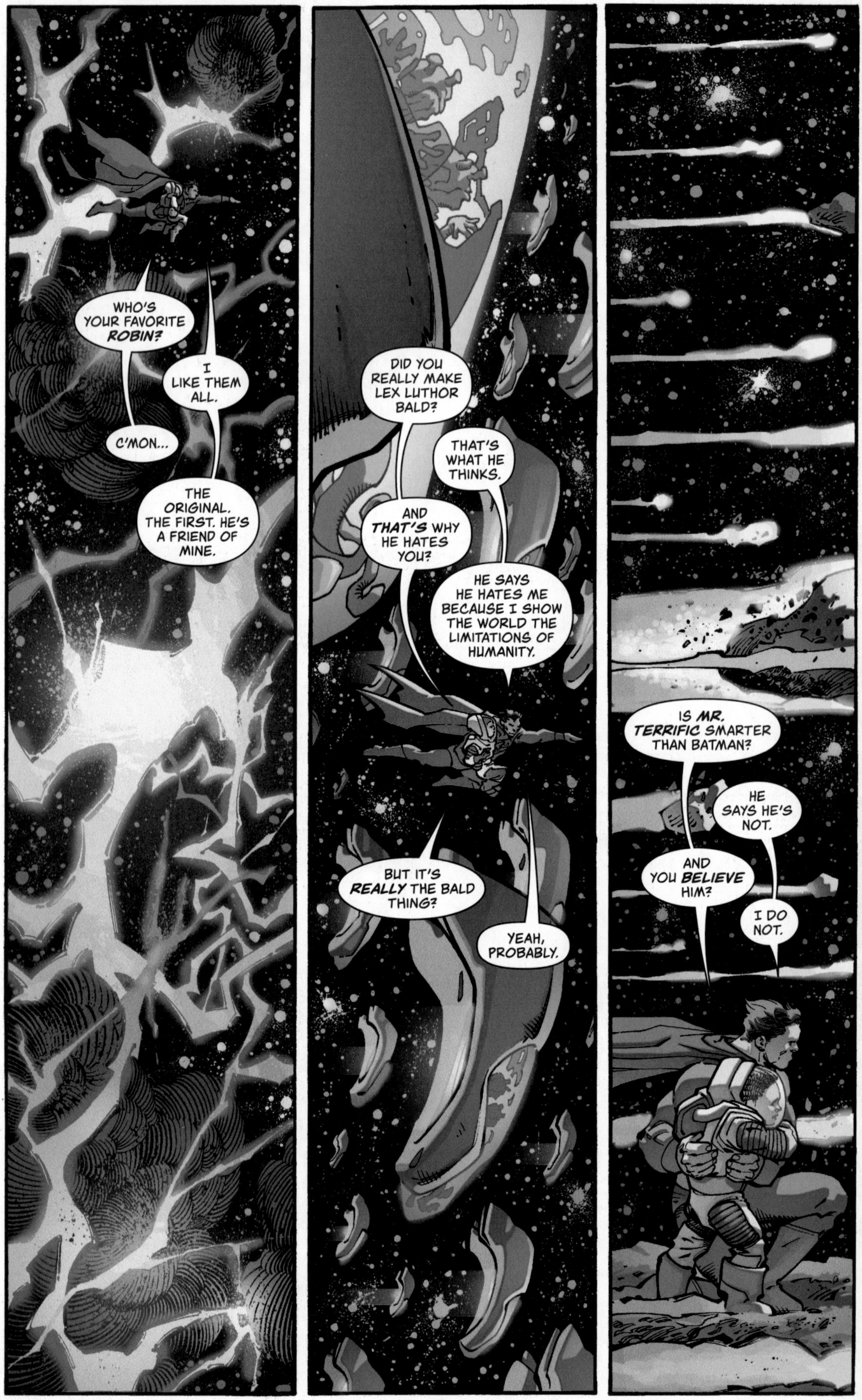
WHO'S YOUR FAVORITE ROBIN?
I LIKE THEM ALL.
C'MON...
THE ORIGINAL. THE FIRST. HE'S A FRIEND OF MINE.
DID YOU REALLY MAKE LEX LUTHOR BALD?
THAT'S WHAT HE THINKS.
AND THAT'S WHY HE HATES YOU?
HE SAYS HE HATES ME BECAUSE I SHOW THE WORLD THE LIMITATIONS OF HUMANITY.
BUT IT'S REALLY THE BALD THING?
YEAH, PROBABLY.
IS MR. TERRIFIC SMARTER THAN BATMAN?
HE SAYS HE'S NOT.
AND YOU BELIEVE HIM?
I DO NOT.

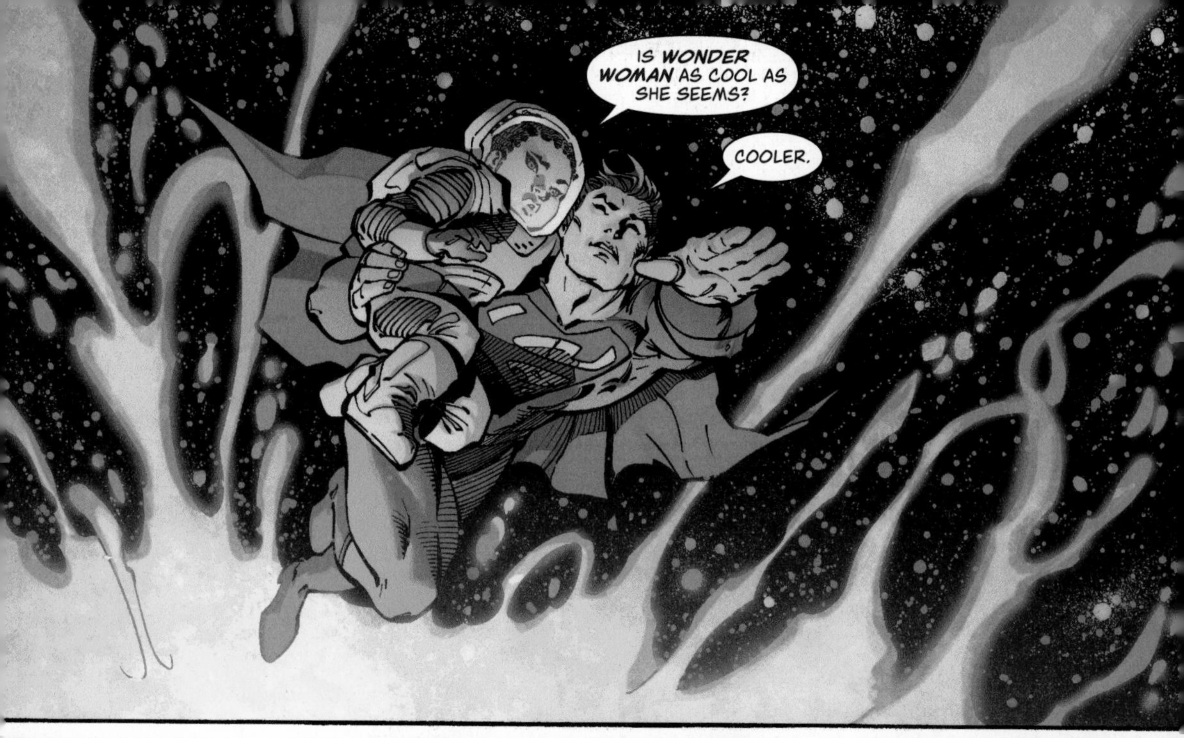
IS WONDER WOMAN AS COOL AS SHE SEEMS?
COOLER.

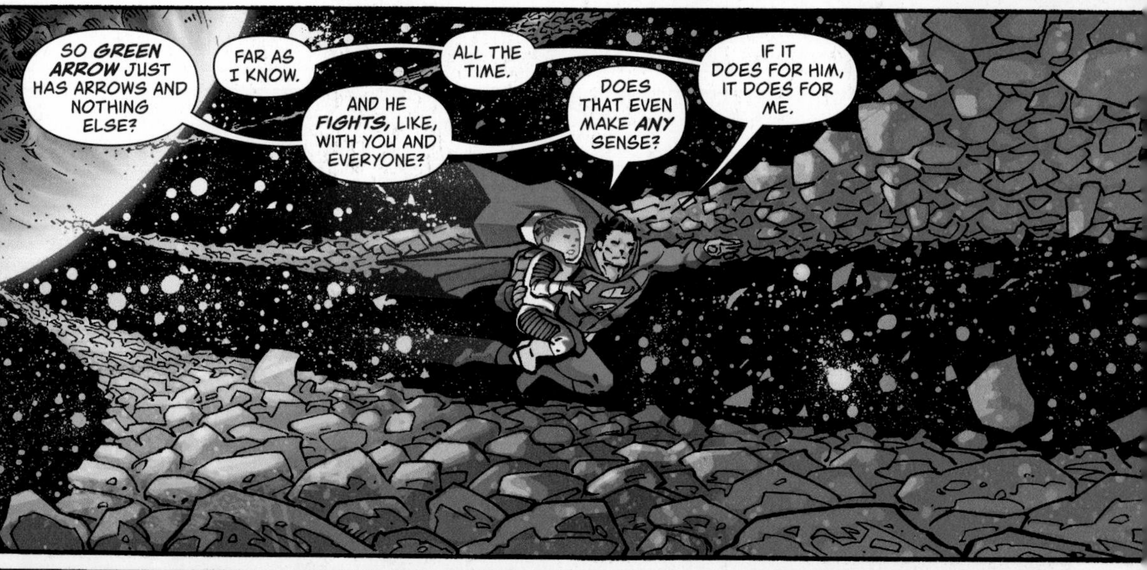
SO GREEN ARROW JUST HAS ARROWS AND NOTHING ELSE?
FAR AS I KNOW.
AND HE FIGHTS, LIKE, WITH YOU AND EVERYONE?
ALL THE TIME.
DOES THAT EVEN MAKE ANY SENSE?
IF IT DOES FOR HIM, IT DOES FOR ME.

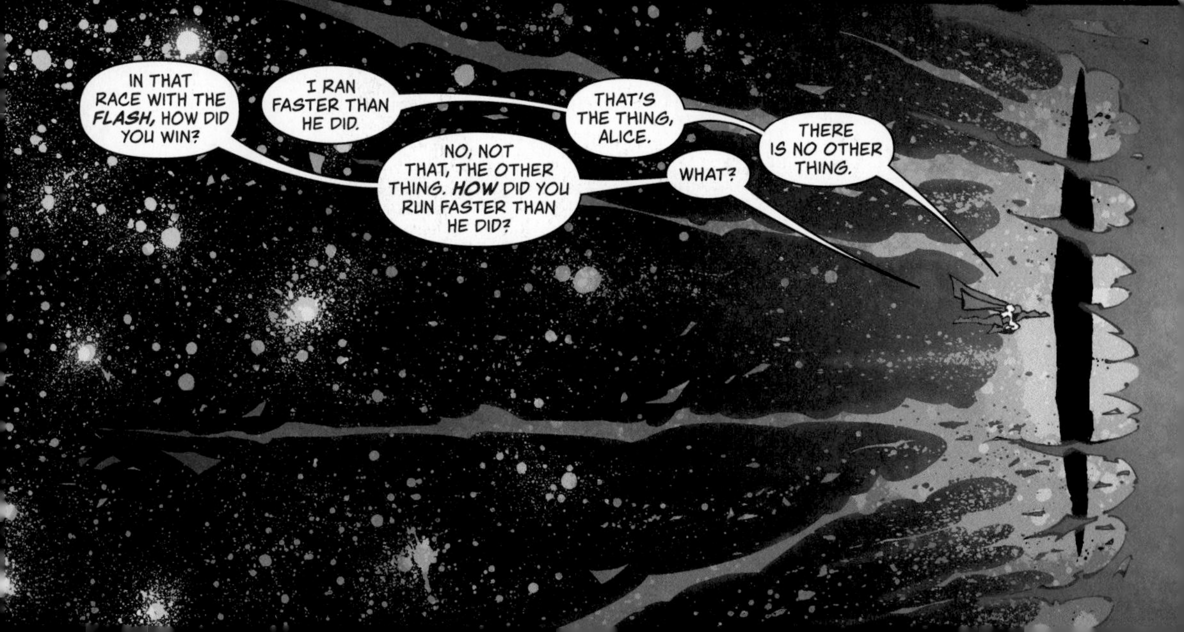
IN THAT RACE WITH THE FLASH, HOW DID YOU WIN?
I RAN FASTER THAN HE DID.
NO, NOT THAT, THE OTHER THING. HOW DID YOU RUN FASTER THAN HE DID?
WHAT?
THAT'S THE THING, ALICE.
THERE IS NO OTHER THING.

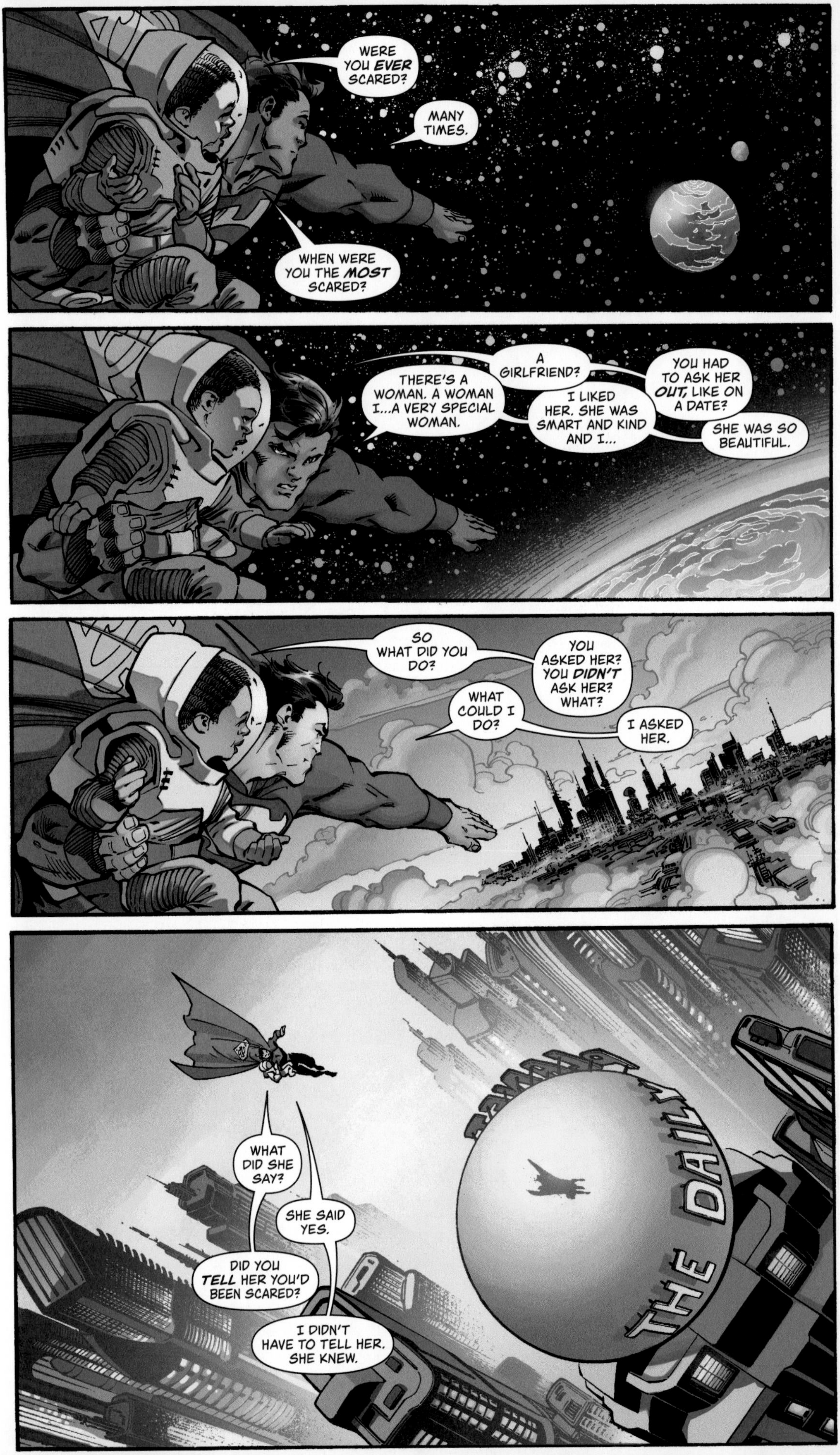
WERE YOU *EVER* SCARED?
MANY TIMES.
WHEN WERE YOU THE *MOST* SCARED?
THERE'S A WOMAN. A WOMAN I...A VERY SPECIAL WOMAN.
A GIRLFRIEND?
I LIKED HER. SHE WAS SMART AND KIND AND I...
YOU HAD TO ASK HER *OUT,* LIKE ON A DATE?
SHE WAS SO BEAUTIFUL.
SO WHAT DID YOU DO?
WHAT COULD I DO?
YOU ASKED HER? YOU *DIDN'T* ASK HER? WHAT?
I ASKED HER.
WHAT DID SHE SAY?
SHE SAID YES.
DID YOU *TELL* HER YOU'D BEEN SCARED?
I DIDN'T HAVE TO TELL HER. SHE KNEW.
THE DAIL

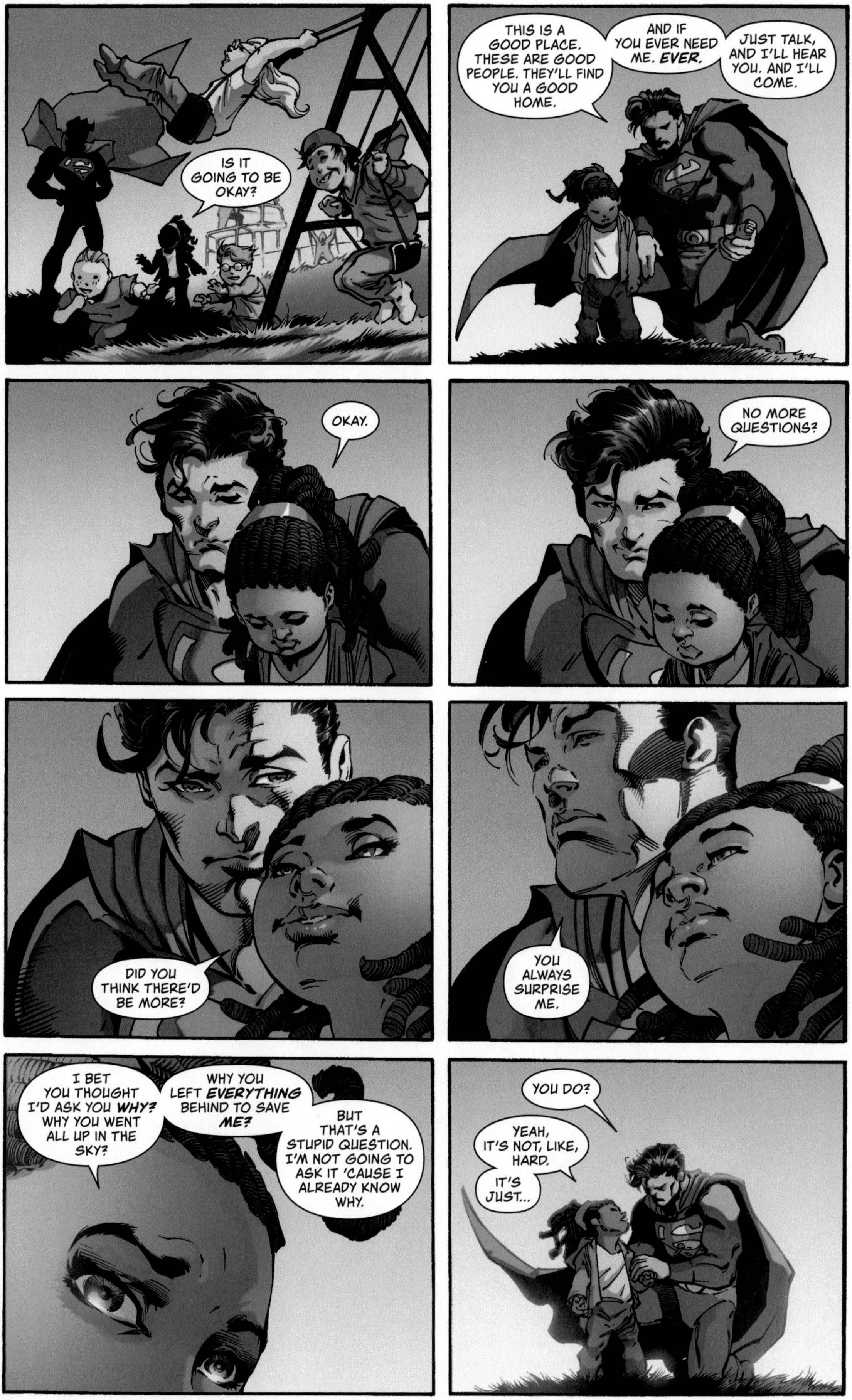
IS IT GOING TO BE OKAY?
THIS IS A GOOD PLACE. THESE ARE GOOD PEOPLE. THEY'LL FIND YOU A GOOD HOME.
AND IF YOU EVER NEED ME. *EVER.*
JUST TALK, AND I'LL HEAR YOU. AND I'LL COME.
OKAY.
NO MORE QUESTIONS?
DID YOU THINK THERE'D BE MORE?
YOU ALWAYS SURPRISE ME.
I BET YOU THOUGHT I'D ASK YOU *WHY?* WHY YOU WENT ALL UP IN THE SKY?
WHY YOU LEFT *EVERYTHING* BEHIND TO SAVE *ME?*
BUT THAT'S A STUPID QUESTION. I'M NOT GOING TO ASK IT 'CAUSE I ALREADY KNOW WHY.
YOU DO?
YEAH, IT'S NOT, LIKE, HARD.
IT'S JUST...

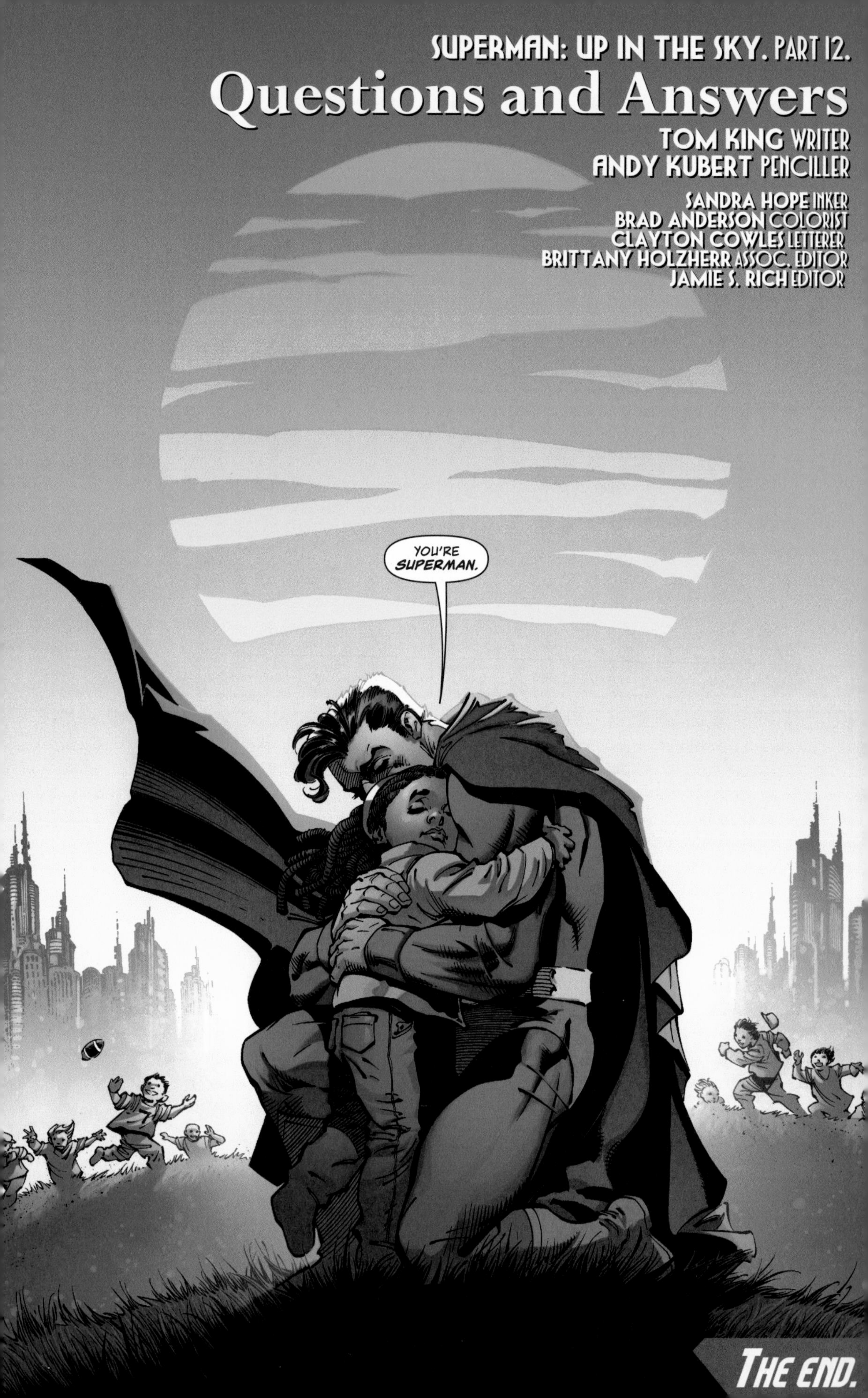
SUPERMAN: UP IN THE SKY. PART 12.
Questions and Answers
TOM KING WRITER
ANDY KUBERT PENCILLER
SANDRA HOPE INKER
BRAD ANDERSON COLORIST
CLAYTON COWLES LETTERER
BRITTANY HOLZHERR ASSOC. EDITOR
JAMIE S. RICH EDITOR
YOU'RE SUPERMAN.
THE END.

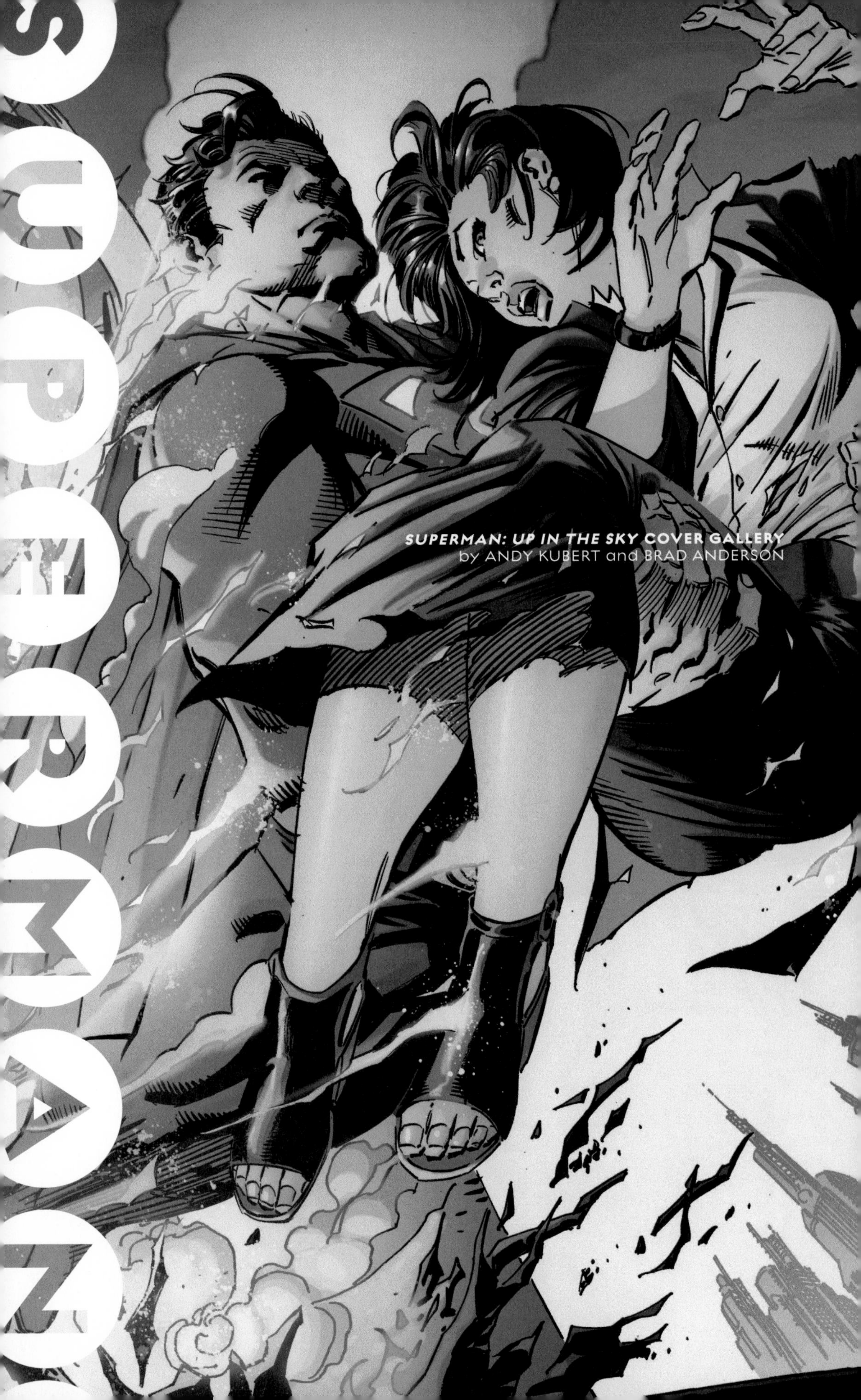
SUPERMAN

***SUPERMAN: UP IN THE SKY* COVER GALLERY**
by ANDY KUBERT and BRAD ANDERSON

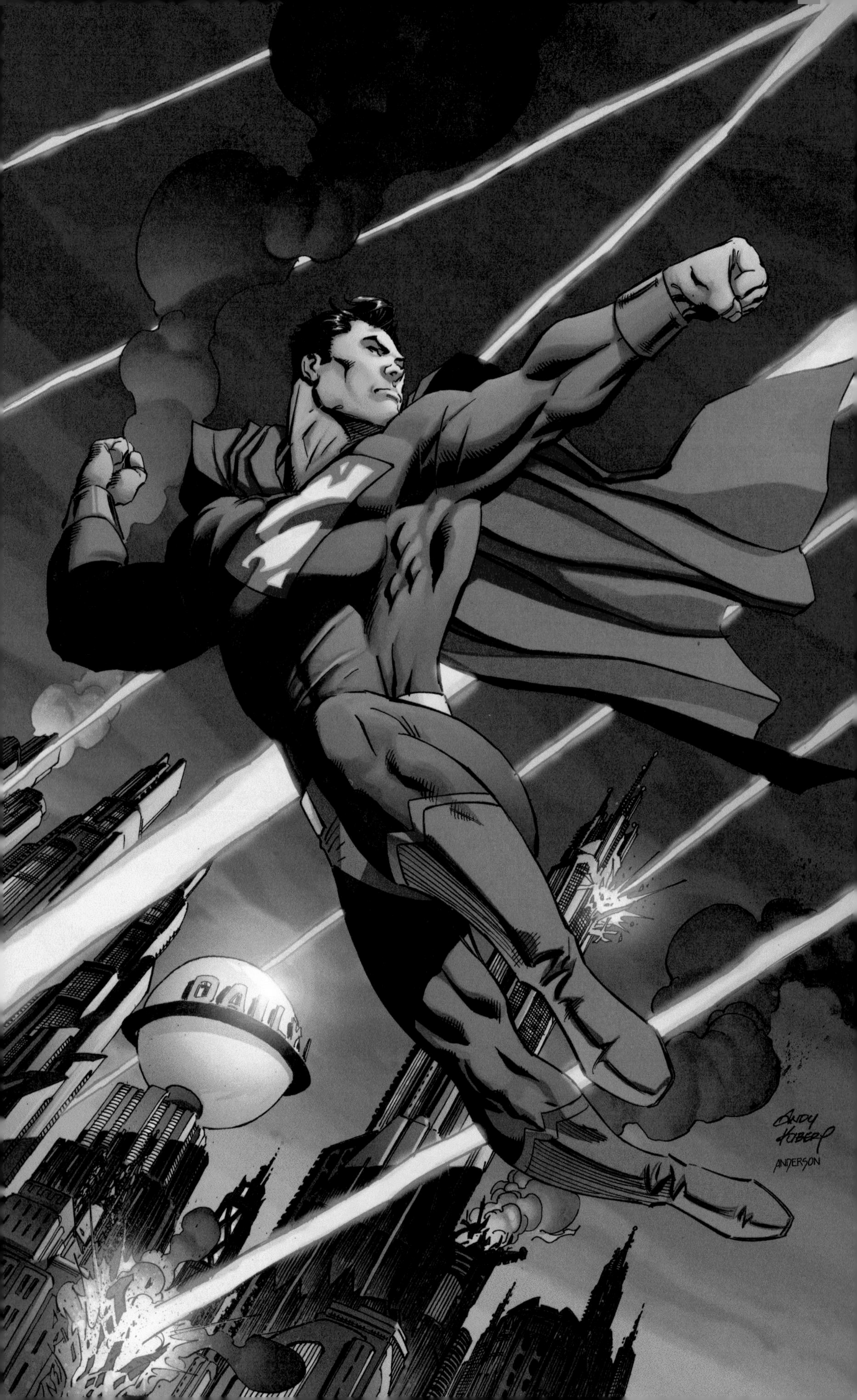
ANDY KUBERT
ANDERSON

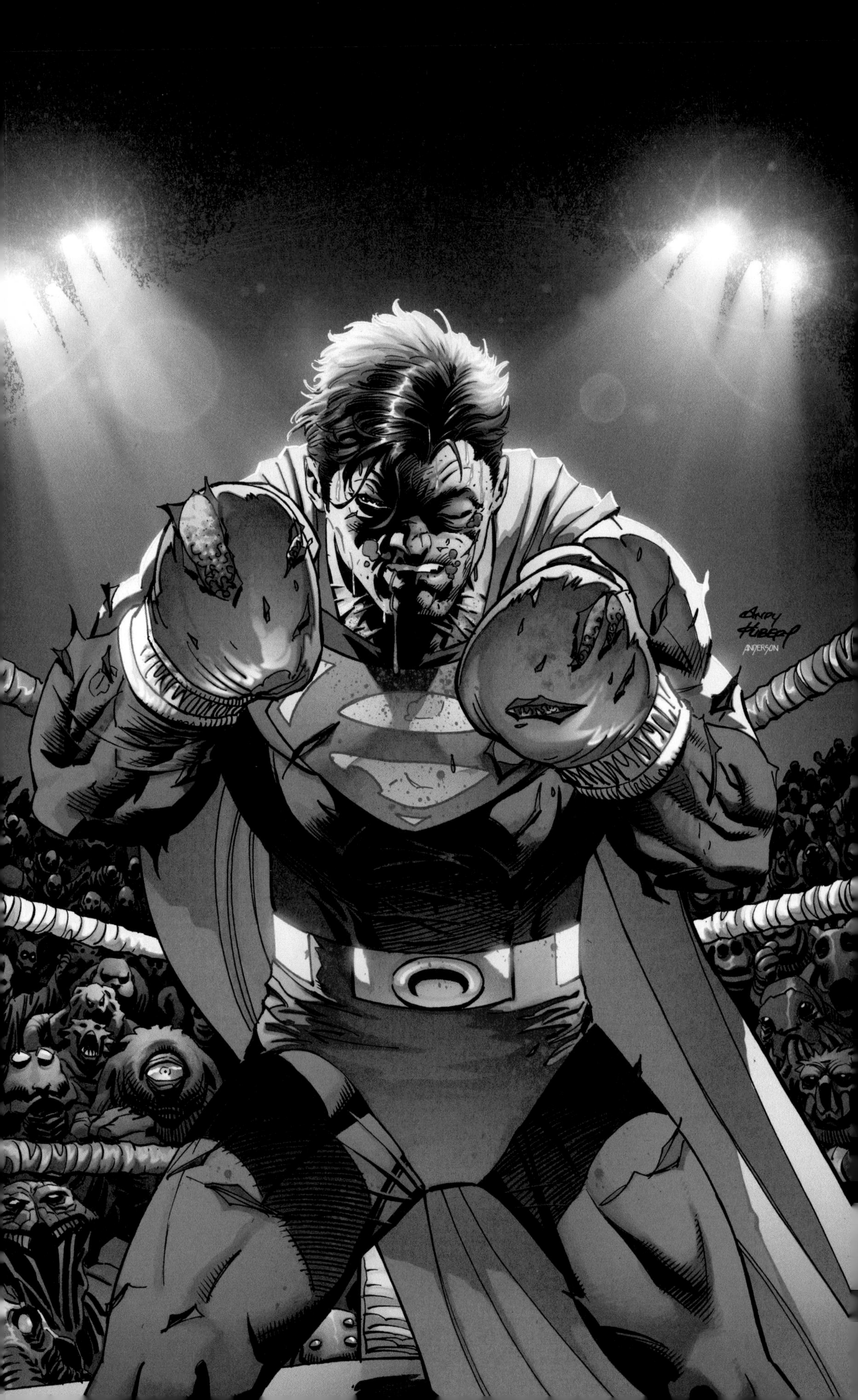
ANDY KUBERT
ANDERSON

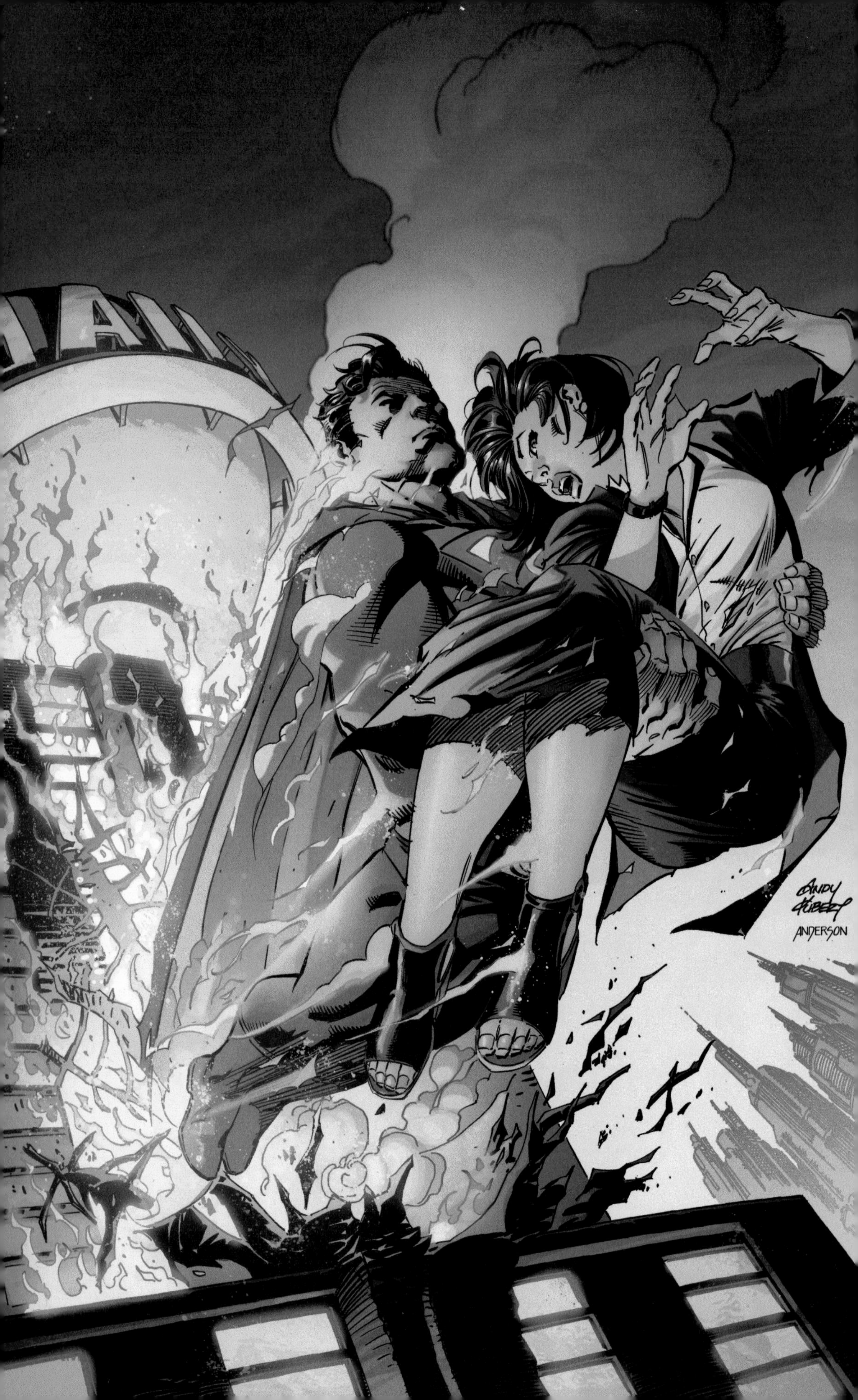
ANDERSON

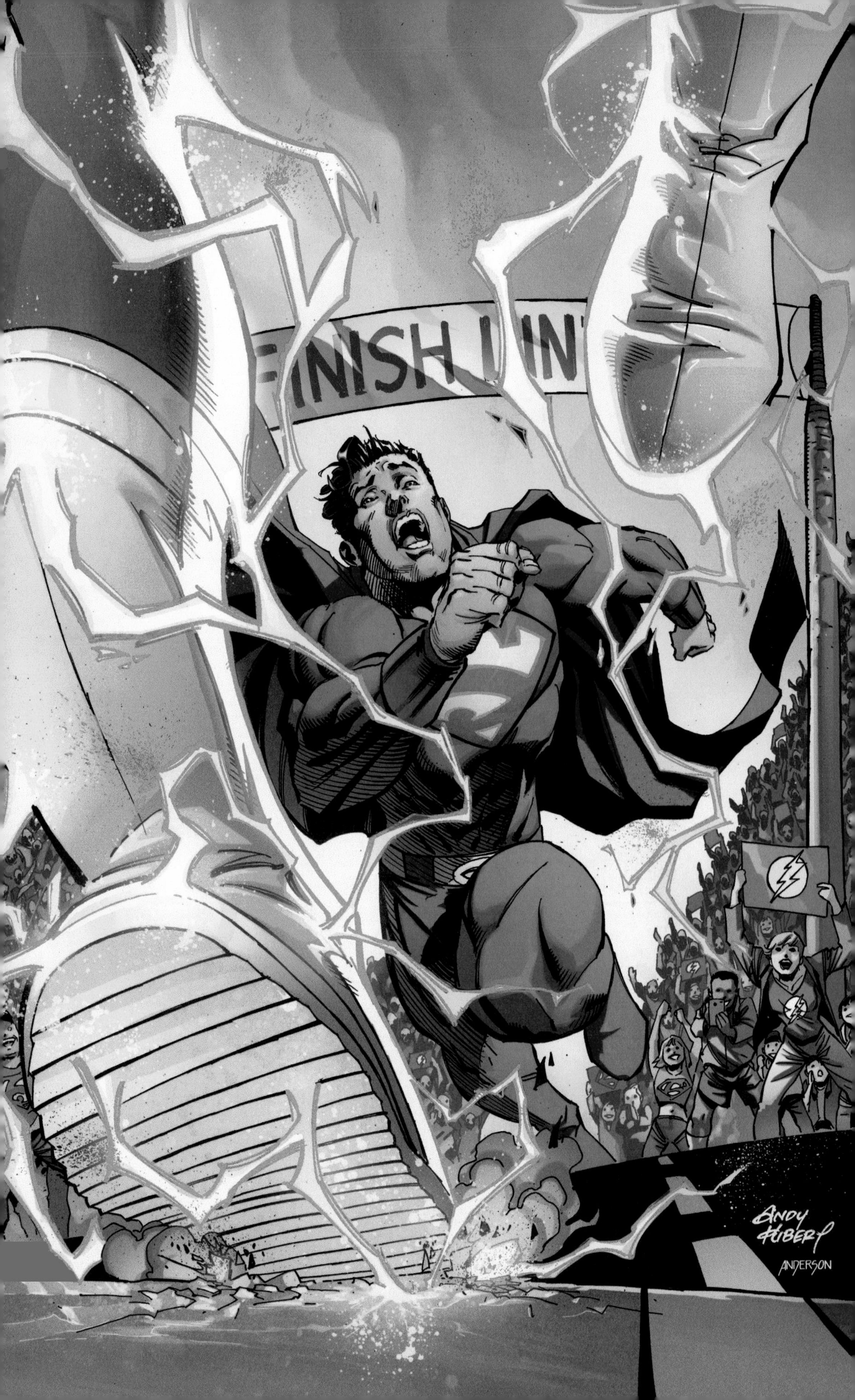

FINISH LIN
ANDY KUBERT
ANDERSON

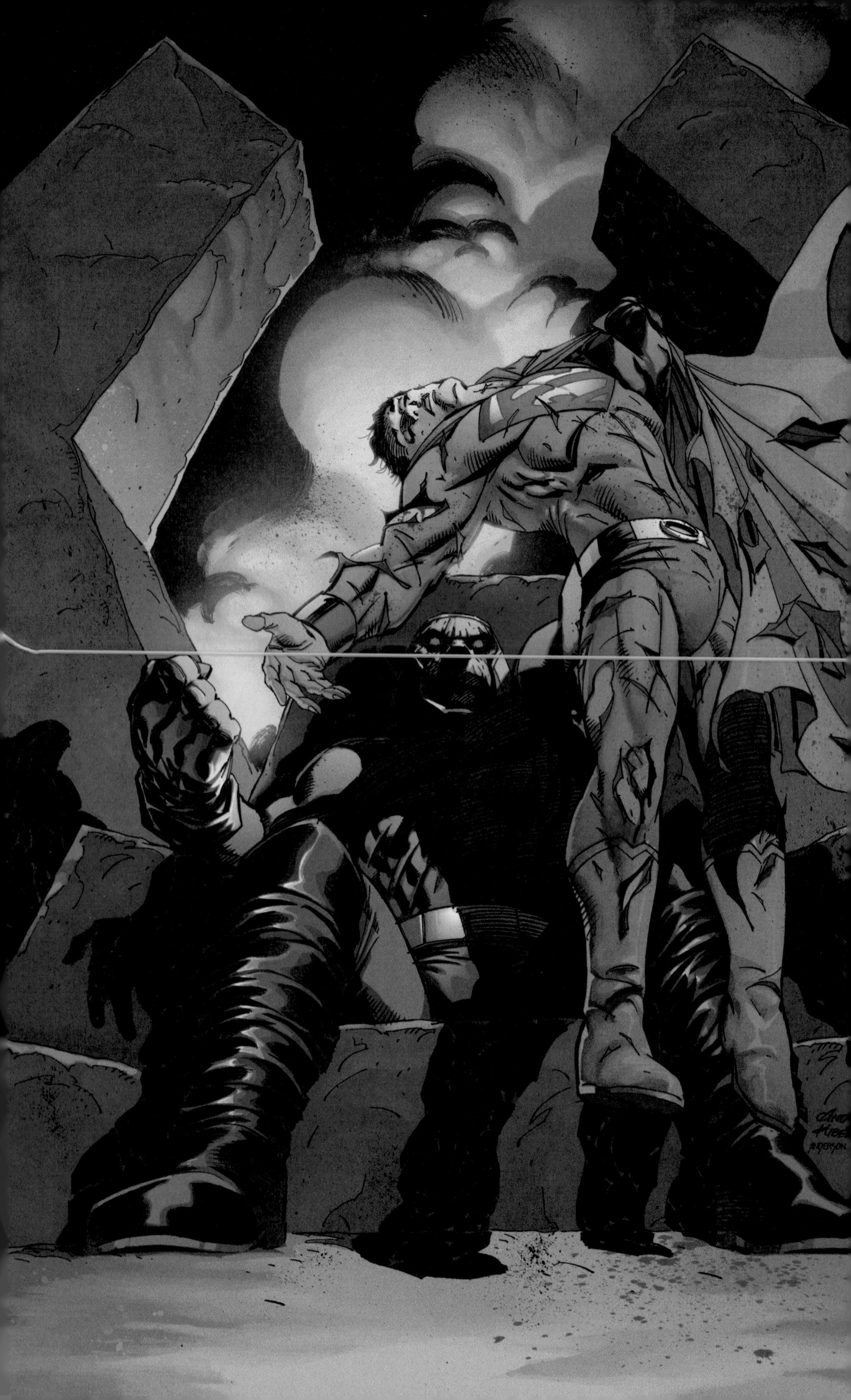
ANDERSON

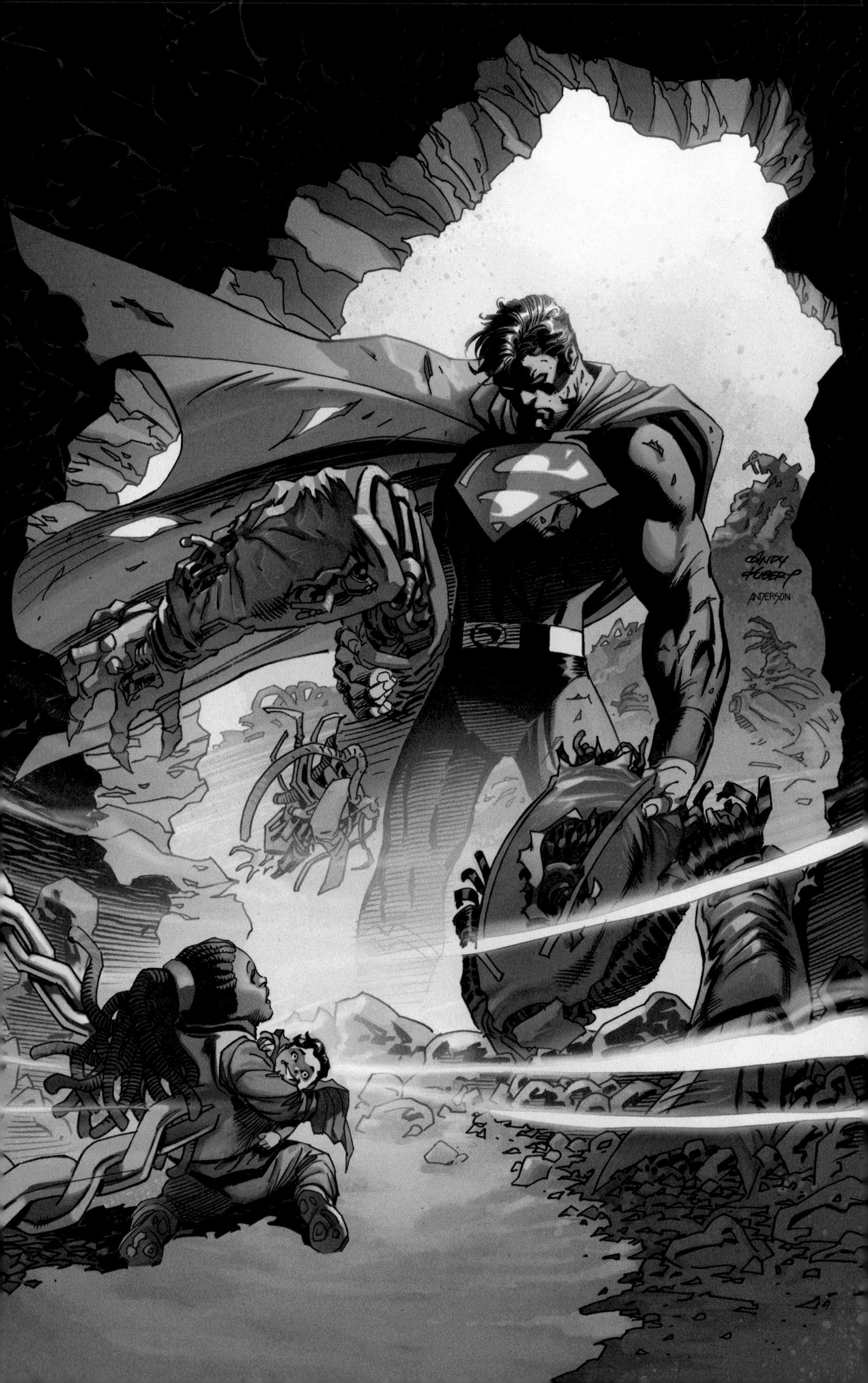
ANDY KUBERT
ANDERSON

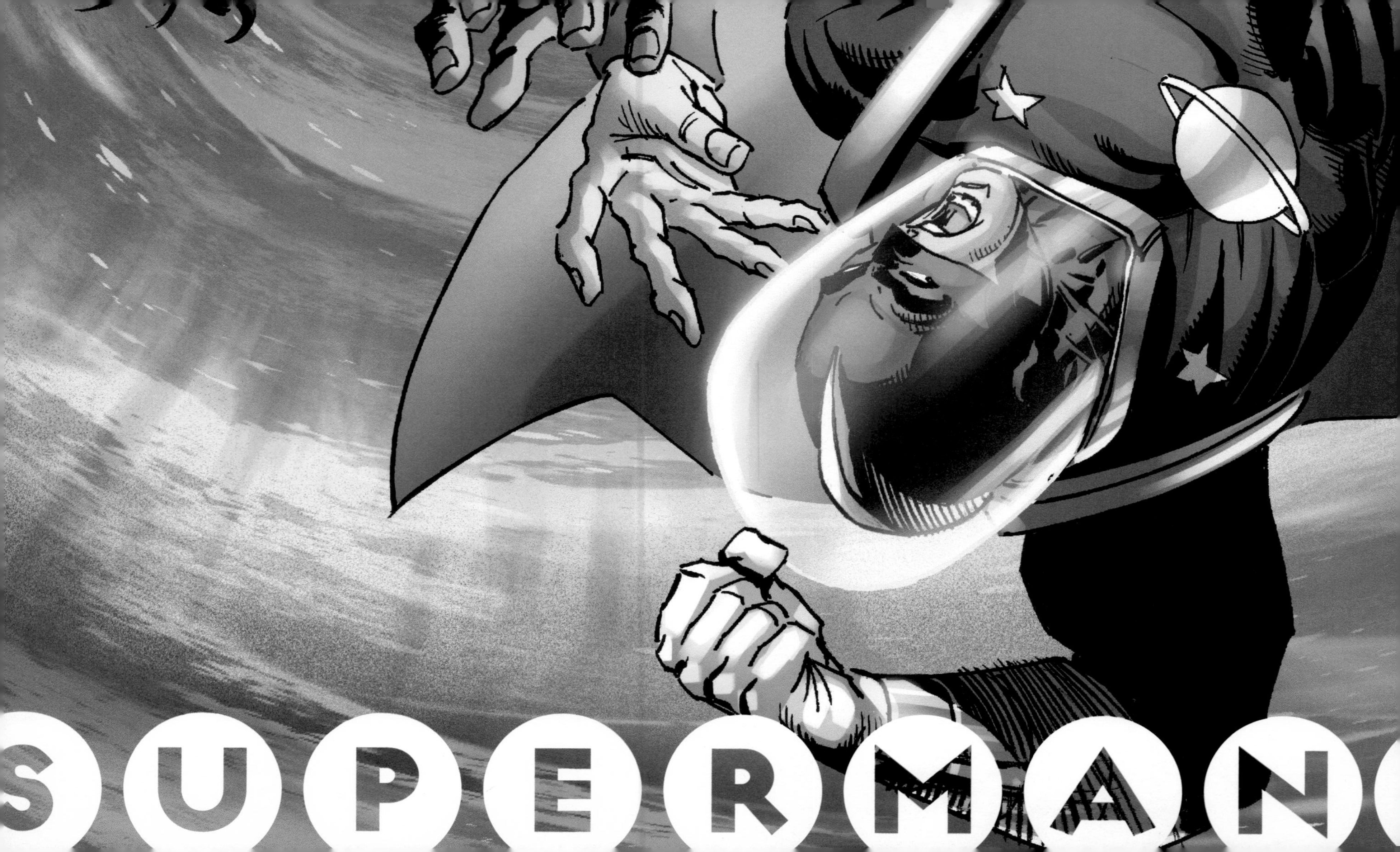
SUPERMAN

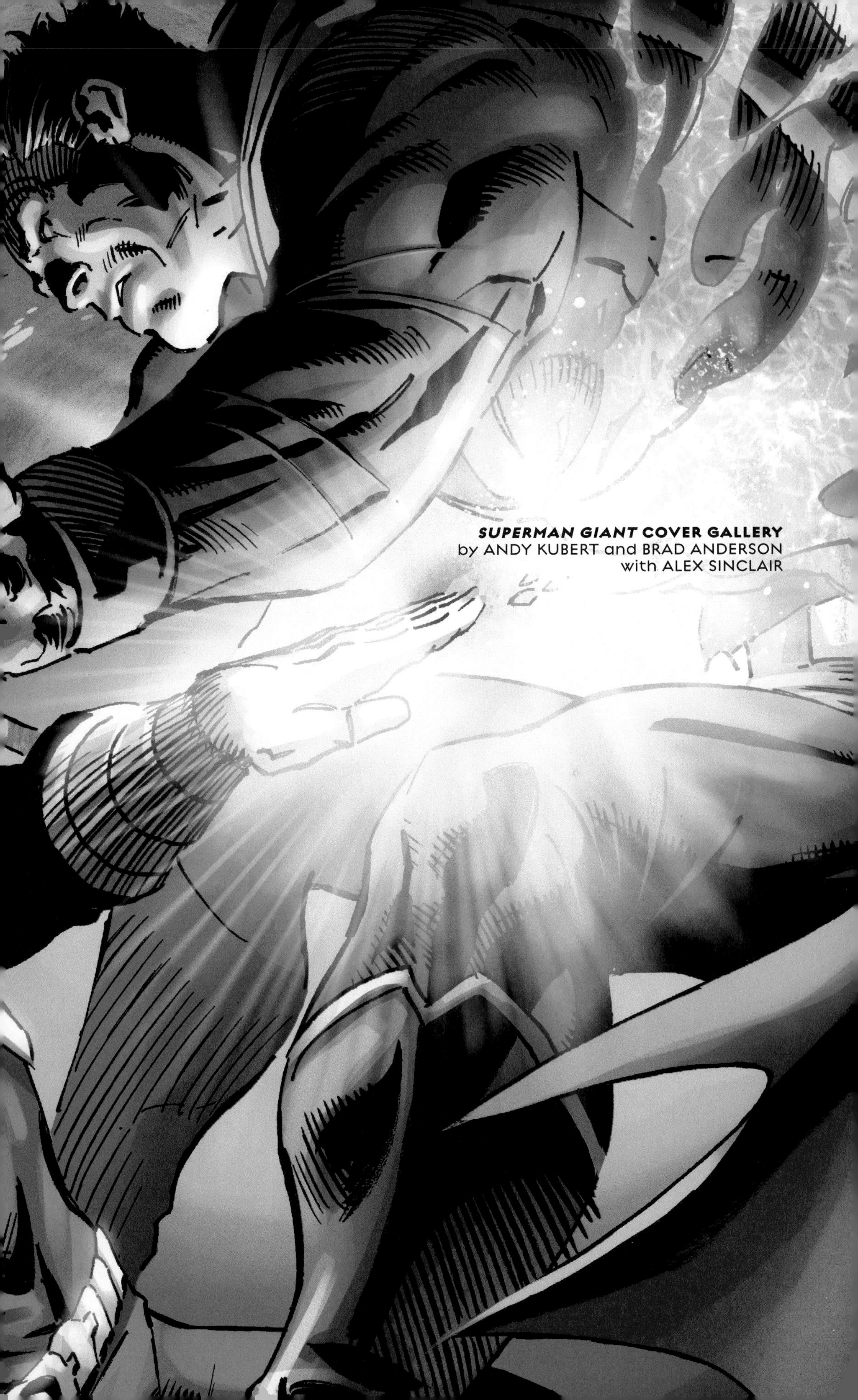

SUPERMAN GIANT COVER GALLERY

by ANDY KUBERT and BRAD ANDERSON
with ALEX SINCLAIR

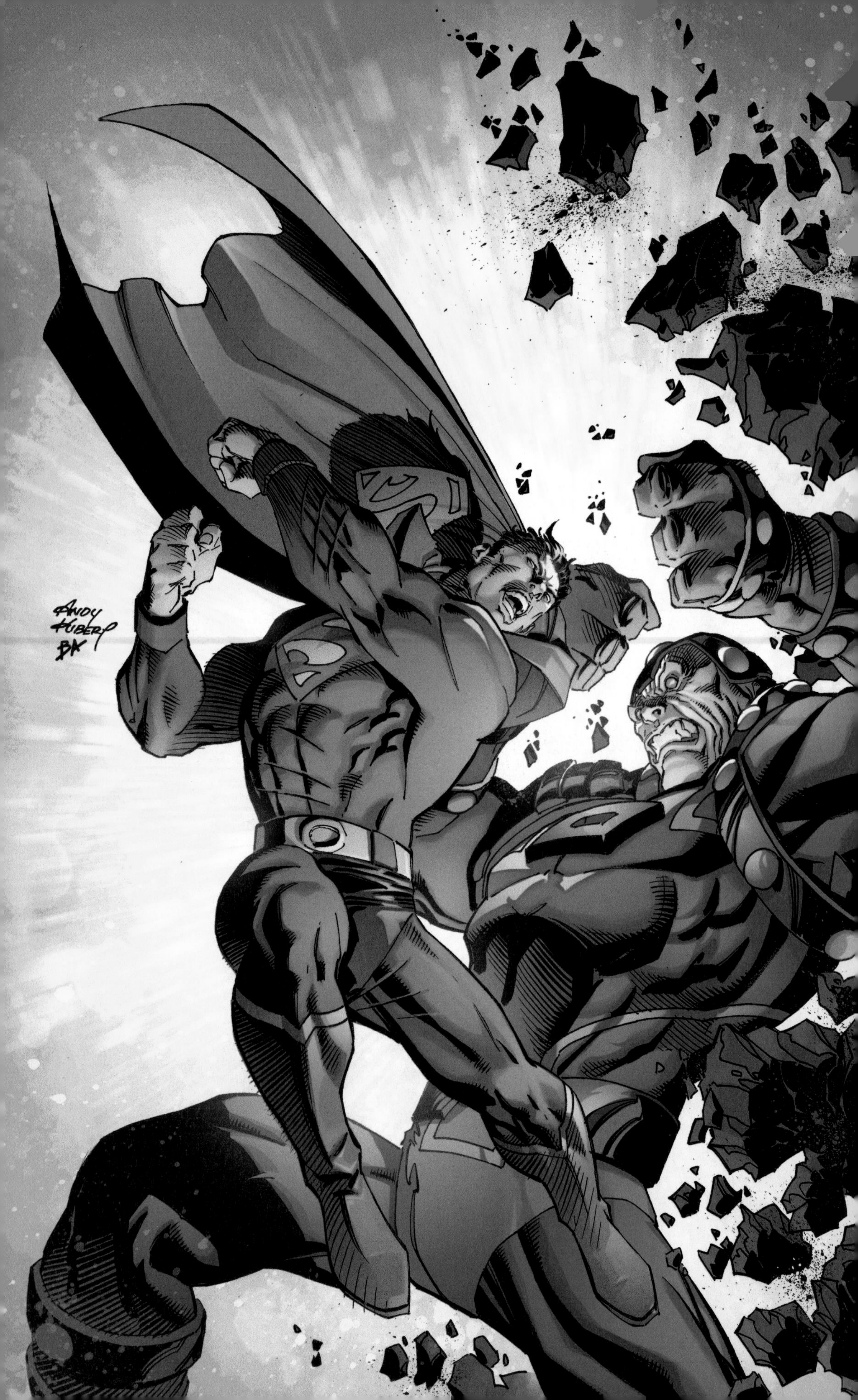
ANDY KUBERT
BK

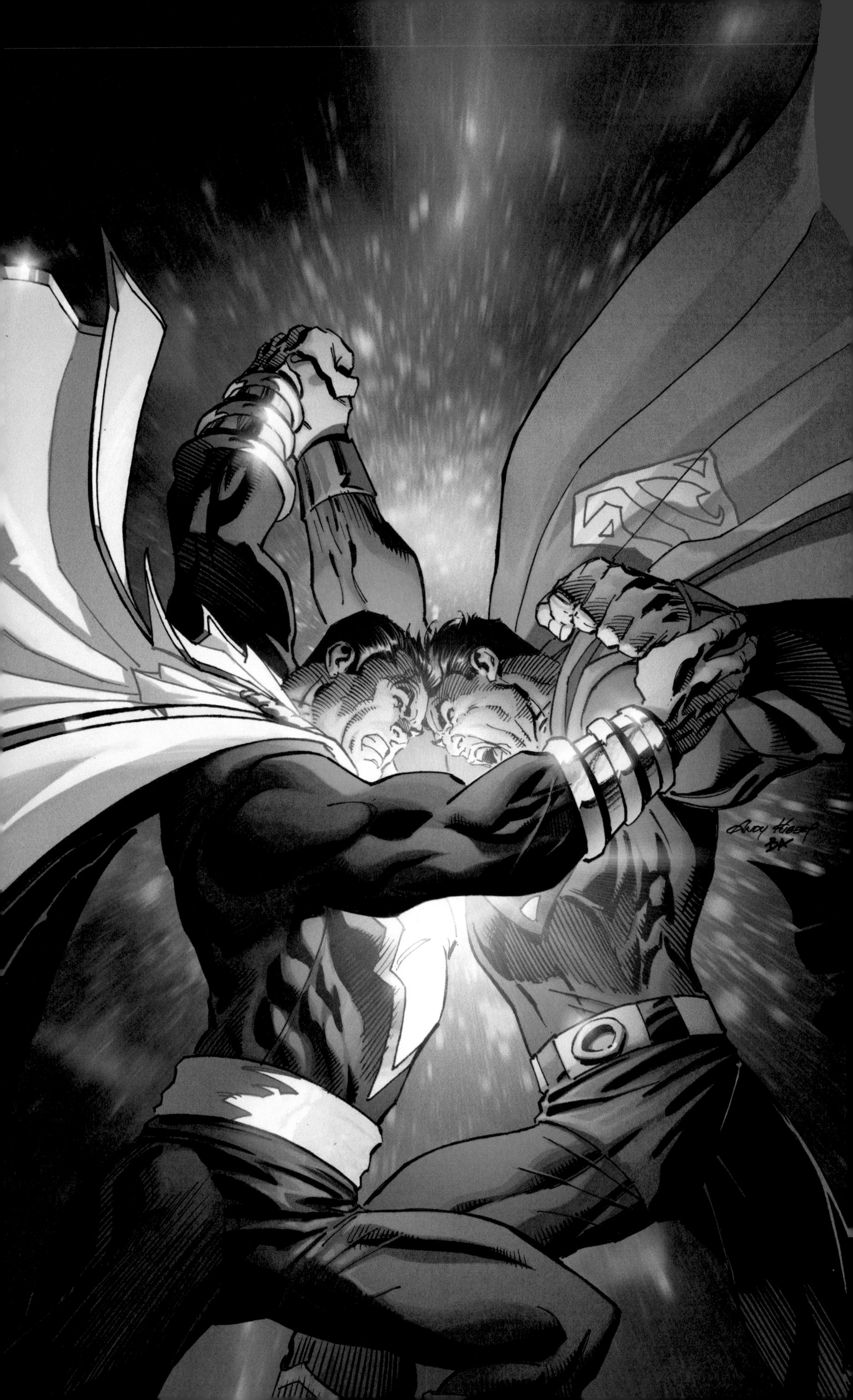

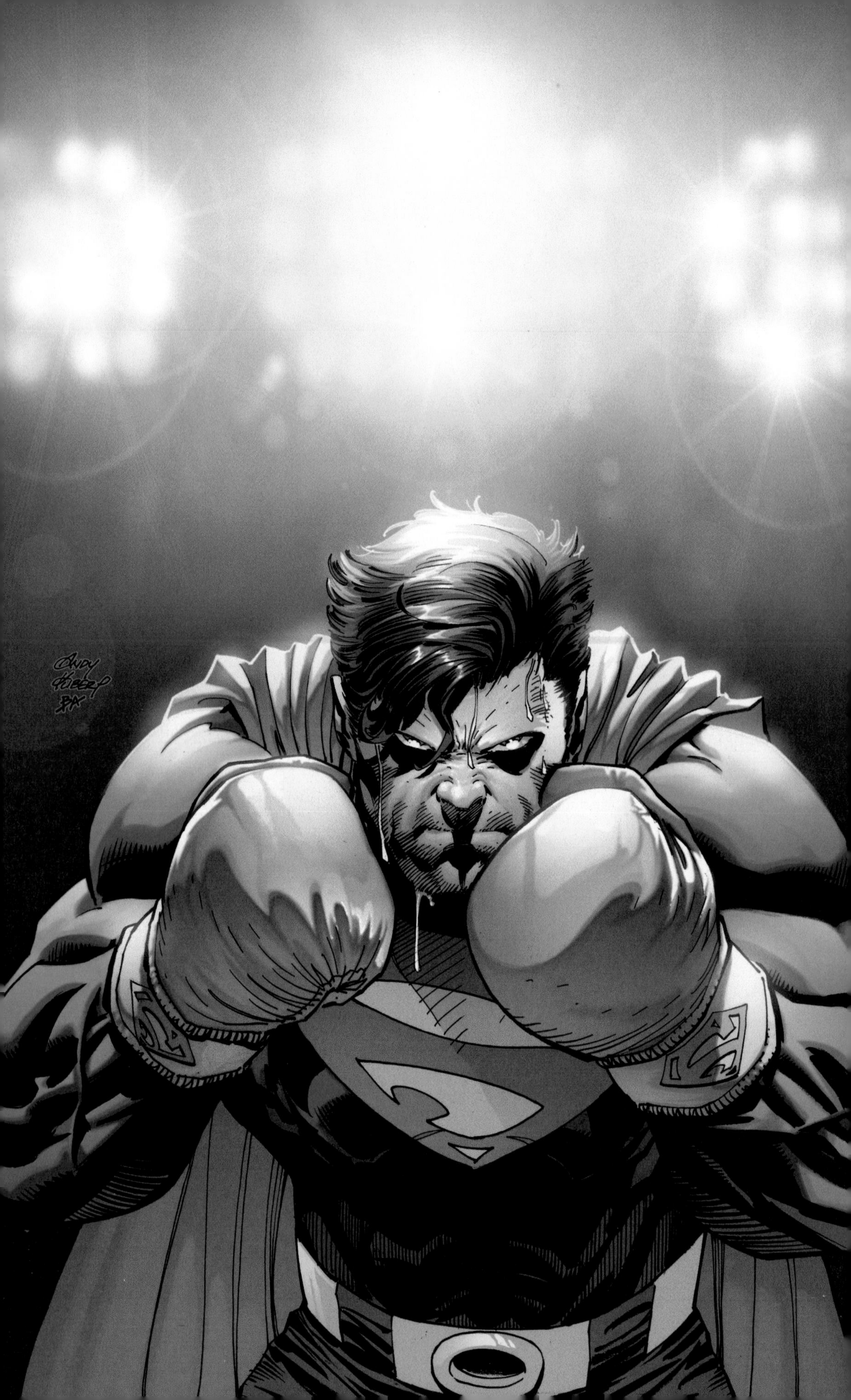

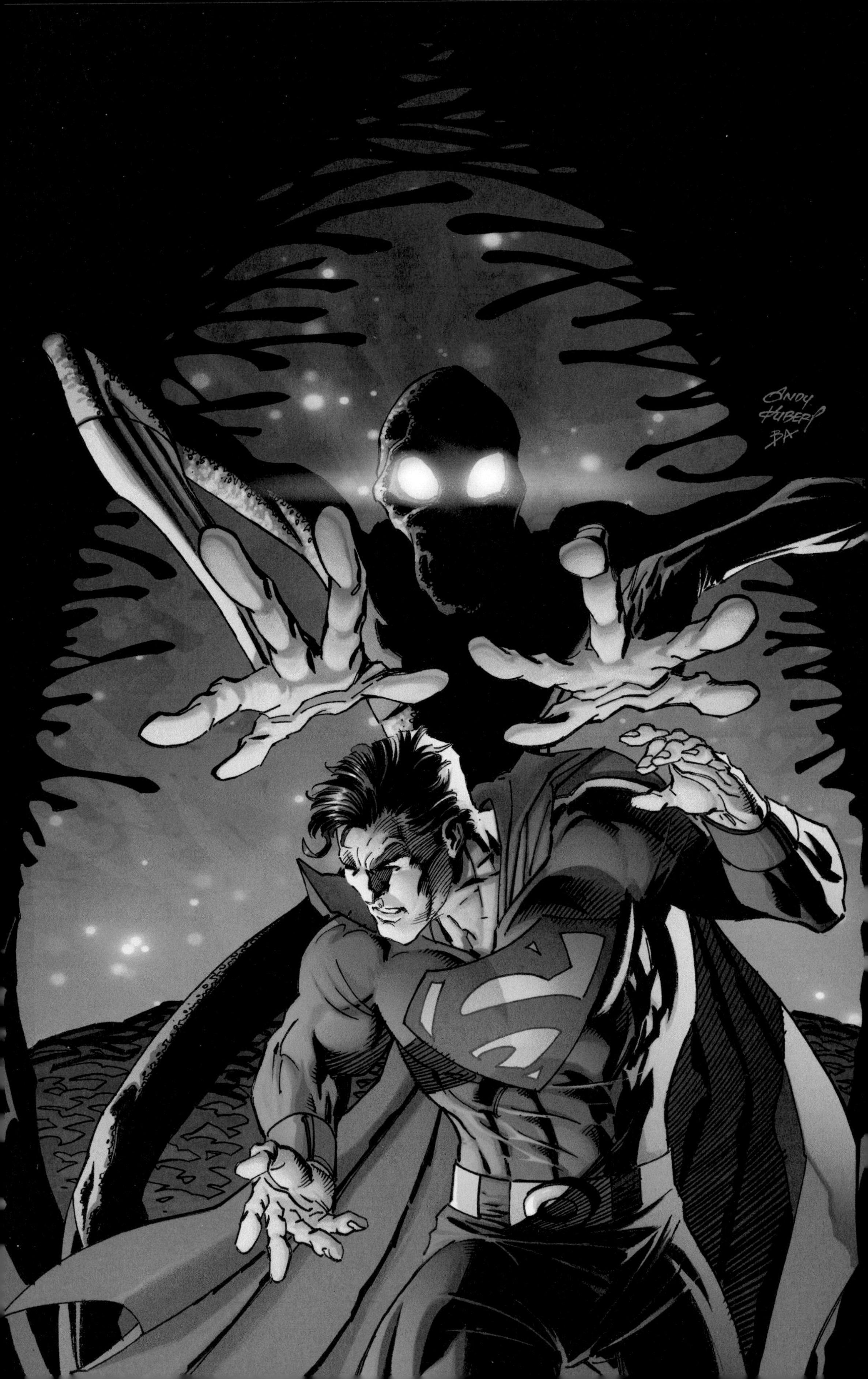

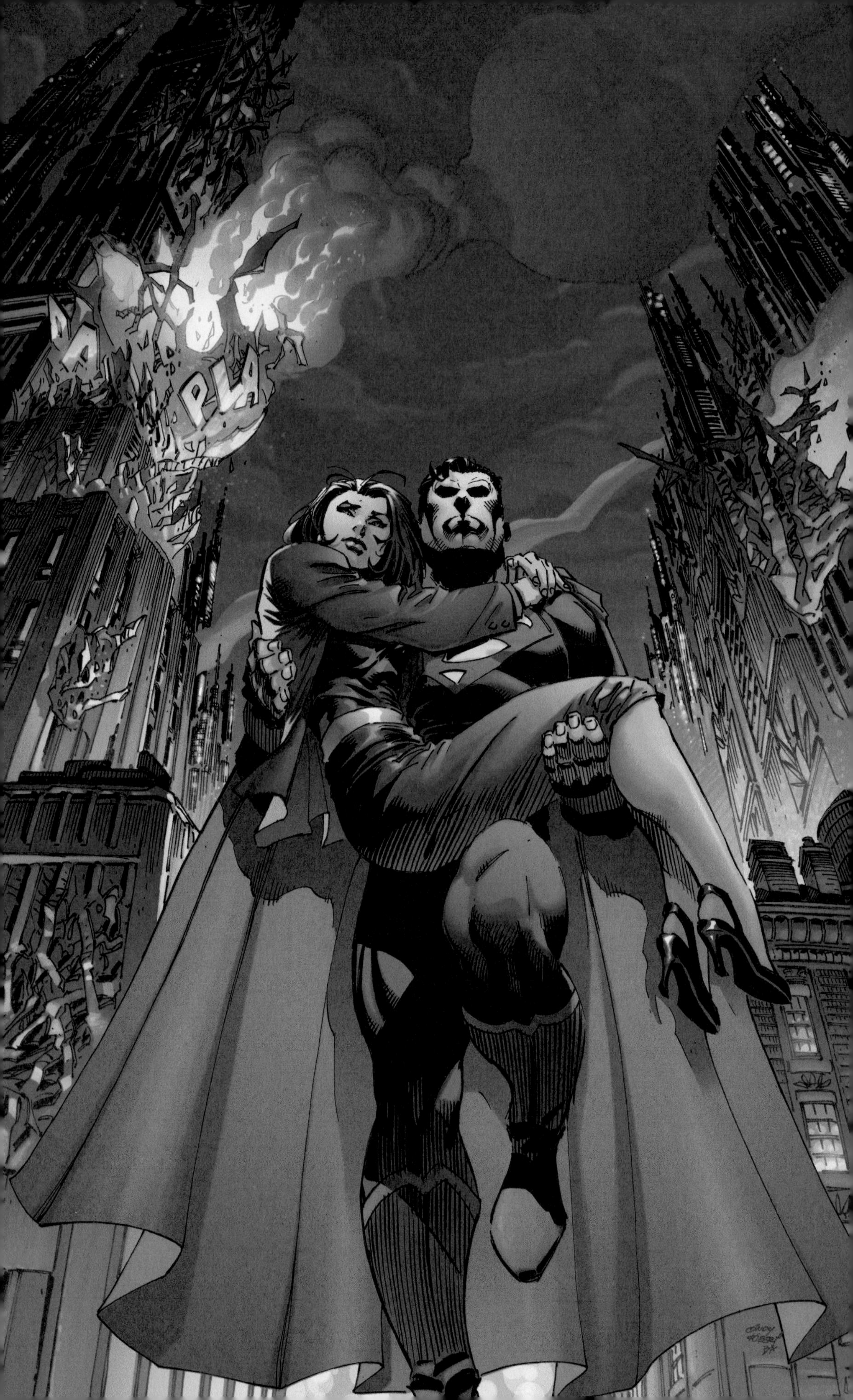

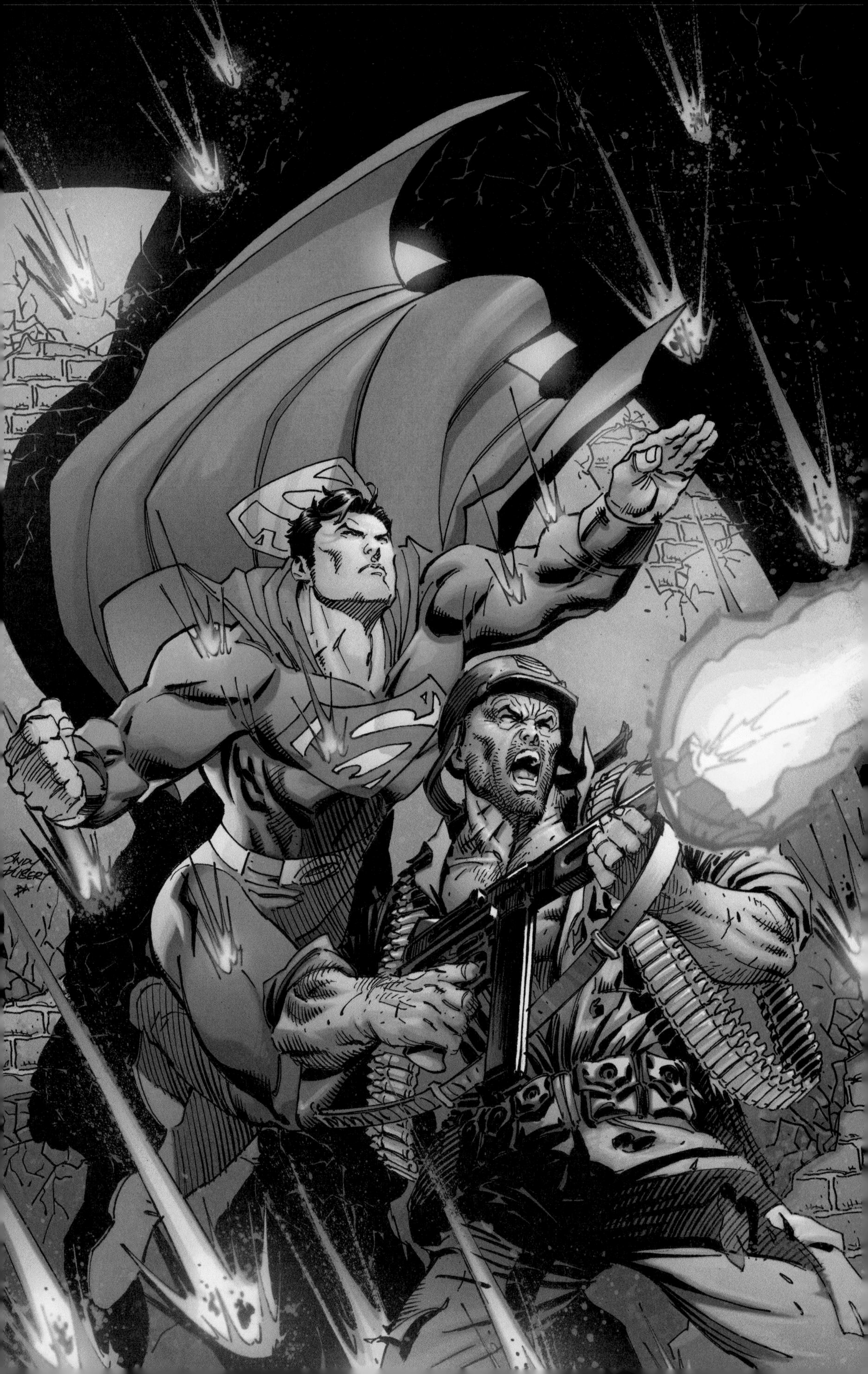

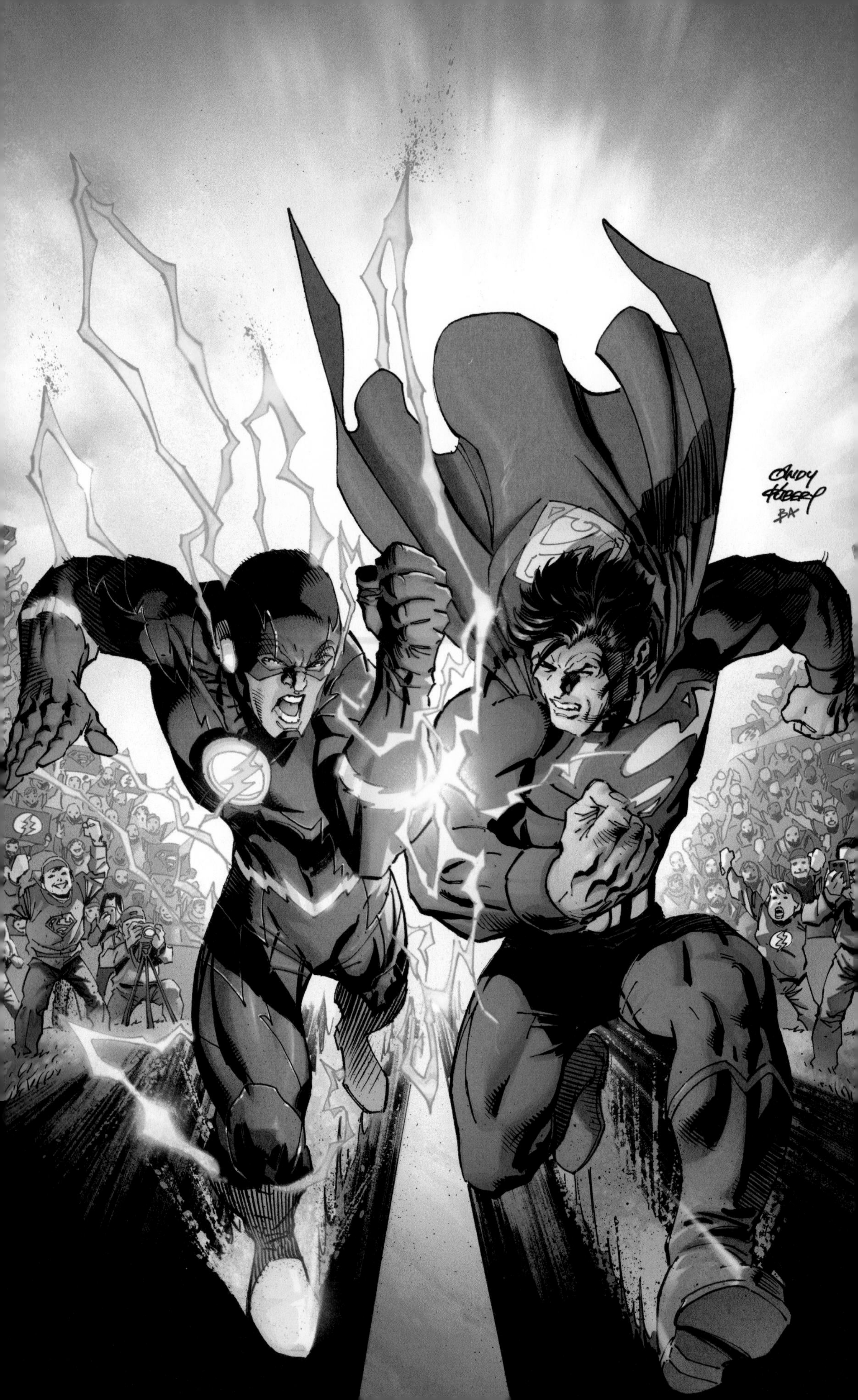
ANDY KUBERT
BA

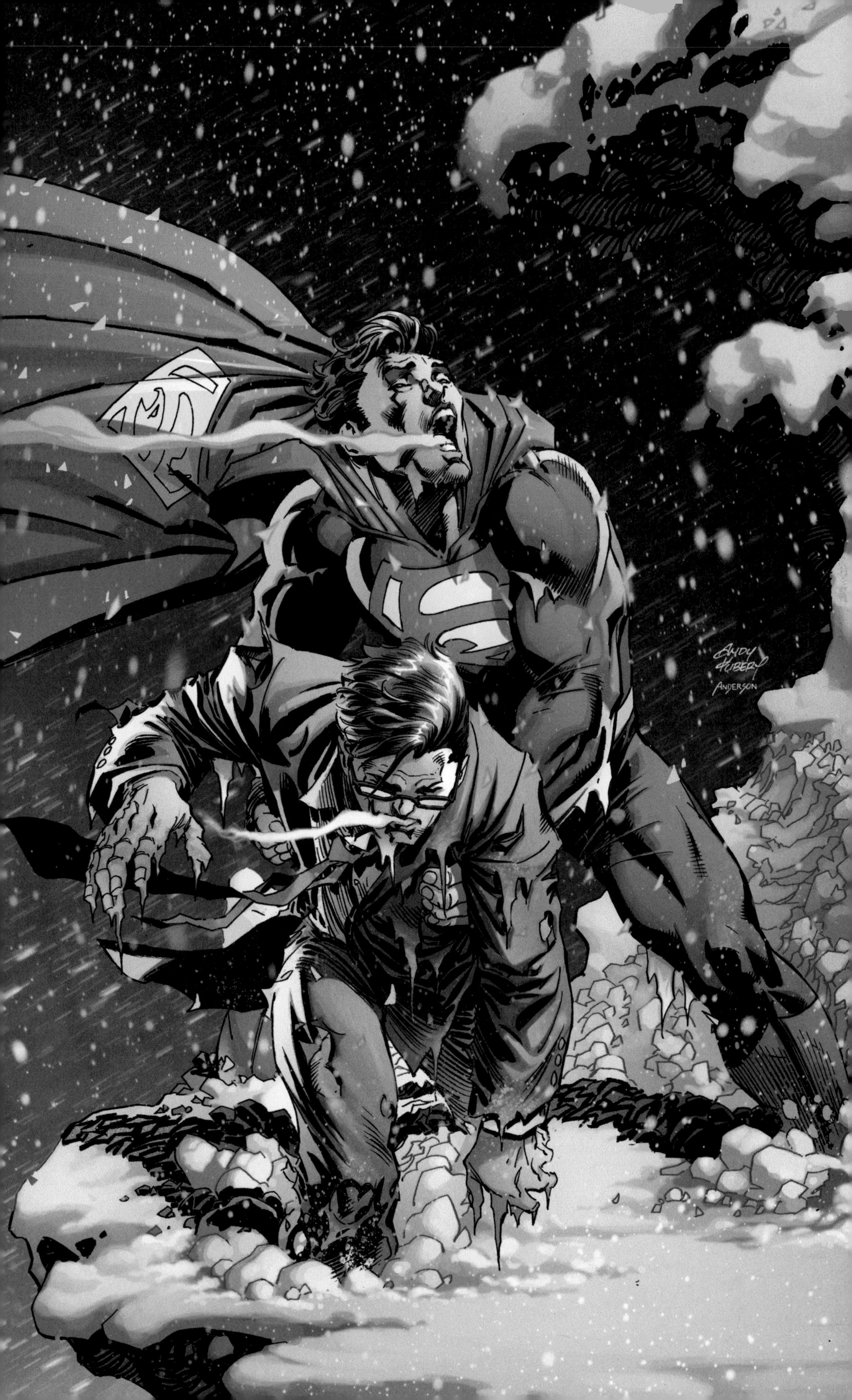
ANDY KUBERT
ANDERSON

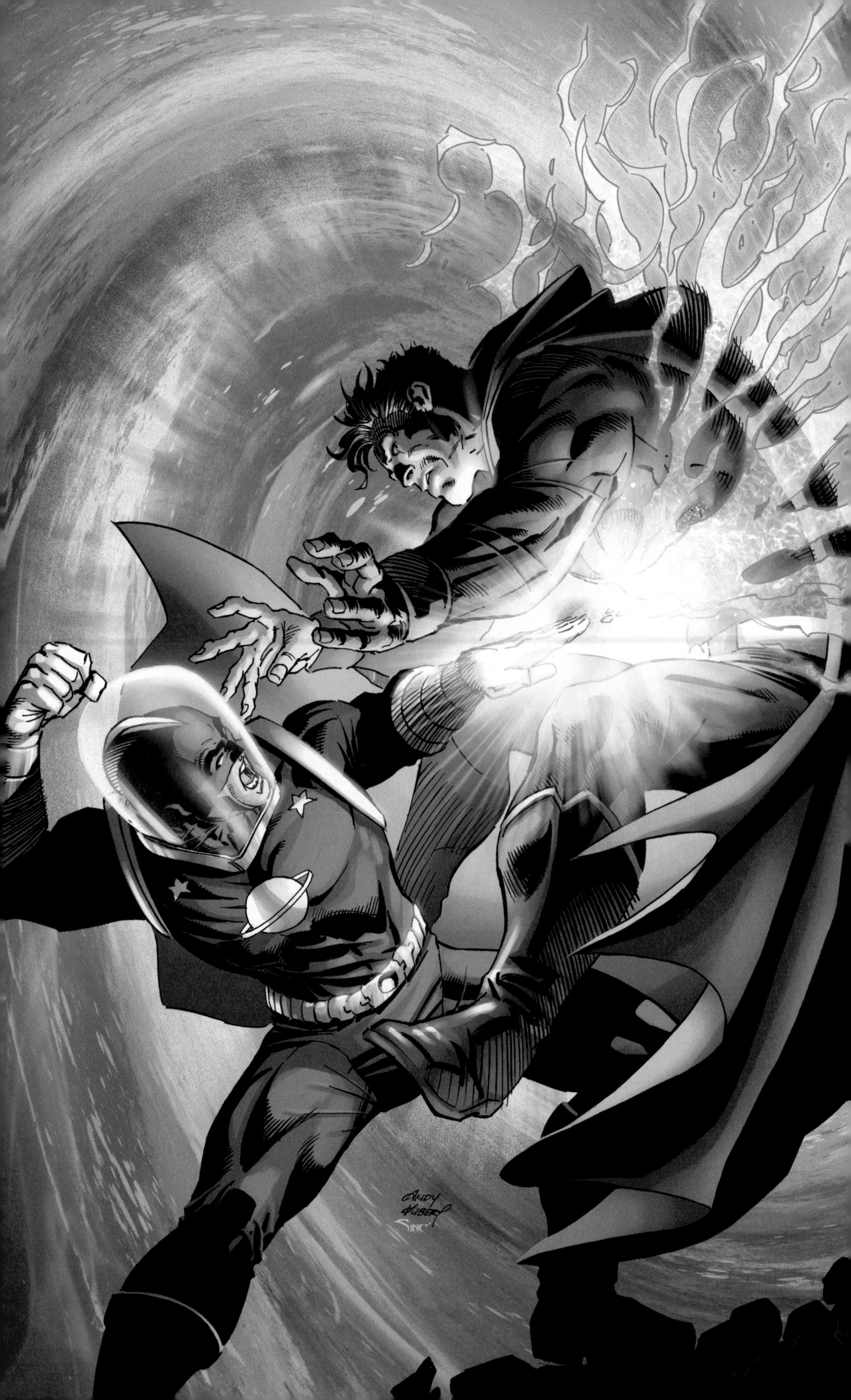
ANDY KUBERT
SINC

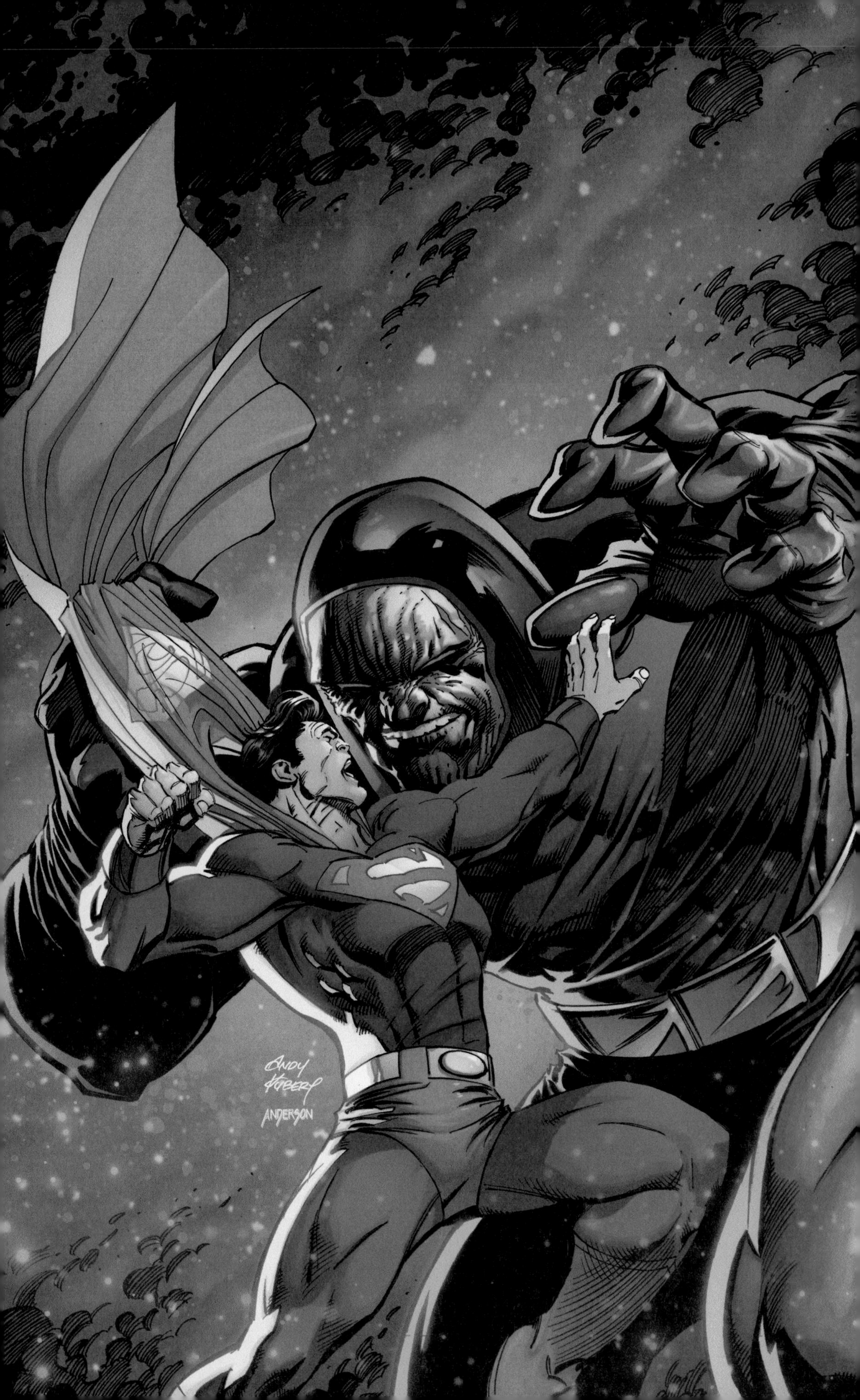
ANDY KUBERT
ANDERSON

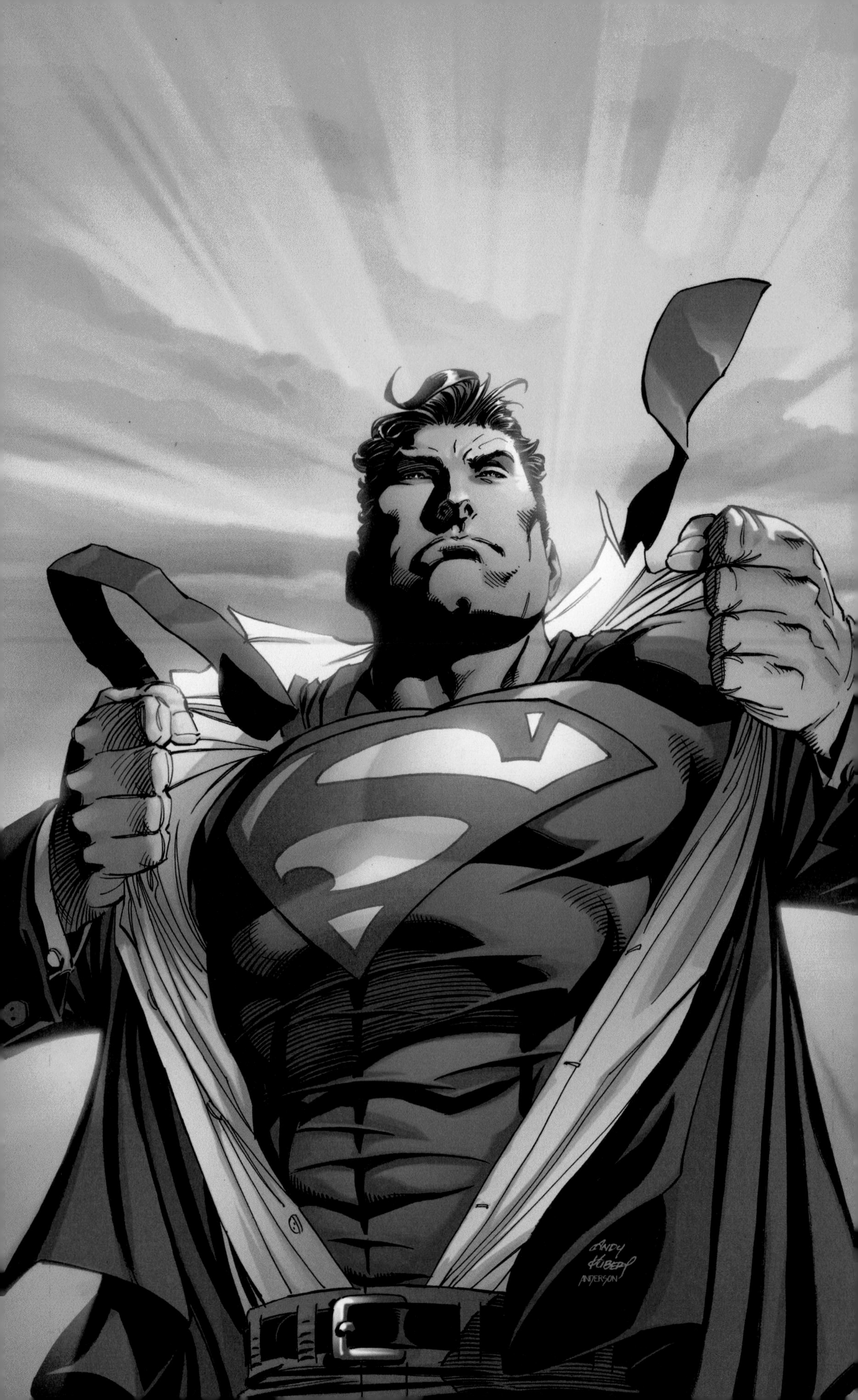
ANDY
KUBERT
ANDERSON

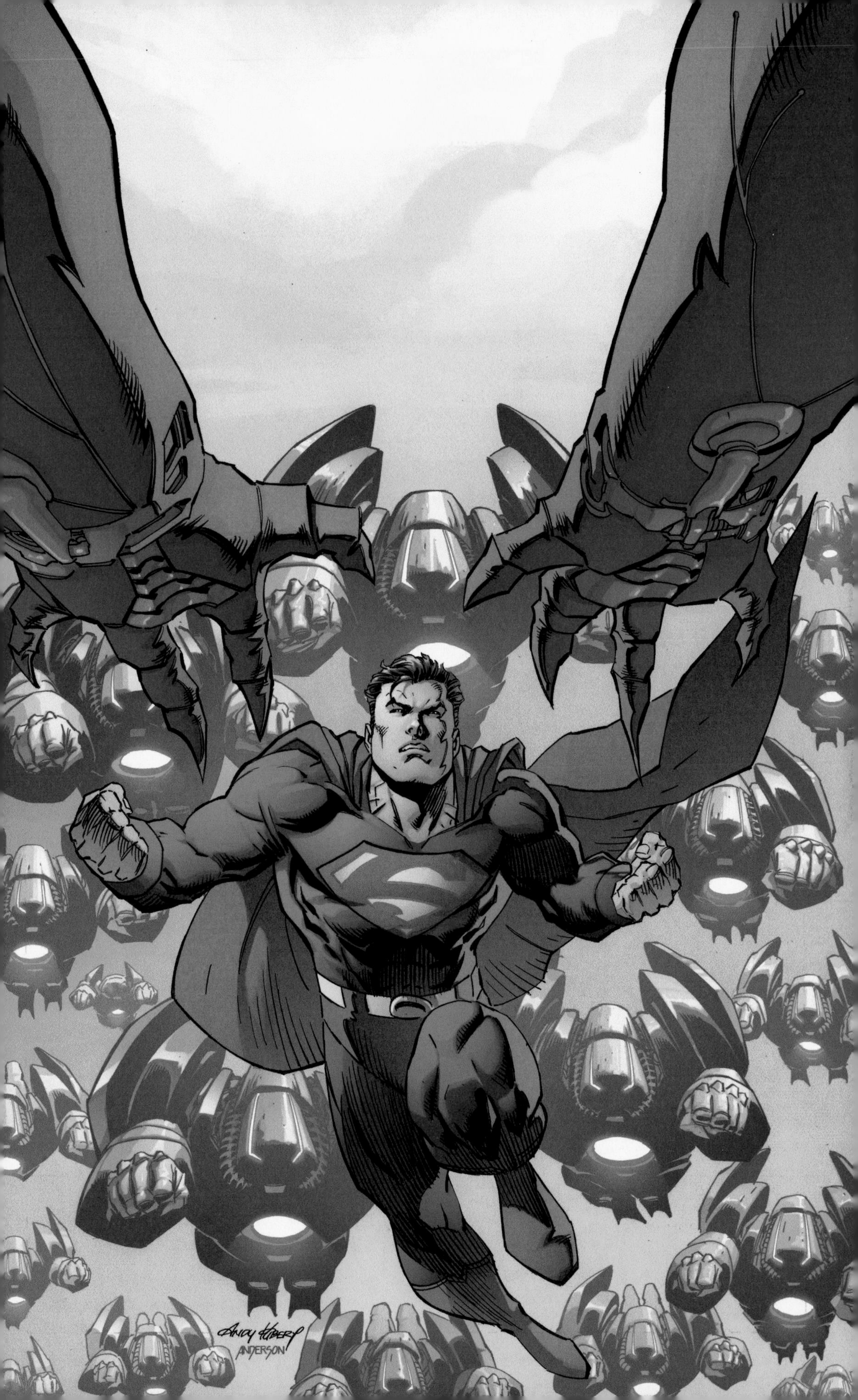
ANDY KUBERT
ANDERSON

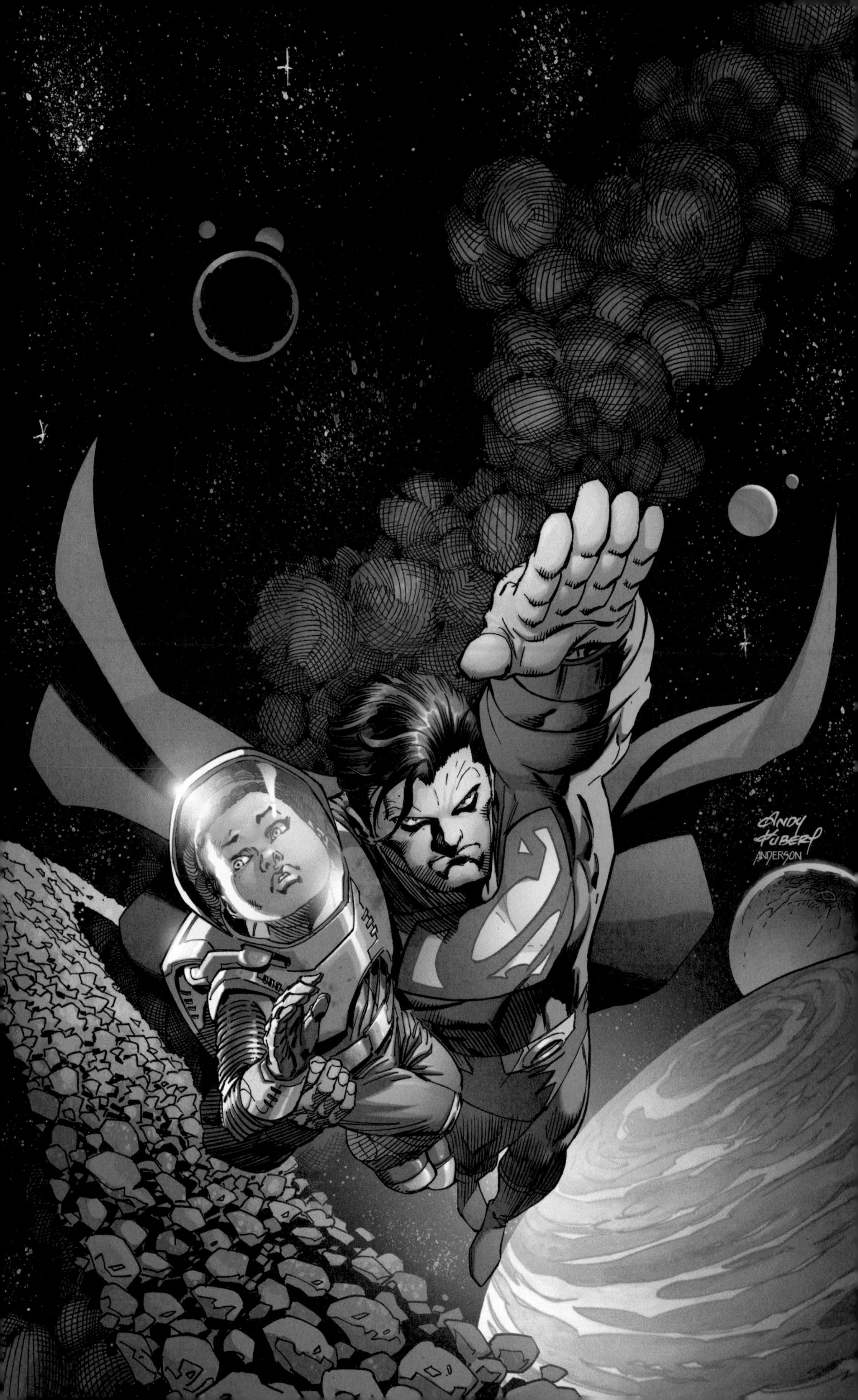
ANDY KUBERT
ANDERSON

SKETCHBOOK
by ANDY KUBERT

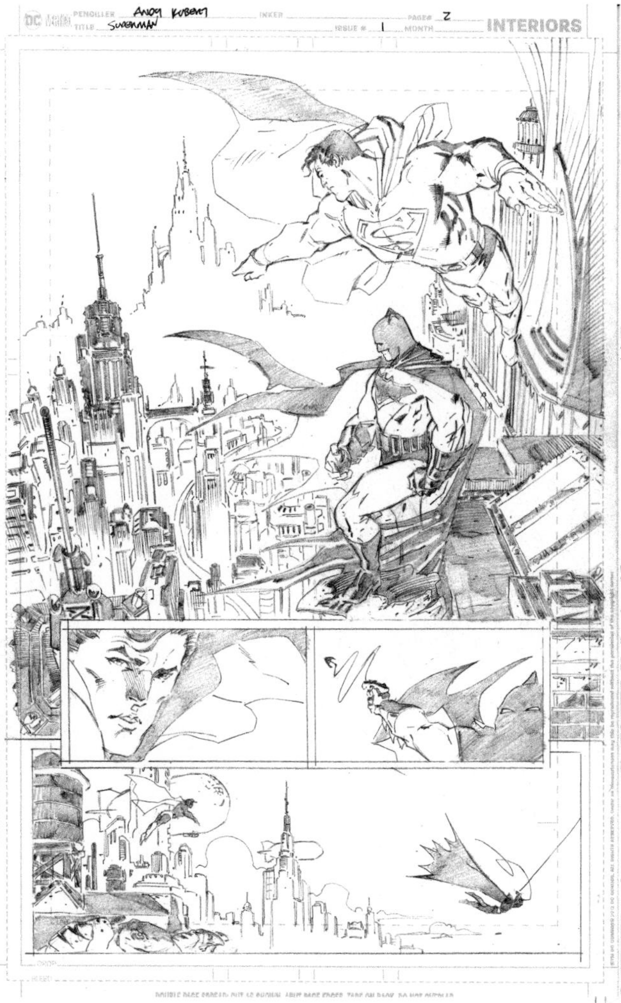
INTERIORS

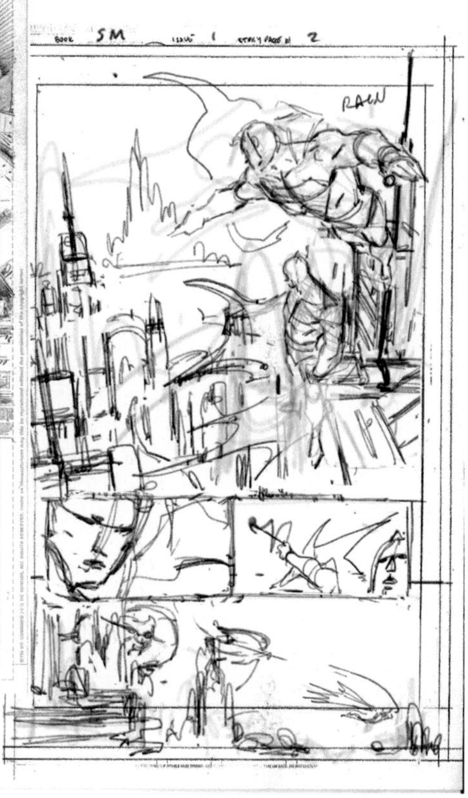

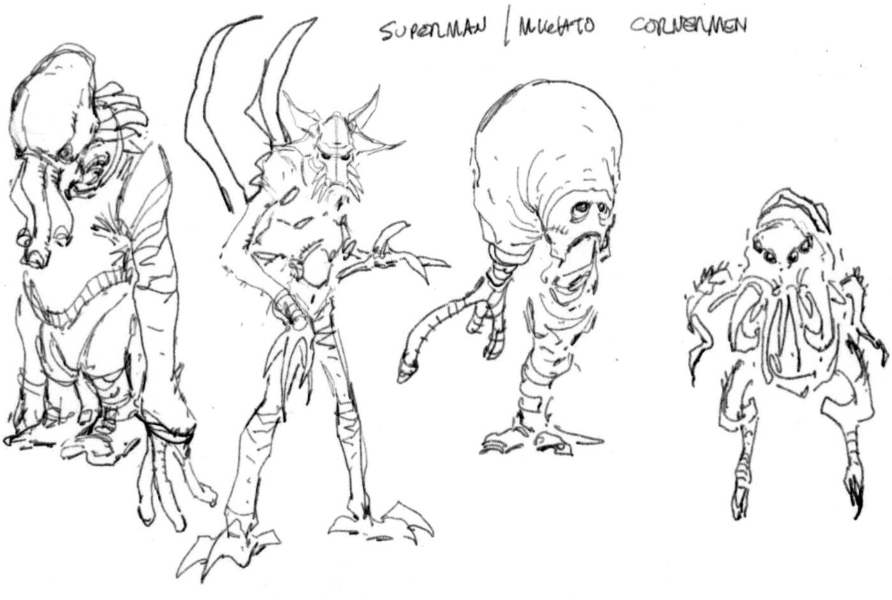

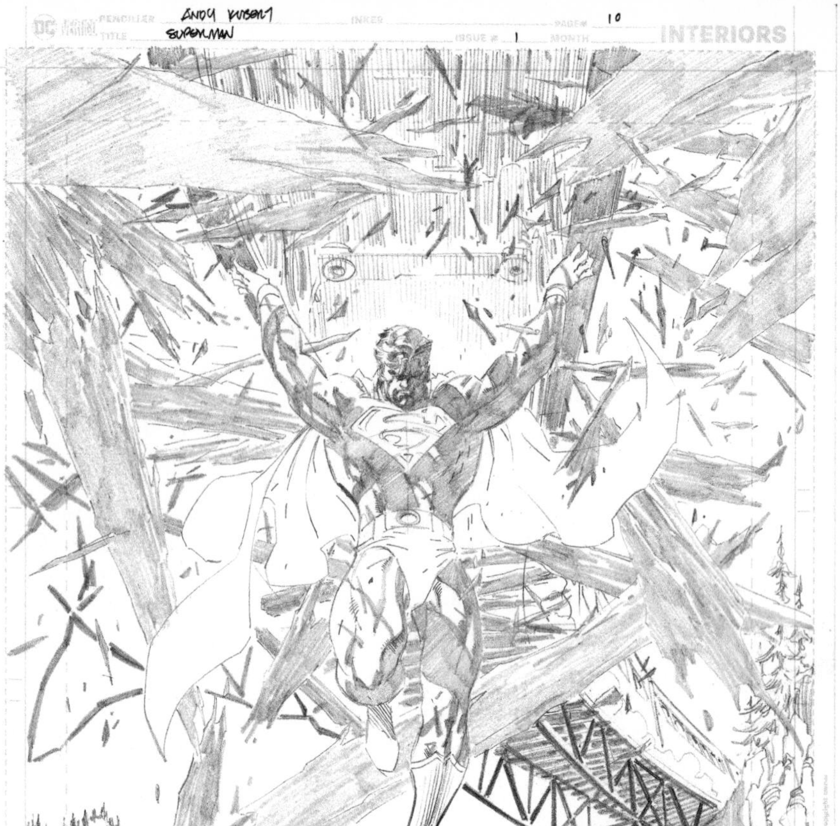
PENCILLER ANDY KUBERT
INKER
PAGE# 10
TITLE SUPERMAN
ISSUE # 1
MONTH
INTERIORS

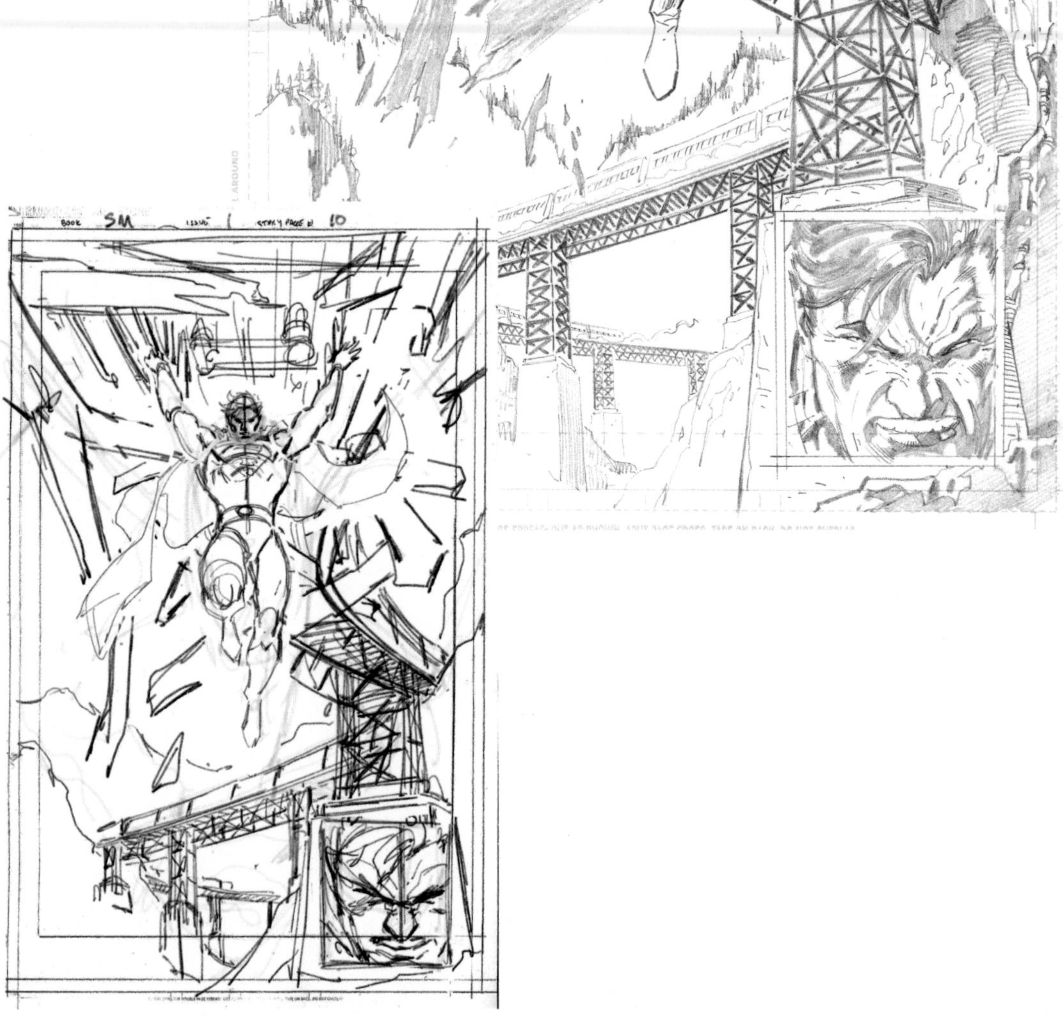
BOOK SM
ISSUE 1
STORY PAGE # 10

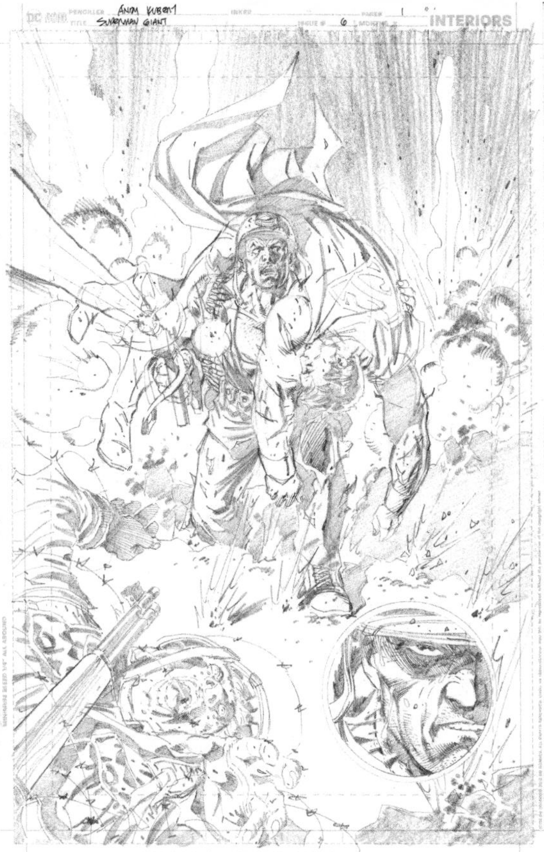
ANDY KUBERT
SUPERMAN GIANT
6
1
INTERIORS
DOUBLE PAGE SPREAD: CUT AS SHOWN, ABUT PAGE EDGES, TAPE ON BACK. DO NOT OVERLAP

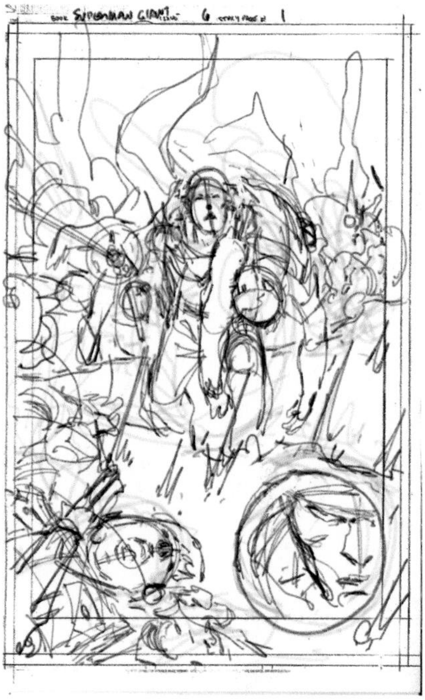
SUPERMAN GIANT
6
1

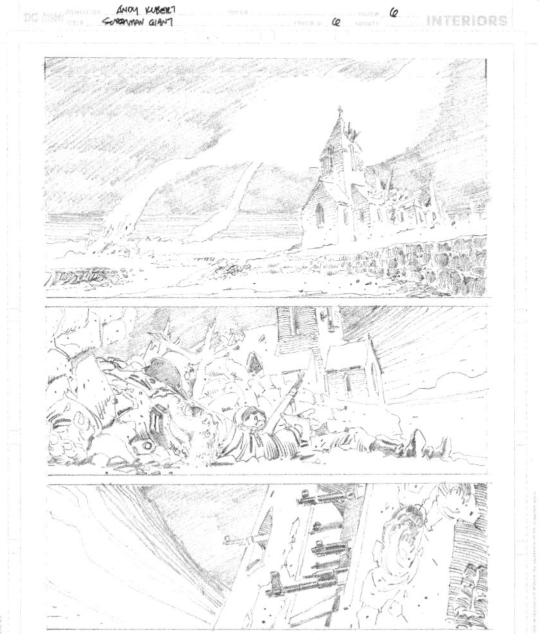
ANDY KUBERT
SUPERMAN GIANT
6
6
INTERIORS
DOUBLE PAGE SPREAD: CUT AS SHOWN, ABUT PAGE EDGES, TAPE ON BACK. DO NOT OVERLAP

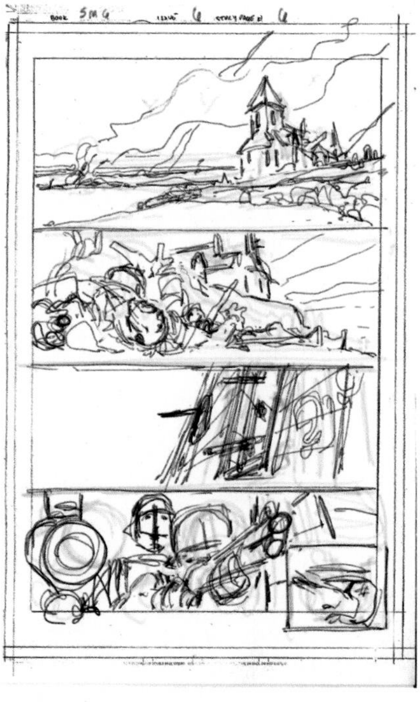
SMG
6
6

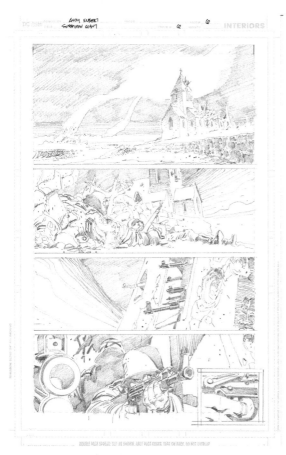